A+

Technician's On-the-Job Guide to

Networking

A+

Technician's On-the-Job Guide to

Networking

Curt Simmons
David Dalan

McGraw-Hill/Osborne

New York • Chicago • San Francisco
Lisbon • London • Madrid • Mexico City
Milan • New Delhi • San Juan
Seoul • Singapore • Sydney • Toronto

*The **McGraw·Hill** Companies*

McGraw-Hill/Osborne
2600 Tenth Street
Berkeley, California 94710
U.S.A.

To arrange bulk purchase discounts for sales promotions, premiums, or fund-raisers, please contact **McGraw-Hill**/Osborne at the above address. For information on translations or book distributors outside the U.S.A., please see the International Contact Information page immediately following the index of this book.

A+ Technician's On-the-Job Guide to Networking

1234567890 DOC DOC 019876543

ISBN 0-07-222777-X

Publisher Brandon A. Nordin	**Proofreader** Mike McGee
Vice President & Associate Publisher Scott Rogers	**Indexer** Jack Lewis
Acquisitions Editor Nancy Maragioglio	**Computer Designers** George Toma Charbak Kelly Stanton-Scott
Project Editor Monika Faltiss	**Illustrator** Melinda Moore Lytle Michael Mueller Lyssa Wald
Acquisitions Coordinator Jessica Wilson	
Technical Editor Kim Frank	**Series Design** Carie Abrew Kelly Stanton-Scott
Copy Editor Dennis Weaver	**Cover Series Design** Jeff Weeks

This book was composed with Corel VENTURA™ Publisher.

ABOUT THE AUTHORS

Curt Simmons (A+, MCSA, MCSE, CTT) is a technology author and trainer based in Dallas, Texas. Curt is the author of over 20 high-level and user-level computing books on a variety of topics. When Curt is not writing about new technology, he spends his time with his wife and children. You can visit Curt on the Internet at http://www.curtsimmons.com or send him e-mail at curt_simmons@hotmail.com

David Dalan (CCDA, CCNA, MCSE) is a technological jack-of-all-trades. Currently, David is earning his keep as an author, consultant and network engineer. David has written books (pretty good ones, he thinks) on topics ranging from Cisco certification to Apache web installation and administration. When he's not pretending to have two jobs, he spends his time with his family or writing music.

I would like to dedicate this book to my family, who put up with the nights and rescheduled events (fortunately few) in order to make this work possible. Heather, Nat and Lou: you are the ballast that keeps me upright and I love you.

-David

CONTENTS AT A GLANCE

CONTENTS

ACKNOWLEDGMENTS

I would like to thank several people who have made this book possible. First, thanks to Nancy Maragiolio for thinking of me for this project. Thanks to Kim Frank for a thorough technical review. Also thanks to Monika Faltiss and Jessica Wilson for keeping things moving in the right direction and bringing the book to completion. A special thanks goes to my co-author, David Dalan. As always, thanks to my agent, Margot, for taking care of the details. And finally, thanks to my family for their support.

—Curt

I would like to extend a special thanks to Curt and Nancy for making me a part of this project and letting me have yet another platform to spout my "geekness" upon the world. I thank the editors (content and technical) for turning my sometimes horribly rough workings into polished gems. And Margot…what can I say about you? You rock! And for those of you who have thrown down some hard-earned coins in questionable economic times to purchase this book, my biggest thanks go out to you. You are the one person that really makes this a possibility.

—David

INTRODUCTION

Networks are ever-growing, ever changing animals, and in today's networking environments, you'll need to know a lot about different networking technologies and configurations. As an A+ technician, or someone who is aspiring to be an A+ technician, you may be faced with the task of supporting network users or even configuring operating systems for networking—or even supporting the network itself. The good news is that networks are more versatile than ever—they do more and they provide more features and options. So, why write a book about networking for A+ technicians? The simple answer – Networks require a lot of knowledge to manage, and you, as the problem solver, are quite likely to run into complex networking issues. Why write a book about networking for A+ techs? To help you do your job!

A+ certification gives you a marketable certification in today's computer support work force. But beyond the standard exam objectives and questions (which now include a lot of networking material), you'll need to support and configure a number of different networking tasks and features. You'll need to know what certain networking components and protocols can and can't do, how to configure it, and perhaps most important, you'll need to know how to solve a number of problems. This is where this book becomes your help and your guide. I've written this book so that it explores the ins and outs of networking and focuses on issues you are most likely to face as an A+ technician.

So what if you are not yet an A+ technician, but you are striving to become one? This book also serves as a great study guide. Although this book is not an exam prep book, it looks at networking in terms of A+ skills. If you have yet to pass your A+ exams, study your A+ certification guides, but also study this book so that you'll have a sharper edge for any networking questions the exam might throw your way.

The *A+ Technician's On-the-Job Guide to Networking* is a new kind of book. It is designed to give you easy to use and easy to find information, most often in a step-by-step, task-oriented format. After all, performing tasks and solving problems is your job, and this book follows you with that same kind of format. You won't have to read paragraph after paragraph of dry, boring text to find information and answers; this book gives you information succinctly about many different networking topics as they relate to the A+ technician's job. In fact, the idea is that you can pull this book off your shelf, find the problem or issue you are experiencing, read about it, and fix it.

You don't have to read this book in any particular order. You can read it from cover to cover if you like, or you can jump around and find answers when you need them—the choice is yours. Just use the table of contents or the book's index to find help on most all important network topics quickly and easily.

This book is for the A+ audience and for those striving to become A+ certified. I expect that you know a thing or two about computers, but I don't expect you to be a networking expert either. If you have passed your A+ certification or if you are moving in that direction, then this book is for you.

To help you along the way, I've also included a few elements that you'll find helpful:

- **Note**   Notes are little bursts of information that give you some additional information. You don't have to read these, but they can help you.

- **Secret**   Secrets are friendly pieces of advice I have thrown in from time to time that can make your work with networks easier.

- **Tech Talk**   These sidebars provide practical insights into specific task options. These sidebars often contain additional steps, workarounds, and other tricks that you can use on the job.

- **Troubleshooting**   These sidebars explore a specific problem and solution. You'll find these scattered throughout the book, and they contain issues and problems that you are most likely to run into. Make sure you pay attention to these!

- **Painful Lessons I've Learned**   And for fun, I've included some light-hearted, but helpful situations and support calls that you may run into when working with networks.

Are you ready? Then let's dive into the world of A+ Networking and your job of supporting networking environments.

Thanks! Enjoy the book!

—Curt Simmons and David Dalan

WORKING WITH NETWORK HARDWARE, CABLING, AND PROTOCOLS

1

In this chapter, we will dive into the basics of networking hardware and their companion protocols that specify how computers should communicate across a network. Think of a network as a house. There is the outer structure (the facility where the network is located), spaces for occupants (workstations and servers), and the wiring, plumbing, and other odds and ends that allow the interior spaces to be usable. While most networks are made of various components such as workstations, servers, printers, routers, switches, network adapters, and cabling, this chapter will focus primarily on the "plumbing" elements. These elements include network-specific hardware such as routers, switches, network interface cards, cables, and the like. This chapter will be slightly less task-oriented than the later chapters, but it is here that we will make sure you get the background on networking you will need for those later chapters. In this chapter, we'll...

- Examine the kinds of network cabling and topology options commonly used in LAN/WAN environments

- Configure the options available with common networking protocols

- Explore in depth the most widespread networking protocol suite, TCP/IP

- Test network connectivity using widely available utilities
- Fix common problems that result from failures of the physical components of the network

NETWORK CABLING AND TOPOLOGIES

Perhaps the most basic set of concepts relating to networking have to do with the cables used to connect hosts together and the manner in which these connections are arranged. Before we go much further, we will briefly define networking. Computer networks are used to connect individual hosts to each other using some kind of cabling medium, often called *network media*. The media is used to communicate binary (1s and 0s) from one computer to another. While the hosts and the end users making use of those hosts may see a file moving across the network, all that actually passes across the network cable is a stream of electrons or light pulses that signal 1s or 0s. The process of moving the digital photo or other file from your home PC to grandma's PC, for example, involves several steps. A protocol is used to define how the steps of this file transfer process translates from a format your applications can use to a stream of binary bits and back again. Network protocols, and a handy method for remembering them, will be outlined later in the "Configuring Network Protocols" section.

Most networks have at least one portion that can be identified as a local area network (LAN). The LAN is defined as a number of interconnected hosts (meaning they can communicate with each other on the network) that reside within a single physical facility. A facility could include a business on one floor of a building, the whole building, or your home. There may be only a single user or thousands of them, but regardless of size it is the constraint to a single location that defines a LAN. There is some gradation between network types, but in general if the hosts all reside at the same mailing address, the network they connect to is a LAN.

Now, suppose that you work for a large company that has many offices throughout the world. Offices in Tokyo, Berlin, Seattle, Oslo, and Moscow each have a LAN. Further suppose that the CIO (chief information officer) has decided that all of the offices should be able to access the same network resources. Once the sites are capable of communicating with each other, a wide area network (WAN) has been created. There are literally dozens of ways to create a WAN, and they have a large number of subtypes. In general, the WAN connects two or more LANs together. If you have ever used a modem to connect your home computer to the office or the Internet, you have made use of a WAN. You made your WAN when you established a connection between your LAN (LANs can have a single host) and the LAN at either your work or ISP. As I mentioned, there are many WAN subtypes as WANs vary greatly in size. For example, two small office LANs connected are a WAN. On the other end of the spectrum, the Internet is a WAN (in fact, arguably the largest WAN of all). Another critical difference between a LAN and a WAN is that compared to LANs, WANs make use of slow connection technology. Where it is common for LAN hosts to use 10-or 100-Mbps (10-100 million bits per second) connectivity, WAN connections commonly make use of 56-Kbps to 1.544-Mbps connections (56,000 to 1.5 million bits per second). WAN connectivity speed tends to be limited because WAN connections often must cross telephone company networks. These networks are often expensive and limited in capacity, thus keeping the capacity of most common WAN implementations relatively low. In Figure 1-1, the various elements of a WAN and a LAN are shown. Take particular note of how the LAN is designated as a piece of the larger WAN. The LANs connected in the larger WAN can vary in size—some may be single users and others entire offices. Either way the relationship is the same.

NOTE   The campus area network (CAN) and the metropolitan area network (MAN) are two of the more commonly referenced WAN subtypes. A good example of a CAN, not surprisingly, is a college campus. Each building would be an individual LAN, and the links between the buildings would define the CAN. Most CANs make use of faster connectivity options than WANs that must traverse the public telephone networks. CANs differ from LANs in that, though they are still geographically defined by a single campus, they are larger than a typical LAN (since they are not confined to a single facility). A MAN is a CAN that spans a single municipal area (a city). The only real difference is that the MAN may make use of public networks if required.

Both LAN and WAN environments can make use of a wide range of cable and wireless connectivity options from fiber optic and copper to 802.11b and licensed spectrum wireless. As far as the hosts on the network are concerned, the underlying network operates in the same manner—the only difference is the kind of equipment and cabling required when using any one of the various options. The manner in which the links and hosts of a network are arranged is known as the *network topology*. Network topology has a huge impact on how the network will operate as a whole, including the kind of capacity the network has, how scalable or easy it can grow, it is, and the degree to which it is reliable and secure. The following sections will explore the wired and wireless connection types available as well as three of the more commonly used network topology types.

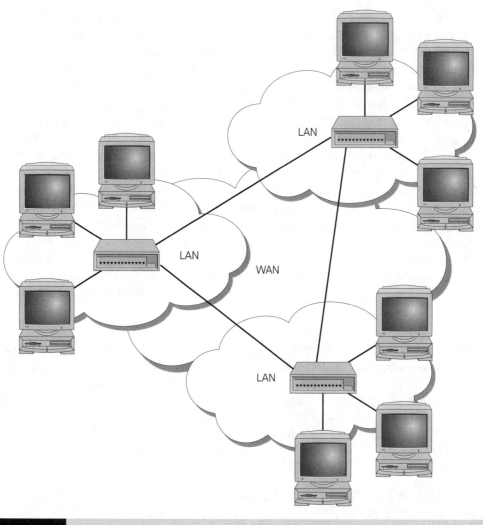

FIGURE 1.1   LAN and WAN

NETWORK CONNECTION MEDIA

There can be a lot of crossover in the jargon used for networking. The terms "link," "connection," and even "cable" can be used somewhat interchangeably. In this section, we will explore connection media. Specifically, this is the media that carries the binary information between any two hosts. All of the available media options fall into one of two categories: either hardwire cables using metal or glass core, or wireless media.

Hardwire cabling is most commonly made up of twisted-pair (TP) copper wiring. This kind of wiring is divided into two forms, shielded twisted pair (STP) and unshielded twisted pair (UTP). STP is used to allow the use of copper-based cables in proximity to devices that generate electrical interference. Since fiber-optic cables are immune to electrical interference and it is not as pricey as it once was, STP has lost its value for most common applications. In any event, UTP is by far the most common iteration of the copper cabling family and is itself divided into groups, known as categories.

There are many categories, but only three of them are of any real importance; Category 3 (CAT 3), Category 5 (CAT 5), and Category 6 (CAT 6). CAT 3 UTP cabling is most commonly used in commercial phone services. For example, most homes use CAT 3 wiring to connect telephones in the home to the public telephone network. CAT 3 wiring has two pairs of twisted copper for a total of four wires. CAT 5 UTP cabling is perhaps the most widespread networking cable in use today. This eight-wire (four pair) cable is used to support a wide range of networking situations, including digital phone services and computer networking. Finally, CAT 6 UTP is also an eight-wire cabling, but is built to standards that improve its capability to transport electrical signaling. In general, the result is that CAT 6 UTP can carry a network signal further than the comparable CAT 5 cable and, far more importantly, is better adapted to handling high-speed/ high-frequency signaling. Depending on the type of technology used with CAT 5 or CAT 6 cabling, such as 10 Mbps, 100 Mbps, or 10,000 Mbps (1 Gbps), the cables can be from 10–100 meters (30–300 feet) in length. In order to make a CAT 5 or 6 cable run longer than this, a signal regenerator (such as a switch or a router) must be used.

In addition to the cabling that makes use of copper wire as the signaling medium, there has been an explosion in the use of fiber-optic cables in smaller network settings. Fiber-optic cabling uses light instead of electricity to transmit the same binary information as copper cables. There are several advantages to this medium and signaling method—most notably is that fiber-optic cabling can be run for many miles without having to use a signal regenerator. Another critical benefit is the fact that fiber-optic media is immune to electromagnetic frequency (EMF) interference. This allows fiber-optic cabling to be run in close proximity to electrical wiring and powerful electrical/magnetic sources (generators, for example) that would seriously interfere with copper-based cabling. When fiber-optic media was first introduced, the cables were very expensive and required specialized skills to install. Since that time, technological improvements have made the production of fiber-optic cabling less expensive and installation less time-consuming. The net result has been the wider adoption of fiber-optic cabling in WAN and LAN environments.

Square Peg, Round Hole

Fiber-optic patch cables typically come with either SC or ST connectors. ST have circular jacks and SC interfaces are round. Keep this in mind—if I had been aware of this, I could have saved a lot of time and hassle. Some networking equipment uses one or the other, and your patch cable must match. When I was working as the senior field engineer (that is, the guy who gets to sleep in a lot of hotels), I was often out in the field working with our customers. Our product required very powerful networks to operate correctly. As such, we were often involved in helping the customers upgrade, troubleshoot, and generally tweak their LANs before and after the sale and installation of the product. On this occasion, I needed to install a 24-port Fast Ethernet switch to improve the performance in their product lab. The existing equipment at the site was a great distance from the lab and a single fiber-optic cable run was used to connect the lab computers to the rest of the network. I made sure that I had a fiber interface on my switch and set off to get the site up and running. Once I had the hosts connected, I grabbed the fiber run to link my switch to the rest of the network— but I could not get the cables to attach. It appeared that I had square connectors on my switch and the cable had round ends. How do you fit a square peg into a round hole? The carpenters answer is "with a hammer," but in this case I needed to explore other options. Since the fiber-optic cable was hundreds of feet long and run through a number of walls and crawl spaces, the installation of a new patch cable was very impractical. Although I had noticed that there were different interfaces for fiber-optic cables, I had assumed I would be able to find a patch cable to match the ends of each device. Oops. So, what did I do? I ordered a replacement part (new adapter for the switch), and returned to finish the installation. A little research could have saved me an extra trip from the West Coast to the East Coast and one fairly irritated customer.

Wireless media all accomplishes essentially the same thing as hardwired media, but wireless makes use of various radio frequency (RF) technologies to transport binary data. Of the wireless options available, 802.11b and 802.11a (both often referred to as Wi-Fi) are probably the most widespread options. The 802.11b option supports a maximum capacity of 11 Mbps and 802.11a has a capacity of 54 Mbps. The uses for these technologies typically apply to LAN environments, but with the capability to support faster speeds (up to 55 Mbps), Campus Area Network (CAN) implementations are on the rise. Think of a CAN as a LAN that spans several buildings that are close together. Even with the 11-Mbps speed, wireless connections can offer a very inexpensive and rapidly deployable option for connecting a small group of users to an existing network.

NOTE   802.11b and 802.11a are not only names used to describe the technology that bear the label, but they are also the ID number for the IEEE (XXXXX) standards used to define how technologies compliant with those standards must operate. In essence, these standards can be thought of as hardware protocols. Each standard specifies features such as signaling and hardware security. For a view into the IEEE standards and the process for developing them, check out the IEEE web site at http://www.ieee.org.

NETWORK INTERFACES

Once you've selected the cabling media to connect your hosts together, you will need to make sure that the appropriate cabling adapters and network interface cards are in place. This is a bigger issue with hardwire media than with wireless media, because there are different technologies that can make use of the same cables—though not at the same time. Most wireless equipment is built using portions of the Ethernet IEEE standard and thus the kind of devices that can share the media are limited. All of the devices using a particular wireless network must be compatible with the standard in use.

With hardwired networks, there are two components used to connect the network host to the cabling. The cable must have a network interface (frequently called an *end*) attached and the host computer will need to have a network card with a complementary interface (often called a *jack*) installed. Typically, the interface connected to the cable inserts into the compatible interface on the network card. The most common network interface used with hardwire cabling is known as the RJ-45. This interface makes use of eight pins to patch the eight wires of the CAT 5/6 cable to the complementary set of pins on a network interface card. Figure 1-2 shows the cable and network card portions of the RJ-45 interface.

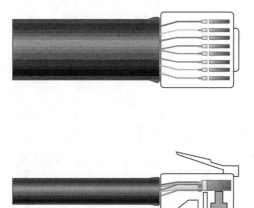

| FIGURE 1.2 | The RJ-45 network interface |

TECH TALK

Make Your Own RJ-45 Cables

While it may be easier to buy a patch cable than to build one, you will be able to save time and money if you can build your own. The length of your cable will depend on your need. If you need to run cable between the floors of a building, or if you just need to patch a router to a switch (that sit next to each other), you will essentially need to do the same thing. In order to build your network cable, you will need to have

- A spool of CAT 5/6 cabling.

- A cable tester.

- RJ-45 ends and an RJ-45 capable crimping tool with a wire stripper.

- A wiring diagram such as the one pictured at http://yoda.uvi.edu/InfoTech/rj45.htm.

Your cabling, ends, crimping tool, and cable tester can be obtained from a wide range of vendors, including just about any business that specializes in networking products. If you would rather not spend money on a dedicated cable tester, you can test any cables you make by using the cable to connect a computer to a switch. If you can get from the computer to the rest of the network, your cable is a success.

The only tricky part of building the cable is getting the small copper wires in the correct order inside the network end. The following steps will outline what you need to do to make the end. Be sure to practice with patch cables before working on wires that may be a hassle to rerun if you end up clipping them too short to attach a network end.

1. Using the wire stripper, remove approximately ½ inch of outer sheath. The inner wires should be exposed, but their individual (color coded) coatings must be intact. If the inner wire coatings are cut, cut the end of the wires off and repeat the stripping operation.

2. Pinch the eight wires between your index finger and thumb until they are arranged in a series (laying flat) that allows you to see all eight wires next to each other.

3. Arrange wires 1, 2, 3, and 6 and clip the ends so they are all the same length.

Make Your Own RJ-45 Cables (continued)

4. While holding the properly oriented wires in one hand, pick up one of the network ends and hold it so you can see the copper contacts.

5. Insert the eight wires into the eight channels in the end. Take your time; this part can be very frustrating if you try to rush. Don't be surprised if the first couple of times you feel like the wires have a mind of their own and seem to go anywhere except where you want them to go.

6. Once the wires are in place, use the RJ-45 crimper to lock the wires in position.

7. Repeat steps 1–6 on the other end of the cable.

8. Test the cable to determine if your attempt has succeeded.

Now that you have a cable with an end, you will need to decide what kind of network adapter to use for your network hosts. The modern LAN makes use mostly of Ethernet and Fast Ethernet, and to a lesser degree token ring and Gigabit Ethernet. Each of these interfaces has a different set of operational capacities and requirements, and we will now take a look at each of them.

ETHERNET

IEEE 802.3 standard, known more commonly as Ethernet, specifies a physical connection, the RJ-45 interface, and a signaling method and process. This standard supports many kinds of cabling, including CAT 5 and CAT 6 UTP and fiber-optic cabling. Ethernet uses half-duplex communication, meaning each node may transmit or receive at a given time, but not send and receive simultaneously. The maximum throughput for any Ethernet connection is 10 Mbps. Any single copper-based cable connection, known as a *segment*, cannot exceed 300 feet in length. The maximum length of Ethernet over fiber-optic cable varies depending on the kinds of fiber-optic cables in use, but generally they can reach upwards of half a mile.

As with all of the Ethernet standards, the carrier sense multiple access with collision detection (CSMA/CD) algorithm is used. Simply put, this algorithm specifies that an Ethernet host will listen to the network segment for a "quiet" period where no other hosts are transmitting. Once that quiet period is found, the host may transmit. This is the "carrier sense" portion of the algorithm. It allows multiple hosts to share a single transmission medium and is known as the "multiple access" part of the equation. If two hosts listen at the same time and both detect a quiet period, they may end up transmitting at the same time. This results in a disruption of both hosts communications attempt—what is known as a collision. Each host will recognize the collision has occurred, wait a random period of time (different for each host), then attempt a retransmission.

In the early days of networking, before switches were widely used, Ethernet networks were slow and severely restricted in size. If more than 20 hosts were on a shared segment, meaning that they were connected to the same hub/repeater, then communications would grind to a stand still. With switching, each host that is directly connected to the switch is not sharing its segment with any host other than the switch. The switch then directs traffic between each attached segment. This has allowed Ethernet to become the most widespread and popular networking specification to date.

FAST ETHERNET

As you may have guessed, Fast Ethernet, IEEE 802.3u, offers increased capacity and the ability to perform full-duplex, or bidirectional, communication. A different electrical signaling method is used to boot the capacity from 10 Mbps (available with Ethernet) to 100 Mbps. Since data may flow in two directions simultaneously, the total capacity of the link is roughly 200 Mbps. Like Ethernet, Fast Ethernet is capable of using a wide range of network connection media such as copper- and fiber-optic-based cables.

GIGABIT ETHERNET

The Gigabit Ethernet (IEEE 802.3z) uses the same general parameters as Fast Ethernet, but has even more tweaked signaling to yield another tenfold increase in capacity. The tradeoff is a technology that, when using copper cabling, has very restricted segment lengths. Gigabit over copper media is typically restricted to 30-foot segments. For segments that must exceed this size, fiber-optic cabling will be required.

TOKEN RING

The token ring (IEEE 802.5) specification uses a special network element, known as a *token*, to identify which host has the capability to transmit on a shared network. A host must have possession of this token in order to transmit, and thus many hosts can share a single segment and not suffer the degradation that occurs with shared Ethernet arrangements. Token ring networks will become less

TROUBLESHOOTING

Signs that You Need More Capacity

If your network users complain of sluggish response from their networked applications, you may be having a capacity issue. Before making changes you will want to analyze the network traffic using either a software monitor such as Hewlett Packard's OpenView or a hardware analyzer such as the One Touch series from Fluke. If you are using Ethernet and your utilization is over 40 percent, and/or broadcasts are consuming more than 25 percent of network capacity, you probably need to move to a faster technology. With token ring, you can push the utilization value to 70 percent before you need to find a route to faster networking.

responsive as more hosts are added, but the performance decay is more graceful than with shared Ethernet—which basically goes from usable to useless with the addition of a few too many hosts. Token ring is capable of operating on both copper- and fiber-optic-based media at speeds of 4 Mbps and 16 Mbps.

WHEN ETHERNET JUST DOESN'T CUT IT ANYMORE

If you are using Ethernet (10 Mbps) over CAT 5, you have several options for upgrading. Fast Ethernet will provide roughly ten times the bandwidth as regular Ethernet and is widely supported. In fact, your network cards may support both 10-Mbps and 100-Mbps settings (autosensing). If this is the case, then by upgrading the network equipment between the hosts to Fast Ethernet (or autosensing) equipment, you can achieve an instant increase in network capacity. Gigabit Ethernet is less widely supported by the typical network card, but it can make use of CAT 5 cabling. If your networking equipment supports Gigabit Ethernet/ RJ-45 interfaces, you can move commonly used resources such as servers to the higher-bandwidth connectivity options.

ADDING SOME ZING TO TOKEN RING

If the old 4 Mbps or 16 Mbps is not cutting it, there are really two options to consider. You can begin migrating to high-speed token ring (100 Mbps) or you can migrate to an Ethernet-based network. The real difference is found in two areas: vendor availability and price. Some vendors, most notably Cisco Systems, have effectively abandoned token ring and no longer support the interfaces with their networking equipment. Notable token ring vendors include Madge Networks and IBM. Ethernet is supported by virtually every network product vendor. Cost is perhaps the most notable factor in choosing one over the other, unless you have unlimited resources. A typical 10/100 Ethernet adapter will cost between $20 and $50 per adapter, whereas HSTR token ring interfaces can cost several hundred dollars per adapter. Even if you have a large investment in token ring, the long-term cost savings of going to Ethernet are fairly evident.

Wireless Ethernet (802.11b and 802.11a) are becoming ever present because Wi-Fi LAN configurations are often simple, inexpensive, and rapidly deployable. Either 11 Mbps or 54 Mbps of bandwidth is available between the wireless host and the central access device, known as an access point (AP). The AP then typically connects back to the hardwired LAN with an Ethernet or Fast Ethernet network adapter. As costs continue to fall for both AP and the wireless network adapters needed by hosts, more and more of these Wi-Fi LANs are being installed. Performance-wise, these technologies are no barn burners, as they can really only effectively support 12 or so hosts per AP. Additionally, there is one serious potential problem to most wireless LANs, and that is security.

Now that we have looked at the kinds of interfaces and cabling in use on most networks, let's take a look at some of the more common (and useful) ways

TECH TALK

Three Holes in Wireless Security

The biggest hole in wireless security is that many users do not bother to implement any form of security. The access point (AP) is added to the LAN and users are given wireless network cards—and that's all. This default arrangement basically negates any physical security measures since it allows anyone with a wireless network card to attach to your network and gain access to any unsecured resources.

When a user enables wireless encryption, such as Wired Equivalent Privacy (WEP), the technology is usually fairly insecure. Some devices use encryption algorithms that have been cracked, or are easily cracked. Some of the encryption processes begin by sending and receiving some information in an unencrypted manner to begin the securing of the data transmission. By using a network sniffer, enough information can be gathered by an unauthorized user to determine how the encryption is implemented and then defeat it. In

Three Holes in Wireless Security (continued)

any event, encryption may or may not prevent a user from attaching to your network. Other user's communications may be secured, but the crooks can still gain physical access to your network.

Now imagine that you are the network administrator, and you have built a nice secure LAN/WAN using good passwords and network design. Imagine that an employee named Bob in your organization gets a wireless AP so he can work outside in the courtyard area right outside his office on nice days. Since the employee knows no better, there is no encryption enabled and anyone can attach the AP—after all he is the only one that knows it is there, right? All is well and good until some curious person drives by with a wireless laptop, a port, and a network sniffer, and discovers the newly available resource. Now your finely tuned secure LAN has a hole in it big enough to drive an 18-wheeler through, and folks are lining up to take advantage of you. Here are a couple of things you can do to securely use wireless on your LAN:

1. Use a secure topology (see "Secure Network Topologies" later in this chapter) to place all of the Wi-Fi users in a DMZ. These users will then connect to the network using the same strategy as any home-based telecommuter (virtual private networking (VPN), for example).

2. Use Media Access Control (MAC) address filtering if your AP includes support. Each network card in the world has a unique MAC address. If it is supported, you can configure your AP to accept connections from only authorized MAC addresses.

3. Finally, you can always change your plans and not use wireless.

to arrange these connections for specific purposes. As mentioned at the beginning of this chapter, these arrangements are known as network topologies.

HIERARCHICAL NETWORK TOPOLOGIES

Hierarchical networks are built using a layer approach, a model that has been widely promoted by networking hardware producers such as Cisco Systems. Essentially, the network is broken down into three layers: the core, distribution, and access layers. Scalability, fault detection, improved manageability, and reduced costs are all byproducts of this design strategy. In Figure 1-3, you can see that there are three distinct layers of devices.

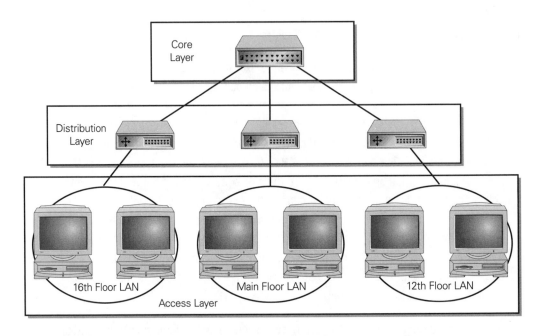

FIGURE 1.3 Sample hierarchical network

At the core of the network, high-speed switching is used. This portion of the network is also known as the backbone in some circles. In the core of the network, all of the various network segments are connected together. The sole purpose of the switches at the core of the network is to move data as quickly as possible between the various segments defined at the distribution layer. Sometimes servers and connections, such as Internet links, that are shared by all of the network users are placed in the core of the network.

At the distribution layer of the network, routers are in use. The distribution layer routers decide if the data coming from the hosts at the access layer need to traverse the backbone to reach another segment or if the traffic is supposed to stay within the network segment that it originated from. In an ideal world, most of the traffic should stay within the network it has originated from. For example, if the 16th floor LAN (in Figure 1-3) has its own mail server, file servers, logon servers, and so forth, the only traffic that needs to traverse the backbone would be destined for resources on one of the other two LANs or the Internet.

The place where all of the workstations, printers, and many of the servers reside is the access layer. This layer is supported by switching of various types—for example, you might have 100-Mbps connectivity to your servers, and 10-Mbps connectivity to the workstations. This would ensure that your servers could accommodate the bandwidth requirements generated by your users.

SECURE NETWORK TOPOLOGIES

A secure network topology is used to create a transitional zone between your private LAN and the Internet. This zone, called a demilitarized zone (DMZ), is used to host publicly accessible servers and services. It is also the location where any Wi-Fi wireless devices should be installed. This arrangement allows users from the Internet or other unsecured networks to gain access to your intended resources, but will prevent those users from getting into the private network without your permission. A DMZ is built using two routing devices and a DMZ device, such as a switch, to attach the routers and hosts in the DMZ together. Alternatively, you can use a multiport firewall device such as the Cisco PIX firewall to perform the role of both the DMZ device and the external router. DMZs are also referred to as isolation LANs. See Figure 1-4 for an example of a DMZ/ isolation LAN.

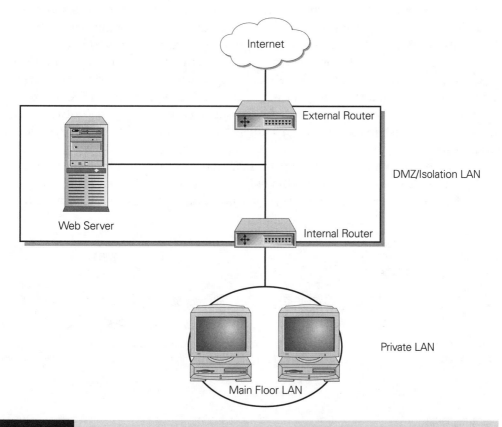

| FIGURE 1.4 | Secure topology example |

An external router is used to control access into the DMZ. It will allow incoming requests destined for the DMZ hosts, but will reject requests destined for either the internal router or internal LAN hosts. Your internal router is situated between the Internet servers and the local network. The purpose of this router is to block access to the internal LAN if it originates from the Internet, DMZ hosts, or the external router. This arrangement protects the internal LAN in the event that the external router or the DMZ servers are compromised.

MAKING USE OF FULL AND PARTIAL MESH TOPOLOGIES

Full and partial mesh network topologies are two commonly used methods for implementing network redundancy. The basic idea is fairly straightforward: by having multiple connections between any two hosts or networks, you can ensure that the failure of any single link will not disrupt the operation of the network as a whole. This kind of network topology is also known as a redundant network because there are multiple paths to some or all of the hosts and networks involved.

The partial mesh is common as a method of adding redundancy to WAN installations. Because WAN links are often expensive, this method is used to develop a middle ground between the expensive and fully redundant full mesh and nonredundant network types. Figure 1-5 shows both full and partial mesh networks. Notice that the links in the partial mesh are used to connect each network to at least two other networks. This is done to most of the networks in the partial mesh example and provides quite a bit of resiliency for the wide area network.

A full mesh is made only when each LAN has a connection to every other LAN in the WAN configuration. This will result in a great deal of protection from the disruptive effects of a network link failure. The downside is that this

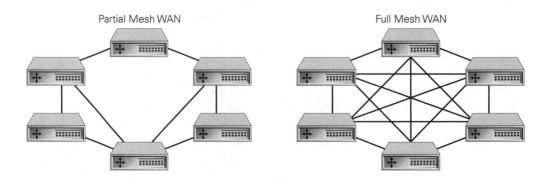

Partial Mesh WAN   Full Mesh WAN

FIGURE 1.5   Partial and full mesh networks

kind of configuration is difficult to maintain if you are to prevent routing and/or switching loops, and can be very expensive because there are a large number of connections required.

CONFIGURING NETWORK PROTOCOLS

Once the physical connectivity has been established on the network, you will need to configure your hosts to make use of one or more higher-level networking protocols. These protocols allow the more complicated components of host-to-host communications, such as encrypting data or changing file formats, to occur.

NETWORK PROTOCOL OVERVIEW

Networking protocols, including those touched on earlier such as Ethernet, are defined within the context of the seven layers of the Open System Interconnection or OSI model developed by International Standards Organization (ISO). This model has seven unique layers, each defining the parameters for a specific part of the network communications process. For example, each of the seven layers defines the functions, hardware, data types, and protocols for the components operating at that specific layer of the model. Each layer is designed to provide services to the layer above and below it in the model. The layers of the OSI model are outlined next.

When you see products advertised with layer designations such as "layer 3 switch" or "layer 2 aware," it is the OSI model that is being referred to.

- Layer 7: Application layer

- Layer 6: Presentation layer

- Layer 5: Session layer

- Layer 4: Transport layer

- Layer 3: Network layer

- Layer 2: Data link layer

- Layer 1: Physical layer

Each of the seven layers provides a different function. At the application layer (layer 7), support exists for the software being used by a user to request network services. The actual applications in use on a computer, such as Microsoft

Word, are not at the application layer, but the services that those applications use to communicate over a network are. Within the presentation layer (layer 6), protocols are defined that allow different computer environments to communicate. For example, Windows and Apple OS computers go about storing files in a very different manner, but protocols at the presentation layer specify how to translate the data from one format to another so that the different systems can interoperate. Within the bounds of the session layer (layer 5), the protocols for establishing and maintaining a logical connection between networked services reside. Services operating at this layer establish, maintain, and manage the communications link between any two network hosts. Protocols and services of the transport layer (layer 4) enable the transportation of data across a network. It is here that data such as text files is first broken into smaller pieces to prepare for network transport. This layer is also the location where the final reassembly occurs of received data, which is then passed up to the session layer.

If you have heard anything of the OSI model, it has probably been in the context of the last three layers. It is here that the most widely known network protocols reside. For example, IP (network layer, layer 3), Ethernet (data link layer, layer 2), and cabling requirements (physical layer, layer 1) reside within this group. At the layer 3, network addressing of all kinds is defined. This is the layer at which routers operate as well. Within the data link layer (layer 2), the interfaces and signaling protocols, such as Ethernet, are defined. The last layer, the physical layer (layer 1), contains the specification for the physical (cables, media types) exist.

In order to prepare to configure network hosts, among the first things you will need to understand are the layer 3 options. The most common protocols used to address clients are IPX, AppleTalk, and (most importantly) TCP/IP. Each of these protocol suites will be examined in the following section. TCP/IP will receive the most investigation since it is the most widespread and is destined to eventually supplant both IPX and AppleTalk on most networks.

IPX CONFIGURATION OPTIONS

The Internetwork Packet Exchange protocol was developed by Novell for its NetWare operating systems. The IPX protocol is supported by NetWare, Microsoft Windows products, and a wide range of Linux and UNIX systems. IPX identifies hosts by making use of an 80-bit host address. This address is made up of two components. There is a 32-bit network number that identifies the segment that host resides on. The second part is known as the node ID. This 48-bit address is used to identify the host uniquely on the network where it resides. The host ID is defined by the administrator when the network is configured, and the node ID is the MAC address of the network card used by the host.

In addition to the address used to locate the host on the network, there is a feature known as a socket number. This feature is used to identify traffic from different applications. For example, if a host is accessing a web page at the same time that it is transferring a file from another LAN host, the socket number is used to identify which data is needed by the web browser and which is needed to complete the file transfer. To use another house analogy, if the computer is the house, the 80-bit address can be thought of as the ZIP code and address of the computer, and the Socket ID is the name of the resident to which incoming mail is destined.

MAKING USE OF APPLETALK

The proprietary network protocol known as AppleTalk uses an addressing scheme that always dynamically assigns addresses to clients. While the user will never need to directly configure an address, there are several variables that can be modified. An AppleTalk host has a node address that is dynamically assigned and makes use of a feature called a socket to identify communications sessions between various applications. Basically, the socket operates in the same manner as the IPX socket ID. Groups of AppleTalk hosts can be configured to operate as members of a common group known as a network. Any hosts connected to the same switch, bridge, or router are considered members of the same network and will be identified by a network number. Apple recognizes two kinds of AppleTalk networks: extended and nonextended. If the network joins multiple physical networks together under a single AppleTalk network number, it is known as an extended network. These networks use what is known as a cable range to identify the participants of the extended network. By contrast, nonextended networks are made of a single physical segment and a single network number.

An AppleTalk zone is a collection of networks. Entire networks and individual hosts can be configured to participate in a zone. Hosts and networks that will participate in the same zone need to be on the same physical network segment.

TROUBLESHOOTING

Problems with Apple and Spanning Tree

Some of the default implementations of TCP/IP on Apple operating systems, such as OS 8.x and OS 9.x, have a known flaw in the way they operate in the presence of the Spanning Tree Protocol (STP). So what is STP anyway? STP is used to connect switches to each other with more than one link. STP makes one of the links inactive until the primary link is taken offline or fails. Then STP brings the standby link online to prevent the disruption of network communications. Computers making use of the defective TCP/IP implementation will experience a number of ill effects, such as file transfers that fail to complete, system bombs, and (in rare circumstances) no network connectivity at all. Apple offers for download an update to their TCP/IP implementation that will resolve the issue. If STP is not being actively used, you could also disable STP on the switch that the Apple PC connects to and the issue will be eliminated.

Many manufacturers of networking hardware have STP enabled on their switches by default. All of the 8.x and most of the 9.x versions of the Apple OS come with the faulty TCP/IP installation by default. So, a user with a number of OS 8.5 workstations that installs a new STP-enabled switch will begin to experience problems soon after the install. One might be convinced the switch is defective, but it may not be the case if the conditions just described exist.

THE TCP/IP PROTOCOL

TCP/IP is the protocol that takes the cake. TCP/IP is supported by nearly every operating system implementation—major and minor—and is the protocol of the Internet. As such, we will take a fairly detailed tour through the protocols of the TCP/IP suite and the configuration options. When configuring network hosts and devices to use the OSI layer 3 component of the TCP/IP protocol stack, IP, you will almost always begin by assigning them an IP address. IP addresses are 32-bit addresses that are typically shown as a four-part decimal number separated by periods—for example, 10.50.200.33. This is just the tip of the IP addressing iceberg, and in the following section we will look at how IP addressing works in detail.

TCP/IP ADDRESSING DETAILS

IP addresses, such as 10.50.200.23, are made of two components: the network ID and the host ID. IP addresses are 32 bits long and are arranged in four groups of eight bits, known as *octets*. Each of these octets can be converted into a more user-friendly decimal number. It is in this decimal form that most IP addresses are displayed, such as 10.50.200.23. While this user-friendly form makes it easier to configure the IP address of network hosts, you do need to know how to translate from the decimal format to the binary format in order to understand how IP addressing really works. For example, the IP address 10.50.200.23 (in decimal form) is represented as 00001010.00110010.11001000.00010111 (in binary form). If you are not familiar with binary to decimal conversions, Appendix A has an explanation of how to convert from decimal to binary numbers.

NOTE   Each of the four octets has a possible value between 0 and 255, or 00000000 and 11111111.

I mentioned earlier that there is a network and host portion to the IP address. In order to identify which portion of the address identifies the host and which part identifies the network, another 32-bit address is used. This address is known as a subnet mask. When the subnet mask and the IP address are added together (in binary from), the result will identify which portion of the IP is network and which portion is host.

Take the IP address 192.168.1.124 and assume that the host using it has been assigned the subnet mask 255.0.0.0. Since we know we need to work in binary, we will convert them. 192.168.1.124 in binary is 11000000.10101000.00000001 .01111100 and 255.0.0.0 is 11111111.00000000.00000000.00000000. To add these numbers together and reveal its secrets, line the binary numbers up like so, remembering that IP is on top and mask is on the bottom:

```
11000000.10101000.00000001.01111100
11111111.00000000.00000000.00000000
```

Before you start adding values together, you need to know the rules of binary addition. Simply put, the rule is as follows: $1 + 1 = 1$, $1 + 0 = 0$ and $0 + 0 = 0$. The result of the addition looks like this:

```
11000000.00000000.00000000.00000000
```

This number, and the result of any subnet/IP addition, reveals the network portion of the address. In decimal form, this is 192. To get this value, you simply need to add the values associated with the particular bits. For example, going from left to right, the eight bit positions have the following values associated with them: 128, 64, 32, 16, 8, 4, 2, and 1. Since the two leftmost bits are set to a value of 1, you simply add 128 and 64 to get 192. All bit positions with 0 values are "off" and have a numeric value of 0. The remainder of the address is the host ID, in this case 168.1.124. Table 1-1 shows a series of IP addresses and subnet masks, and the resulting network and host address components.

This leads into the topic of default subnet masks. Early on in the design of IP, it was found that there was a need to organize how an IP address would eventually be allocated to hosts. To facilitate this, default subnet masks were assigned to IP address ranges. These assignments are known as address *classes*. In order to work with IP on your network, you should understand the three primary classes: class A, class B, and class C. The matching of IP addresses to address classes is based on the binary arrangement of the IP address. But in this case it is easier to just look at the decimal value of the first, leftmost octet. For example, 16.45.233.166 would be a class A address because the number 16 (the value of the first octet) is within the established range for class A addresses. Using the first octet of the address, the classes are defined as follows: class A includes 1–126; class B, 128–191; and class C, 192–223. Each of these classes has a default subnet mask assigned as well: 255.0.0.0 for class A, 255.255.0.0 for class B, and 255.255.255.0 for class C. So, our previous example 16.45.233.166 is a class A address with a subnet mask of 255.0.0.0. This means the network portion of the address is 16 and the host address is 45.233.166.

Along with these established classes, there are a few reserved and special-purpose address groupings. First off, you may have noticed that addresses beginning with 127.0.0.0 are not in any of the default classes. This is because the address 127.0.0.1 is reserved as the loopback address. When the address is used by a host, it identifies the host itself. This address is useful when troubleshooting IP on a host. If a host cannot reach the 127.0.0.1 IP, that host is having some serious IP protocol-related problems.

Other specialized addresses include reserved experimental IP address classes. Any IP address beginning with the value 224–254 is reserved for an array of special purposes and should never be assigned to a workstation or server unless

IP Address	Network Mask	Network Address	Host ID
192.168.1.22	255.0.0.0	192.0.0.0	168.1.22
192.168.1.22	255.255.0.0	192.168.0.0	1.22
172.16.125.1	255.0.0.0	172.0.0.0	16.125.1

TABLE 1.1   IP/Network Mask Addition Examples

you understand the use of the addresses. Aside from these specialized classes, there are several IP address ranges designated as private IP addresses. These ranges reside (one each) within each of the major address classes (A, B, and C). A private address is only usable on a network that does not connect to a public network directly. A router must be used to connect a network using a private IP address range with a public network such as the Internet. The reason for these private ranges is simple—as the use of networks increased, it became apparent that eventually there would be no more IP addresses left for host assignment since there are a finite number of addresses possible. Private IP addresses can be used in multiple networks because a router translates between the private and public network. For example, the Boston branch of a company can use 192.168.44.0 as its network address pool and the Seattle branch can use the same exact address pool, especially if each site has only one Internet-routable IP address and all internal hosts are masked by the office's Internet router/firewall. If the offices will connect directly to each other using private lines, each would need to use different IP subnets. The private IP address ranges are 10.0.0.0–10.255.255.255 (class A), 172.16.0.0–172.32.255.255 (class B), and 192.168.0.0–192.168.255.255 (class C).

I would be remiss at this point if I did not mention one other related concept, the port number. Port numbers are used with layer 4 TCP/IP protocols to identify the communication session for multiple applications on a single host. This is identical to the socket ID (IPX) and socket (AppleTalk). We will look at commonly used port numbers in the following section, which examines the protocols of the TCP/IP protocol suite.

PROTOCOLS OF THE TCP/IP SUITE

Each of the protocol suites mentioned in the chapter (IPX, AppleTalk, and TCP/IP) contains various subprotocols. Most of the features of IPX and AppleTalk are rarely components of modern networks. IPX will occur commonly as a feature of networks using NetWare servers. NetWare (and IPX) are the subject of Chapter 11. Right now we will examine the protocols of the most common networking protocol suite, TCP/IP. While there are literally dozens of TCP/IP-related protocols, we will focus on the more common elements of layers 7, 4, and 3.

APPLICATION LAYER PROTOCOLS

The application layer is where the software you use first comes into contact with the protocols and services that allow networked communication. The protocols of the TCP/IP suite that reside at this layer are probably familiar to you already.

Some of the more common layer 7 protocols are Domain Name System (DNS), File Transfer Protocol (FTP), Telnet, Hypertext Transfer Protocol (HTTP), Simple Mail Transfer Protocol (SMTP), and Simple Network Management Protocol (SNMP). Each of these protocols is identified by a port number. As mentioned repeatedly, ports allow a host to have more than one communication session at a time. These ports are defined at layer 4 of the OSI model, but they are used solely for identifying the layer 7 processes that use them. The following is a list of the ports used for the previously mentioned TCP/IP protocols:

- DNS: Port 53
- FTP: Port 21
- Telnet: Port 23
- HTTP: Port 80
- SMTP: Port 25
- SNMP: Port 161

These port assignments are the protocol defaults. In most cases, a server can be configured to use another port for a particular type of traffic. This allows a server to host a service on a port that is not widely known. This is not really a good way of implementing security, because many networking tools could be used to discover the new port. Nonetheless, if you wanted to keep most users away from an FTP server you were hosting, you could configure your FTP server to listen to a port other than 21. This way, in order for a user to connect to the FTP, they would need to know the IP address and the port number. If you should decide to do this, keep in mind that all of the hosts using the service with a nondefault port assigned will have to be configured to use the new port assignment. Now let's take a look at some of the services proved by the application layer protocols mentioned earlier.

The Domain Name System (DNS) uses a hierarchical and distributed database to provide hostname-to-IP address resolution service. The host uses a service called the resolver to query the DSN database for information. For example, when you open a web browser and type in an address, such as www.yahoo.com, a resolver process on your computer makes a query. The resolver then gets the IP address, port, and other assorted details and returns this information to the web browser, which then goes out and gets the web site using HTTP.

The File Transfer Protocol (FTP) is the "go-to guy" protocol of the TCP/IP suite. FTP is most often brought into the mix when the user needs to move files from one computer to another. The FTP service can also be used to perform basic file management tasks such as creating and deleting directories and browsing directory contents. In addition to being a protocol, FTP is also an application (called FTP) on most commercial operating systems, including Microsoft Windows, Linux, and UNIX.

Telnet is very simple protocol that has be used in a wide range of settings to enable remote management of hosts. Telnet is used to provide terminal emulation that allows a local host to interact with a remote host as if the remote host were in the same location as the local host. This kind of connectivity can allow a user at one location to monitor and configure devices located anywhere in the world as long as they are reachable across a common network. Many switches, routers, and other network devices support remote management via telnet. Telnet can be used in conjunction with FTP so that a user can not only manage the remote computer, but also move files between the remote and local host.

The HTTP protocol is used to allow users and applications to access files on the World Wide Web. This protocol is designed to specify how to handle various web page elements, such as HTML code used to make web pages, and move files from a web server to the requesting host. Internet URLs (Universal Resource Locators) such as www.yahoo.com begin a set of characters used to identify the protocol that needs to be used with the URL. The http:// in http://www.yahoo.com tells your computer to look on port 80 of the IP associated (in DNS) with the URL. Some web browsers support using alternate prefixes such as ftp:// to specify other ports and services.

The ever-popular electronic mail service (e-mail) depends on the Simple Mail Transfer Protocol (SMTP). SMTP defines the logical processes used to get e-mail messages from the originating source to the destined user. Much of it is accomplished by relaying e-mail from one SMTP server to another. For example, your ISP probably has an e-mail server with a SMTP interface that allows you to send e-mail to other users. You send the mail and it is delivered to your SMTP server. That server in turns takes care of getting your e-mail to the correct host.

SNMP (the Simple Network Management Protocol) is used to standardize how information about network health and operation is reported. This protocol allows network monitoring software and hardware from a wide range of vendors to collect information in a standardized way.

TRANSPORT LAYER PROTOCOLS

The layer 4 protocols used by TCP/IP are made up of the Transmission Control Protocol (TCP) and the User Datagram Protocol (UDP). Each has its own properties and uses, and most of the layer 7 protocols use one (and only one) of them to segment and reassemble data for network transport.

TCP is used to provide a reliable connection over a network, since networks can be a fairly unreliable means of sending information. Basically, TCP addresses the fact that hardware cannot always be trusted to get data from point A to point B without losing a few bits here and there. TCP compensates by implementing error detection and correction. When two hosts begin to establish a session using TCP, the hosts negotiate a set of criteria that will allow each of the participating hosts to determine if all of the data they send makes its way to the intended recipient.

One of the variables the hosts establish is how much data can be sent by the sending host before the receiving host sends an acknowledgement; this is known as the TCP window size. By sending an acknowledgement back to the sender, the sender can determine the last piece of information, which is called a segment, that was received by the target host. Segments are always sent in sequence, and a complete sequence must be received in order for it to be properly reassembled. For example, if host A sends 25 segments to host B and the receiving host acknowledges packets 1–17, the original sender knows that 18–25 did not make the trip. In fact, if the receiver did not get segment number 18, it would then ignore 19–25 even if they did make it, since they need to be in the proper sequence for reassembly. So, once the window size has been agreed upon, the TCP process on each host will establish a session, known as a virtual circuit, between the hosts. With the known window and acknowledgement procedure, detecting errors and retransmitting lost segments is fairly simple.

Another option that TCP uses to ensure delivery of information is the use of flow control. Flow control works like this: Host1 and Host2 establish a virtual circuit. Host1 begins to transmit data to Host2, but the data is being delivered faster than Host2 can handle. Host2 begins to drop packets and issues the computer equivalent of "Whoa, stop!" to Host1. Host1 then reduces the rate at which it is sending the packets and Host2 can now effectively process the received information. The flow of packets was manipulated, or controlled, in a manner that ensures both hosts are functional.

All is not perfect with TCP, however. This reliability comes with a price, and that price is called overhead. In order to maintain the virtual circuit, some of the network bandwidth is consumed by TCP control traffic. This is not data moving from one application to another, but is instead data moving from one TCP process to another to maintain the virtual circuit. This is not a big concern if the network has high capacity with lots of bandwidth. On slow or highly reliable links, another layer 4 protocol may be more appropriate—the User Datagram Protocol (UDP).

If TCP is regular, reliable, and sometimes a touch inefficient, like the U.S. Postal Service, then UDP is like the Pony Express. Things move quickly, but your stuff gets dirty and occasionally doesn't show up at all. No virtual circuit is established with UDP, and the sender could care less if the receiving host gets all of the segments. So how does a protocol like this do anything useful? Fortunately, some layer 2 elements (such as Ethernet) have built-in error detection features. UDP simply leaves the task of delivery verification up to either the layer 7 process that initiated the transmission or the layer 2/1 elements delivering the data. UDP just breaks down and reassembles segments. This allows UDP to carry very little overhead and have a minimal negative impact on any connections that use UDP.

NETWORK LAYER PROTOCOLS

Protocols of the network layer (layer 3) are mostly concerned with path determination. Essentially, this means these protocols are used to locate other hosts on the network. Since these protocols allow hosts to find each other on the network, they and the processes that use them are very useful when configuring or troubleshooting an IP-based network. Three protocols are particularly important, the Internet Protocol (IP), the Address Resolution Protocol (ARP), and the Internet Control Message Protocol (ICMP).

Internet Protocol (IP) is the most significant protocol in use in modern networking. It is used to address hosts on a network so that interhost communications can occur. Virtually every networking operating system supports it, and without it there would be no Internet. We examined IP in some detail earlier, but it bears mentioning again that IP is used to uniquely identify hosts within the confines of the networks where they reside. Popular technologies such as the World Wide Web, instant messaging, e-mail, and streaming audio/video depend on IP to operate. IP sets the stage for one host to make contact with other hosts. But even with the IP address of a target in hand, a network application will still need to resolve the MAC address of that host, or the device that can get the host in touch with its desired target, before a host can actually establish communication.

The Address Resolution Protocol (ARP) is used to discover the MAC address associated with a particular IP. Where an IP address is unique to a host within the confines of a network, the MAC address is unique to the host among all other devices on the earth. ARP is used to send a broadcast requesting the MAC address associated with a particular IP address. If the IP is on the same network as the host making the ARP request, the host will reply to the ARP request and send the MAC address of its network adapter to the requesting host. If the target host should reside outside the network, then the process is a bit different. When a host makes an ARP request in this scenario, the network gateway (a router) responds with its MAC address. This router (often called the default gateway) is acting as an intermediary so that the requesting host can communicate with a remote host.

NOTE MAC addresses are supposed to be unique, but this is not always the case. There are network adapters that share the same MAC address, but they are few and far between. In order to cause trouble, the duplicate MAC addresses would need to reside on the same network, which is very unlikely. A MAC address is stored in hexadecimal and is part manufacturer ID and part device ID. The manufacturer ID is common to all of the devices from one vendor, and the device ID is the supposedly unique portion of the MAC.

One of the most useful basic troubleshooting tools is the ping utility. A ping is properly named "ICMP Echo Reply." ICMP is short for Internet Control Message Protocol and it (ICMP) is used to collect a wide range of information about the status of IP processing on network hosts. The ICMP protocol-based tools will be examined in the next section.

TROUBLESHOOTING HARDWARE AND PROTOCOLS

Most of the problems that occur with computers, whether they are on a network or not, relate to software in some way or another. Problems are often caused as the result of incompatibilities with hardware, conflicts with other software, or just good old-fashioned file corruption. But software is not the source of all the woes of the networked world. Sometimes software is behaving just fine, moving data to and from hosts, and the physical components of the network begin to misbehave—causing what appears to be a software malfunction since what the end user sees is software not doing what it is supposed to be doing.

This section will look at some of the common problems arising from hardware, cabling, and protocol problems. We will also spend some time looking at ways to verify where the fault is occurring and what can be done to fix the issues found.

COMMON CABLING PROBLEMS

Most cabling problems arise during installation. Perhaps the cabling is roughly handled during installation (which is a particular problem for fiber-optic cabling), or the cable ends are not properly attached, or the copper wiring is run too close to sources of EMF interference. The symptoms that arise may be intermittent communication failures, long initial logon times, and, most commonly, inoperable links. The simplest method for finding the source of a cabling problem is a good cable tester. Cable testers will let you know if a signal is passing successfully across the wire. If there is a break in the wire, a good cable tester will be able to identify how far from the place where the cable tester is attached the break exists.

Several good cable testers are available—one of my personal favorites being the Fluke OneTouch series. This device is more than just a cable tester, as it also offers layer 2 and layer 3 network protocol traffic analysis. Though this device is full of fairly neat features, you will pay for the privilege as the device ranges in cost from $5,000–$6,000. Another good testing solution is the Belkin Multinetwork Cable tester. This device will allow you to verify that the ends of a cable are attached correctly (the wires are in the correct order) and that there is a continuous signal (or not) across the wire. It is not as fancy as some of the other cable testers, but it gets the job done and costs less than $100.

NOTE   Most network testing equipment is designed to work with copper cabling. Testing fiber-optic cabling will often require somewhat expensive add-on components or additional specialized tools. If you do not have a large number of fiber runs, it may be more cost effective to have a contractor come out and test suspect lines than buying expensive tools that may not be used regularly.

Once you have used a cable tester and you have found a problem with the cable, the options for fixing the problem are fairly limited. If the ends are not correctly attached, you can probably attach replacement ends. If the cable is broken at some point, your only choice is to replace the cable. This is not a big deal for a short patch cable, but if you have 50-foot cable runs through a ceiling or crawl space, this could be a serious chore.

TESTING NETWORK CONNECTIVITY

OK, suppose you have eliminated the possibility of cabling problems but there is still some kind of connectivity issue. The next step is to see which hosts the

TROUBLESHOOTING

Mystery Problems Caused by Bad Power

Poorly installed electrical wiring can cause all kinds of havoc, and often the disruptions are almost random in nature and frustrating to isolate. In fact, if you have no direct reason to believe that power is the source of your networking problems (such as brownouts), it might never occur to you to check it out. Fortunately, most electrical supply and hardware stores sell a handy little device that is, in essence, a small and simple multimeter. It looks like a fat, three-pronged plug with LEDs instead of wires attached and is commonly called something like "GFI Electrical Outlet Tester." When placed into an outlet, the LEDs will show where power is running through which wire. If the wiring has been improperly done, you may find certain electrical no-no's such as power being conducted on the ground prong. If electrical problems are identified or suspected, contact a certified electrician to have the problem corrected.

computer experiencing communication problems can contact, if indeed it can contact any hosts at all. One basic means of testing this is the ICMP echo reply tool, commonly called *ping*. Under most operating systems, you can run some form of the ping utility. For example, in Windows 2000 you can open a command prompt and type the following command, where IP address is the host you want to try connecting to:

```
Ping <IP Address>
```

Typically, you would attempt to ping other hosts on the same network, the default gateway, and then some remote hosts to see where the communication breakdown is occurring. To see if the IP protocol is operating properly on the host you are performing testing on, try pinging the loopback address (127.0.0.1). If this succeeds, IP is working. If it fails, something is seriously wrong with the IP support on the host in question. Often, a simple fix is to uninstall and reinstall the TCP/IP protocol stack. If you can successfully ping some hosts and not others, the problem probably lies within the network and not with the host itself. For example, if the connection to the internet has gone offline, you will probably be able to ping local hosts but not remote ones.

TROUBLESHOOTING

Using the ping Command on Windows

The following steps will show you how to execute the ping command from within the Windows operating system environment. In this example, we will be using the loopback address, 127.0.0.1, but feel free to repeat this exercise while substituting the IP address of another host.

1. Open a command prompt.

2. At the prompt, type the following command: **ping 127.0.0.1**

3. Press the ENTER key.

The results you receive should be similar to the example shown in Figure 1-6. The value after the "time" statement in the output, "time<1ms" in this example, is the time in milliseconds it takes for data to get from your host to the remote host and back again.

```
C:\WINNT\System32\cmd.exe                                    _ □ X

C:\>ping 127.0.0.1

Pinging 127.0.0.1 with 32 bytes of data:

Reply from 127.0.0.1: bytes=32 time<10ms TTL=128
Reply from 127.0.0.1: bytes=32 time<10ms TTL=128
Reply from 127.0.0.1: bytes=32 time<10ms TTL=128
Reply from 127.0.0.1: bytes=32 time<10ms TTL=128

Ping statistics for 127.0.0.1:
    Packets: Sent = 4, Received = 4, Lost = 0 (0% loss),
Approximate round trip times in milli-seconds:
    Minimum = 0ms, Maximum =  0ms, Average =  0ms

C:\>_
```

FIGURE 1.6   Ping output

Should the ping test reveal that there are one or two hosts you cannot reach, then with many operating systems you might be able to make use of the traceroute utility. The traceroute utility will attempt to get a response from every device and host that lies between the host you are testing and the host that you are trying to reach. As devices respond, a list will be generated.

TROUBLESHOOTING

Finding Where the Data Transport Fails

In Windows 2000, and many other operating systems, there is a traceroute command named tracert. By opening a command prompt and running the following code with the proper IP address inserted, you will see a list of devices, called hops, that lie between your local host and the remote host:

```
Tracert <IP Address>
```

If one of the devices has failed, the chain will be broken and your list will stop providing useful information at the last active host. An example of the output of the tracert (to www.yaoo.com) is shown in Figure 1-7.

```
C:\WINNT\System32\cmd.exe                                              _ □ ×

C:\>tracert www.yahoo.com

Tracing route to www.yahoo.akadns.net [66.218.71.81]
over a maximum of 30 hops:

  1    <10 ms    <10 ms     16 ms   198.239.158.241
  2     31 ms     32 ms     47 ms   198.239.158.249
  3       *         *         *     Request timed out.
  4     31 ms     32 ms     31 ms   198.187.0.66
  5     31 ms     47 ms     31 ms   198.187.0.178
  6     78 ms     78 ms     94 ms   198.187.0.162
  7     31 ms     47 ms     47 ms   198.187.0.218
  8     31 ms     63 ms     47 ms   ccar2-wes-FE1-2-1-0.pnw-gigapop.net [198.107.144.9]
  9     31 ms     47 ms     31 ms   cnsp1-ads-ge-0-1-0-0.pnw-gigapop.net [198.107.151.4]
 10     31 ms     47 ms     63 ms   unknown.Level3.net [209.247.84.37]
 11     31 ms     47 ms     47 ms   so-0-0-0.gar1.Seattle1.level3.net [209.247.8.161]
 12     32 ms     62 ms     47 ms   so-7-0-0.mp1.Seattle1.Level3.net [64.159.1.81]
 13     47 ms     62 ms     63 ms   so-2-0-0.mp2.SanJose1.Level3.net [64.159.0.218]
 14     47 ms     63 ms     47 ms   gige10-0.ipcolo3.SanJose1.Level3.net [64.159.2.41]
 15     47 ms     78 ms     94 ms   unknown.Level3.net [64.152.69.30]
 16     47 ms     78 ms     47 ms   w2.scd.yahoo.com [66.218.71.81]

Trace complete.

C:\>_
```

| FIGURE 1.7 | Tracert output |

WRAPPING UP...

In this chapter, we took some time to review some basic networking concepts and information about the physical components of a network. Specifically, we looked at the kinds of cabling available and spent time learning the ins and outs of making the needed components to the most common LAN media type, Category 5 copper cabling (CAT 5), using the most common interface (RJ-45). Along with this, we looked at the benefits and limitations of some of the other available media types, including fiber-optic and wireless media. In order to ensure the physical network is well organized, maintainable, and able to grow (also called scaling), we looked at three common network topology forms: hierarchical, secure, and redundant.

In order for two computers on a network to communicate, there has to be a common, known, and agreed upon set of communication rules. These rules are known properly as protocols. We looked briefly at the IPX and AppleTalk protocol, and took our time with the granddaddy of them all, TCP/IP. Finally, we looked at some of the tools available for testing basic network connectivity and possible strategies for troubleshooting problems with the physical components of a network.

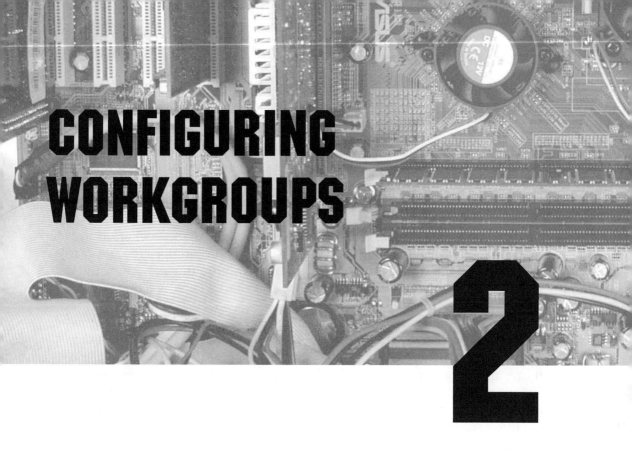

CONFIGURING WORKGROUPS

2

In the recent past, workgroups were considered an easy networking fix for small offices and home networks. They consisted of connecting a few computers together for the purpose of sharing files and printers. Security was generally weak and, for the most part, workgroups didn't do much else. However, in the constantly changing computing environment, larger offices consisting of 20 or more computers often use a workgroup model to avoid the expense of server hardware. Home networks have become more complex as well, with different networking topologies and the need to connect different operating systems. Along with the need for file and printer sharing are the issues of Internet connectivity and security. As you can imagine, home and small office networks—also called workgroups—have become more complex, but also more needed and more important. In fact, there are entire books just on workgroup configurations and options. As an A+ technician, you are likely to be faced with managing and implementing a small office network, or even setting up a home network. The good news is there are more options and more flexibility than ever before. In this chapter, we'll...

- Explore workgroups
- Understand workgroup topologies
- Configure workgroups and services

WORKGROUPS 101

A workgroup is a collection of computers that are networked together for resource sharing purposes. There is no single-server computer and no centralized authentication system. Users are authenticated with user accounts on the local machine and can then use network resources according to permissions established for those resources. Basically, each computer user is responsible for managing his or her shared resources and for managing the network as a whole. However, the definition becomes a little fuzzy because some workgroups are rather large. In fact, some have a part-time administrator who keeps things working the way they should (often along with a number of other tasks, such as fixing the copy machine!).

It is important to note here that the term "workgroup" has been intermingled in the past few years with the concepts of "small office network" and "home network." In truth, there is no difference between these network terms and the term "workgroup," because all of the computers function in a peer-to-peer fashion without centralized security and administration. Regardless, the basic definition of a workgroup still applies in today's diverse computing environments, but the management of the workgroup and the need for the workgroup have changed dramatically. For example…

- Some workgroups exist to share files and printers. This was the original design and need of the workgroup, and continues to be a driving force for workgroups today.

- Some workgroups share files and printers, but need strict security for shared resources. Rather than the network allowing basic access to all resources, users can place restrictions on users and more finely control the use of resources.

- Internet connection sharing and access has become a driving force in workgroup environments. Many smaller environments need to share a single broadband connection, such as a DSL or cable Internet connection, while protecting the network from Internet hackers.

- Some workgroups need to combine different workgroup topologies and even operating systems for sharing purposes.

As you can see, the need for workgroups remains all important, but the use and physical setup has changed a bit over the years. In actuality, workgroups have become more diverse and provide more services, and there are more hardware devices available (such as routers and residential gateways) that are designed to meet the needs of Internet connectivity and security. Operating systems themselves can also provide these services, and in the never-ending race for the consumer's dollar, operating systems often provide more workgroup features and flexibility than ever before. This is all great news for workgroups today, because the flexibility and options are plentiful.

NOTE As with anything in the computing world, it is important to make a clearly defined list of what you need in a workgroup, then find the equipment and software that will meet those needs. In an attempt to be all things to all people, many operating systems now provide numerous networking functions designed for the home or small office. If you are faced with the task of designing a workgroup, make sure you understand all of the networking needs (the possible restrictions or problems) and have a clear view of the budget before you begin your planning.

UNDERSTANDING WORKGROUP TOPOLOGIES

As I mentioned in the previous section, workgroups today have more flexibility than ever before. This is true in terms of network use and topology options. Remember that the "topology" of a network refers to the physical layout of the network and how computers are connected to one another. There are four primary topology methods available today for connecting computers in a workgroup together. The following sections explore those options.

ETHERNET

Ethernet is a tried and true network topology and essentially all computers today support Ethernet networking. Ethernet has been around practically forever, and most workgroups in use today use the Ethernet standard. In fact, most larger networks use Ethernet as well. Ethernet networks have been around since the mid-1970s, when Xerox first introduced the Ethernet standard. The Ethernet standard is a set of specifications that define what hardware and what transmission speeds can be used on an Ethernet network. From those standards, hardware manufacturers develop NICs, cabling, hubs, and routers. Ethernet networks break data into small pieces of data called data frames. Each frame contains between 46 and 1,500 bytes of data. Each data frame contains header information that includes the destination for the frame, where it came from, and a cyclical redundancy check (CRC) that checks the data frame for accuracy or problems with corruption during transit. Ethernet is a stable, effective workgroup solution, and you will find numerous hardware products on the market that support it. In fact, many computers today ship with a standard Ethernet card already installed.

Ethernet networks use RJ-45 connection cables and require the use of a centralized hub for communication on the workgroup. Because of this design, Ethernet is considered a bus topology, or more commonly a star-bus topology because all of the computers connect to a centralized hub, as shown in Figure 2-1.

SECRET

Ethernet networks use an access method called carrier sense multiple access with collision detection (CSMA/CD). CSMA/CD is a method where computers listen to the network to see if the network is clear before sending data frames. Should two frames collide on the network, the CD portion of the access method can detect the collision and resend. CSMA/CD is a standard part of the Ethernet, and you'll see the CSMA/CD specification often listed on Ethernet routers and residential gateway documentation, letting you know the access method is supported by that device.

Of course, one of the most important options to consider when looking at any networking topology is the supported speed. With Ethernet, you have three standard options, and you can readily find the necessary hardware to support these speed standards:

- **Standard Ethernet (10BaseT)** Standard Ethernet is capable of transmission speeds up to 10 Mbps. This standard is the original Ethernet standard and is what you typically find with a standard Ethernet NIC.

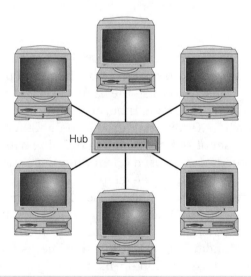

| FIGURE 2.1 | Star-bus topology |

- **Fast Ethernet (100BaseT)**   Fast Ethernet is capable of 100-Mbps transfer. In order to use Fast Ethernet, all NICs and hubs must support the 100BaseT standard. Most NICs and hubs sold today are sold as 10/100 Ethernet, meaning they can support Standard Ethernet or Fast Ethernet.

- **Gigabit Ethernet (1000BaseT)**   Gigabit Ethernet is capable of 1-Gbps transfer, and is an excellent option for networks that use a lot of multimedia transfer and streaming media. In order to use Gigabit Ethernet, you must install Gigabit Ethernet cards in all workgroup PCs and use a Gigabit Ethernet hub. You'll pay a little more for the faster service, but depending on your networking needs, the speed may be well worth the money.

Considering the vast support and availability of Ethernet products and the fact that virtually all PCs support Ethernet NICs, is there any real reason to use another topology? That all depends on your needs, but for the most part Ethernet remains the fastest and most reliable workgroup topology you can implement. However, in some offices and homes, the issue with cabling becomes a problem. What do you do if you need to establish an office network in an existing building with five different rooms? You have to have the cable run in the walls and installed (which can be costly), or you have to allow cables to run along the floor and baseboards, which can be unsightly. Due to the possible problems with using cables and hubs, there are now some other options, which can be quite useful in the right circumstances. These are explored in the next few sections.

HOMEPNA

HomePNA (Home Phone Network Alliance) is a networking standard that first became popular a few years ago as an inexpensive alternative to Ethernet. Like Ethernet, HomePNA networks use an internal or external network interface card (NIC), but the difference is the NIC plugs into any standard phone jack using standard RJ-9 telephone cabling. Rather than using a hub, the HomePNA clients use the existing home or office telephone wiring as the network wiring. This option solves the cabling and hub problems that often occur when using Ethernet. In home networks, the solution works great because you can connect to the network from any room in the house as long as a phone jack is available nearby. The best part of the solution is no hub is needed and the network communication does not interfere with regular voice communication—you can use the network and talk on the phone at the same time without any interference.

HomePNA networks are considered "daisy-chain" topologies. The computers do not connect to a centralized hub, so communication simply follows the home's internal phone wiring, as you can see in Figure 2-2. The downside of HomePNA

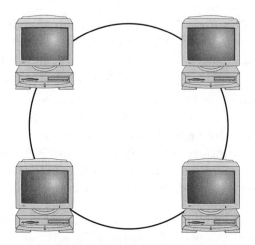

FIGURE 2.2	Daisy-chain topology

networks, however, is the speed. HomePNA networks are limited to 10 Mbps and do not support the 100-Mbps or 1-Gbps speeds of Ethernet. However, in many home and small office networks, the 10-Mbps speed is plenty. If typical network sharing, Internet usage, and printing are the primary functions of the network, 10 Mbps is all you need. In networks where a lot of multimedia is transmitted, application sharing is used, or other forms of high-bandwidth transmissions are in use, 10 Mbps may be a little slow. For most homes and small offices, though, HomePNA is a viable solution that is rather inexpensive.

NOTE HomePNA kits are readily available from most computer stores for around $50. The kit contains several NICs and setup software, aimed at the home consumer.

POWERLINE

Powerline networking is a lot like HomePNA—you use an existing network in your home or office, but instead of using phone lines, you use electrical lines. That's right—Powerline networking provides a NIC that plugs into a standard ac outlet. Other computers in your home plug into other outlets, and communication between the computers occurs over the electrical lines without disrupting any other electrical services.

Powerline networking also provides speeds of around 8–14-Mbps transfer, so the system is compatible with HomePNA. So why use Powerline? The main reason for Powerline networking is that ac receptacles are more readily available in homes and offices than phone lines, which gives you more networking flexibility.

While many homes or offices have only a few physical phone jack ports, there are usually several ac receptacles in every room. In terms of networking, Powerline is all about flexibility.

If you are considering HomePNA, is Powerline a better, more flexible choice? Not really. You face the same speed and Internet connection challenges as HomePNA, but Powerline networking can be problematic, although sales brochures might tell you otherwise.

Powerline technologies have had a lot of problems in the past due to noise and distortion on traditional power lines within the home. For example, the home network might work fine until someone turns on a hair dryer or a toaster. Then, the static and interference would bring the network to a standstill. However, recent developments in the ways that Powerline NICs use frequencies over the cabling enable the Powerline network to adjust frequencies on a need basis so that network disruptions are not as problematic. Also, some providers use an encryption method for all network communications in the event that data gets out of the local home or office and onto the main power line.

As you can see, Powerline networking is an interesting and viable alternative, and one that continues to mature. In fact, you may see more and more Powerline offerings, including broadband Internet over power lines in the near future, so this is certainly a technology to keep your eye on. For the home and small office network, the technology does work, although you can expect some hiccups from time to time. If you think that Powerline networking might be right for you, I would suggest that you certainly purchase a recognized manufacturer, such as HP or Linksys.

WIRELESS

Wireless networking has become more popular and commonplace in workgroups during the past few years. Wireless networks are obviously sought after due to the flexibility they provide. You can easily move computers around and communicate with network computers without having to worry about connections and cables. Most wireless networks today support the 802.11b wireless standard. You can use an ad hoc mode where computers outfitted with a wireless radio NIC can communicate with each other in a direct fashion, or you can use an infrastructure mode option where a wireless access point (which is the same as a hub) is used to manage wireless traffic. The wireless access point can even be used to connect to a wired Ethernet network through the wired Ethernet hub. Windows XP supports all of these wireless features, and other operating systems, such as Apple's OS X, support similar technologies and features (called AirPort).

Compatibility and Support

Probably the most important actions you can take when you are looking at workgroup networking is compatibility and support. Although Powerline networks may help you, or you may want a wireless network, you are going to have to take a hard look at what operating systems are supported. If you are using the latest and greatest in the Windows world—Windows XP—you'll find vast support for all of these options. Older operating systems such as Windows 9x are much more limited. The same is true with other operating systems such as Linux and Macintosh. Make sure the hardware and networking software is supported by the operating system before you move any further into deployment. Although you can solve a lot of problems in the networking world, compatibility is always going to be a major roadblock (if not the end of the road, in some cases).

NOTE See Chapter 10 to learn more about Windows XP's support of wireless networking.

NOTE With all operating systems, keep in mind that you can configure direct cable connections using a null modem cable or even the computer's modem. If the computer is outfitted with an infrared port, you can exchange information this way as well. See the operating system's help files for specific information, but always keep the direct connection option in mind for quick, temporary network solutions.

WORKGROUP HARDWARE

Workgroup hardware is fairly simple, but it is important to understand the options available to you. In order to determine what hardware you will need, you'll have to first decide on the kind of topology that you want and the specific needs that you have. For the most part, however, hardware is rather simple in workgroups.

NETWORK INTERFACE CARD (NIC)

For any computer to communicate on a network, the computer has to be outfitted with a NIC. The NIC handles all of the translation of data as it leaves the computer bound for the network and as it arrives at the computer from other network hosts. The NIC contains some kind of jack that you connect the appropriate cable to, and then you connect the cable to the hub or the wall outlet (in HomePNA networks). If you are using a wireless network, you still use a NIC, but the NIC contains a small antenna that is used for radio communications with other wireless NICs. As I mentioned earlier, most computers sold today ship with a standard Ethernet NIC. If not, you can readily find internal PCI NICs or even external USB NICs at any computer store that supports the Ethernet standard. If you want a HomePNA network, wireless network, or Powerline network, you'll need to purchase and install the appropriate NICs for those networks. Again, most computer stores even sell NICs in the form of a kit, which is easy for small office or home network setup. For installation of NICs, simply purchase what you need, make sure it is compatible with the operating system you are using, and follow the manufacturer's instructions.

HUBS/ACCESS POINTS

Ethernet networks require the use of a centralized hub, whereas wireless networks functioning in infrastructure mode require an access point. The two items are basically the same thing—the hub or access point functions as a traffic cop of sorts to manage traffic over the network. Hubs are small devices that have a row of ports for the Ethernet connections. Access points look about the same, but you have an antenna instead of connection ports. Hubs are typically sold with 8, 12, 16, and 24 port options and you can even daisy chain some hubs together so that more computers can be connected. Hubs, however, are a lot like cars—you can buy basic models for around $70 or deluxe models that provide Internet gateway, cable, and DSL modem connections, DHCP services, firewall services, and other networking services for upwards of $500. So, depending on your needs, you'll need to make a decision about the kind of hub that is most useful to you. Like a NIC, the transfer speed of a hub will drive up the cost as well (10/100 Ethernet hubs are much less expensive than gigabit hubs).

ROUTERS AND GATEWAYS

As Internet connectivity has become commonplace in workgroups, the need for hardware to manage shared broadband connections has become more and more important. In today's marketplace, you'll find a number of routers and residential gateways that are designed to manage workgroup connections and a broadband connection to the Internet. The router or residential gateway acts as a "meeting place" of sorts by separating the Internet connection from the network connections. For example, as you can see in Figure 2-3, the router handles all of the network connections as well as the connection to the Internet, provided you are using a DSL modem that supports this kind of configuration.

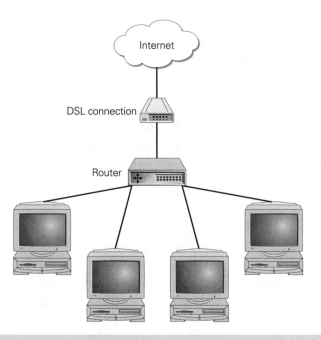

FIGURE 2.3	Router or residential gateway

As you can see in Figure 2-3, the router/residential gateway sits between the workgroup and the Internet. No computer is directly connected to the Internet, but the router/residential gateway handles all of the traffic between the Internet and workgroup. If you are using a Windows workgroup, the first question is why would you use a router or residential gateway? After all, Windows computers can use Internet Connection Sharing (ICS) to share an Internet connection, thus removing the need for the additional hardware expense. If you are using Windows XP, you can even use Internet Connection Firewall (ICF) to firewall the connection and protect the network. True enough—and in reality, there may be no benefit in using a router or residential gateway. However, routers and residential gateways sold today for the small office and home environment also offer a number of additional advantages, such as the following:

- Because the router or residential gateway handles the connection to the Internet through a broadband connection, such as a cable or DSL modem, no single computer is responsible for the connection. Under the ICS model, the sharing computer must remain on at all times (and actually work at all times), or no clients have a connection to the Internet. In other words, the Internet connection is only as strong as the hosting computer. If the hosting computer is offline, the Internet is offline. With a router or residential gateway, the device handles the connection, thus freeing the users to shut down their computers and move them around as needed, and because the router/residential gateway handles the connection, no single computer must carry the traffic burden of handling Internet requests.

■ Many routers and residential gateways on the market today provide DHCP services to workgroup clients. This means that the router or residential gateway can manage the dynamic IP addresses assigned to clients, rather than using a dynamic IP address assignment scheme (such as APIPA in Windows networks).

■ In addition to handling the routing of Internet requests, many routers and residential gateways use Network Address Translation (NAT), which is an addressing scheme. When NAT is used, the router or residential gateway hides all of the internal IP addresses of the computers on the network. Should a hacker attempt to attack the network from the Internet, the IP address used on the Internet is simply a fabricated address configured by router. For example, let's say that the computers on your network all have an IP address in the range of 10.0.0.1–10.0.0.30. Rather than using an address in this range, NAT will give the router a different address in a different range, such as 131.107.2.200. In other words, the hacker is not attacking a real computer on the network, but rather the router, which leads to no attack at all. NAT management is completely handled by the router's software, so there is nothing for you to configure.

■ Some routers and residential gateways are designed to work with additional third-party security software, such as Zone Alarm (www.zonealarm.com), which provides additional security from Internet threats.

As you can see, routers and residential gateways provide a number of services to workgroups and can be very helpful in terms of Internet access and security. As with any hardware device, you'll need to take a hard look at your network and determine if a router or residential gateway is right for you. You can learn more about the features and options at any computer store, and you'll find that Linksys makes several different kinds of routers and residential gateways. Check them out at www.linksys.com.

BRIDGES

A bridge is a hardware device that is designed to connect two dissimilar network segments. For example, let's say that your workgroup resides in an

TROUBLESHOOTING

Issues with Routers and Windows XP

If you want to use a router or residential gateway with Windows XP clients, you'll need to make sure that you purchase one that supports Universal Plug and Play (many new models do). Windows XP uses Universal Plug and Play with several different services, particularly Remote Assistance and Windows Messenger. If the router or residential gateway does not support UPnP, these services will not work over the Internet. As always, make sure you do your homework before buying a router or residential gateway. Check compatibility information with the router/gateway and your network clients. The best place to start is at the manufacturer's web site, where you can get lots of downloadable information before making a purchasing decision.

office building. The original workgroup is Ethernet, but you have recently added a HomePNA network to accommodate several classrooms that are not outfitted with Ethernet jacks. A bridge can connect the Ethernet and HomePNA network together for seamless communication between the two networks. In the past, bridges were used to connect large LAN segments using dissimilar topologies, but you'll see small bridge devices developed for the same problem in workgroup environments.

WORKGROUP CONFIGURATION SCENARIOS

Now that we have taken a look at the workgroup topologies available to you and the network hardware you are likely to work with, let's turn our attention to some network topology and setup options and diagrams. As you are designing a workgroup, consider these options, which may be right for the workgroup you are configuring.

STANDARD WORKGROUP

In a standard workgroup configuration, the computers are connected to each other as determined by the network topology you are using, as shown in Figure 2-4. Each

TECH TALK

Windows XP as a Bridge

In workgroup environments, Windows XP can also act like a bridge, due to the bridge feature now included with Windows XP. Returning to our previous example, let's say part of your network is Ethernet and part is HomePNA. You simply install the Ethernet NIC and the HomePNA NIC in the Windows XP computer; then, in Network Connections, you choose to bridge the two NICS. Clients on each network can then communicate with each other over the Windows XP computer. Of course, for the bridge to work, the Windows XP computer has to be turned on and working at all times. This option, however, is easy to configure and can certainly save you some money. See Chapter 10 to learn more about Windows XP's networking features.

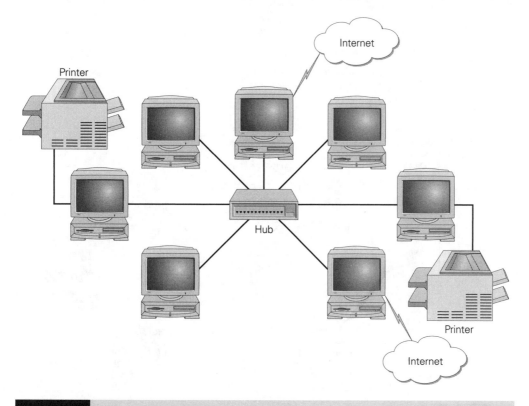

FIGURE 2.4   Standard workgroup

computer shares the desired resources, such as files and printers. There is no centralized Internet connection, so different computers may connect to the Internet via broadband or dial-up connections. Computers on the network that do not have an Internet account/connection hardware are unable to access the Internet.

CENTRALIZED INTERNET CONNECTION WITH ETHERNET

In a centralized workgroup, there is one shared Internet connection, as shown in Figure 2-5. The shared Internet connection is configured through an operating system feature, such as Windows ICS, or through some kind of third-party product. Clients that need to connect to the Internet access the shared Internet connection. In order for the clients to have the necessary connectivity, the Internet host computer must remain available at all times. Depending on the software used,

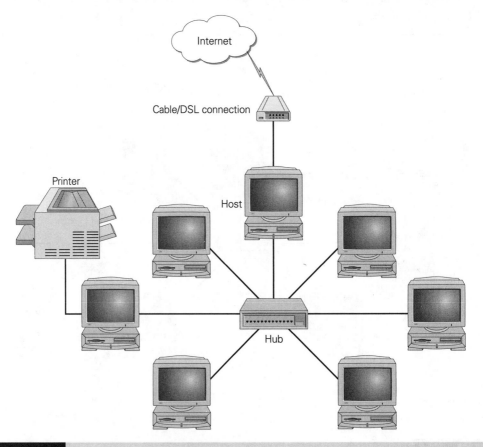

FIGURE 2.5   Shared Internet connection

the host and the network clients may require certain static IP addresses. For the example, when Windows ICS is used, the ICS host always has an IP address of 192.168.0.1. The other clients also have an address in this range, but they are configured to always see the 192.168.0.1 address as the default gateway. Other software products may configure the clients differently, but the point is there is one Internet connection shared by all clients. Firewall software can also be used on the Internet host as a security measure.

ROUTER/RESIDENTIAL GATEWAY

As we discussed in the previous section, a router or residential gateway can be used to manage the connection to the Internet, rather than the shared connection being managed by one of the workgroup computers. See the previous section for details.

ETHERNET/WIRELESS NETWORK

In an Ethernet/wireless network, part of the network uses a standard wired Ethernet topology, while a second part of the network is wireless, as shown in Figure 2-6. This option is often used in workgroups where laptops are employed that need to move from room to room. For example, let's say a small company has ten office computers that are wired as an Ethernet workgroup. The company also has five classrooms where instructors use laptop computers. Rather than having to worry about wiring, the laptops can be configured with wireless NICs in infrastructure mode. The wireless NICs communicate with the access point, which is connected to the Ethernet hub. The instructors can then move about with their laptop computers while staying connected to the network. In this network, a shared Internet can be used, and wireless clients can access the shared connection as well.

NOTE   Don't let the concepts of wired Ethernet and wireless networking confuse you. Wireless networks conforming to the 802.11b standard are still Ethernet networks—they are simply wireless Ethernet networks. For this reason, the access point is used to connect to the wired Ethernet hub seamlessly.

BRIDGED NETWORK

A final portion of the workgroup puzzle that may be necessary is a bridge. Remember that a bridge is a device that can connect to dissimilar networks, such as an Ethernet and HomePNA network. Windows XP can also function as

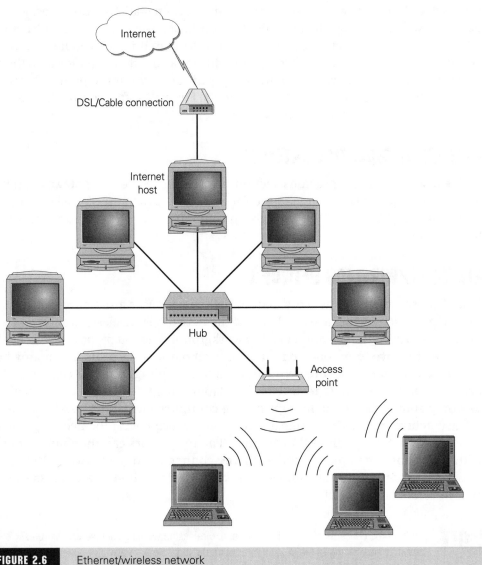

FIGURE 2.6	Ethernet/wireless network

a bridge for this purpose. In Figure 2-7, you see that a Windows XP computer is bridging the two networks, wireless clients are also used, and there is a shared connection to the Internet. This configuration, though it appears complicated, is actually easy to configure.

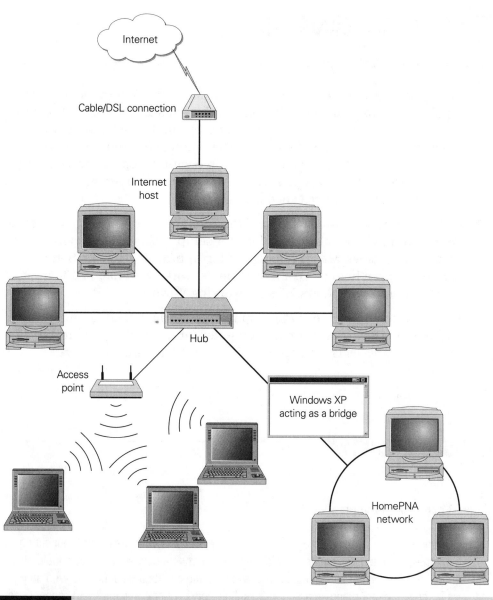

FIGURE 2.7   Bridged network

SETTING UP A WORKGROUP

Setting up a workgroup generally involves three different tasks:

- First, purchase and install the necessary hardware. Determine the kind of topology that you will need, then install the NICs as necessary. If required, connect the computers to the hub and power on the hub. As always, follow the manufacturer's instructions for installation and setup, and make sure you are using products that are compatible with the operating systems you are networking. If you are unsure, check out the computer manufacturer's web site—that is usually a good place to start.

- Once the hardware is installed and the computers are connected, refer to your operating system's instructions for setup. Most modern operating systems (Windows, Macintosh, and so forth) provide you with Setup Wizard that can help you configure the network. See Chapter 10 for a walk-through of Windows XP's Networking Wizard.

- If you are setting up the workgroup manually, you'll need to configure an appropriate IP address for each computer (or use APIPA) and install any necessary services (such as File and Printer Sharing in Windows networks).

TROUBLESHOOTING

Client Connection Problems

If you are configuring a workgroup and you are having problems with the clients connecting to one another, use the ping command to test for basic network connectivity. You should also check the IP addresses and subnet masks to make sure the clients are configured with an IP address in the same range and an appropriate subnet mask. Check all cables and connections and make sure the hardware is installed as it should be. Also, make sure your DNS and gateway addresses are correct. If you continue to have problems, consult the operating system's help files for specific instructions and troubleshooting steps that may be available to you.

If you are creating a workgroup of mixed clients, you'll have some additional obstacles to tackle. The simple reality is networking functions best when you use the same operating systems—Windows computers network freely with Windows computers, Macs network freely with Macs. However, client computers may be able to connect to your primary network, depending on the operating system and your network base. For example, let's say that you are using a Windows workgroup. However, there are two Macintosh computers that need to access network files. Can this be configured? The answer is yes—with the right operating system. Using Mac OS X, you can connect to a Windows computer on the network using Server Message Blocks (SMBs). This feature allows the Mac client to access shared files on a Windows computer and store files in a shared folder. As you can see in Figure 2-8, use the Go menu to choose the Connect to Server option, then enter the address you want to connect to in the form of smb://*host/share*. You can also connect to Windows computers from a Linux computer in a similar fashion. The point is that you will have to study the particular operating system's help files for details about connectivity.

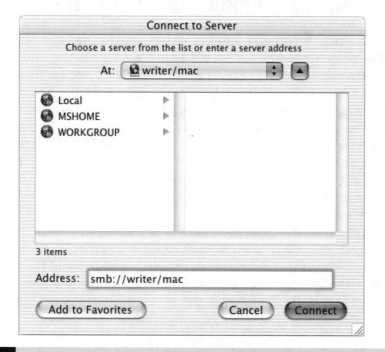

| FIGURE 2.8 | Mac OS X connection to a Windows computer |

PAINFUL
LESSONS

I'VE LEARNED

Operating Systems and Networking

The painful reality is networking in workgroups when mixed operating systems are in use is difficult. You can access shared network files from one client to another, but sometimes using a Windows client to connect to other operating systems is difficult. Also, using shared printers across different platforms is complicated, and oftentimes difficult. Although larger networks using different servers (such as Linux's Samba server) have additional connection and networking options through the server, you are rather limited in a workgroup. The key point to keep in mind is that mixed operating system environments never provide you with seamless networking that you'll enjoy—you'll face many problems and limitations. The simple lesson is to try and keep the operating systems the same—you'll see much better results and fewer problems, complications, and restrictions.

WORKING WITH RESOURCES AND SECURITY

Once the network is set up and running, you can begin sharing resources and managing security for those resources. The process for sharing and managing security is different, depending on the operating systems used on the network, but there are some basic similarities. Typically, you simply share the resource, then set any desired permissions or restrictions on that resource for your network.

For example, let's say that you want to share a folder called Documents, stored on a Windows XP computer. To share the folder, simply right-click it and click Sharing and Security, then click the Sharing tab, shown in Figure 2-9. You can choose to share the folder and allow users to make changes to the folder contents and files. If you do not want users to make changes to the folder's contents, simply do not select the option.

As you can see, however, there are not many security options, and this is the typical approach you will find when configuring workgroups. The network users have the option to view the information, or you can allow them to change it, which includes write access and even permission to delete the files. Because workgroups are typically small and house people who trust each other, the security settings on shares is usually not an issue.

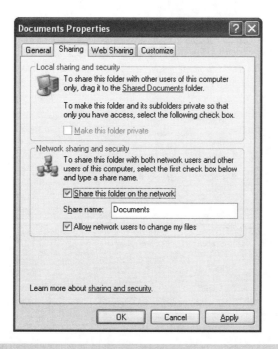

FIGURE 2.9   The Sharing tab

TECH TALK

Simple File Sharing in Windows XP

Let's say you are hired to create a workgroup for a client. The network consists of Windows XP computers. The client wants to share folders and files, but the client wants specific control over which users can access the files and how they are used. Can it be done? Perhaps—that depends on the operating systems. If the network is using Windows XP Professional, you can turn off Simple File Sharing and apply NTFS permissions to the networked files. This way, you can control exactly which users can access a file and what the users can do with the file once they access it. By default, Simple File Sharing is configured to make file sharing easy for end users in a workgroup, on Windows XP Professional, you can turn off simple file sharing and use NTFS permissions. Open Folder Options in the Control Panel, and on the View tab clear the Use Simple File Sharing option. Once Simple File Sharing is turned off, the Sharing tab of each resource will change, shown in Figure 2-10, so that you can share the resource, then use the Security tab to configure individual NTFS permissions for the share.

Documents Properties [?] [X]

| General | Sharing | Security | Web Sharing | Customize |

You can share this folder with other users on your network. To enable sharing for this folder, click Share this folder.

○ Do _n_ot share this folder
◉ _S_hare this folder

_S_hare name: `Documents`

_C_omment: ``

User limit: ◉ _M_aximum allowed
○ Allo_w_ this number of users: `` ▲▼

To set permissions for users who access this folder over the network, click Permissions.   [_P_ermissions]

To configure settings for offline access, click Caching.   [_C_aching]

[OK]   [Cancel]   [_A_pply]

FIGURE 2.10   The Sharing tab

TROUBLESHOOTING

Security in a Workgroup

In the past, workgroups had major problems with security—after all, under most operating systems, any user who could get to a computer could access data on the network. Newer operating systems, however, such as Linux, Windows 2000/XP, and Macintosh OS X are all user-based operating systems. This means that you can configure various accounts in order for users to log on to the local computer, and thus access the network. Since there is no centralized logon server in a workgroup, the responsibility for network protection falls on each user managing a desktop. Accounts must be created (protected with effective passwords), and desktops cannot be left unattended while a user is logged on. Depending on the workgroup, such security measures may not be necessary at all, but if security is an issue, keep these important user points in mind—and use operating systems that support these features!

WRAPPING UP...

Workgroups in today's networking environments have become more complex, but also more feature rich. You can employ several different types of inexpensive network topologies and you can share resources, including Internet connections. Newer operating systems all support a number of important workgroup options and features that are rather important in today's diverse workgroup environments. As with all aspects of networking, careful consideration, study, and a hard look at budget constraints are a must when configuring workgroups, but with the features available today, you can configure effective, secure workgroups that can meet most any need.

NETWORK OPERATIONS AND TOOLS

3

During the course of this chapter we will look at the kinds of tools that can be used to both configure your network devices and measure the overall health of the network. We will examine the kinds of information you will need to have access to in order to ensure the expected, and hopefully peak, performance of our network. As a network manager, having both quantitative and qualitative information about your network will be important, because you cannot hope to manage what you cannot measure. Information is just the first step, and here we'll examine some approaches for making management decisions using the information you have on hand. In this chapter, we'll...

- Define the kinds of information that needs to be collected, and practice organizing that information in a useful manner

- Practice using some of the more common software and hardware tools for measuring network performance

- Solve network bandwidth problems

- Resolve media access and network bottleneck problems using hardware and software solutions

- Design and implement network device configurations

GATHERING NETWORK PERFORMANCE DATA

In order to manage the network, evaluate the performance of your networking hardware, and in general ensure that the network is working properly, you will need information. In this first section, we will examine what information needs to be collected. We will also look at a method for organizing this information, including the idea of using a baseline. You will need some kind of software or hardware product to collect the information you need to organize. Because this is the case, we will look at several features and usage guidelines for some of the common hardware and software tools.

WHAT INFORMATION DO YOU NEED?

There is virtually no end to the kinds of information that you can collect about the performance of the various computers and other devices that make up your network. In the majority of situations, the information you need to have handy will fall into three categories: broadcast/multicast traffic, network latency, and the error rate.

BROADCASTS AND MULTICASTS

Broadcasting on a network is conceptually very similar to the broadcasting of a radio signal. With radio broadcasts, any listener tuned to a particular station will receive all of the information being sent from the radio station. In the case of networks, all of the hosts on the same logical network segment (such as a computer in the same IP subnet) are considered to be on the same station. Any host on the network can perform a broadcast, and all of the hosts on that same segment will receive and process the transmission. There are other occasions where a host will receive all of the traffic generated by other hosts. For example, if a multiport repeater, or hub, is used on an Ethernet network, all of the hosts that are sharing the same physical segment will receive every bit sent and received from every other host connected to the same repeater. This is not the case if the hosts are connected to a shared network switch, because each port on the switch is its own Ethernet segment. In contrast, broadcasts are transmissions that specify "all hosts" as the target rather than a single communication partner, and as such, all hosts that receive the broadcasted information must process the data. Regardless of whether the host is connected to a switch or a hub, they will all receive and process the transmission.

Multicasts are a specialized form of broadcasting. In fact, multicasting allows a single host, sending the multicast traffic, to connect to multiple hosts that share a particular common configuration. The multicasting computer sends only one copy of the data, and that data is then processed by all the hosts that are members of the same multicast group. While each host does not have to process a multicast that occurs on that hosts segment, all of the network devices such as routers and switches must.

NOTE   Multicast traffic requires the use of a special range of IP addresses beginning with 224.0.0.0, and collectively called class D addresses. Hosts that are participating in the multicast session use these addresses to join a multicast group. All members of the group receive the multicast sent by the multicast server/application.

Because broadcasting and multicasting involves large numbers of hosts, and both add to the load on all of the involved network routers and switches, they must be carefully controlled. The measurement of broadcasts and multicasts is typically done in the form of a percentage of total traffic. We will get into specifics later, but generally speaking you want to have less than 25 percent of all network traffic to be the result of broadcasts and/or multicasts.

LATENCY

Latency is also known as delay, and sometimes as responsiveness. Though the definition varies slightly depending on whom you ask, latency can be defined as the round-trip time for data transmission between any two hosts. For example, host A sends data to host B (see Figure 3-1) and then host B replies.

The time elapsed between the transmission of data from host A to the return of a response to host A from host B is the latency of the path between host A and host B. By obtaining the round-trip time between various hosts on a LAN or WAN, you can determine the responsiveness of various network paths. There are many things that affect the latency of the communications between any two hosts, including network utilization, CPU utilization on the hosts, and transmission problems.

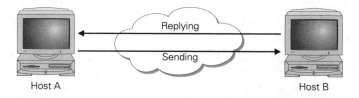

| **FIGURE 3.1** | Latency |

ERROR PERCENTAGE

During the course of normal network communications, bad things occasionally happen. Sometimes the data from one host does not survive the journey to its intended destination. This data loss is known as an error. When an error occurs, the sending host must resend the lost information. The retransmission of some information is not a big problem if it does not occur often. However, if large numbers of errors force hosts to spend a lot of time retransmitting data, the capacity of the communicating hosts to send and receive data can be greatly reduced. Generally speaking, error rates above 10 percent should be considered a potential issue.

SIMPLE NETWORK PERFORMANCE TESTS

Even without the use of specialized hardware or software, there are some simple things you can do to informally evaluate the status of your network. This informal analysis makes use of the ping utility, as introduced in Chapter 1, and a good old-fashioned file copy between network hosts. What you want to collect from the ping utility is the "time" value that is given as a part of the output. This is the time it has taken for data to go to the host and then return to the originating computer. On a LAN, hosts should be found in less than 10 ms. Greater round-trip times are indicative of poor network performance. In a WAN environment, round-trip time should not exceed 500 ms.

The file copy is used to estimate the bandwidth available, and to a degree the level of network utilization. In order to use the file copy to evaluate the link between the sending and receiving hosts, you will need two hosts on the same network, a stopwatch and a file of 1–100MB in size. Here is what you will do: You initiate a file copy between the two hosts. You time how long it takes the file copy to complete. Then, you record both the size of the file and the time it takes to move the file from one particular host to another. You will also want to record any identifying features of the test, such as the route the data is taking to get between the hosts and so forth. To find the route, or path through the network, that the data is traveling, you can use the tracert command. This command is explained in Chapter 13. Basically, the command output will show you how many devices are involved in the communications process and how much delay is occurring at each point.

If you are testing the transfer over the Internet or other WAN, you may need a smaller file. For testing a high-speed WAN connection or for a LAN, larger files (as large as is practical) are definitely preferred. Larger files minimize the effect of human error. If your timing is a few seconds off, with a 25-minute file transfer you will see less error than if you are a few seconds off on a 1-minute file transfer. Record your timing results in seconds. Once you have the data, divide the file size by the time it takes to copy the file. Remember that most computers show file size in kilobytes and megabytes (KB/MB) and network links are most often rated using kilobits and megabits (Kb/Mb). In order to ensure that you are working with the correct size, you will need to know that there are eight bits for each one byte. In most cases, you will save some serious headaches by using megabits as your units.

Once you have made the needed calculation, you will have the rate at which your file was moved across the network in megabits per second (Mbps). Divide your number by the throughput rating (also Mbps) of the slowest link between the hosts (see Figure 3-2 for some guidelines) and then multiply by 100 to yield a percentage.

For example, if you got 6 Mbps during your file copy and the slowest link between the hosts was 10 Mbps, the result would be .6 × 100 = 60 percent. Because this means that 60 percent of the 10 Mbps capacity was available for your file transfer, the link was approximately 40 percent utilized. This calculation needs to be taken with a large grain of salt. Protocol overhead, latency induced by network hardware, and other conditions reduce the theoretical maximum transfer significantly. Also, it is not true that your file transfer will be able to consume all of the available bandwidth. But this method is for rough estimation, as tools exist for more precise

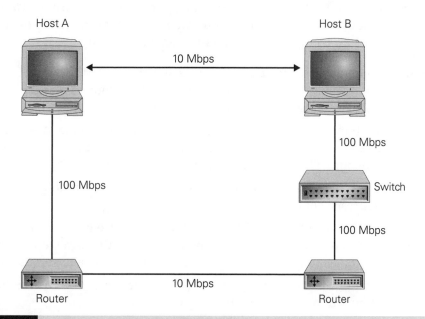

FIGURE 3.2   Identifying the slowest link

measurements. With Ethernet network segments, the most you can reasonably expect to find available is about 70 percent of the rated line speed. Token ring and some WAN technologies can push this to 90 percent. So in our example, we found 60 percent of the theoretical capacity of 10 Mbps was available. In practical terms, this means that we were able to consume 85 percent (6 Mbps/7 Mbps) of the link, meaning that the link was previously only 15 percent utilized.

NOTE WAN technologies include frame relay, Asynchronous Transfer Mode (ATM), and Demand Dial (ISDN and Modem), as well as xDSL and point-to-point wireless connections.

Once you have the rough utilization value, you can compare to the recommended maximum utilizations. Ethernet is considered overutilized if utilization exceeds 40 percent. Token ring and WAN technologies become overutilized at 70 percent. Once these thresholds are exceeded, a bottleneck has developed. Dealing with the results is a subject we will tackle later in this chapter. While this method of roughly estimating network utilization is not 100 percent accurate, it is fast and works well if you find yourself in a location where more advanced networking tools are not readily available. In a pinch, this can save you time when trying to identify the general health of the network.

Just to make sure you're comfortable with the process, we will step through the data collection and calculation process for performing an informal evaluation of the network utilization. For this test, you can use any operating system you are most comfortable. To complete the evaluation on a LAN host, follow these steps:

1. Search your computer for a file that is larger than 100MB in size. Once located, either make note of its location or make a copy of it and place the copy in an easy to find location such as the desktop. Note the exact file size.

2. Locate another host on your network that will allow you to place files on it from a remote host. This receiving computer could have file shares or maybe even an FTP server allowing you to send files.

3. Make sure you have a stopwatch, PC clock, or other time-telling instrument that measures seconds.

4. Perform a file copy, start an FTP session or otherwise begin a transfer of the file selected in step 1 to the receiving host identified in step 2. Time how long it takes to make the transfer. Record the time elapsed in seconds.

5. Convert the file size from megabytes (MB) to megabits (Mb) using the following equation: MB × 8 = Mb.

6. Divide the number of megabits transferred by the time elapsed in seconds using the following equation: Mb/s = Mbps.

7. Divide the resulting Mbps value (obtained in step 6) by the line rating of the slowest segment between the hosts. See Figure 3-2 for a refresher, if needed. Use the following equation to calculate the amount of capacity your file transfer consumed: [Mbps (transfer)/Mbps (rating)] × 100 = % of capacity consumed.

8. The percentage you now have tells you roughly how much bandwidth (capacity) was available to consume. By subtracting this value from 100 percent, you will obtain your approximate network utilization. This value should be below 40 percent for Ethernet networks and below 70 percent for WAN and token ring segments.

Since this method for determining network health is not really adequate for day-to-day management or precise analysis, we will look at some more powerful network monitoring tools. These tools fall into two general categories, software-based and hardware-based.

SOFTWARE NETWORK MONITORS

Software network monitors are widely used to log daily activity, pinpoint trouble spots, and even configure network devices remotely. These tools are made by a wide range of vendors, including IBM, Hewlett Packard (HP), and Microsoft.

HEWLETT PACKARD: OPENVIEW

OpenView has been a virtual standard in large- and medium-scale networking management for many years. There are many individual components to this software suite, each with its own applications and potential uses. In this section, we will examine some of the general features available with the basic elements. For information about the multitude of configuration options available with the OpenView package, check out the OpenView web site at http://www.openview .hp.com/.

The OpenView suite has components that enable (among other things) the measurement of broadcast/multicast traffic, network utilization, host configuration information and inventory, and remote server and network device configuration. Additionally, there are elements for managing networkwide "quality of service" levels for various network services and resources. Such tasks as network device configuration and managing networkwide data backups are also possible. Most of these features are accessible by a pleasant graphical user interface, typically on a dedicated monitoring station. By no means do you have to dedicate a computer, or computers, to the task of running OpenView, but various processes such as network discovery will noticeably tax the resources of the computer running it. If you're playing Unreal Tournament III on the same box where OpenView is running, you'll notice serious performance degradation (in UT3).

IBM: TIVOLI

Much like HP OpenView, IBM's Tivoli is a comprehensive suite of network management tools. Of the many individual software products sold under the Tivoli moniker, the Enterprise Console product is probably the most comprehensive network/systems monitoring and management tool. This tool will allow you to monitor servers, network devices (switches/routers), and network clients. Other products allow enterprise-wide storage and backup management (Storage Manager), web site transaction and health information (Business Systems Manager), and mainframe systems monitoring (NetView Performance Monitor).

QUEST SOFTWARE: BIG BROTHER

Big Brother 1.9 is a product of Quest Software (not to be confused with Qwest communications) that provides a large number of remote monitoring features. The status of the network, including servers, network performance, and other essential bits of information are available to the administrator via a web interface. Big Brother will also page an administrator when specified events (link failure, server response failure, and such) occur. While the last two features listed are available to varying degrees with OpenView and Tivoli, the big difference is cost. Big Brother is "free" for many users and for those who need to purchase a commercial license, the cost is considerably less than the packages from IBM or HP. Check out http://bb4.com/ for more information on licensing and purchase options.

PAINFUL LESSONS I'VE LEARNED

The Network Tool that Broke the Camel's Back

Some network analysis tools have topology discovery functions. Basically, these discovery tools send out various kinds of broadcasts and protocol messages to discover which devices are attached to the network. Unfortunately, as I learned, these discovery sessions can generate a substantial load on the network. In an attempt to resolve a connectivity issue I was having once, I decided to run a discovery session and find out exactly which workstations and servers were connected to my network, and generate a topology map. The result was that my network went from limping to belly up almost instantly. Once I figured out what was going on, I ended the session and made a mental note to perform network topology discovery when nobody else would be using the network.

OTHER SOFTWARE PRODUCTS

Of course, there are also more frugal options for monitoring the health of individual segments of your network and individual hosts on your network. Many operating systems include tools for doing just this. In particular, Microsoft Windows NT family of operating systems (NT, 2000, XP, and .NET) has a useful tool called Performance Monitor, or simply Perfmon. While this tool is probably nothing new to you, some of the network-related features might be. In the following section we will outline the procedure for monitoring the utilization of various network- related components of a Windows 2000 Server. To perform this exercise, you will need a computer with Windows 2000 installed that has configured a network adapter. The MS loopback adapter can be used, but no data will be recorded.

1. Log on to the computer with administrative credentials (domain administrator if appropriate).

2. Right-click My Computer and select the Manage option from the context menu that appears.

3. In the displayed window, called the Microsoft Management Console or MMC, click the plus symbol next to the entry titled Performance Logs and Alerts to expand the menu.

4. Click the Counter Logs Entry. Click the Action menu again and select New Log Settings. A box will appear prompting you to provide a name. Type in the word **Sample** and click the OK button.

5. Once you have clicked the OK button, a configuration window will appear. Click the Add button in the middle of this window. In the Select Counters window that appears next, choose which system elements to monitor.

6. In the Performance Object drop-down, select the Network Interface object. In the bottom pair of option lists, select the network adapter that is in use (lower-right portion of the current window) and the Bytes Total/sec entry and click the Add button.

7. Next, click the Current Bandwidth entry that is immediately below the Bytes Total/sec entry and click Add again. Click the Close button.

8. Click the Log Files tab that is visible at the top of the configuration window. Note the location where windows will store the log file. By default, it is C:\perflogs, and if this directory has not already been created, you will be prompted to do so when leaving this window.

9. Click the General tab to return to the main configuration screen.

10. From within the General Settings screen, change the interval setting at the bottom of the window from the default of 15 seconds to a value of

1 second. Click the OK button, which should close the Configuration window.

11. In the main MMC window, titled Computer Management, you should see your sample log with a stack of green disks next to it, indicating that the system is now logging the elements you just configured. If this if not the case, right-click the Sample entry and select Start from the menu that appears.

12. Let the log record data for 30–60 seconds. While it is logging, you should browse the network, Internet, send/receive e-mail, or otherwise generate some network activity.

13. Returning to the Computer Management window, right-click Sample, and select the Stop option to end logging. Close all open windows.

14. Click the Start button and select the Run entry. In the box, type **perfmon** and click the OK button.

15. A new window, the Windows Performance Monitor, will open. Click the View Log File Data icon circled in Figure 3-3.

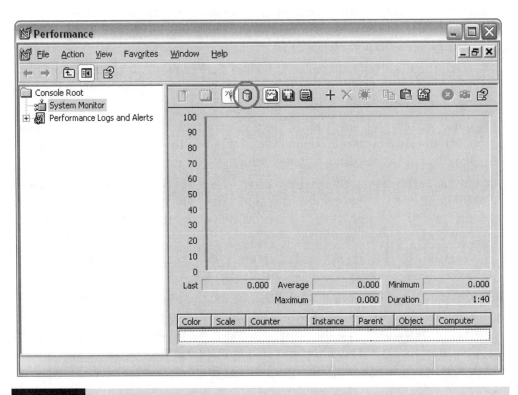

FIGURE 3.3 The Performance Monitor window

16. Browse the File Open window to the C:\PerfLogs directory if it does not open by default. Select the log file named "sample_00000x" where "x" is the highest number listed. Once highlighted, click the Open button.

17. You will now need to add the counters to the displayed graph. Click the Add button, as seen in Figure 3-3. In the window that appears, click the bullets next to All Counters and All Instances and click the Add button.

18. Click the Close button.

19. The graph will now show colored lines to designate the various counters you recorded. The bandwidth line should be flat and next to the corresponding setting for your network adapter. For example, the value would be 10 for 10 Mbps by default. You should see some variation in the other line that represents the incoming and outgoing traffic from your computer during the monitoring cycle.

By changing the values logged (steps 6 and 7), you can monitor a wealth of data concerning the network performance of the host as well as CPU, memory, and hard disk utilization. One thing you should keep in mind, though, is the fact that logging consumes resources. For our test, we used a 1-second sample interval. This is not recommended if you will be logging for a long period of time. If you will be logging for long periods of time, such as 5–10 hours, intervals of 15–60 seconds would be preferable, as this will reduce the impact on the system's performance and greatly reduce the size of the resulting log file.

HARDWARE NETWORK MONITORS

One of the shortcomings of software tools is the need for a desktop computer or server to house the software. This can hinder the flexibility of the solution as well as limit the ability to move the monitoring system between discontinuous networks. Hardware meters, on the other hand, can be ultraportable and are almost entirely platform independent. Additionally, since they are relatively simple devices, they have an extremely long mean time between failure (MTBF) values. These values are a rough measure of the reliability of the particular component. One of the most prevalent providers of hardware network monitors is Fluke. Fluke produces networking tools that range from small signal generators and cable testers to rack-mounted network traffic analysis devices. The OneTouch series of portable network analyzers probably represents as much of a flagship product as anything that Fluke produces. Fluke is not the only manufacturer that produces reliable and powerful hardware for monitoring a network. Agilent makes another hardware-based product, the FrameScope 350, which also provides a wide range of network monitoring and analysis features. These devices are capable of discovering hosts and network devices, monitoring traffic in terms of utilization, broadcast/multicast values, and error and data collision rates, and sorting traffic by protocol type (IP, IPX, and AppleTalk). In addition, they list all discovered network nodes in order of the volume of network traffic they produce. The net result is a quickly obtainable and concise analysis of the health of the network and quick identification of problem hosts and devices.

USING A BASELINE

You now have an idea of the kinds of information that will be useful when monitoring the performance of your network. You also know some of the tools available for helping you collect that information from informal assessments to precise, real-time data collection tools. But what do you do with the information you have? How can you ensure that the time spent monitoring the network and collecting data will actually be useful in the event that some problem arises? The answer is that you will use the data to build a baseline. The following list shows the minimum information you should include for each of the three information-gathering samples listed shortly:

- Network utilization

- Percent of traffic that is broadcast/multicast

- Error rate (percent of transmissions that encounter an error)

- Protocols in use on the network

- Ten hosts/devices (nodes) generating the most network traffic

A good baseline is a document of some kind that contains information describing your network under "normal" conditions. Normal is, of course, a vague term when it comes to networks, so you should be as detailed as possible in describing the "normal" conditions of your network. This will help identify issues that are variances from normal conditions versus actual network issues. A baseline is made of information collected during three different periods of network usage:

- Low network utilization

- High, or peak, network utilization

- Long-term

First, information is collected when the network is least utilized. This means different things to different networks, but an example might be a LAN within a grade school from 8:00 P.M. to 4:00 A.M. This overnight sample would give the administrator a picture of the "background noise" present on the network. The idea of this kind of sample is to assess the volume of nonuser-generated traffic. You will want as many of the hosts and servers on as possible, especially those that are used on a daily basis. Keep in mind there is probably always some kind of user influence, even when there should be no users. For instance, someone may have walked off leaving their favorite web-based radio station playing on their computer.

The next period to collect information on your network is peak utilization. Find the time that your users are putting the hurt on your LAN/WAN the most and then start logging the assorted variables. This is the time you will find out if you're exceeding the broadcast or utilization thresholds for your network. If there are future problems waiting to happen, this is the time you will be able to identify them. Typically, the biggest hit to your network will occur when large numbers of users are logging in (morning and after lunch), as well as if they are making use of networked applications in large numbers at the same time. Predict the peaks and make sure you are recording data before they occur, during the event, and afterwards.

Finally, you will want to make a map of how your network traffic changes over the course of a day, week, or month. If your users do pretty much the same thing from day to day, a daily average should suffice. If there are behavioral patterns, such as product releases, that vary network usage over a week or a month, then you will need to take a longer sample. Generally, this kind of data collection has a long interval between samples. There is no need to sample the network every 15 seconds if you will be collecting data for days. Every few minutes or even hours will suffice for your long-term average. The peak- and low-usage samples will give you the fine detail you need.

The baseline should be updated on regular intervals. This interval depends on how often the network will undergo changes in usage. After there are significant changes in network design or usage, you should build a new set of baselines. This new information will not only give you a fresh set of data to use for troubleshooting purposes, but it can also be used as a comparative tool to assess the effect that the change has made on the health of the network.

SOLVING BANDWIDTH PROBLEMS

One of the issues you may identify during your network analysis is network congestion or a shortage of bandwidth. Typically, this shortage is manifested by links that are highly utilized. Recall that Ethernet networks using over 40 percent of the available bandwidth are considered overutilized and token ring/WAN networks reach the same point as 70 percent utilization. When this threshold is reached, you will need to complete a number of tasks to resolve the issue. But why resolve the issue, you ask? Overutilization typically generates a never-ending steam of end-user complaints stemming from slow, unresponsive, and crashing networked applications. Unless you feel a need to be berated by your users, including your boss, this is an issue you will look forward to resolving. To return your end user to network nirvana, you will need to first find the source of the problem and then implement a solution.

SEGMENTATION SOLUTIONS: ROUTING

If your network is having problems supporting the number of hosts present, segmentation may be the easiest, most effective solution. Segmenting is accomplished by breaking the network hosts into smaller groups and thus effectively increasing the amount of bandwidth available to each host. Using a router, or changing the way the router connects hosts on the network, can have a dramatic impact on how the network performs. A good "rule of thumb" is the 80/20 rule. Any host should spend 80 percent of its time communicating with hosts and servers that reside on the same network segment. Only 20 percent of the communication time should be spent contacting hosts on other network segments. The key reason for this is the fact that most routers have a limited capacity to handle network traffic. Network segmentation helps ensure that the router is only used when absolutely needed. Segmentation falls into two broad categories that often overlap: logical segmentation and physical segmentation.

LOGICAL SEGMENTATION

If your router and hosts are all connected to a single switch and you are making use of two or more IP address subnets on your LAN, your network is making use of logical segmentation. Though the devices are physically sharing the same device (the switch), they logically are on separate networks—each with its own IP subnet. Logical segmentation will allow you to control the passage of broadcast traffic on the network without having to physically relocate hosts and servers. If your network traffic is more than 25 percent broadcast/multicast, logical segmentation can be used to improve your network's performance significantly. Two of the key benefits of this solution are cost and time. Logical segmentation will not require the addition of hardware if you already have a router. By readdressing the hosts that will be placed in a new subnet and then configuring the router to route between the new and existing network subnets, you can painlessly segment the network.

The downside is that the new segment and the old one share the same hardware. All of the data that is carried by a switch is processed by a component called a *backplane*. The backplane has a limited capacity to handle traffic. For example, many multiport switches commonly have a 1-Gbps (gigabit per second) capacity or more. If your switch is housing 15 hosts that each have 100-Mbps connections to the switch, there is a potential for the hosts to overwhelm the backplane since the hosts can theoretically consume 1.5 Gbps (1,500 Mbps) of capacity. If the hosts are generating traffic that is pushing the backplane capacity, logical segmentation is not likely to provide any improvement in performance unless you also replace the existing switch with one having a greater backplane capacity.

PHYSICAL SEGMENTATION

If your network hosts are running your network hardware ragged, you may need to move some of your hosts to another physical network segment. Not only will physical segmentation yield the same benefits as logical segmentation, but you will also reduce the load on the individual networking devices. The catch here is that you will need to purchase and install new networking hardware. If your network is having trouble with high utilization rates, physical segmentation offers you the chance to greatly expand the bandwidth available.

Along with the two solutions for bandwidth issues listed earlier, there is a third solution that is a mixture of the concepts of the previous solutions. This solution is known as the virtual local area network (VLAN). VLANs are similar to the logical segmentation described in previous sections. Unlike simply hosting multiple IP subnets on a single device, as with logical segmentation, VLAN-enabled devices can treat groups of attached hosts as if they were on separate physical devices.

TROUBLESHOOTING

Solutions to Broadcasting Problems

If you have found that there is a problem with broadcast traffic on your network, you can implement any and all of the following solutions as they apply to your network configuration to help resolve the problem:

1. Use a router to segment the network. By default, routers do not pass broadcasts from one connected network to any of the other networks to which they are connected.

Solutions to Broadcasting Problems (continued)

2. Remove protocols that communicate heavily with network broadcasts such as NetBEUI, AppleTalk, and IPX/SPX.

3. Install a DNS server and configure hosts to use it for all hostname resolution requests. This will help minimize hosts sending network broadcasts to resolve hostnames.

4. Install a WINS server to provide NetBIOS name resolution. This will reduce the volume of network capacity consumed by NetBIOS resolution traffic, which can be significant on large networks.

SEGMENTATION SOLUTIONS: VLAN

Virtual LAN will allow you to take advantage of an improved form of logical segmentation. VLANs allow you to group individual switch ports into groups. None of the data generated by any of the hosts within a particular VLAN group (VLAN1, for example) will pass to any port not in that same VLAN group. Hosts on the same switch share the backplane still, but individual interfaces will not receive transmissions from hosts outside their VLAN group. A router is connected to a switch port that is then made a member of each configured VLAN, and thus the router will enable communications between the VLANs.

NOTE Do not confuse a switch backplane with a network backbone. The backplane is the device that centrally connects all of the components of a switch. The backplane is roughly analogous to a computer motherboard.

BENEFITS OF VLAN

Many VLAN configurations make use of large-capacity switches that have 144 or more switch ports. This "network in a box" configuration can improve performance and reliability and greatly simplify network management. One of the ways that performance is improved is that these large switches typically come with robust backplanes and data moving from one host to another can take advantage of this high-speed backplane to have extremely fast access to other hosts. Reliability and ease of management are closely linked in this scenario. With fewer individual components, there is less to configure, less to fail, and you can monitor network traffic from a single point. The downside is that your network has a single point of failure. For example, should the switch's power supply fail, your network will go offline.

For those switches that can make use of a routing module, such as a Route Switch Module in a Cisco 4000 series switch, the performance of routing between VLAN hosts can be greatly improved. Because the route module is connected directly to the same backplane as the hosts, data can be moved much faster (up to 3 Gbps) than would be possible with the 10–16-Mbps capacity available with most routers.

NOTE   Switches make use of application-specific integrated circuits (ASIC) to move data between the individual switch ports. The ASIC is used to make the logical determination about which port the data is supposed to go—that is, where the intended recipient is located. Because this decision is made with hardware circuitry and not software processing, the result is blazing speed.

Solutions that take advantage of internal route processors are not always appropriate. Because these one-unit solutions are often relatively expensive, they really should only be used if needed. If there is little communication between the various VLANs, a less expensive external router should be used. The external router can be configured to participate on each of the VLAN segments and will provide basic connectivity between them.

DEVICES THAT SUPPORT VLAN

Maybe you're now considering VLANs for your network, so let's take a look at some of the devices that support the use of VLANs. We'll take a look at products from Cisco Systems, Hewlett Packard, and a few other manufacturers that support VLAN configurations.

Cisco Systems makes a dizzying array of networking products—from small home networking products to huge enterprise network routers. The Catalyst series of products (Cisco's Switching line) has many units that support VLAN configurations. The 2948G, 2980, 4000 series, 4800 series, 5000 series, and 6500 series all (among others) support VLAN. This ensures that networks of all sizes can make use of VLAN functionality.

Much like Cisco, Hewlett Packard (HP) makes a substantial assortment of networking products. Of the switching products that they make, the following is a list of some of the more commonly used devices (all Procurve models) that support VLAN operation: 2524/2512, 4000M, 5300XL series, and the 8000M.

Many other manufacturers make networking products that support VLANs. Linksys, IBM, 3Com, and Madge Networks make a variety of switching products, from small workgroup Ethernet devices to large enterprise token ring products. To determine which is best for your situation, you will need to balance product options such as the backplane capacity, available ports, and configuration options with the cost of the unit.

CONFIGURING THE VLAN

On a Cisco Catalyst switch that supports VLAN, the steps to enable this feature are relatively straightforward. The following steps will create VLAN with a VLAN ID of 4 on a Catalyst 4000 series switch, on module 3 and ports 1–48 of that module. Each VLAN must carry a unique identifier known as a VLAN ID. This ID is an arbitrary value (you choose). Many of Cisco's switching products are modular in nature, making use of a central chassis and swappable units (called modules) that carry different network interfaces. Connect to the switch through a terminal session and follow these steps:

1. Type **enable** and press ENTER. When prompted, enter the **enable** password.

2. Type the command **set vlan 4 2/1-48** and press ENTER.

This is only one example of enabling a VLAN. Switches from other vendors do not use the same syntax. In fact, some of Cisco's switching products do not use the same commands. Depending on the hardware you are working with, you will need to obtain the proper documentation of the operating software. If the relevant

TECH TALK

Causes of "Destination Unreachable" Messages

When using the ICMP ping utility, you may occasionally find that the error message "Destination Unreachable" is returned when you attempt to test connectivity to a host. This error message can result from a couple of conditions. The most obvious are that the host may not be online or the IP address may have been mistyped. Routing problems can also cause this error to arise, even when the host is actually online. This situation occurs when one of the routers between your host (sending the ping) and the recipient (replying to the ping) does not have routing information needed to forward data back to the originator of the ping. If the router has no route to the host you are trying to ping, or if the host is configured to ignore ping requests, the message you will see is "request timed out." What you should take away from this is the fact that a "Destination Unreachable" message does not really tell you much except that the ping test is failing.

Secret Host Files Defeated My Router

Once upon a time I made some router configuration changes and readdressed a number of network clients to increase the capacity of the network. Once all of the network changes were in place, I went home satisfied that all of the users would be blissfully unaware that any change had been made, except perhaps to notice that the network was a bit more responsive. Well, they noticed the change all right. Come the next morning my phone was literally blowing off the hook with complaints about inaccessible servers and an inability to access the Internet. As it turns out, users in the development group had taken it upon themselves to modify the local hosts file on their computers. The modifications contained name-to-address mappings for the network domain, file servers, and the device responsible for firewalling, proxy, and Internet access. Since many of these resources had been readdressed, the host entries were no longer valid and left the users stuck because many had also disabled the use of DNS on their workstations. To add injury to insult, the host file was processed before the DNS server is queried. Any bad, or good, host file entry would be used in lieu of DNS hostname resolution. Once DNS was enabled and the hosts file entries removed, all was well with the world and it only took me half a day to figure it out.

documentation does not accompany the equipment when it is purchased, you can typically obtain the information from vendor web sites or by calling product support.

TROUBLESHOOTING THE NETWORK BOTTLENECK

Sometimes the problem with network access has nothing to do with bandwidth. Very often a single (or a couple) of devices that are responsible for passing traffic between hosts and these devices are not up to the task. These devices become bottlenecks in the communications process.

HOW TO IDENTIFY BOTTLENECKS

The symptoms of a bottleneck include slow response times (high latency) and poor data transfer speed (unusually low bandwidth). Sometimes the most obvious sign of a bottleneck is a network-based application that becomes unresponsive or crashes. If these issues occur, you can take your baseline data and network monitoring tools to assess the situations. Typically, a user will report a problem when performing a specific task such as accessing a server or running the aforementioned networked application. This in itself will help you focus on a small section of the network. Your analysis will need to focus on the section of the network between the host computer experiencing the problem and the network resource that the host is accessing. First, test the overall path from the host to the resource. If the network path between the host and the resource traverses multiple network devices and or subnets, test each section until the smallest testable portion has been measured. One (or if your really unfortunate, more than one) link will show signs of underperformance.

BOTTLENECK SOLUTIONS

When the bottleneck has been identified, you will have a couple of solutions at your disposal: upgrade hardware and/or reconfigure. Each of these solutions has associated benefits and shortcomings. You will need to assess your particular situation and make a determination about which of the solutions will best suit your situation.

Hardware upgrades are particularly useful if your bottleneck problem is the result of adding new services or users to your network. In this kind of a scenario, the device that became a bottleneck when the new resources or hosts were added was not an issue in the prior configuration. Let us look at a hypothetical scenario. Assume that you have a 24 port, 10/100 Ethernet switch with a 500-Mbps backplane, two servers with 100-Mbps network adapters and ten end-user computers with 10-Mbps adapters. You add ten more end-user computers with 100-Mbps adapters and two more servers with 100-Mbps adapters. Almost immediately users begin to complain that access to the new servers is sluggish. In this case, the problem is that the new users are consuming more bandwidth than was left available on the backplane of the switch. The only solution that will have any meaningful effect, while allowing the various hosts and servers to operate at maximum capacity, involves upgrading the switch to a model that has a more robust backplane.

If such a problem does arise on your network, you can temporarily alleviate the problem by manually configuring the network adapters of all of the client computers to 10 Mbps.

Design-based solutions are usually only an option if the network is composed of multiple network devices. This solution type involves reorganizing the way the devices on the network interconnect and/or changing the configuration (port settings, routing options, and such) of the existing network hardware. One of the most basic configuration changes involves the idea of managing aggregate traffic. The idea is fairly simple: any network servers should be able to accommodate all of the data traffic that client connections generate. An example of this would be a network making use of a 40-port 10/100 Ethernet switch to house 30 clients and 4 servers. If the servers and host both make use of 100-Mbps network adapters, it is theoretically possible for a single network client to monopolize one of the servers. By forcing all of the client computers to 10 Mbps, it would now require ten clients simultaneously connecting to the server (and no other hosts or servers) to overwhelm the server. With the client network interfaces restricted, it becomes very unlikely that one of the servers in the above scenario will be come overutilized.

UNDERSTANDING MEDIA CONTENTION PROBLEMS

Media contention is a problem on most network types. Media contention is literally competition among networked hosts for access to communicate on the network. When any networked host wants to communicate on a network, it must have exclusive access to the network for the few milliseconds that it takes to send a portion of the data it wants to send. When there are too many hosts vying for network access, the process of network communications begins to break down. In this section, we will look at media contention on Ethernet and token ring networks.

Ethernet networks are probably the most sensitive to media contention issues. Ethernet depends on the carrier sense multiple access with collision detection (CSMA/CD) algorithm to determine when a host can transmit on the physical network segment. Basically, this algorithm specifies that a host who wants to communicate must perform the following steps:

1. Listen to the network to see if any device is currently transmitting. If there is a transmission going on, the host will wait a specified period of time and then listen again.

2. If no other device is transmitting, the host is allowed to make a transmission.

3. If two hosts should end up sending at the same time, the data from both hosts will be corrupted in what is called a *collision*. Each host will begin the communications process all over again—after waiting a random time interval—following the collision's occurrence.

If the number of collisions becomes large, this algorithm is not capable of sustaining functional communications. Users will see slow access to network resources and abnormally long file transfer times, and they may have trouble using the network at all. Because of the limitations of the CSMA/CD algorithm, no more than 20 Ethernet hosts should be connected to a single Ethernet segment. All of the ports on a repeater/hub share the same segment, for example.

Token ring networks use a technique known as token passing to determine which host is allowed to communicate. A special piece of data (an OSI layer 2 frame) called a *token* is literally passed between hosts and servers on the network. In order to transmit, a computer must have possession of the token. The data that the host wishes to send is appended to this special frame and then passed back on to the network. Because each host must have the token in order to communicate, there is no chance for a collision to occur. This allows token ring networks to scale very well to large numbers of users gracefully. While the token segment will continue to get slower as more hosts are added, there is a gradual reduction in performance rather than the dramatic drop as is experienced with Ethernet.

SOLVING MEDIA CONTENTION WITH SWITCHING

So what do you do if the Ethernet or token ring network you are in charge of becomes overcrowded? The best solution is to break up the individual physical segments with switching. Let's clarify our definition of a physical segment at this point. It is probably most useful to look at this in terms of how it relates to network equipment. All of the ports and the hosts connected to them on

PAINFUL LESSONS

I'VE LEARNED

Chain of Pain

In a time long gone it was generally accepted among casual networkers that one could connect Ethernet hubs (repeaters) in a chain to increase the number of available ports. This is probably the result of applying token ring network practices to an Ethernet environment. Unfortunately, because of the CSMA/CD behavior of Ethernet, this is an extremely poor idea. Once while at a customer site I was trying to resolve some horrendous and mysterious networking problems, almost to no avail. Then one of the customer representatives casually mentioned that there was one wiring closet I had not been shown. I decided to investigate. To my amazement I found three 24-port Ethernet hubs connected in a chain from one hub to another. Almost every port on every hub was connected to a host somewhere in the facility. While the theoretical maximum number of hosts per Ethernet segment is 20, they had nearly 50 hosts sharing the same segment. Once the hubs had been reorganized with a switch linking each 24-port unit to the LAN, the mystery performance issues vanished.

TECH TALK

Removing Unused Protocols

Many network devices come with a host of networking protocols enabled by default. These protocols include IPX, IP, AppleTalk, NetBEUI, and occasionally others. To ensure efficient use of your networking resources, any of these protocols that are not used should be disabled. The following list identifies some common devices that come with multiple networking protocols enabled by default:

1. External network print servers

2. Internal network print servers

3. Network attached storage and storage area network products

an Ethernet repeater or a token ring multiaccess unit (MAU) share the same physical segment. Even if some of the hosts are spread across different logical segments (IP subnets, for example), they would still share the same physical subnet if connected to a common repeater or MAU. On a switch, each of the ports is its own physical segment. The backplane of the switch and the switch-processing engine handle the movement of data between the communicating devices. While it is possible to overwhelm the backplane of a switch, the problem of Ethernet collisions is eliminated for the hosts connected directly to a switch port. In a token ring environment, the capacity of the network is greatly increased since each switch port has its own token.

CONFIGURING NETWORK HARDWARE

Regardless of the kind of network that you are in charge of maintaining, new hardware installations always pose something of a dilemma. Most of the time the network is functional, and adding new hardware always invokes the specter of failed configurations and network disruption. Unless you are in the unpleasant position of replacing failed equipment, you are probably going to be of a mind to take to heart the old cliché "If it ain't broke, don't fix it." But fear not! If you have a plan in place, and you implement it carefully, the impact of new hardware should almost always be a positive one.

MAKING A PLAN

As you prepare to implement your new hardware, there are several kinds of information that you need to keep tabs on. You should use some kind of tool, be it paper or electronic, to record the configuration plans and other related information for future reference. Having thorough documentation will save you a lot of headaches should something go awry after you implement the new hardware. Should a problem occur, you can take a look at your proposed configuration and see if there is anything that might result in the issues you are having. Even if there is nothing obvious about the configuration, your documentation will allow you to double-check the configuration of your new devices and see if you have actually done what you had planned. Many times it is not the plan that is defective. Sometimes it is something as simple as forgetting to save your configuration changes before exiting or rebooting the device you just configured.

NOTE You will also want to document thoroughly the configurations being used by your current devices, if your plan requires changing them. You always want the ability to "go back" if needed.

TESTING AND IMPLEMENTING

When you are to the point where your network design appears to be solid, you need to make sure that the plan will work in a real-world implementation. There are two basic ways to test your design. Which of these options you choose depends on the scope of the changes and the risk that they might present to your network.

PILOTS AND PROTOTYPES

A network pilot is used to verify that the basic features of the network design are sound. This kind of network test involves building a small part of the proposed network change and testing to see if it behaves as expected. For example, if you were planning to install four new switches and a router to add new network capacity, you might configure a single switch and the router, then attach hosts to them and run some basic performance tests (such as building a baseline) to see if the desired results are being achieved.

By contrast, a network prototype is a complete test of the proposed network changes. This method is typically more time-consuming and costly than building a pilot network. Using the same scenario mentioned in the pilot explanation, you would configure and deploy all four switches and the router. Hosts would

TECH TALK

Crossing Over

When connecting network pieces together, it is important to remember which links will need to make use of crossover cables and which ones will require straight-through connections. Here are the rules:

1. Switch to switch requires a crossover.

2. Router to switch requires a straight-through cable.

3. Host to switch requires straight-through cable.

4. Router to router, host to host, or host to router require a crossover cable.

be attached and the performance assessed. If this upgrade was planned for multiple separate LANs, building a prototype at one location might be a good way to ensure a smooth deployment at the other locations.

UPDATING CONFIGURATION INFORMATION

It is almost inevitable that during either a pilot or a prototype test you will discover some configuration options you want to tweak a little before beginning the live implementation. It is important that you update your documentation with these changes. Of particular importance is the change information that includes the reasoning behind the alterations of the original plan. This information will aid you and anyone else that must troubleshoot the newly configured or installed network, because they will be able to take your logic into consideration when correcting any issues that might later arise.

NETWORK HARDWARE ACCESS OPTIONS

For the majority of network hardware components, such as switches and routers, there are two or three options for accessing and configuring the device itself: direct access with a console port, a telnet session, or http "web-based" access. Each of these options has an impact on how easily you can keep tabs on your networking hardware and make changes if needed.

Most commonly networked hardware is configured, at least initially, with the use of a console port of some kind. The port is one of the interfaces on the

TECH TALK

Getting Basic Information from a Cisco Router

When working with a router, it is often useful to check its configuration to see how the various interfaces are configured. This might be done either to plan for a network change or to troubleshoot an existing problem. To use the following command, connect to your router and then log on with any valid account. The show config command will show the current active interfaces, configuration information about those interfaces (IP addresses), the protocols in use on the router, and some other information, including the networks (IP subnets) for which the devices are providing routing services.

networking hardware and may look like a typical serial interface (RS-232), or it may be in the form of an RJ-45 interface. Regardless of the physical connection on the network hardware, the port is a serial interface. If the RJ-45 port is installed on the networking hardware, as is the case with nearly all Cisco hardware, then you will need a cable that can connect the RS-232 serial interface of your computer to the console interface of the hardware. To access the hardware, you will initiate a terminal session using software such as HyperTerminal and configure the session to use the port where the console cable is connected. Once the session is established, you will have access to the command line interface of the networking hardware. One of the shortcomings of this method is that the individual configuring the hardware must be physically near to the networking hardware.

One of the things often done first to network hardware when it is configured is the enabling of telnet access to the device. If this feature is enabled, you or any other administrator of the networking hardware will be able to access the device from anywhere on the network. This can be a really useful feature if you are in charge of monitoring and managing hardware on a large network. There are some inherent risks in this approach, though. If you can telnet to the device, so can someone else. It is for this reason that you should never, under any circumstances, enable or leave enabled telnet-based access on any network hardware that is directly connected to insecure networks such as the Internet. The security benefits gained by closing this potentially serious security risk far outweigh the cost of having to trudge over to your Internet gateway to configure it manually.

TROUBLESHOOTING

Don't Toss Your Console Cables Out

Most network hardware that has a console port of some kind is accompanied by a cable that will allow you to connect a computer of some kind to the hardware for configuration purposes. Unless you happen to be located within a short distance of a vendor who can provide the sometimes unique cables, you will want to keep them handy. In the event that one of your devices fails or is not configured to allow access by means other than the console port, you will not be very happy should you be unable to find the right cable in a pinch. Though these cables are far from unique items, when time is an issue you don't want to have to hunt for a replacement.

WRAPPING UP...

In this chapter, we examined the kinds of information you should have on hand about your network. Utilization rates, traffic characters such as the percent of overall traffic that is broadcast-based, and error rates are among the more important pieces of information to have about your network. There are several ways to go about collecting this kind of information, from informal testing to full-featured hardware and software network analysis tools. We also looked at one particularly useful way of arranging the information you have—the baseline. The baseline gives you a "known good" configuration analysis to aid in troubleshooting networking issues should they arise.

In addition to exploring ways of measuring network performance, we spent some time examining how to isolate bandwidth- and media contention-related networking problems. From quick and dirty fixes to full-blown network redesigns and deployment, we looked at a wide sample of options for solving these fairly common and disruptive situations.

CONFIGURING DIAL-UP NETWORKING AND VIRTUAL PRIVATE NETWORKING

4

Dial-up networking and virtual private networking (VPN) are both remote networking technologies that remain important in today's mobile network environments. Although both dial-up and virtual private networking have been in use for a number of years now, they continue to be a driving force in network environments, many of which have large numbers of mobile users who must be able to securely connect to the network and access its resources. Virtually all modern operating systems support dial-up networking and virtual private networking, including Windows, Linux, and Macintosh. In this chapter, I'll be using Windows XP as a reference, but if you are using another operating system, you can adapt the concepts and steps we explore to your system. In this chapter, we'll...

- Install and configure modems
- Work with dial-up connections
- Use virtual private networking

INSTALLING AND CONFIGURING MODEMS

Dial-up connections use modems, which are designed to modulate and demodulate data for use on a phone line. Essentially, a modem converts digital data to analog data for transfer over analog phone lines, and back again to digital data when it reaches the desired computer. This kind of connection, limited to 56 Kbps (with a real-world reality of about 48 Kbps), is slow by today's broadband standards, but it continues to be a driving force in networks because the technology is readily available and inexpensive. As you are well aware, most all computers sold today ship with a standard modem. In the past, installing and configuring modems could be a real chore, but in today's plug-and-play environments, modem installation and configuration is generally a much less painful task.

In modern operating systems, such as Windows 2000 and Windows XP, you simply insert or attach (in the case of external modems) the modem to the correct port, and Windows can automatically install it—generally without any assistance from you. In the case of problematic modem installation, you can use the Add Hardware Wizard found in the Control Panel. You'll need the manufacturer's driver for the installation.

NOTE   Windows XP has the most extensive driver database of any Windows operating system. Most modems are automatically detected and installed. However, if you are having problems, always download the correct driver from the manufacturer's web site. Also, check the Windows HCL for information about compatibility, found at www.microsoft.com/hcl.

Once the modem is installed, it appears in Phone and Modem Options in the Control Panel as an installed device, as well as in Device Manager. If you open Phone and Modem Options, click the Modems tab to see the installed modems and the port the modem is attached to, as shown in the following illustration. If you need to install a new modem, click the Install button (if Windows XP does not detect it). This opens the Modem Installation Wizard, which you can also use from within the Add Hardware Wizard. Again, you will not need to use the wizard options in most cases, because Windows XP can automatically detect and install most modems.

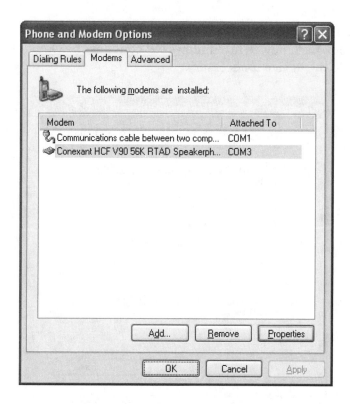

Once the modem is installed, you can access the properties dialog box and configure the modem. Many times, the default configuration is all you need, but there are some important options you should be familiar with that help you solve some specific problems. On the Modems tab, select the modem you want to configure and click the Properties button. The following sections explore the options you find.

NOTE   You can access this same properties dialog box from within Device Manager. Simply open Device Manager, expand the Modems category, then right-click the modem and click Properties.

THE GENERAL TAB

The General tab of modem properties, as shown in the next illustration, provides basic information about the modem. You can open the Windows troubleshooter from this tab if you are having problems with the modem, but the main action you can take here is to simply disable the modem. If you are having problems with hardware conflicts, or if you need to create a hardware profile, you can easily disable the modem using the Device Usage drop-down menu. This action disables the modem, but it does not uninstall the modem from the system. Each device in Windows XP contains the General tab so that you can disable the device if necessary.

THE MODEM TAB

The Modem tab provides you with three configuration options:

- **Speaker Volume** By default, modems play connection noise that you can hear when you are connecting. If you like, you can increase or decrease the volume of the connection noise, or turn it off completely.

- **Maximum Port Speed** Port speed determines how fast programs can send data to the modem. This setting does not affect the speed at which the modem communicates with another modem. Typically, this setting is fixed at 115200, which is the proper speed for most programs. However, if a program using the modem requires a faster speed, you can set the value as needed.

Windows CE devices often require faster modem speeds to work properly. This is one practical application of this setting. In most circumstances, however, the default speed of 115200 is correct.

- **Dial Control**   The Dial Tone check box tells the modem to wait for a phone line dial tone before dialing the number. Under most circumstances, this check box should remain enabled. However, if the modem seems to be having problems detecting the dial tone or dialing out, you can try clearing this option.

THE DIAGNOSTICS TAB

If you are concerned that the modem is not working properly, you can access the Diagnostics tab to run a diagnostic test on the modem. Essentially, the diagnostic test runs a series of query commands that the modem should accurately respond to, as you can see in the following illustration. The diagnostic test is saved in a log file, which is saved in %systemroom\Modemlog_*modemname.txt*. Click the View Log button to see the log file. You can open the log file with any text editor and take note of any communication errors listed. This information might give you some clues about possible problems with the modem.

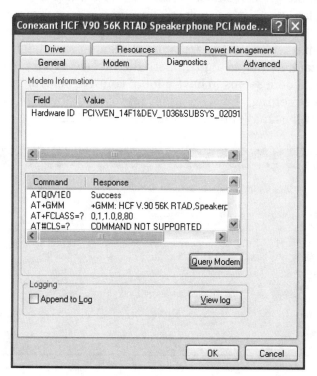

Although the log file can be difficult to read unless you are familiar with modem commands, you can scan the log file and look at the test performed. If the tests complete properly, you'll typically see an "OK" listing after each test.

THE ADVANCED TAB

On the Advanced tab, you can enter additional initialization commands. In the past, initialization commands were commonly used to get certain modems to operate with Windows and connect as they should. For the most part, most modems today do not require initialization commands, but the option appears on the Advanced tab to support modems that do. If you are having problems with the modem, check the modem's documentation about the use of initialization commands. Then you can try some of the documentation-recommended commands, which might resolve certain problems you are experiencing.

You can also select the country/region the modem is used in, and you access the Advanced Port Settings button or the Change Default Preferences button. The latter two items can be useful in some specific troubleshooting circumstances. First, when you click the Advanced Port Settings button, you see the Advanced Settings dialog box for the particular port the modem is using. As you can see in the next illustration, you can adjust the First In First Out (FIFO) buffer. The FIFO buffer is a standard used on practically all universal asynchronous receiver-transmitter (UART) chipsets. These settings determine the speed at which data is buffered when traveling to and from the modem—essentially a type of flow control. The default setting is high on both the receive and transmit buffers. However, if the modem seems to have a lot of connection problems, you can try lowering these settings. Lower settings may cause slower performance, but the lower settings may solve the connection problems.

![Advanced Settings for COM3 dialog box. Checkbox "Use FIFO buffers (requires 16550 compatible UART)" is checked. Text reads "Select lower settings to correct connection problems." and "Select higher settings for faster performance." Receive Buffer: Low (1) to High (14), set at (14). Transmit Buffer: Low (1) to High (16), set at (16). COM Port Number: COM3. Buttons: OK, Cancel, Defaults.]

You can also click the Change Default Preferences option on the Advanced tab. This opens an additional dialog box where you see General and Advanced tabs. Again, the default preferences are usually best, but you can change these in order to meet specific needs and solve specific problems. The General tab, as seen in the following illustration, gives you several options, which are described in the following list:

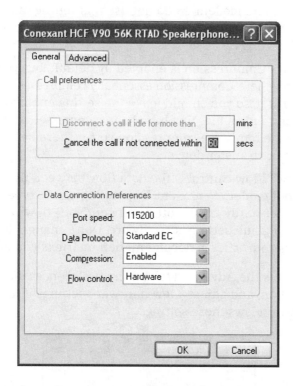

- **Call Preferences** This option allows you to set an automatic disconnect if the call is idle for a certain period time. In other words, if there is no connection activity for a specified period of time, the computer automatically disconnects the modem. Although useful in some cases, this setting can be the cause of aggravating automatic disconnects, and by default this setting is not enabled.

- **Port Speed** Under Data Connection Preferences, you see the same port speed option that you found on the Modem tab. By default, the speed is 115200, and you do not need to change the port speed unless you are having problems with applications communicating with the modem. Check the application's documentation for more information.

- **Data Protocol** Under Data Protocol, you can choose either Standard EC or Forced EC, or you disable data protocol altogether. The setting controls how protocols are used when modems communicate with each other, and the default option is Standard EC, which is the best setting for most modems. Forced EC is a specific type of error control that uses a correction method called V.42. Forced EC, though, will hang up the connection if V.42 is not used on the remote modem, so do not use this setting unless the computer you are connecting to requires Forced EC. Most all modems use the Standard EC settings.

- **Compression** Compression is enabled by default, but you can disable it using the setting here. Compression essentially compresses data automatically for faster transfer, so you should leave the setting enabled. However, if you are transferring a lot of files that have been compressed with Zip technology, try disabling the hardware compression setting here because it may actually slow the transfer down.

- **Flow Control** Flow control is the data flow between the modem and the computer—not modem to modem. Depending on the type of modem you are using, either hardware or software (Xon/Xoff) flow control can be used, and the default setting is Hardware. Don't change the flow control setting unless your modem documentation instructs you to do so.

You can also access the Advanced tab on the preferences dialog box, shown in the next illustration, and adjust a few hardware settings if necessary. The following bullet list reviews those settings:

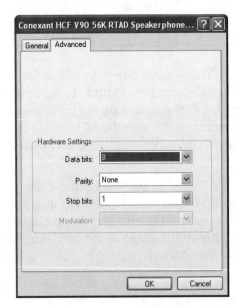

- **Data Bits** The Data Bits setting refers to the number of bits that are used to transmit each character of data. When two modems are communicating, they must have the same Data Bits setting. The default is 8, so generally you should leave this setting at the default. However, if you are communicating with a modem or an online service that requires a different Data Bits setting, you change it here.

- **Parity** Parity is a type of error checking where a parity bit is appended to data that is sent, then checked by the receiving modem for accuracy. In order for parity to work, the modem you are communicating with must use parity checking as well. Online services typically do not use parity, so the default setting here is None. Again, do not change this setting unless the modem you are communicating with uses parity.

- **Stop Bits** A stop bit is a bit of information that tells the receiving modem that one byte of data has been sent. The default setting is 1, and this is the correct setting unless the modem you are communicating with, or even your ISP, requires a different Stop Bit setting.

- **Modulation** Modulation refers to how data is changed from analog to digital and vice versa. Standard modulation is generally used, and depending on your modem, the option to change may even be grayed out.

THE DRIVER TAB

The Driver tab of modem properties is like any other Driver tab found on a device. The Driver tab allows you to get information about the current driver, update the driver, roll back the driver, and uninstall the current driver (which effectively uninstalls the device from the computer). Should a new driver for the modem be released, you can install updated drivers here by clicking the Update Driver button, in which case a wizard appears to guide you through the process. If you are using Windows XP, you can also roll back to the previous driver should the new driver cause you problems.

THE RESOURCES TAB

Windows XP and Windows 2000 computers automatically handle hardware resources, such as IRQ settings when you install a new device. In the past, the manual assignment of these resources left many users and even technical personnel pulling their hair out. Today, through plug and play, you do not have to manually configure resources—unless there is a conflict. The options on the Resources tab, shown in the following illustration, are all grayed out unless there is a conflict between two devices. In this case, you can use this tab to manually assign the resources so that the conflict will not exist. As you can see, there is no conflict, so the option to change the settings is grayed out.

NOTE In some cases, you may also see a Power Management tab, depending on the operating system configuration. The Power Management tab allows you to specify that activity from the device can bring the computer out of standby mode.

CREATING DIAL-UP CONNECTIONS

You can easily create dial-up connections to an ISP, a network dial-up server, or directly to another computer, or you can configure your computer to accept incoming dial-up connections in the event that you want to connect to a home or office computer remotely. Regardless of the operating system you are using, modern operating systems such as Windows XP/2000, Macintosh, Linux, and NetWare all provide an easy wizard approach to configuring dial-up connections.

The following steps show you how to create a dial-up connection using Windows XP:

1. Click Start | Control Panel and open the Network Connections folder.
2. In the Network Tasks dialog box, click the Create a New Connection link.
3. The New Connection Wizard appears. Click Next.
4. In the Network Connection Type window, you can choose the kind of connection that you want to create, such as a connection to the Internet or a connection to your workplace. In this example, I am creating a connection to my workplace.

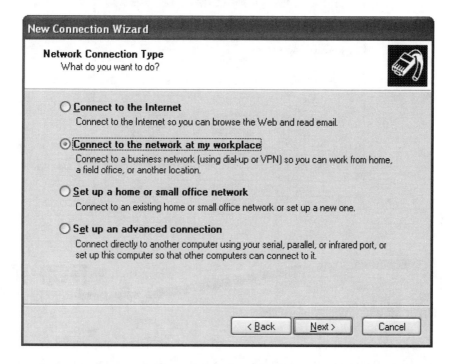

5. In the next window, choose to create a dial-up connection or a VPN connection. Choose the dial-up radio button and click Next.
6. In the Connection Name dialog box, enter a name for the connection and click Next.
7. In the Phone Number to Dial window, enter the phone number that should be dialed and click Next.

8. The Connect To dialog box appears. Enter a username and password as needed and click Connect to start the connection.

TECH TALK

Windows XP and Connection Access

Windows XP Professional provides the option for secure local accounts, and the same principle holds true for dial-up connections. Let's say that three different people use your computer at work. However, you sometimes use a dial-up connection to connect to a certain server at another office. This connection is meant for you only, and the other users of your computer should not be able to use the connection. No problem—when you open the connection to be dialed, choose the Save this Username and Password for the Following Users option, then choose Me Only. This will ensure that only your user account will be allowed to dial the connection.

Aside from connecting to a remote computer or remote server, you can also configure your computer to accept incoming connections. This feature can be very helpful when a computer is used at home or small office and you need to access it remotely, such as in the case when you travel with a laptop computer. To configure your computer to accept incoming connections, you once again return to the Network Connections folder in Windows XP and use the New Connection Wizard. If you are using a different operating system, see the Help files for specific instructions. If you are using Windows XP, follow these steps:

1. Click Start | Control Panel and open the Network Connections folder.

2. In the Network Tasks dialog box, click the Create a New Connection link.

3. The New Connection Wizard appears. Click Next.

4. In the Network Connection Type window, choose the Set Up an Advanced Connection option and click Next.

5. In the Advanced Connection Options window, choose to accept incoming connections and click Next.

6. In the Devices for Incoming Connections window, select the devices you want to use for incoming connections.

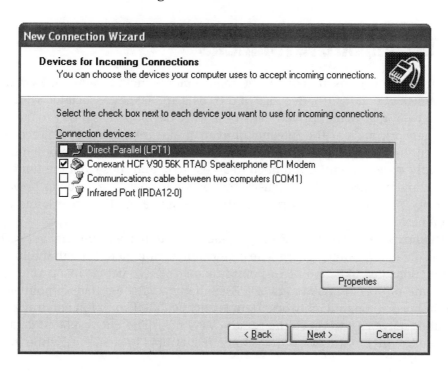

7. In the next window, you can choose to allow VPN connections on the incoming connection, if desired. Make a selection and click Next.

8. In the User Permissions window, select the local users that have permission to make a connection to the computer. You can also create new local users here by clicking the Add button. Click Next.

9. In the Networking Software window, choose the networking software that you want to enable on the connection. For example, if you want the connecting client to be able to use file and printer sharing over the connection, enable that service. Make your selections and click Next.

10. Click Finish.

Once the connection is created, you can access it and its properties dialog box from within Network Connections. Keep in mind that you change every setting you configured with the wizard by simply accessing the properties dialog box. This includes adding and removing users who can access the connection.

NOTE You can configure dial-up connection properties, and you can also configure dialing rules. See Chapter 5 to learn more.

VIRTUAL PRIVATE NETWORKING

Wide area connections are costly. The requirements include WAN links and the expense of bandwidth. Because of the costs and issues associated with WAN networking, virtual private networks were developed as a way to use a public network, such as the Internet or even an intranet, to send and receive data securely. For example, let's say your home office is in Houston but you frequently work in Seattle. You need to access data and files from the home network, and you need to use a dial-up connection to do it. The problem, however, is security. Your files and information are traversing a public network and can be stolen.

Virtual private networks (VPNs) provide a way to use a public network while keeping data private and secure. The connection is tunneled through the Internet and functions just like a point-to-point link on a WAN, such as in a frame relay, leased line, or even an ATM network. Essentially, a VPN emulates a point-to-point link using a public network. Data is encapsulated so that it can travel the public network and reach the remote VPN host. The encapsulated data is encrypted so that in the event that someone attempts to steal data while in

TROUBLESHOOTING

Dial-Up Connection Problems

The very nature of dial-up connections dictates that there will be connection problems. After all, you are using a public phone system, and each time you need to use dial-up networking, you must generate a connection. The connection speeds that you end up with are largely dependent on the quality of the phone line, traffic, and modem that you are connecting to. As you are working with user complaints about dial-up networking, it is important to educate users as you work—most dial-up networking problems are simply out of your control. However, there are a few items to check when you are troubleshooting dial-up connections:

- Make sure the username and password is correct for failed connections. If the connection appears to attempt to connect, the problem may be with the remote computer.

- If the connection disconnects frequently, there may be a lot of noise on the phone line or a problem with the remote computer. Also, check to make sure that the modem, as well as the connection, is not configured to disconnect after a certain idle time has passed.

- If the connection is slow, first assess whether or not all connections are slow. If all connections are slow, check the modem driver and make sure you are using the latest version. Also, check the modem documentation about possibly using extra initialization commands.

transit, the data is useless without an encryption key. When connected, the user accesses the remote network just as if he or she were locally connected. As you can imagine, VPNs can use broadband connections for private networking, while using the free public Internet as the networking medium. This design can save companies thousands of networking dollars because there is no need to deploy a WAN network or lease expensive WAN links.

UNDERSTANDING TUNNELING

The VPN is built on the concept of a tunnel. The tunnel is the process of moving data from one host to another over the public network, such as the Internet. The tunnel essentially encapsulates private network data into PPP frames for Internet transfer. The encapsulated data is encrypted. To the Internet, the encapsulated data appears as a typical PPP frame. When the encapsulated frames reach the VPN host, the VPN host strips the encapsulation away and decrypts the data, and then normal network traffic resumes. To the user, the VPN tunnel is invisible and it appears as though he or she is actually accessing the local network.

There are two primary protocols used to create VPN tunnels. The first is the Point-to-Point Tunneling Protocol (PPTP), and the second is Layer Two Tunneling Protocol (L2TP). PPTP is the most common protocol used, but L2TP provides additional security features through IPSec. The following bullets explain the differences between PPTP and L2TP:

- **PPTP** Microsoft first developed PPTP as a way to move data securely across an insecure network, which includes the Internet, an intranet, or even a WAN connection of some kind. PPTP provides encapsulation of data packets, essentially in a secure wrapper. When the PPTP packet travels over the PPP network (such as the Internet), the encapsulated data is hidden inside. When the PPTP packet reaches its final destination, the secure wrapper is discarded, revealing the data.

- **L2TP** Cisco developed a networking protocol called Layer 2 Forwarding Protocol, which moved data from one point to the next over an insecure network. Microsoft's work with PPTP and Cisco's work with L2F was combined to create the new industry standard, L2TP. L2TP provides the same functions as PPTP. L2TP is sent as a UDP message and is used with IPSec in Microsoft networks. It is more secure than PPTP and is becoming the standard VPN protocol today.

 Not all computers support L2TP. For example, if you wanted to use Windows XP to connect to a Windows NT VPN server, you'll have to use PPTP because L2TP is not supported on Windows NT. The point is to make sure you know what operating system you are connecting to and if the OS supports L2TP. If not, simply use PPTP.

CONNECTING TO A VPN SERVER

In order to generate a VPN connection to a server, the computer uses a VPN connection, just as you would use a dial-up connection. The VPN connection essentially tells the computer how to format data and to use either PPTP or

TECH TALK

VPN Tunnel Types

There are two basic types or forms of VPN tunnels that can be created—voluntary and compulsory. One or both of these tunnels may be used on your network, depending on your needs. The first type, voluntary, is the most common type of VPN tunnel and is typically what we think of when we say "VPN." In a voluntary tunnel, the VPN tunnel is created by the connecting client and the server. In this case, the tunnel connects these two endpoints so that communication can take place. Whenever you think of one VPN client connecting to a VPN server, you are thinking of a voluntary tunnel because this type of tunnel is "voluntarily" made.

   The second kind of tunnel is called a compulsory tunnel. In a compulsory tunnel, a hardware device, such as a router, acts as a VPN client to a VPN server. The hardware device is the endpoint. Any client computers using the router to access the VPN server are using a VPN, even though the actual VPN connection is not generated on their computers. For example, let's say a router exists in a remote office. The router has a static compulsory connection to a VPN server in another office. Clients in the first office simply use the router to connect to the VPN server, but a voluntary VPN tunnel is not needed because all traffic flowing over the router is sent through the VPN tunnel. Again, users are not aware of the VPN tunnel in this case. In fact, the local client computers can access the router and use the VPN tunnel without even being configured with VPN software or protocols.

L2TP. The actual steps for creating a VPN connection vary according to operating system, but most provide you with some kind of wizard help. In the following steps, you can see the process for configuring a VPN connection on a Windows XP Professional computer:

NOTE VPN connections work with an existing dial-up or Internet connection. In order to start the VPN connection, you must already be connected to the Internet or have a dial-up session in progress. Note that you'll need a valid username and password to access the VPN server.

1. Click Start | Control Panel and open the Network Connections folder.
2. In the Network Tasks dialog box, click the Create a New Connection link.

3. The New Connection Wizard appears. Click Next.

4. Click the Connect to a Network at My Workplace option and click Next.

5. On the page that appears, choose the Virtual Private Network connection and click Next.

6. Enter a name for the connection and click Next.

7. On the Public Network page, you can configure Windows to automatically dial one of your existing dial-up connections when the VPN is launched. If the computer uses a DSL or cable connection to the Internet, you may not need to use this option. Make your selection and click Next.

8. In the VPN Server Selection page that appears, enter the fully qualified domain name (FQDN) or IP address of the VPN server that you will connect to. Click Next.

9. Click Finish. The VPN icon now appears in Network Connections. You'll see a dialog box asking you to connect.

TROUBLESHOOTING

Default Gateway Problems

Let's say that each time you launch a VPN connection, other Internet applications such as your browser and mail applications stop working. What's the problem? As you might guess, it's the default gateway. In this case, the VPN connection is configured to use the default gateway on the remote network. If you needed to access the Internet through the remote network, this configuration would be helpful. However, if you simply need to access the VPN server and have your other applications use the local Internet connection, you need to change the default gateway. In Network Connections, right-click the VPN icon and click Properties. Click the Networking tab. Select Internet Protocol (TCP/IP) from the list and click the Properties button. Clear the Use Default Gateway on Remote Network check box and click OK.

CONFIGURING WINDOWS XP PROFESSIONAL AS A VPN SERVER

In most cases, clients will connect to a VPN server, such as Windows 2000 Server running the Routing and Remote Access Service. However, Windows XP Professional can also function as a VPN server so that VPN calls can be received. This feature is very helpful in small networks where server software is not used, but where you still need secure remote connections. The process to configure Windows XP Professional to act as a VPN server works basically the same as configuring the computer to accept incoming connections.

Firewalls can cause you some problems when configuring the VPN server. If the computer is protected by a firewall, you must configure the firewall to allow incoming traffic on port 1723. You should not use ICF with the VPN connection.

To configure Windows XP as a VPN server, follow these steps:

1. Click Start | Control Panel and open the Network Connections folder.

2. In the Network Tasks dialog box, click the Create a New Connection link.

3. The New Connection wizard appears. Click Next.

4. In the Network Connection Type window, choose to Set Up an Advanced Connection and click Next.

5. In the Devices for Incoming Connections page, select the modem or broadband device you want to use to allow incoming connections. Click Next.

6. On the next page, choose to allow virtual private connections and click Next.

7. On the User Permissions page, choose the user accounts that are allowed to access the VPN connection. Click Next.

8. On the Network Software page, choose the networking software that you will allow over the connection. Click Next.

9. Click Finish.

WRAPPING UP...

Dial-up networking and virtual private networking continue to be important parts of networking environments today. Fortunately, dial-up and VPN networking are so popular that most modern operating systems give you easy wizard tools to configure these networking features. Keep in mind that dial-up networks and VPN networks, though often more troublesome in terms of connection problems, give you easy solutions for wide area networking that would otherwise be costly with expensive WAN links. In the next chapter, we'll take a look at Internet networking.

INTERNET NETWORKING

5

As the Internet has grown and developed, the importance of Internet networking and its place in corporate environments cannot be understated. Many companies today rely on Internet access for business transactions, and employees often use the Internet for a variety of business purposes. Corporate Internet access can be quite costly, and corporate security can be quite an issue as well. Due to security and management issues, most corporate environments use a firewall or proxy server to manage Internet connections. From a local computer point of view, connecting to the Internet requires the proper hardware and connection configuration. In this chapter, we'll take a look at Internet networking from the standpoint of the local computer. If you are managing a firewall or proxy server, I suggest you locate a book that explores the firewall or proxy server product that you are managing. Also note, Internet connections are slightly different from operating system to operating system, but the same basic principles apply. Here, I'll be using Windows XP and Internet Explorer as references, but if you are using another operating system, you can adapt the concepts and steps we explore to your system and browser. In this chapter, we'll…

- Create an Internet connection
- Configure broadband and dial-up connections

- Manage dial-up connection properties
- Manage browsers

WORKING WITH INTERNET CONNECTIONS

An Internet connection is a service that you configure on a computer. Using the connection, the computer can make a physical connection to an Internet service provider (ISP), which gives the local computer access to the Internet. The connection is essentially designed to work with some kind of connection hardware, such as a modem, DSL modem, satellite connection, and so forth. In order to create an Internet connection on a computer, you need a few basic items:

- **Hardware** In order to connect to the Internet, the computer must have the necessary hardware for the connection, such as a modem, DSL modem, cable modem, or satellite modem. The Internet connection uses the hardware to connect to the ISP.

- **Account** Since the ISP charges you for the connection, you'll need a valid account in order to connect to the ISP. This typically means that you'll use a username and password to connect.

- **Connection** If you have the hardware and an account, you must then use the computer to create the connection, which uses the hardware and your account information to connect to the ISP.

You may need to enter the IP addresses of the DNS servers that should be used. Refer to your ISP's documentation for details.

In terms of corporate Internet access, the process is basically the same. Corporations typically use an ISP connection, but connectivity for network clients generally occurs through a proxy server. The connection to the ISP typically consists of some high-bandwidth backbone connection, such as a T1 or T3 link. The proxy server manages the connection, and all clients connect to the Internet through the proxy server. Since the clients do not directly connect to the ISP, all the client computers need is a standard NIC because the connection to the proxy server is simply another network connection. Through the proxy server, all client connections can be managed, and depending on the server software, you can also use a firewall and even impose certain rules and restrictions on clients—and even clients from the Internet.

NOTE Again, proxy server and firewall product specifics are beyond the scope of this book, but you'll find plenty of books and online documentation about the kind of proxy server or firewall product that is in use in your environment. If you are faced with managing the proxy server or firewall in your network, pick up a product-specific book to help you.

TYPES OF CONNECTIONS

If you need to configure individual client computers for connections to the Internet, you'll need to make some decisions about the kind of connection that you want to use. If you are configuring Internet connectivity in a small office environment, you may also need to make some decisions about using Internet connection sharing or some kind of Internet proxy software so that all computers on the network can use the same Internet connection. If you are using Windows XP, you can use Internet Connection Sharing and Internet Connection Firewall (which you can learn more about in Chapter 10) to protect your network and share a single Internet connection. If you are using another operating system, you'll find a number of third-party software products that can provide the same services.

If you are faced with the task of choosing a connection type, you'll find the following types of connections and service plans available, depending on your area:

- **Dial-up** Dial-up service requires a modem and a phone line, where your computer dials a phone number to connect to an ISP server. Dial-up connections are the most common type of Internet connections used today, and dial-up connections are available worldwide. Most dial-up connections will cost you around $20 per month for unlimited use, but the greatest problem is that all modem connections are slow by today's standard. Phone line limits restrict modems to 56-Kbps transfer, with around 45-Kbps transfer being the reality. This speed is rather slow, but it is still the most common type of Internet connection in use today. Additionally, if you are using a lot of multimedia applications over the Internet, or if you are sharing the Internet connection, the connection will be slower.

- **DSL** Digital subscriber line (DSL) is a broadband technology that provides broadband throughput, with speeds between 400 Kbps and 1 Mbps. DSL is an "always on" technology, meaning the computer is always connected to the Internet and there is no need to dial a connection. DSL also works with public telephone lines, but different channels are used to transmit high-speed data. Since different channels are in use, the same line can be used for Internet access and voice conversations; however, note that download rates are faster than upload rates. DSL service typically costs around $40 per month, but it is generally limited to metropolitan areas at this time.

- **Cable** Cable Internet uses a typical coaxial cable attached to your computer, just as you would use a coaxial cable with your television. Access to the Internet is performed over the cable connection, and the cable company or service provider provides an always-on service, just as you would receive with cable television. In the past, cable connections worked well, but often did not have the bandwidth of DSL. However, with new cable implementations, the cable access speed is just as fast as DSL and sometimes faster. Like DSL, you can expect to pay around $40 a month for cable Internet.

- **Satellite** Satellite connections are new in the Internet market and are available in the continental United States. Satellite connectivity is a good broadband solution, providing on average 300-Kbps transfer. However, it is not as fast as DSL and cable and costs considerably more. The satellite disk equipment generally costs around $500 and monthly unlimited access is around $70. Still, for users who cannot get other types of broadband, satellite may be a great solution. See www.starband.com to learn more.

NOTE For satellite, DSL, and cable connections, you may have specific setup instructions. Make sure you follow the ISP's setup instructions for the type of connection you are creating.

CREATING AN INTERNET CONNECTION

Once the hardware is installed and you have an account with your ISP, you can then create the connection. Once again, you should review the ISP's instructions and setup information, and you may even need to use connection software from your ISP. Regardless of the operating system you are using, you can create a connection to the Internet using the appropriate ISP software or the operating system's own internal software. Since Internet connections are commonplace, most operating systems provide you with a simple wizard to help you connect. The following steps show you an example of how to create an Internet connection on Windows XP.

1. Click Start | Control Panel and open the Network Connections folder.

2. In the Network Tasks dialog box, click the Create a New Connection link.

3. The New Connection Wizard appears. Click Next.

4. In the Network Connection Type window, you can choose the kind of connection that you want to create. Select the Connect to the Internet radio button and click Next.

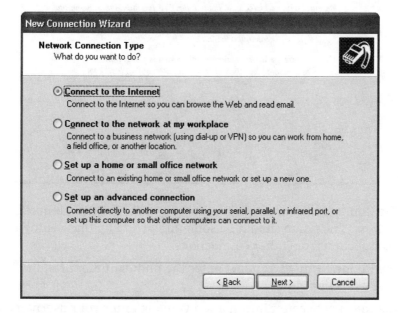

5. In the Getting Ready window, you can choose from a list of ISPs if you do not have an account. This process opens a connection to a referral service so that you can sign up with available service providers on the Internet. If you have an installation CD, you can also choose the option to run setup from the CD. Finally, you can choose the manual setup option, which is shown in the rest of the wizard steps here.

6. In the Internet Connection window, choose the type of connection that you are using, such as a dial-up, broadband that is always on, or broadband that requires a username and password. Make your selection and click Next. Since you are most likely to use the New Connection Wizard to set up modem connections, the rest of the steps focus on that option.

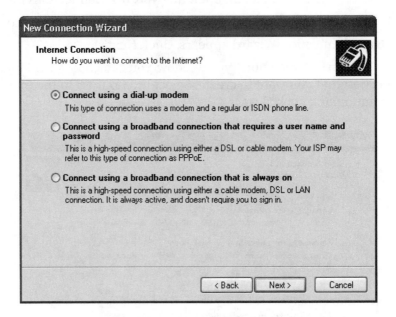

7. In the Connection Name window, enter a name for the connection and click Next. The name should be something friendly that distinguishes the connection from other connections.

8. In the Phone Number window, enter the phone number required to dial the ISP and click Next.

9. In the Internet account information window, enter your username and password and click the check box options that you want to use. Note that the account can be used by anyone using your computer, or just you. You

can also make the connection the default connection, and you can turn on the Internet Connection Firewall. Make your entries and selections and click Next.

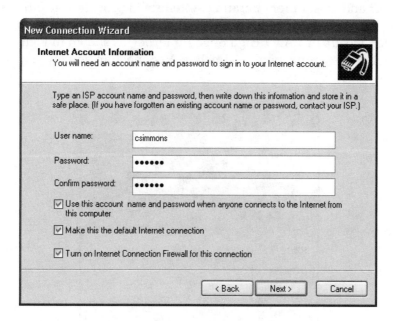

10. Click Finish. The new connection now appears in the Network Connections folder.

LAUNCHING A CONNECTION

Broadband connections are typically "always on, always connected." This means that you do not have to dial a connection or worry about disconnects. You simply launch a browser or your e-mail client to connect. However, if you are using a dial-up connection, a connection to the ISP must be established each time you want to connect to the Internet. To launch the connection, you can use the Connection icon that now appears in the Network Connections folder in Windows XP, and most other operating systems will provide you with a simple connection icon. In Windows XP, the icon is displayed in the Network Connections folder under dial-up or LAN / High Speed Internet, as shown in Figure 5-1.

Double-click the connection to launch it. A connection window appears, shown here.

Enter your username and password for the ISP. Notice that you can choose to save the username and password so that you do not have to retype it each time. You can save the password for Me Only, which will only allow the connection to be used with your user account, or you can choose to allow anyone who uses the computer use of the Internet connection. Again, this connection window is specific to Windows XP—the one you see will look somewhat different depending on the operating system.

FIGURE 5.1   The Network Connections folder

CONFIGURING DIAL-UP CONNECTION PROPERTIES

Dial-up connections, though the most common, tend to be troublesome types of connections. The problems you'll face, of course, reside in the fact that the connection is not always on, or always connected. Each time a connection is required, the connection has to be manually established. Regardless of operating system, you can manage dial-up connection properties so that the connection acts in a particular way that meets your needs. Again, in this section, I'll use Windows XP as an example, but you'll see the same kinds of dial-up connection options.

In Windows XP, if you right-click an Internet connection in the Network Connections folder, you can click Properties, which opens the properties pages that manage that particular Internet connection. The properties pages have a number of settings that determine how the connection operates, so we'll take a look at those in the following sections.

THE GENERAL TAB

On the General tab of the connection's properties, you have a few different items, such as the modem configuration, phone numbers, and notification, as you can see in the following illustration.

Concerning phone numbers and dialing rules, it is important that you understand the options and features dialing rules bring to the table, since you may be required to support configurations like this in your network. Dialing rules simply tell an operating system how to handle area codes, long distance calls, and even calling cards. In other words, area code rules help the computer know what calls are "local," which ones are "long distance," and which special treatment should be given certain phone numbers. The following steps show you how to set up and configure dialing rules.

1. On the General tab, click the Use Dialing Rules check box, then click the Dialing Rules button.

2. The Phone and Modem Options window appears. On the Dialing Rules tab, you see the current location that is configured. You can choose to edit the existing location or create a new one by clicking the appropriate button. Regardless of whether you choose to edit a current location or create a new one, the same configuration dialog box appears.

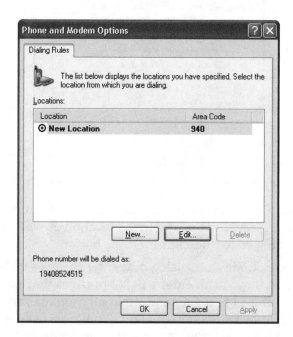

3. On the New or Edit Location window that appears, you see a General tab with several setting options. On this tab, enter the area code and country/region the area code is found in, then use the Dialing Rules boxes to

determine the rules concerning the use of the area code. You can also choose to disable call waiting and select tone or pulse dialing.

4. Click the Area Code Rules tab. Area code rules determine how phone numbers are dialed within your current location as well as other locations. To create an area code rule, click the New button.

5. In the New Area Code Rule dialog box, enter the area code to which this rule applies. Then, you can enter a list of prefixes that can be used with the area code, or accept the default—that all prefixes you use can work with the area code. For example, let's say the area code is 214. You only want to use 564 and 569 prefixes with the area code. In this case, click the Include Only button and click Add to enter those prefixes. If you do not place any prefix restrictions, Windows XP will assume that any prefix you dial can be used with the area code. At the bottom of the dialog box, use the check boxes to determine if a 1 should be dialed when using the area code, and if the area code should be dialed when using the prefixes. For example, if a dial-out number is 214-564-1234, and the area code is required each time you dial the number, click the Include the Area Code check box. Click OK.

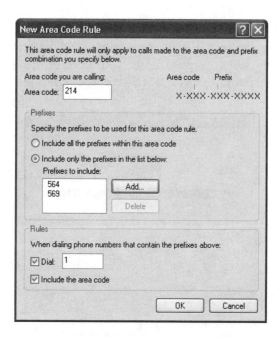

6. The new area code rule now appears on the Area Code Rules tab. You can
   create new area codes and edit existing ones at any time on this tab.

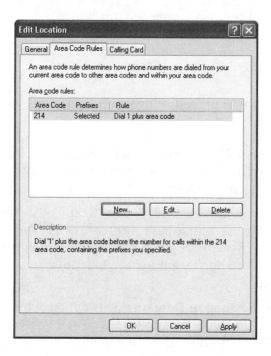

7. Click the Calling Card tab. If you need to use a calling card to make the connection, such as in the case of dialing a long distance number when you are traveling with a laptop, enter your card information as necessary on the Calling Card tab. Click OK to save your changes.

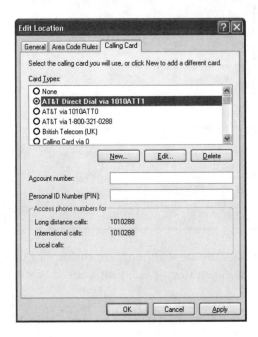

THE OPTIONS TAB

The Options tab, shown in the following illustration, gives you a few dialing and redialing options:

- **Display Progress While Connecting** Lets you see the connection process as it occurs. If it is cleared, you'll not see any progress information during the connection process.

- **Prompt for Name and Password, Certificate, etc.** If you want to be prompted for the username, password, certificate, and so forth during the connection, check this option. If this information is entered in the connection and you don't want to have to reenter it each time, do not use this option.

- **Include Windows Logon Domain** This option, which can only be used in conjunction with Prompt for Name and Password, Certificate, etc., requests the Windows domain for logon purposes. Generally, when dialing to an ISP, you do not need this option.

- **Prompt for Phone Number**   This option allows you to see, modify, and select the phone number that will be used when dialing the connection. If you only use one phone number, you can simply clear this check box option.

- **Redial Attempts**   If the first dial connection is not successful, Windows can automatically redial the number. Use the selection box to determine how many times Windows tries to redial the connection before stopping. The default is three.

- **Time Between Redial Attempts**   By default, Windows XP waits 1 minute between each redial attempt. You can change this value if desired.

- **Idle Time Before Hanging Up**   If you want the connection to automatically disconnect after a certain period of idle time, enter the value here. Use Never if you do not want the connection to automatically disconnect.

- **Redial if Line Is Dropped**   If you lose the connection, this option will have Windows XP automatically try to redial the connection.

- **X.25**   If you are logging onto an X.25 network, click the X.25 button and enter both the X.25 network provider and remote server information as required.

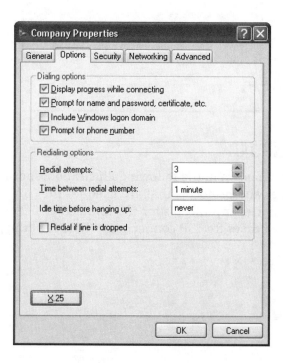

THE SECURITY TAB

The Security tab, shown in the next illustration, provides security settings for the dial-up connection. The Typical connection options are used, by default. The Typical connection option validates your username and password with your ISP without any additional encryption. Do not change any of the settings on this tab unless explicitly instructed to do so by your ISP. Incorrectly changing these settings will stop your computer from successfully logging on to the ISP.

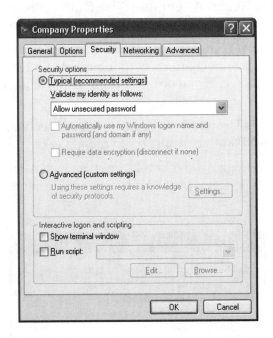

THE NETWORKING TAB

The Networking tab, shown in the following illustration, shows you the current networking services and protocols that are used for the connection. If you need additional services or protocols for the connection, use the Install button to add them. In most cases for ISP connections, there is nothing you need to configure here.

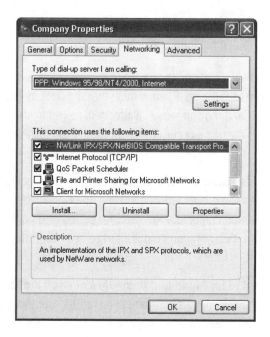

THE ADVANCED TAB

The Advanced tab on Windows XP computers enables you to turn on Internet Connection Firewall and Internet Connection Sharing. See Chapter 10 to learn more about ICF and ICS.

TROUBLESHOOTING

Common Connection Problems

Dial-up connection problems are, unfortunately, common, and they are often out of your control. Congested phone lines and busy ISPs account for busy signals and dropped connections. However, there are some actions you can take. The following list gives you a number of common dial-up problems and their solutions:

■ **Connections are slow**   Modem speeds at your ISP, phone line congestion, and even phone line noise can contribute to this problem. If the modem seems to always connect at a low speed, make sure you have the correct modem driver installed. Otherwise, call the ISP for support.

Common Connection Problems (continued)

- **Connections drop** Due to problems with phone line noise and/or problems with the ISP, connections can be dropped. Keep in mind that the Options tab enables Windows XP to automatically redial if the connection is dropped, so you might want to make sure this option is enabled. If the drops occur often, you should call technical support at your ISP for assistance.

- **Users' connections automatically disconnect** As a safety measure to keep connections from staying connected when in use, the Options tab has an autodisconnect option. After the connection is idle for a certain period of time, the connection is disconnected automatically. If you do not want to use this option, however, simply disable it on the Options tab.

- **The user is prompted for name and password at each dial-up session** Keep in mind that you can have Windows XP prompt you for the username and password, and even the phone number, each time a connection is made to the ISP. If you do not want to use these options, turn them off on the Options tab.

- **The logon fails each time during authentication** If the logon fails during authentication, make sure you are using an appropriate username and password for the connection. Also, check the Security tab and make sure you are using settings that are compatible with the ISP. If all seems to be in order, contact the ISP for assistance.

- **A 1 is always dialed when dialing phone numbers** If a 1 is always dialed, you need to edit the area code rules properties from the General tab.

WORKING WITH INTERNET EXPLORER

Internet Explorer 6 is designed to be a flexible piece of software that you can use to connect to intranet and Internet web sites. As such, it is designed to work with LAN connections, modems, broadband connections to the Internet, and just about any other type of remote network connectivity that is available. In most cases, IE's connectivity options are readily configured and available. In other words, IE is good at determining what Internet connections are available on your computer and using those connections.

However, IE 6 also provides you with a number of important configuration options that can provide specific features and services that might be useful. Again, we'll look at IE 6. Open Internet Explorer, then click Tools | Internet Options. This opens several Internet Options tabs where you can configure a number of features, which we will explore throughout the remainder of this chapter. If you click the Connections tab, shown in the next illustration, you see that you can manage dial-up/broadband connections, and you can even configure IE for proxy server access.

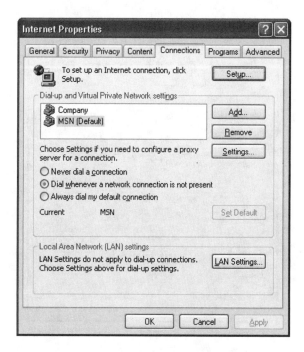

NOTE Although this section focuses on Internet Explorer 6, the current version of IE at the time of this writing, you'll also find similar features in other browsers, such as Netscape and Opera.

In the first portion of the Connections tab, you can configure dial-up and virtual private network connections. Any existing dial-up or VPN connections that you have configured also appear on this tab, listed in the dialog box provided. This tab essentially allows you to select the connection that you want to use, so if you need a different connection, first configure it using Network Connections. You can also directly create a new connection from the Connections tab by clicking the Add button, or click the Setup button at the top of the window to configure a connection.

There may be instances where you need to connect to a proxy server in order to access a dial-up or VPN connection. In this case, you can click the Settings button and enter the proxy server contact information in the Settings dialog box, shown in the following illustration. This dialog box, however, is used only for dial-up and VPN connections that must be made through a proxy server. Do not use this option when you need to connect via a typical LAN proxy server or with a broadband connection. Instead, use the LAN Settings button at the bottom of the Connections tab, which we'll explore later in this section.

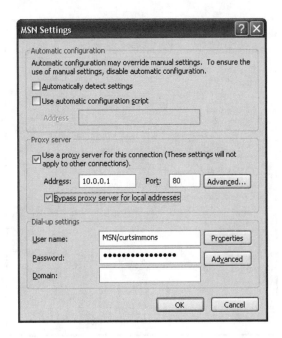

Note the option to Bypass Proxy Server for Local Addresses setting. This option can be used to access local resources on your network without accessing the proxy server, which typically speeds up access and resolves connectivity problems. If users are complaining that they are having problems accessing local resources using IE, you may need to enable this setting when a proxy server is in use.

The Connections tab also gives you three radio button options that allow you to manage how the dial-up/VPN connection functions. First of all, you can choose to never dial a connection. This option prevents IE from automatically dialing a connection when it is launched. If you choose this option, you must first manually connect to the dial-up/VPN connection using Network Connections. Then, you can use IE. If clients complain that IE never connects to a dial-up/ VPN connection when it is first opened, check this setting and disable it. Next, you can choose to dial whenever a network connection is not present. This setting, which is your best default setting, simply tells IE to dial the default connection when no existing Internet connection is available. In other words, when you launch IE, it will launch the default Internet connection if the computer is not currently connected. Finally, you can choose to always dial your default connection. If you do not want IE to use any Internet connection, choose this option. If you open IE and there is a current connection to the Internet, IE will still try to dial the default connection.

In the lower portion of the tab, you see the LAN Settings button. If you need to connect to a proxy server for Internet connectivity, or if you are using a broadband connection, click the LAN Settings button. This opens the Local Area Network Settings dialog box. You can configure access to a specific proxy server by IP address, or through automatic discovery. You need to check with a proxy server administrator to determine how these settings should be configured.

NOTE   Keep in mind that network group policy can also impact the settings you see here. If you are having problems configuring proxy settings, or the settings keep changing, the odds are good that a site, domain, or OU policy is in use.

CONFIGURING INTERNET EXPLORER SETTINGS

Internet Options provides you with several settings that govern how Internet Explorer behaves. Overall, these settings are not complicated, but you should be familiar with them because users may complain about the different settings. The following sections explore them.

CONFIGURING GENERAL SETTINGS

If you access Internet Options, you'll see a General tab where you can configure several standard IE settings. The General tab, shown in the following illustration, contains settings for the home page, temporary Internet files, and history, as well as some other basic settings.

The home page starts Internet Explorer with the URL that is entered in the provided dialog box. In other words, each time the user opens IE, the browser connects to this page. Temporary Internet files refer to web page files and graphics that Internet Explorer caches. These files and graphics are cached in an attempt to make web surfing faster. In other words, if IE caches files and objects, there is less information to download each time the user connects to that particular page, giving the illusion that the Internet is working faster than it actually is. You can choose to delete all temporary files and cookies from this location by simply using the Delete buttons. You normally do not have to do this since IE does a good job of managing its own cached content. If you click the Settings button, a Settings dialog box appears that allows you to configure how the cache is managed. By default, IE checks for new pages automatically, but you can change this behavior by choosing a different radio button so that IE checks for pages more often, or even never. A more often setting gives you more accurate data but increases traffic, so you'll have to find the balance that works best for you. You also see the amount of disk space that is used for temporary Internet files, and you can use the buttons provided to move the temporary Internet files folder to a different location (which can preserve disk space on your primary drive). You can even view the files.

On the General tab, you can also manage the History. Internet Explorer keeps track of all web pages that are visited for easy access. This feature allows users to surf the Web and quickly return to previously viewed pages, which are simply stored as links.

NOTE   By default, history is maintained for 14 days, but you can adjust this setting here, and you can manually delete the history as well.

MANAGING CONTENT

The Content tab, shown in the next illustration, of Internet Options contains three features that can help you manage content: Content Advisor, Certificates, and Personal Information.

The Content Advisor is used to control different kinds of questionable or objectionable content in Internet Explorer. Content Advisor works through voluntary site ratings. Web site administrators complete a form provided by the Internet Content Rating Association (ICRA) that determines a content rating for the site. IE examines the content rating of the site found in the site's HTTP header information, and then determines whether or not to block the site. ICRA ratings are based on language, nudity, sexual content, and violence. Using

IE, you simply enable the content advisor, then adjust the level of content you want to make available (or not). The following steps show you how to configure the feature.

1. Choose Tools | Internet Options | and select the Content tab. Click the Enable button.

2. The Content Advisor window appears with four configuration tabs. On the Ratings tab, shown in the next illustration, you see a listing of rating categories. Select a desired category, then move the slider bar to the desired level of content you want users to be able to see. Note that each category defaults at level 0, which is the least offensive setting. Adjust the categories as desired, then click the Approved Sites tab.

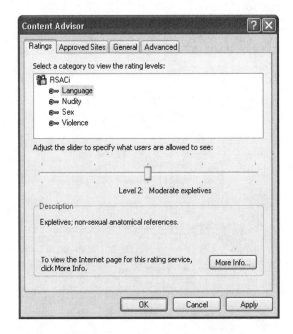

3. On the Approved Sites tab, you can override the settings that you configured on the Ratings tab by entering a desired web site address and clicking the Always or Never button. Never will always prompt for an administrator password in order to see the site, and Always will allow anyone to see the site without an administrator password.

4. On the General tab, you have a few different configuration options. First, you see two important check boxes that will allow users to see unrated sites and a supervisor override option. The first option should not be used if you are trying to secure the computer from harmful content. Just

because a site contains inappropriate content does not mean that they have a rating, so if a site does not have a rating, a prompt will appear for the administrator override. This may cause some surfing difficulty, but it is the safest setting. You should always keep the supervisor setting selected so that you can override any site prohibits if needed. If you need to change your supervisor password or find rating systems used by other companies, you can use the additional options found on the General tab. Keep in mind that the administrator password you assign is used to control and even turn off content management, so keep up with it.

5. On the Advanced tab, you see the option to locate and employ a ratings bureau and use PICSRules. A ratings bureau is an Internet site that can check a rating of a site if the site is not rated by ICRA. This, however, can seriously slow down browsing time. You can also import PICSRules, which are labels that can help you determine if sites can be viewed or not. There are no default rules configured, but you can import them if desired.

NOTE While the Content Advisor can help control objectionable material, it is in no way foolproof. If you are working with children, you may consider using additional third-party products to help control content, such as Net Nanny, found at www.netnanny.com, or CyberSitter, found at www.cybersitter.com.

NOTE If you decide that you no longer want to use Content after you have configured it, you can always return to the Content tab and click the Disable button. You'll need to provide your administrator password to turn off the feature.

Internet Explorer allows the use of digital certificates for identification purposes. The certificate is an authentication method that allows the user to prove his or her identity before access to a site is granted. In cases where

TECH TALK

Forgotten Passwords

If you should forget the Content Advisor password, you can override it with a registry edit. Navigate to HKLM\Software\Microsoft\Windows\CurrentVersion\policies\Ratings and delete the Key Value that you see. If you are worried about other people deleting the key to gain access to content management settings, you can use Group Policy to prohibit access to the registry or you can even use registry permissions (Edit menu) to control access to the key.

certificates are used, a user can obtain a digital certificate from a certificate authority, such as VeriSign. The certificate can then be imported into Internet Explorer using the Certificates option on this tab. Then, when the user attempts to access the secure site, Internet Explore can provide the user's certificate to the web site.

Another IE feature is AutoComplete. AutoComplete allows Internet Explorer to remember information that you have entered when using the Internet, such as URLs, names, passwords, e-mail addresses, and other information that you might have typed into web forms. IE remembers this information, then tries to identify and automatically complete it for you when you are entering the same information at a later time. On the Content tab, you can click the AutoComplete button and determine the kinds of information that you want Internet Explorer to remember. On the AutoComplete Settings dialog box, enable or clear the check boxes to adjust how AutoComplete works.

SETTING DEFAULT PROGRAMS

Internet Explorer gives you the Programs tab, shown in the following illustration, in Internet Options so that you can set default programs that Internet Explorer should use. For example, by default, Outlook Express is used as the default e-mail program and newsgroup reader. However, you may be using Eudora or some other e-mail program. In this case, you can use the Programs tab to select the alternative program that you want to use. Just use the drop-down menus to change the default programs to the programs that you want.

CHAPTER 5   INTERNET NETWORKING   **131**

WORKING WITH ADVANCED SETTINGS

Internet Explorer gives you a number of different advanced settings, organized by category, which you can access on the Advanced tab of Internet Options, shown in the following illustration. The default settings here are typically all you need, but the options can solve particular problems or give IE some additional functionality if needed. You can browse these to get familiar with them, but the following bullet list points out the more useful settings.

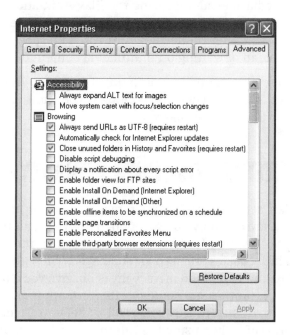

- Under Browsing, the Automatically Check for Internet Explorer Updates setting is not selected by default. If you have a broadband or network connection to the Internet, consider enabling this setting so that Internet Explorer can periodically check Microsoft.com for updates. The feature checks for any new version of IE that is available, and if you select the option, it checks the web site every 30 days.

- Under Browsing, consider disabling the Enable Page Transitions option if you are using a slow Internet connection. Some web sites have page transitions configured so that one page fades into another. These transitions can waste your bandwidth and time, so disable this feature if the connection is slow.

■ Under Browsing, consider enabling the Enable Personalized Favorites Menu. If you use Favorites a lot, the list can become long and junky. The Personalized Favorites menu hides the favorites you haven't used in awhile so that the list is easier to see and use.

■ Under Browsing, if you want Internet Explorer to help you autocomplete web addresses that you have used before, click the Use Inline AutoComplete check box option.

■ Under Multimedia, consider clearing the Play Animations in Web Pages, Play Sounds in Web Pages, and Play Videos in Web Pages check boxes if you have a slow Internet connection. This will help speed up your browsing experience instead of waiting on multimedia content download.

■ Under Security, consider using the Empty Temporary Internet Files Folder when Browser Is Closed check box option if you want to keep Internet Explorer clean and cookies deleted.

MANAGING INTERNET EXPLORER SECURITY

As an A+ technician, security configuration may be a major part of your work. Internet connections are certainly no exception to this rule, and Internet Explorer 6 provides a number of security features that manage how Internet Explorer uses different sites and how cookies are used and managed. These features, in a further attempt to control online piracy and privacy invasion, give you a number of controls that can be very important from a home or office situation. Internet Explorer does not provide antivirus software or firewall protection. To make certain that a computer is always safe when using the Internet, third-party antivirus software should always be running and you should also enable the Internet Connection Firewall to prevent hacker attacks.

CONFIGURING INTERNET EXPLORER ZONES

Internet Explorer uses four different security zones, which you can access on the Security tab of Internet Options, shown in the next illustration. On the Security tab, you see the Internet, Local Intranet, Trusted Sites, and Restricted Sites zones. If you select a zone, you can see the current security level of the zone in the lower portion of the window.

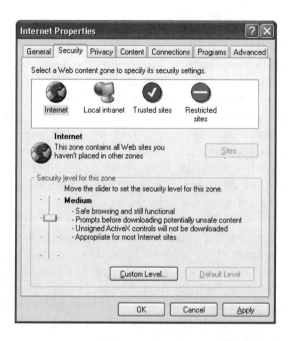

There are four preconfigured levels of security that you can select for each zone by simply moving the slider bar. They are

- **High**   Using this setting, all features that are less secure are disabled. This is the safest way to use the Internet, but it provides you with the least amount of functionality. All ActiveX content is disabled along with all downloads. Additionally, there are a number of restrictions on accessing data and requesting data.

- **Medium**   The Medium setting does not allow the downloading of unsigned ActiveX controls, and you see the familiar prompt before downloading potentially unsafe content. Browsing is safe yet functional under this setting, and in most cases this is the best setting to use.

- **Medium-Low**   The Medium-Low setting will run most content without prompts, but still does not allow unsigned ActiveX controls. This setting is safe for intranet use.

- **Low**   The Low setting provides basic warning and few safeguards. All active content can run. This setting is not recommended unless the site is one you completely trust.

You can configure different settings for each zone by simply selecting the zone and moving the slider bar. However, you can also custom create the settings by clicking the Custom Level button. This opens the Security Settings window. You can scroll through the list of settings and choose the Disable, Enable, or Prompt option for each security setting. This enables you to create a custom security setting that invokes the features you want instead of the default options. If you want to see what settings are used under one of the default options (such as High, Medium, and so forth), click the Reset To drop-down menu at the bottom of the Security Settings window and click Reset. You can then see how each of the custom settings are applied under one of the default security options and customize the settings as you wish.

For the Internet zone, the Medium setting is the best. You have the best browsing functionality, but you still have enough controls in place to keep the computer reasonably protected. You can, of course, customize the settings as needed, but as you are working with the Internet zone, it is a good idea to keep in mind the highest security settings possible, but maintain good usage features. Low security settings may make browsing easier, but you are asking for problems. The opposite is also true—settings that are too high are very secure, but they hinder browsing capabilities.

The default setting for the Local Intranet zone is Medium-Low. You can basically use the intranet in any way, but unsigned ActiveX controls will not be allowed. In some cases, you may even want to use the Low setting, if you are certain all of the content on your intranet is safe. If it is, then the Low setting will not prevent any active content from running. If you select the Local Intranet icon on the Security tab, you can also click the Sites button and select/deselect a few other options. You can choose to include all local sites not listed in other zones, include all sites that bypass the proxy server, and all network paths. The default setting enables all three of these options, and you should typically leave these enabled. You can also click the Advanced button and add web sites to this zone.

If you use a particular site often and know that content from the site is safe, you can add the site to your Trusted Sites zone. The Trusted Sites zone is made up of sites that you deem trustworthy. When a site is added to the trusted sites list, then the Low security setting is used when that site is accessed. This allows you to freely use the site without any security restrictions. Of course, you should make absolutely certain that a site is trustworthy before adding it to your Trusted Sites zone; otherwise, you have no security protection for that site.

The Restricted Sites zone works like the Trusted Sites zone, except in reverse. Sites listed in the Restricted Sites zone are given the High security level in order to protect the computer from harmful content. You can select the Restricted Sites zone and click the Sites button in order to add sites to the zone that might use harmful content.

WORKING WITH PRIVACY SETTINGS

Privacy Settings, which is a new feature in Internet Explorer 6, gives you a way to manage cookies that are used by Internet Explorer. A cookie is a text file that is exchanged with your browser and a web site. Cookies can contain personal information about you and even your surfing/access habits.

Although cookies are very useful and even required by some sites, they do pose certain security risks. If the cookie information gets in the wrong hands, you have just given someone personal information about you. That's where the problem comes in—cookies personally identify you on the Internet, which can cause problems. Cookies account for many different kinds of privacy invasions, including a lot of the spam that users receive in their e-mail inbox.

Internet Explorer 6 provides a collection of settings that can restrict and control cookies. These settings, when effectively used, can help safeguard your information but allow you to use sites that manage cookies in an appropriate manner. Internet Explorer 6 uses a standard called the Platform for Privacy Preferences (P3P), which enables Internet Explorer to inspect cookies, determine how they will be used, and then decide what to do about them. The feature is not perfect, but it does help control cookie usage and the user's privacy. Before you configure privacy settings, there are a couple of concepts that you should get familiar with:

- **Compact Privacy Statement**   A Compact Privacy Statement tells how cookies are used on the site and the lifetime of that of particular cookie. When you access a web site, the Compact Privacy Statement is contained in the HTTP header of the web site and Internet Explorer can read the Compact Privacy Statement when you first access the site.

- **First-Party Cookie**   A first-party cookie is a cookie that is generated and used by the site you are currently viewing. First-party cookies contain information about you and your browser, and are commonly used to tailor site content to your needs. First-party cookies are commonly used on online store sites.

- **Third-Party Cookie**   A third-party cookie is used by a site other than the one you are currently accessing, such as a banner ad or an advertisement. Third-party cookies can be a problem because you do not really know who is using them or what they will do with the personal information contained in the cookie.

- **Session Cookie**   A session cookie is generated during a single session with a web site, and then deleted once the session has ended. In many cases, you cannot use a web site unless a session cookie can be generated.

■ **Implicit and Explicit Consent**   Implicit consent means that you have not blocked a site from using a cookie—in other words, you have not granted permission, but you have not denied it either. On the other hand, Explicit consent means that you have acted to allow a web site to use or gain personal information about you.

Privacy settings are managed on the Privacy tab, shown in the next illustration. You have a slider bar option that enables you to select a desired privacy setting.

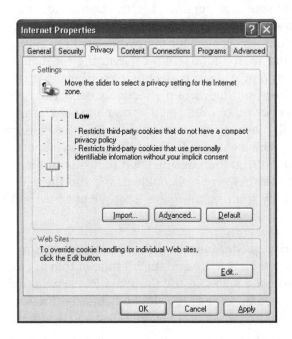

The standard privacy setting options that are available are as follows:

■ **Block All Cookies**   All cookies are blocked. Web sites cannot generate any new cookies and no existing cookies can be read. This setting will prevent access at some web sites.

■ **High**   No cookies that use personally identifiable information can be generated without your explicit consent. Web sites that do not have a compact privacy statement cannot generate cookies.

■ **Medium High**   First-party cookies that use personally identifiable information are blocked without your implicit consent. Cookies are blocked from third-party web sites that do not have a Compact Privacy Statement.

Also, third-party cookies that use personally identifiable information are blocked without your explicit consent.

- **Medium**   First-party cookies that use personally identifiable information without your implicit consent are allowed, but they are deleted when you close Internet Explorer. Third-party cookies that use personally identifiable information without your implicit consent are blocked as well as third-party cookies that do not have a Compact Privacy Statement. The Medium setting is the default Internet Explorer setting.

- **Low**   The Low setting accepts all first-party cookies. Third-party cookies are blocked from sites that do not have a Compact Privacy Statement. However, third-party cookies that use personally identifiable information are allowed without your implicit consent, but the cookies are deleted when you close Internet Explorer.

- **Accept All Cookies**   All new cookies are allowed and all web sites can read existing cookies.

The Advanced button gives you the Advanced Privacy Settings window. The Advanced Privacy setting essentially allows you to override how cookies are handled for this particular zone. You can choose Accept, Block, or Prompt for First and Third-Party Cookies, and you can also always allow session cookies. For some users, the automatic cookie handling settings do not provide the right support. In this case, you can override these settings and choose how you want to handle all first- and third-party cookies at all sites, regardless of the Compact Privacy Statement. For the session cookie, you should typically allow session cookies to be generated so that the web site can keep up with your surfing selection while you are there. Session cookies are typically harmless and you may find that web surfing is hindered without them.

If you choose to use automatic cookie handling, you can override the privacy settings for certain web sites. For example, let's say that there is a site you regularly use that contains first- and third-party cookies. However, the site does not have a Compact Privacy Statement, and your current cookie settings prohibit the use of first-party cookies on sites with no such policy. Rather than changing your entire policy, you can simple create an exception for the web site.

On the Privacy tab, click the Edit button. You see a Per Site Privacy Actions window. Simply enter the URL of the web site and click the Block or Allow button. Web sites that you have added appear in the managed web sites list, which you can edit and change at any time.

WRAPPING UP...

Internet networking is an important part of business networking today. The good news is the Internet can provide all kinds of resources and features that business networks need, and with modern operating systems, configuring and managing Internet connections, security, and browsers does not have to be the complicated chore that it once was. For the A+ technician who is often left with these kinds of details, this is certainly good news. As you are working with Internet connections, keep in mind that the operating system that you are working with is designed to manage connections and general web usage. All you typically need to do is configure the options that are right for your network.

NETWORK SECURITY

6

One of the most pressing issues in computing today is security. Your network will face a number of potential security risks, both internal and external. Virus and worm developers are poised to take advantage of your users. Hackers are almost always willing to show you the shortcomings of your publicly accessible server configurations. In fact, your own end users may be your biggest threat. Accidental and intentional data destruction by current (and perhaps soon-to-be former) employees results in millions of dollars of lost productivity every year. To address these issues, we will look at methods to design, implement, and evaluate security solutions for your network. In this chapter, we'll...

- Configure a server operating system to enforce a password policy
- Change the access allowed to a set of files and folders on a server
- Install a software firewall and design a secure LAN/DMZ
- Select and install antivirus software
- Configure and schedule a backup of server data

MANAGING USER ACCOUNTS AND PASSWORDS

Controlling who can and cannot access your networked resources is the first line of defense, so to speak. When using a Windows 2000 domain, there is often a tendency for user accounts to accumulate over time. As users come and go, you should make a habit of disabling or deleting accounts that are no longer active or needed. If the user is not likely ever to return, you should delete the account once any needed information has been recovered. The reason you will want to recover information before you delete the account is this: some operating systems allow encryption based on user account. In many cases, the user account that enabled the encryption is the only user account that can decrypt the information. If the account exists on the domain, an administrator can reset the password of the user in question to gain access to data that has been encrypted in this manner.

NOTE If you are using Windows 2000 in a workgroup environment, resetting or deleting a user account that has been used to encrypt files will make those files forever inaccessible. If your user is gone and you do not know the password, or worse yet if you have already reset the password, you will need to consult Microsoft for additional information about recovering the encrypted files. The Knowledgebase document (support article number 290260) provides some additional guidance on the topic. As of this writing the article is located at http://support.microsoft.com/ default.aspx? scid= kb;en-us;290260

However, if the account is deleted prior to data recovery, the data may be lost forever. If you might need the account later—for example, if you have an intern during the summers—you can simply disable the account during the time that the user is not using network resources.

Once you get beyond the issues with accumulated accounts, you can focus on user account password policies. The biggest security risk to your network is weak user and administrator passwords. The tendency for users to use simple, repetitive, or intuitive passwords poses a greater threat to your network than all of the hacking tools, viruses, and flawed software combined. By having the ability to guess or logically deduce your user's passwords, a hacker can gain instant access to network resources. For this reason, you need to develop a good, clear, and enforceable password policy. While your users still need to have passwords they can remember, your password policy needs to encourage passwords that are strong enough to resist cracking by the ever-present "script kiddies" (a novice hacker of sorts). These intruders make use of premade hacking tools to guess user passwords, using what is known as a "brute force" attack.

DEVELOPING A PASSWORD POLICY

When building a password policy, it is important to keep in mind the need for balance between security and usability. While you certainly want to keep unauthorized users from getting in where they do not belong, you don't want your users calling you every couple of days to reset their passwords because they forgot them. Worse yet, you don't want your users writing their passwords on a sticky note and attaching it to their computer monitor. With this in mind, you need to evaluate six elements of any password policy:

- Password length
- Use of repeating characters
- Use of both alpha and numeric characters
- Banning dictionary words
- Password expiration policies
- Automatic account lockout policies

PASSWORD LENGTH

One of the most basic elements of a password policy is password length. Generally speaking, users should not be allowed to use passwords that are fewer than six characters in length. On the flip side, you should not require your users to recall passwords longer than 12 characters or you will spend a lot of time resetting forgotten passwords. The reason for this password length requirement is twofold. First, it is true that longer passwords have more possible character combinations and are hopefully harder to guess. Additionally, longer passwords also help support the policy of the banning of dictionary words. As the password length increases, you will end up reducing the number of common dictionary words that can be used as a potential password.

NOTE   For a variety of reasons, from the mathematics involved to common behavior of network users, a password that is seven or fourteen characters in length tends to be the hardest to crack. Since most users do not find a fourteen-character password easy to recall, seven typically is the magic number.

REPEATING CHARACTERS

Once you have decided on the password length requirements, you will need to decide if your users will be able to use repeating characters. If you banned the use of repeating characters, a user would not be able to use a password like j33na2 since the number 3 is repeated. Typically, the ban on repeated characters does not forbid all kinds of repeating characters—only sequential recurrence of a character. For example, while j33na2 would not usually be allowed, je3na32 would be all right because the duplicated characters are not adjacent to each other in the password. This particular policy is not as important as password length, but it can be a powerful deterrent to using easy-to-guess passwords.

ALPHA AND NUMERIC CHARACTERS

The next policy to implement in nearly all cases is requiring your users to include both numbers and letters in their passwords. As with all of the other password policies, the goal of this requirement is to reduce the chances of an unauthorized user gaining access to network resources by discovering a valid user's password. In the preceding section, we saw the password je3na32. This password is essentially a user's name, Jeena, with numeric characters added in various locations. As an added precaution, you can encourage your users to make use of capital and lowercase characters as well. Some operating systems are case sensitive about usernames, but nearly all of them are case sensitive when it comes to passwords. For example, Je3na32 and je3na32 would be considered different passwords on most Windows, Linux, and UNIX-based systems.

NOTE   There is a common practice among Internet users to substitute certain numbers for certain letters. For example, *e* is replaced with 3, *a* with 4, *s* with 5, and *t* with 7. The result is that a word such as "sweaters" might become 5w347er5. This fact is not lost on would-be hackers. Using this direct replacement system is almost no better than using the regular dictionary word that it replaces. Using this replacement system and random numerical characters can yield a strong password. For example, 3sw3at3rs4u could be remembered with the mnemonic "three sweaters for you."

BANNING THE USE OF DICTIONARY WORDS

Because we are in the business of making strong passwords, we will need to prevent users from making use of passwords that are common dictionary words. In fact, here are some of the most common passwords used by network users: love, sex, god, secret, default, nobody, unknown, and wizard.

Because many users make use of the same weak passwords, hackers have developed applications called "crackers" that in part make use of long lists of known passwords as part of their system for gaining access to user accounts. These text files often contain hundreds of passwords, and most users would find it disturbing how many of the passwords they currently use (or previously have used) are on these lists. One might be prone to thinking that there is great variation in the passwords that users select, but in fact most of the time there is not much difference at all. Essentially any password on one of these lists should probably be banned. Some network administrators have gone as far as deploying a password-cracking tool against their own users. In most cases, any account that is cracked is either disabled or set to force the user to change their password. In either event, the user is notified that there password was insufficient.

PASSWORD EXPIRATION POLICY

No matter how good a user's password is, periodically they should be required to change to a new password. Over time, users may leave themselves logged in or perhaps they might give the password to another user for some reason or another. Additionally, if there are network intruders attempting to discern the passwords of your users, it will be just that much harder if the users' passwords change regularly. While there is no solid guideline for how often your users should change their passwords, you can assume that forcing them to reset their passwords more often than once a month will probably drive them nuts. On the other hand, if they only change passwords every three months or more, there will be ample time for the passwords to be compromised. As a rule of thumb, users should be forced to change their passwords every 45–60 days.

PASSWORD LOCKOUT POLICIES

The last element of any sturdy password policy is the existence of an account lockout requirement. Basically, if a user enters their password incorrectly a number of times over a specified time period, their account will be locked out. It is fairly common for users to lose access to their accounts if they enter the wrong password more than three times in a 30-minute period. The lockout duration will vary, but it should be longer than the previously mentioned interval of 30 minutes. One of the things stopped dead in its tracks by a policy like this is a brute force password hack, because accounts will be disabled after a few bad password submissions.

TECH TALK

Watching the Watchers

An unfortunate fact is that some administrators are the worst violators of the password policy. In particular, they may exempt themselves from the password expiration policy. This is a serious hazard because the administrative users typically have the power to do serious damage to networked systems if the password is compromised. Because the threat to the network is significant, regular auditing of administrative user accounts should occur to ensure that the proper policies are being followed.

SELLING THE POLICY TO USERS

One of the biggest challenges to implementing a password policy is selling the importance to critical users. In an ideal world you would be able to convince all of the network users of the importance of your password policy, but alas this is not a perfect world. At the bare minimum you need to obtain buy-in from the users who can help encourage other users to follow the password policy. Your organization's management is a prime target for ensuring your policy will have the needed backing to survive. It is almost a guarantee that new password restrictions will bring about some complaints and possibly some disruption of the users' day-to-day operations while they are adjusting to the new policies. In a worst-case scenario, management will probably have the means to help enforce the policy should the users stray from the new policy.

TECH TALK

Tools for Auditing Passwords

There are several good tools for auditing passwords to ensure that they are not overly simple. While it is true that the particular tools I am about to mention have a certain appeal to would-be hackers, they are in fact more useful as security auditing tools. Each of the following tools requires the person running them to have administrative/root access to the system that they are running in order to successfully use the tool.

For Windows-based operating systems, there is a product called L0phtCrack ("Loft Crack" or "LC"). This product was developed by the research arm of the security company @stake ("At Stake"). L0phtCrack can be used to scan the Windows SAM database that stores usernames and passwords, or it can be used to extract usernames and password hashes. Hashed passwords are basically an encrypted version of the user's password. The program then uses common passwords and some testing algorithms to decrypt the hashed passwords. To obtain a 15-day trial of this product, check out the @stake software download web site at http://www.atstake.com/research/lc/download.html.

If you are using a UNIX-based operating system, one of the best password auditing tools available is simply called Crack. This program operates in a manner similar to LC and like LC can easily determine oversimplified passwords.

ENFORCING PASSWORD POLICIES

If you are using a Windows 2000/.NET–based domain, you have at your disposal the tools needed to force everyone who logs on to your domain to use passwords that meet criteria you specify. In order to use the Domain Security tool, you will either need to be logged on to a Windows domain controller (Windows 2000 or .NET Server) or have the Windows 2000 Administrative tools installed, if using Windows 2000 Server. You will need to log on as a user who is a member of either the Domain or Enterprise Administrators group(s). Then, follow these steps:

1. Open the Domain Security console by clicking Start and selecting Programs, then Administrative Tools, and, finally, click Domain Security Policy.

2. Click the plus symbol next to Security Settings, then Account Policies.

3. Click the Password Policy entry.

4. You will see the screen shown in Figure 6-1.

5. From this point, you can right-click any of the items in the right-hand portion of the Domain Security window to enable and/or configure any of the options for use.

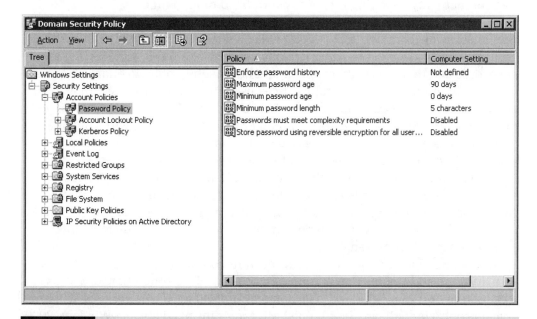

FIGURE 6.1   The Domain Security Policy screen

There are six options in the domain password policy. These options are

- Enforce Password History
- Maximum Password Age
- Minimum Password Age
- Minimum Password Length
- Passwords Must Meet Complexity Requirements
- Store Passwords Using Reversible Encryption for All Users In the Domain

The Enforce Password History option does exactly what you might think: it turns password policy use on or off for the entire domain. In order to make use of the other five options for domain password management, you will need to enable this option. The Maximum Password Age option determines how long a user may continue to use a particular password before it expires and the user is forced to change the password. In Figure 6-1, the maximum age is set to 90 days. This particular option is important because even with account lockout enabled, users need to regularly change their passwords. This setting ensures that all users will be forced to change their passwords instead of relying on a user's ability to keep track of manually changing their password from time to time.

The next option is Minimum Password Age. This value is used to prevent user passwords from being changed before a specified duration has passed. This option is not widely used, but if your users have a tendency to change their passwords and then forget them, this might be a useful option to enable. The next option, Minimum Password Length, forces users to use passwords with as many or more characters as this option specifies. Users should use passwords longer than five characters and probably not longer than twelve. Passwords outside of this range are either too easily guessed or they are too hard to recall easily.

The last two options will allow you to enable complexity requirements and password storage using reversible encryption. If, for example, you wanted to specify that user passwords must include both characters and numbers, the complexity requirements can be used. Encryption is useful for protecting the integrity of the user passwords if your network security policy dictates this level of security is required.

Now we will look at another very important component of password security—the account lockout settings. First let's walk through how to access these settings on your Windows 2000 domain. You will need to log on to a Windows domain controller or have the Administrative tools installed if using Windows 2000 Server. Again, you will need to use an account that is a member of either the Domain or Enterprise Administrators group(s).

1. Open the Domain Security console by clicking Start and selecting Programs, then Administrative Tools, and, finally, clicking Domain Security Policy.

2. Click the plus symbol next to Security Settings and then Account Policies.

3. Click the Account Lockout Policy object to reveal the individual options.

4. You will see the screen shown in Figure 6-2.

The options here determine the policy used when a user enters the incorrect password for a valid username. Since some basic hacking tools use a known username and try a large volume of passwords, you probably do not want a user to be able to enter an invalid password without limitations. If the legitimate user has a weak password and the hacker is allowed to freely try a brute force or dictionary password attack (lots of password guesses), they will probably compromise the user's password in a short period of time. If the account locks out after a few failed attempts, the usefulness of such brute force attacks is lessened. There are three options you can alter. The first option sets the Account

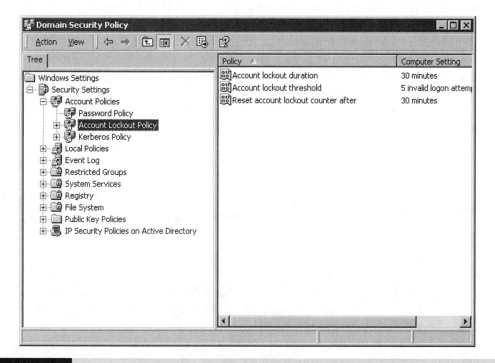

FIGURE 6.2   Account lockout options

Lockout Duration. This value determines how long the user's account will remain inaccessible after the specified number of bad logon attempts have been met or exceeded during the lockout counter period. In the example shown in Figure 6-2, the lockout duration is 30 minutes.

The next configurable value is the Account Lockout Threshold, which is the number of failed authentication attempts allowed during the counter period before the account is locked out. In Figure 6-2, the option has been configured to allow five connection attempts before locking out the account. Finally, the Reset Account Lockout Counter After option defines the period within which the failed logon attempts (five in the case of Figure 6-2) must occur. The net results of the options shown in Figure 6-2 are as follows: a user account will be locked out for a duration of 30 minutes if the user enters their password incorrectly five times within a 30-minute window.

It is important to note that you want to make sure that the Lockout Duration value is equal to or greater than the Reset Account Lockout Counter After value. If the duration is shorter than the reset interval, you will run into some nasty complications. Because the counter may not reset before the lockout ends, the account could be automatically relocked because, as far as the counter option is concerned, the same conditions exist as when the account was first locked out. To correct this condition, an administrator would need to intervene. If your password policy requires users to change passwords, you could have a real mess on your hands because any user that is locked out will be locked out for a long time— at least double what is planned—which may result in an added administrative burden.

TECH TALK

Making Policies Stick

An unfortunate fact is that some administrators are the worst violators of the password policy. In particular, they may exempt themselves from the password expiration policy. This is a serious hazard because the administrative users typically have the power to do serious damage to networked systems if the password is compromised. Because the threat to the network is significant, regular auditing of administrative user accounts should occur to ensure that the proper policies are being followed.

TECH TALK

Who Needs Passwords? Use Biometrics!

If you are interested in putting most of the problems with passwords behind you, it might be in your best interest to think about *biometric* options. Biometric devices can use voice, fingerprint, retinal (eye), or other physically distinct characteristics to authenticate users. Devices such as thumbprint scanners come in a wide array of designs, from USB to PCMCIA (PC card), and support every major operating system currently on the market. While it should never be assumed that any solution is foolproof, biometrics can go a long way towards securing not only supercritical resources but also everyday user access. Typically, the cost of a thumbprint scanner, which is the most common and cost-effective biometric option right now, is less than $200. Some computers from major manufacturers such as IBM now come with biometrics equipment as an optional component with new computer purchases.

If enforcing the user password policy has become a serious challenge, or there is a security need that dictates more powerful measures, there are some alternatives. One useful option is to restrict the time of day or night that a user can log on. Another technique is to restrict the computers that a user can authenticate to locally. While you want your network users to have use of network file and applications servers, you probably don't want them to be able to log on locally to the server. Lastly, there is an alternative that does a good job at reducing your dependence on passwords or improving the strength of your system's security: biometrics.

Rather than being an option for replacing passwords all together, biometrics are more commonly used as a powerful means of fortifying the existing authentication processes. But as the technology continues to advance and prices on the hardware continue to fall, you may someday be in a position to do away with the vast majority of passwords on your network. Keep in mind that you will have to deal with end users. While biometrics may solve a number of issues, users may not warm to the technology initially. You should be especially prepared for end users' objections to the digital storage of identifying information such as fingerprints because this may bother some people. Assuring them of the security of the stored information will go a long way to helping them buy in to the idea of biometrics.

PAINFUL LESSONS I'VE LEARNED

Single Sign-on Nightmare

If you are in a situation where your users authenticate to multiple vendor systems (Linux, Windows, NetWare, OS400), you may find that it is easiest to make passwords uniform for each user across the various servers. Some systems integrate fairly well with OS-included software, and some must be done manually. Once upon a time, I worked in a mixed Windows 2000/IBM AS400 environment. Because of inexperienced staff (myself) and a lack of feasible alternatives (no money), we opted to synchronize the passwords for the AS400 and Windows 2000 domain accounts manually. A little problem resulted. If a user's Windows 2000 password expired and the user changed both the Windows and AS400 password, all was well. If they were unfortunate enough to change just the Windows password and then log off, they could not log into Windows again. To make a long story shorter, it turns out that the AS4000 client software (when a single sign-on was enabled) was trying to log on with the new Windows password, which of course was no longer the same password used by the AS400 account. Rather than generate an error or crash, the AS400 client would just halt the system. After two OS reinstalls and a few phone calls, we realized the solution was simply resetting passwords. The moral of this story? Shell out the cash for synchronization software if needed, but avoid manually tracking passwords between systems at all costs.

MANAGING FILE ACCESS

Once you have a system in place for ensuring that only the proper users have access to your network, you will probably need to organize what resources authorized users have access to. Typically, not all users need access to all of the network resources. In many cases, there are resources that are reserved for certain users and groups, and they need to be secured from unauthorized access. In order to ensure that your file access requirements are met, you will need to make a plan, implement that plan, and then take special consideration for remote users accessing public resources.

MAKING A FILE ACCESS PLAN

Planning is just as important for your file access configuration as it is for setting a password policy. Fortunately, it is not as complex a process as building a password policy. You will need to build a representation of how the network users are organized. Figure 6-3 shows an example of an organizational chart that has the basic divisions for a company.

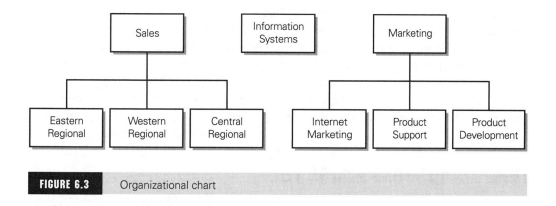

FIGURE 6.3   Organizational chart

The chart in Figure 6-3 shows three general groups: Sales, Information Systems, and Marketing. Assuming that users from each group do not need access to resources used by the other groups, you could design a file structure that has separate storage areas for each of the three groups. If there were some common shared resources, these resources could be placed in a fourth location accessible by all groups. So now you have an idea of how to organize the files for each group, but in practical terms, how is this done? In order to ensure the most efficient use of computer disk space and to simplify the management of file access rights, you should create a file structure that mimics the organizational chart of your organization. The folders/directories created within the structure should be hierarchical. The following steps outline the general steps for making this kind of file storage arrangement using the information on the organizational chart in Figure 6-3:

1. Locate the drive or volume where you will store the user files.
2. Create three folders/directories. Name one Sales, another IS, and the last one Marketing.
3. Within the Sales folder/directory, create a folder titled Western, Eastern, and Central.
4. Within the Marketing folder, create three new folders named IM, PS, and PD.
5. Within each subfolder (Western, Eastern, Central, IM, PS, and PD) and the IS folder, create a folder named Common.

Users in each division would be given their own folders for their work materials. Shared documentation would be placed in the common folder for each division. This type of arrangement can be used to accommodate the most complex of organizations. This logical arrangement of the file structure will not only make it easy to find resources used by a particular group or user, but it can also aid in troubleshooting permissions problems because the arrangement is hierarchal. If there are resources that are restricted, such as management and human resources information, the folders/directories should be placed at the root. If in our previous example there was a need for a restricted file storage location for human resources, a folder/directory called HR could be created alongside the other root folders (Sales, IS, and Marketing). Permissions could then be assigned to the HR folder that would be unique from the other root-level folders.

IMPLEMENTING YOUR ACCESS PLAN

So, now you have a plan of action about how to build a good file structure. Next, you need to assign permissions to those folders in order to complete the process. The following steps will walk you through the process for assigning permissions on a Windows 2000 Server. In order to make use of file-level permissions, the folder or file must reside on a hard disk partition using the NFTS file system. If FAT is used, these steps will not work.

1. Using Windows Explorer, open one of the computer hard drives.
2. Right-click any file or folder located on that drive. You may want to create a new one to prevent issues with existing file access or application operation.
3. Select Properties in the menu that appears.
4. Select the Security tab.
5. In the Window that appears (see Figure 6-4), you may add or remove users (to or from the Access Control List or ACL) as well as modify their permissions to the resource.

NOTE Changing permissions under Windows XP Professional is accomplished in a similar manner. In order to use the steps just outlined, you will need to disable simplified file sharing. To do this, open the Control Panel and then the Folder Options applet, and then select the View tab. At the bottom of the options list there is a check box you can clear to disable simplified file sharing. This option is not available with Windows XP Home Edition.

If you are making use of a UNIX/Linux-based operating system, you will probably be using the chmod command to alter the access rights available to a particular user. The chmod command is used to change the permissions list for any directory specified in the filename variable of the command. For example, the command chmod /usr/local/myfiles 642 would change the access allowed to the myfiles directory. The variable 642 specifies the permissions granted to

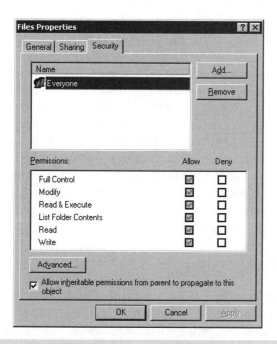

FIGURE 6.4   The Permissions window

the user who created the folder (6 in this case), the members of the same group as the creator (4), and other users (2). The leftmost number always indicates the permissions granted to the owner of the file, the middle bit relates to the users who are in the same groups as the owner, and the rightmost bit pertains to all users other than those covered by the first two groups.

This numerical code is made of four options. Read permission is indicated with 4, write with 2, execute with 1, and no access with 0. So, for example, if a user was assigned read and write permissions and all other users were denied access, the numeric value would be 600. This numeric value which is the sum of the four values (0, 1, 2, and 4) is used to thus specify the permissions. To change the permissions of a folder on your Linux/UNIX systems, follow these steps:

1. Open a terminal session and change in to the directory of your choice.

2. Execute the command chmod *file/directory* 744. The *file/directory* variable can be any file or directory you choose. The result will give you (the owner of the files) full control and everyone else read-only access.

PUBLIC SERVERS: PREVENTING UNAUTHORIZED ACCESS

What about servers which by their design allow virtually anyone to access them? It's all well and good to secure resources by using strong passwords and file access control, but how do you manage a server such as a public web or FTP server that allows broad access. In order to secure your publicly accessible resources and ensure that they do not compromise the security of your private resources, you need to make good infrastructural design choices. After your design has been implemented, you will want to tune your servers to reduce the number of potential security risks. Finally, you want to make sure that you are logging enough of the user activity to track down the source of any issues, such as intrusion attempts, that might occur.

SECURING PUBLIC RESOURCES

If your network will provide publicly available resources such as web or FTP access, you need to take extra precautions to avoid allowing either the servers or your private network being compromised. One of the most meaningful measures of keeping outside users outside is through the use of a secure LAN topology, commonly called a DMZ (demilitarized zone). In Figure 6-5, you see that there is an external router and an internal router. Public resources are placed in the DMZ between the routers. Access lists are configured so that the following items are in place:

- Inbound traffic arriving at the external router is forwarded to specific hosts on the DMZ or rejected all together.

- The internal router will not accept inbound connections from either DMZ hosts or the external router. Traffic designated as a response to a request from the internal LAN will be passed back to the internal/private LAN user. This allows FTP, web browsing, and such.

The net result is that Internet users can access only designated servers on the DMZ. Should a hacker compromise either the external router or a DMZ device, the internal router still protects the private LAN from intrusion by rejecting incoming requests from the DMZ and external router.

There are many options for building a DMZ. You can use hardware routers from any of a number of vendors (Cisco, AlliedTelesyn, and Nortel, for example) or you can use comparatively inexpensive PC-based routers that use a product

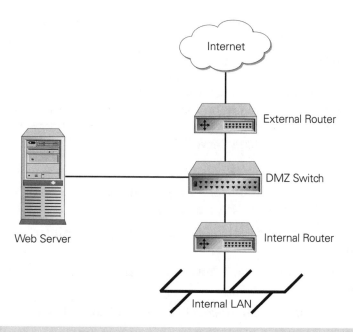

FIGURE 6.5   A secure LAN/DMZ example

like ZoneAlarm with Windows, or any of a number of firewalling products available for Linux systems. Adding a firewall to the router configuration will give you expanded abilities to manage and monitor traffic. In most cases, it is not a requirement, but if you are using PC-based routers, a firewall on the internal DMZ router is highly recommended.

Before going on to third-party solutions, however, let's look at the options available right out of the box if you are making use of Windows 2000 or .NET server. The Routing and Remote Access (RRAS) application can be used to turn any Windows 2000/.NET server into a router. If the server has two or more routers, a useful DMZ router can be constructed. By enabling RRAS (see Chapter 13 for details), you can make use of this routing capability to build the two routers needed for a DMZ configuration.

NOTE   If you are planning on building a DMZ for a production environment, you would be best served by a dedicated routing/firewalling product such as one of the units produced by Cisco, 3Com, HP, and others. Software/PC-based firewalls are easier for would-be hackers to compromise and, typically, the PC-based firewall is a good temporary solution.

While the Linux variant is probably more secure, especially for the external gateway, neophytes will probably find configuring a Windows-based product easier. If you depend on resources located in the DMZ for day-to-day operation, you should invest in dedicated hardware firewall solutions.

So, now you know about some methods for keeping users of your public resources from being a problem for your private network. Since we talked about using ZoneAlarm, we will now walk through the process of downloading and installing it on a Windows 2000 Server. To get ZA installed and running, follow these steps:

1. Log on to the server as a user with administrative rights. Open a web browser and go to http://www.download.com.

2. At the top of the page in the Search box, type **ZoneAlarm** and then click the Go button.

3. A list of items will appear. Find the ZoneAlarm 3.1.x entry and click the link.

4. On the page that appears next, click the Download Now link.

5. A box will appear prompting you to save the ZoneAlarm installer. Click the Save As button and select a location to save the file.

6. Browse to the directory where the file was saved and double-click the file to execute. The file will be named something like "zasetup_1001.exe."

7. The first window that appears will ask you to select a location for the install. If needed, make a change; otherwise, just click the Next button.

8. Next, the application collects some basic registration information (hey, it's free!). Fill out the fields and click the Next button.

9. If you're ready, check the I Agree check box, and then click the Install button.

10. At the end of the installation, you will be asked to fill out a little survey. Select some answers and click the Finish button.

11. When prompted, you can opt to start ZoneAlarm by clicking the Yes button.

TECH TALK

Not Just a Firewall

My favorite "pet" firewall is ZoneAlarm, if you haven't guessed. Not only is it free in many applications, it has a superb ability to granularly control inbound and outbound traffic. If you install ZoneAlarm with the highest default security settings, you will be able to tune the application as you go to allow various services to operate. With the highest security settings, you will be prompted to approve inbound and outbound communications sessions. For example, if your Internet gateway is running ZoneAlarm and your users begin using a new messaging program, ZoneAlarm will block the new outbound traffic since neither the application nor the port it is using would be authorized to pass the firewall. With this ability, you can granularly manage what kind of traffic is allowed to pass your firewall and thus conserve often expensive bandwidth.

PAINFUL
LESSONS

I'VE LEARNED

Oh, that Anonymous Account!

First off, I happily admit that this is not actually my painful lesson, but one that I had the somewhat humorous task of witnessing. A number of years ago I was asked to configure an FTP server for use by our sales department. The server would be located in my NOC but managed from afar. They needed a server that would allow their Customer Relationship Management (CRM) software to synchronize the field user's data with the corporate data server. I set up the server and was told they would take care of configuring user access. When I was done with it, there was a single management account available. Many months went by and I received a phone call from the would-be-sales-FTP-admin and it seemed there were some directories he could neither access nor delete, and they had strange names. He was sure that he had not created the files. Using a local admin account, I logged onto the server locally and took a peek. It seems that someone had managed to compromise the server and had been using it to share a variety of items from a French copy of the movie *Lethal Weapon* to pornographic images. I removed the offending content and disabled the FTP server. When I began researching the issue, I found that my coworker in the sales group had indeed configured the access accounts to allow user access. In fact, he gave 'anonymous' users the ability to read, write, and modify files and directories. To add insult to injury, he left the access account with a blank password. Anyone who bothered to try and connect to the server would find that they had the power to do as they pleased.

TROUBLESHOOTING

Keep out the Bad, Let in the Good

If you do not have a firewall between your private LAN and the Internet, get one. Once the firewall is in place, you will have gained the ability to keep out intruders while still allowing your users to make full use of the Internet. For example, many firewalls make use of Network Address Translation (NAT) to conceal users of the internal network from devices on the Internet. Typically, this blocks all inbound connections from the Internet to your private LAN. If you need to allow inbound connections, or some service/software is failing after installing a NAT firewall, the port filters may be the solution you need. Most firewalls will allow you to permit inbound connections based on the TCP port number (FTP is 21, for example) and then specify which host the firewall should direct that connection attempt towards. The steps for configuring this functionality vary from one device to the next, but in most cases it is a fairly straightforward operation.

SELECTING OS SERVICES

Most operating systems have as a part of their default installation configuration a number of system services that you may or may not ever use. Because services sometimes provide routes for hackers to exploit operating system vulnerabilities, it is a good idea to disable the services that you know you will not be using. Under Windows 2000, follow these steps to disable the telnet server service:

1. Click the Start button.
2. Select Settings and then click the Control Panel entry.
3. From within the Control Panel, open the Administrative Tools applet.
4. In the window that appears, select and open the Services applet.
5. In the right-hand portion of the window, browse down the list and locate the Telnet entry.
6. Right-click the entry and select Properties from the context menu that appears.
7. Change the Startup Type drop-down menu to Disabled. Click the Apply button and exit all windows.

Other services can be disabled in basically the same manner. In addition to the telnet service, many other services should, and can, be disabled if you are not actively using them. The following is a list of some of the best "get rid of them if you don't use them" services.

- Messenger Service
- Net Logon
- Network DDE
- Remote Registry Service

Of course, Windows is not the only system where you might need to disable stray services. The following steps outline the procedure for disabling a service on a Linux OS system:

1. Open a terminal window and go to the /etc/ directory.

2. Open the inetd.conf file with the text editor of your choice—for example, you can run pico inetd.conf or vi inetd.conf to open this file with either the Pico or vi text editor.

3. Once you are in the file, place the pound symbol (#) in front of any services that you need to disable. For example, to disable the local FTP server, you would make an entry that looks something like #ftp.

4. Hit all of the services you deem unneeded and save the file.

5. Restart your server and the new configuration changes will take effect.

TROUBLESHOOTING

Restoring Services

So, you went a little wild when you disabled the operating system services, and now you would like to restore some of them. In order to do this on a Windows 2000/XP/.NET system, you will need to enter computer management and then access the system services. Not only should you start the services you now realize you need, but you should configure them to automatically start with the system.

On a Linux system, you can restore the use of services disabled in the /etc/inetd.conf configuration file by removing the # symbol used to comment out the symlink for the service back into the file and then restarting the services manually or restarting the server.

KEEPING OS AND FIRMWARE CURRENT

Regardless of the platform that you are working with, such as Windows, Linux, NetWare, or Apple OS, you will probably want to regularly check for OS updates and security patches. By keeping current on fixes and software changes, you greatly improve your chances of surviving an intrusion attempt. Many hacking exploits are dependent on known and often fixed vulnerability. By obtaining current updates, you successfully close the door on some of the methods for invading your network. Each operating system environment has an associated web site where security fixes and product updates can be obtained. While updates are important to continued system integrity, you should not begin applying patches if you are unsure what effect the patch will have on system performance. If there is any question about the wisdom of applying a given patch, deploy it first in a testing environment and spare yourself the pain of having to rebuild or repair a working production server.

WINDOWS 2000/.NET SERVER

Updates and security fixes can be obtained from one of two places. http://windowsupdate.microsoft.com/ will provide ready access to more common patches and upgrades, but you may need to investigate the Microsoft downloads site to obtain a comprehensive list of available patches and updates. This site is located at http://www.microsoft.com/downloads.

LINUX (GENERAL INFORMATION)

One of the best places for updates on issues and updates relating to Linux is http://www.linux.org. This site not only contains information about the status of Linux modifications and patches, but it also has a wealth of general user information and documentation.

REDHAT LINUX

If you are using the RedHat distribution, you should keep your eyes on http://www.redhat.com for system updates and patches.

APPLE OS

If you are using any of the Apple computer operating systems, you can find information about firmware and software updates at http://www.info.apple.com/. This site is more of a general-purpose users' support area as opposed to just providing updates.

NOVELL NETWARE

Users of the NetWare product family can go to the Novell File Finder site at http://support.novell.com/filefinder/ and search for their version of NetWare to obtain the latest security fixes, service releases, and supplementary software.

TRACKING THE CULPRIT WITH LOGGING

On both Windows Servers and Linux/UNIX systems, logging of user activity is prevalent out of the box. If an unauthorized user has gained access to your systems or is attempting to do so, information in the log files can be helpful in identifying how they are trying to get in (if not who the attacker is). Windows can be used to log a variety of application, system, and even user security activity (log0/logoff, privilege use) by default.

To view the information collected, as well as manage some of the logging variables, you need to access the Windows Event Viewer. To access this information, follow these steps:

1. Click the Start button, then select Settings and open the Control Panel.

2. Double-click the Administrative Tools icon and then the Event Viewer icon.

3. A window will appear showing three classes of log entries: Application, Security, and System. Click each one to see the individual entries in each group.

4. Right-click the Application log entry in the left-hand portion of the window and select Properties from the context menu that appears. From here, you can set the variable parameters for the Application log by using the filter options. Repeating the previous steps for the other two logs will allow you to set parameters for them as well.

5. To view the contents of any of the three log files, simply click the log file in question and the entries will appear in the event viewer. Three classes of notifications may appear. Informational items simply display routine transactions. Warnings record information about events that could potentially be a problem, such as a failed replication between servers. An error entry indicates that some kind of system event failed to occur or complete successfully.

Linux systems log a wealth of information. Typically, a variety of log files are stored in /var/log/ directory, and sometimes monitoring these logs can be difficult since they can be numerous and are essentially flat text files. Tools exist to ease the interpretation of these log files, and such a tool is recommended if you need to work with Linux log files on a regular basis. One such tool is LogSentry. This tool allows the visual analysis of a wide range of standard and proprietary log types. For more information on the LogSentry product, check out http://www .psionic.org/products/logsentry.html.

Dedicated hardware firewalls and many routing products also offer a wealth of logging options. By logging incoming IP connections, you may be able to obtain far more detailed information about the source of any network intrusion attempts. Regardless of the kind of firewall you employ, take the time to get familiar with the logging features so that in an emergency you have the tools to hunt down the source of your problems.

TROJANS, VIRUSES, AND WORMS

Worms, viruses, and Trojans, or what I collectively call "infectionware," are probably the most potent plague that has ever been bestowed on the unprepared network manager. No matter how they get on your network—be it by e-mail, infected user files, or pirated software—these critters can cause a ton of problems in a hurry. While some of these "infectionware" applications can destroy data or sack a mail server by sending thousands of e-mails, the most disturbing infections involve those elements that install backdoor software. Worms, such as some variants of the Klez worm, have demonstrated this ability. The backdoor allows the worm developer to take control of, or otherwise gain access to, the infected system. The backdoor tool works even in the presence of a firewall because the infected host makes an outgoing connection to some host specified in the worm. Since firewalls almost always allow incoming traffic that is in reply to an internal host request, the worm is able to establish a connection with the hacker's designated host.

Once the tool has connected to the clandestine server, remote control tools can be uploaded and the infected host becomes a tool waiting to do the worm developer's bidding. The hacker may then have long-term and unfettered access to network resources, or a willing "Zombie" to use in later distributed denial-of-service (DDoS) attacks against other networks. With diligence and good network protection tools, you can avoid this potential nightmare.

TECH TALK

Worm-Resistant Systems

Unfortunately, the more widely used a platform is (particularly by home users), the more attention it seems to garner from virus writers. Certain operating systems that have widely known virus and worm issues are not solely the victim of popularity, but also sometimes questionable development. Alas, there are some operating systems that have a very low occurrence of Internet spawned "bugs." Of these systems, Linux is probably the most noteworthy. As a server platform, it has proven to be extremely flexible and reliable, and has had the benefit of a dedicated development community that takes some pride in the fact that Linux is less prone to security exploits than other operating systems. While Linux has yet to garner mass appeal as a desktop platform, it is under continued development and may yet prove useful in this arena. Another system that has proven to be unpopular for virus writers is the Apple Computer Apple OS. Virtually no viruses exist for Apple OS 7.x/8.x/9.x, making it a fairly reliable system to use where virus encounters have been (or are) an issue. This fairly user-friendly OS is a relatively popular solution for desktop systems, but is not generally a good server-side solution.

PROACTIVE PREVENTION

The first step to saving yourself from infectionware headaches is having your defenses in order. You want virus detection and cleaning tools in place before your users inadvertently begin introducing the latest worm to your network. Every computer should have virus protection software installed. If the hardware is relatively new, the real-time file access scanning should be enabled. If the hardware crawls and crashes with such settings enabled, the software need to be configured to scan all removable media on access as well as e-mail. Various e-mail gateway applications can scan all inbound mail messages (if you have your own mail server) and eliminate the majority of threats before they even reach your network. Not only are known viruses detected, but the mail scanners can usually be configured to filter out certain attachment types. Generally speaking, attachments that are not within an archive (.zip, .gz, .tar, .rar, .arj) should be summarily blocked. Since there is almost no way to make an archive automatically execute, there is little threat from these attachment types.

TECH TALK

System-wide Virus Scanning

When protecting your network from viruses, worms, and their kind, you might not believe how handy centralized management can be. Products such as Symantec Antivirus Corporate Edition and MacAfee AVSS (Active Virus Scan Suite) both offer server and client tools for managing your virus scanning software for a large organization from a single location. Typically, enterprise or corporate editions will allow an administrator to control the behavior of individual workstation and server copies of the scanning software. The administrator can manually or automatically initiate scans, virus definition updates, and software upgrades, all from the comfort of the management station. This not only saves time but greatly improves the protection afforded the network, because often it only takes a single infected host to wreak havoc.

SELECTING PROTECTIVE SOFTWARE

Choosing a virus scanning software package is almost a matter of taste. The real value in the packages is how often they are updated and have fresh virus definitions installed. If your virus definitions are a year old, the virus scanner might as well be uninstalled. Packages exist for Windows, NetWare, Apple, and a host of other operating systems. Some of the more popular scanning suites come from Symantec, Sophos, MacAfee, and Dr. Solomon.

DISASTER RECOVERY

If your system is compromised, the hardware fails, or a user accidentally deletes the file they have to have for a meeting in 20 minutes, you will be happy you have a backup of the network information. The following are the steps for using the Windows NT backup software to make a backup of existing data. Many more robust and flexible software options exist, but this product is "free" with Windows, and if you have Windows, you can begin backing up files ASAP.

1. Click Start | Programs | Accessories and click the Backup icon.
2. Windows backup will open.
3. Click the Backup Wizard button. Click Next in the window that appears.
4. In the following screen, you will choose the kind of backup: everything, selected files, or the system state. Click Next.
5. If backing up selected files, check the box next to the appropriate entries.

6. If doing a full backup, select the backup device and then click Next. If doing selected files, you will need to check the box next to the appropriate items and then select the backup location.

7. Click Finish to run the backup.

Linux also comes with an out-of-the-box backup solution, the tar utility. The command-line-driven application is basic, but it is common to nearly all UNIX and Linux systems and is thus worthwhile to keep in mind when working with backups in this kind of environment.

The tar command is used to copy existing files into a *tar archive*. This archive can exist on any media (removable, networked, or local) and can be copied freely once it has been created. The options used with the example command include Create New Archive (-c), Specify Filename (-f), and Verbose Mode (-v), which displays the file creation progress. To make a backup of a particular file or directory, execute the following command, where *filename.tar* is the name of the archive you will create and [files/directory] is the location of the data you wish to back up.

tar –cfv *filename.tar* [files/directories]

PAINFUL LESSONS

I'VE LEARNED

You Only Miss Your Backup When It's Not There

I cannot stress enough the importance of a good system backup. A good, usable backup will save lost production time and will spare you the task of answering nasty questions from users and managers about why there was no backup of missing data. In one of my previous positions as the director of a technical support and software development group, one of the items I had been tasked with was the implementation of backup software. Previous managers had never seemed to accomplish this basic task, and there was great fear that products could be left high and dry in the event of a system failure. I delegated the matter to one of my bright, if somewhat disorganized, technicians and went about my business. Some months later the unthinkable happened: a developer overwrote the production version of the code with an older version. I won't say anything about the development process that encouraged the kind of behavior that caused this, but I figured we'd restore from backup and be up and running in no time. Unfortunately, with the support call load being what it was, the technician had not implemented the backup solution yet. Fortunately, another justifiably paranoid programmer had made the habit of copying the production version of the code to his hard drive every night and we were able to recover. I had to eat lots of crow, since I had not made this a priority, but the solution was up, running, and tested less than three days later. I found the time, and you should too.

TROUBLESHOOTING

Recovering from Infections with "Fix" Tools

If you find your system infected by a pernicious worm or virus, you may find that (1) your virus scanning software is not working and (2) you cannot reinstall the virus scanner. Because many worms first attempt to nuke your protection, you may need to make use of virus-specific removal tools. By browsing to http://securityresponse.symantec.com/, you can obtain removal tools for the more common and resistant bugs. These tools are a true blessing when your system is down and you can't seem to get it cleaned up.

WRAPPING UP...

In this chapter, we spent quite a bit of time working on developing your own password policy. We covered the critical elements, from minimum password length to the regular expiration of existing passwords to ensure that unauthorized users will have a very difficult time compromising your users' passwords. We also examined a process for developing a meaningful and organized file storage arrangement. We changed access privileges on folders and directories to ensure that users would have the appropriate access to any particular resource. Since the topic is network security, we also spent some time looking at ways to protect your network resources from Internet-based intrusion attempts through the use of secure LANs. We also looked at virus detection and repair tools to protect you from the seemingly endless supply of worms, Trojans, and viruses.

Another topic touched on was firewall hardware and software. As integral components of network security, firewalls help prevent attacks from succeeding and can help track the source regardless of the success or failure of the attempt. This brings us to the topic of logging, which can be very useful when dealing with network intrusion. Logs can be used to help identify the manner in which an attack occurred, should you ever become the victim of network intruders. Finally, we looked at some disaster recovery methods—primarily, having a good system backup. In a worst-case scenario, a backup can really save your bacon, so to speak!

SHARING DATA ON THE NETWORK

7

A big benefit of networks is the ability to share information between various users and systems. The advantages of this kind of arrangement are numerous. Users can work collaboratively on documentation without having to manage multiple copies of the files in multiple locations. All of the files being worked on collectively can be stored in a single location on a network and, depending on the network capabilities, literally be accessed from anywhere in the world. Not only is access to the files provided, but if user data files are kept on a centralized server, the data can be protected by regular system backups. Some devices can also be shared in this manner (in particular, printers). Rather than installing and maintaining printers for every user on a network, groups of users can share a single device. This not only provides cost-effective printing resources for network users, but it also reduces the number of devices that must be maintained and repaired. In order to make file and printing resources available to users, several configuration changes are needed. In this chapter, we'll…

- Share files, folders, and printers from network servers while managing user access to shared resources

- Establish file quotas for users accessing networked resources

- Audit user access to networked resources
- Make a plan for placing servers on the network
- Examine the pros and cons of sharing resources from workstations

SHARING FILES AND FOLDERS

One of the first things we need to explore is creating file shares on a network server. In this section, we will create file shares on a Windows 2000 Server, a Windows XP Professional workstation, and a Novell NetWare server. We will look at some of the kinds of problems that can arise from improperly configured file- and share-level permissions and how to both identify and resolve them. We will also explore the topic of monitoring share access through auditing and logging. It is important to make sure that the right users have access to the appropriate resources and that unauthorized users do not have access to files and directories that they should not have. Finally, we'll configure quotas on a volume. By adding a quota, you will be able to place automatic limitations on how much data can be stored in a given location by a particular user. This will allow you, as the network administrator, to keep tight reigns on the amount of disk space consumed by your users, if you need to do so.

ESTABLISHING A NETWORK SHARE

Because providing access to shared files and directories is a basic function of almost any kind of server, creating a share is typically a simple process. We will do a quick review of the files-share creation process and then explore some platform-specific tips and tricks, as each of the three mentioned options have some unique benefits and limitations.

WINDOWS 2000 SERVER

In order to create a file share on your Windows 2000 Server, follow these steps:

1. Log on as a user with rights to create a share, such as a member of the domain or local administrators group.

2. Double-click My Computer and then double-click the drive containing the folder you wish to share.

3. Right-click the folder you want to share and select Sharing from the context menu that appears.

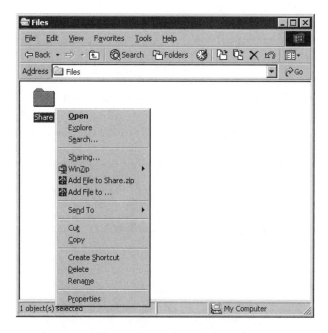

4. The Share Properties window will appear. Click the bullet next to the Share this Folder entry.

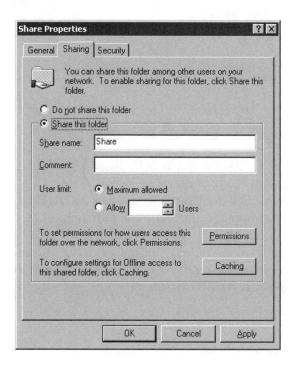

5. Either leave the share name as the default, or change it to a name that users will find meaningful for the share. For example, if you were creating a share for the Sales department to store files, you might call the share Sales Files.

6. Click the Permissions button in the lower right-hand portion of the screen and notice that the default settings allow all users, "everyone," full control. The limiting of access is accomplished under the Security tab.

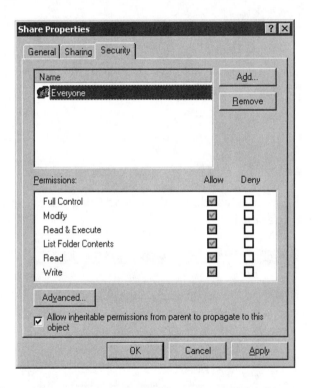

So, now you know that you can use hidden shares to gain access to resources in a pinch. But if you have administrative privileges, there are more options available. If you right-click My Computer and select the Manage option from the context menu that appears (opening the Management Console) you can manage the shares of that computer. Once the MMC is open, expand the Shared Folders entry and then click the Shares entry. The shares, including hidden ones, will appear in the right-hand portion of the MMC. You will see the name of the share, where the share is linked to, the type of share

TECH TALK

The Administrative Share

File shares from a server can be useful for supporting a wide range of network data access needs. But what if you need to get to files on a remote computer and there are no file shares, or the files you need do not reside within the share? If you are a nonadministrative user, you'll need to get help from your administrator. If you have administrative rights to your Windows NT/2000/XP/.NET computer, you can make use of "administrative shares" to get to your files. By default, all of the local hard drives have a hidden share configured at the root of the volume. For example, the C:\ drive of a Windows 2000 server is shared as c$. The $ prevents the share from appearing in normal computer browse lists. Were you to open the browse list and view an NT/2000/XP/.NET computer, you will not see the hidden shares. However, if you open an explorer session and enter ***servername*\c$**, you would be given access to the root of the C:\ drive on the target computer.

In addition to the default administrative shares, you can create your own hidden shares by creating a new share with a name *sharename*$, where *sharename* is the name you decide to assign the share. So, if you had a Windows XP Professional PC called XPStation and you created a hidden share secret$, you could access the share by opening Explorer and entering **\\xpstation\secret$**.

(what clients can make use of the share), and how many clients are connected to the share.

In addition to the Shares object, there are two other entries under the Shared Folders entry of the MMC. The Sessions option allows you to view all of the users connected to a file share on the computer you are managing. This can be especially useful if you need to quickly determine which users are connected to your server—for example, if you need to perform an unscheduled restart of the computer. The other option under the Shared Folders entry is Open Files. Rather than sorting the connections by users, you can use this option to sort which files are being accessed. If you needed to make sure that a file was not in use before opening and updating it, this option would reveal all of the users currently connected to the file. You could then contact the users and ask them to close the connections to the file before you begin working with the file.

Service Packs Matter

PAINFUL LESSONS I'VE LEARNED

At one point in the past, I was tasked with supporting a Windows NT 4.0 network that had Windows and Apple OS clients in use. In fact, much of the product development that was going on was performed on the Apple PCs. As such, we had file shares on the NT servers that were used to provide access to data on both the Windows and Apple clients. One day the primary file server seemingly rebooted by itself several times. Nothing useful was found in the event log as far as the actual error, but in tandem with the server reboots, a user complained about having trouble copying files to and from the server. I sent one of the other technicians to watch the server while I asked the user to repeat the file copy. Sure enough, about two minutes into the copy of a large (200MB) data file, our server reset itself.

One of the long-time developers seemed to recall an issue like this occurring before, but they could only recall that they eventually reinstalled the operating system to resolve the issue. This was hardly a practical solution, so off to my fellow admins and technical documentation I went. It turns out that the issue is known and was corrected sometime around Service Pack 5. Funny thing was, I had SP 6a installed. It finally occurred to me that I had enabled the File Services for Macintosh after installing the service pack. In NT 4.0 days, the service packs only updated installed services, so the files providing file services for the Apple computers (macfile) were basically Service Pack 1. I reapplied the service pack and found our users again able to move large Apple OS files around without tanking our server. Sharing information is an essential use of any network, and it is important to keep it working to keep your users (and yourself) happy. In order to keep things running smoothly, you will need to be prepared for anything. If the configuration appears to be correct, but the desired effect has not been achieved, check, double-check and don't hesitate to interview network users for their view of the symptoms if you are unable to make headway. They may have seen something you could find useful.

WINDOWS XP PROFESSIONAL

When creating a file share under Windows XP Professional, your ability to configure the details of NTFS permissions at the file and folder level will only be fully accessible if the Simplified File Sharing feature has been disabled. Windows XP Home and Professional come with this feature enabled by default.

Essentially, the simplified sharing system allows a user to create a file share without having to work with the details of the Windows ACL. For the casual or new user, this can be a very useful feature. If, however, you need to manage the access to a resource with complex access rules, simplified sharing will not be useful at all. The following steps will walk you through the process of disabling simplified file sharing. You should note that simplified file sharing can only be disabled on Windows XP Professional. If you have XP Home Edition, you will not be able to manage the ACL options in any detail.

1. Log on as a user with administrative rights.

2. Click the Start button and open the Control Panel, as depicted in Figure 7-1. If your Control Panel appears different, you may need to click the Switch to Classic View option.

3. Double-click the Folder Options icon within the Control Panel.

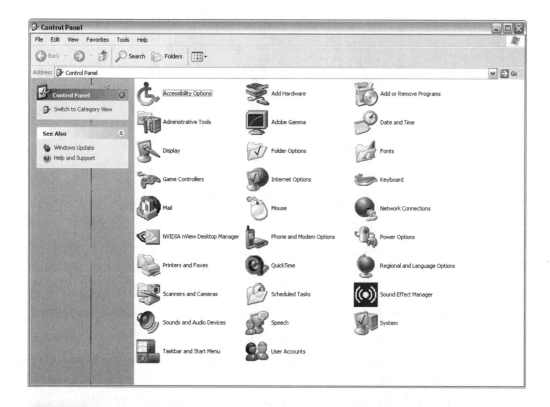

FIGURE 7.1   The Control Panel

4. In the Folder Options window that appears, click the View tab.

5. Within the Folder Options window, scroll to the bottom and uncheck the box next to the Use Simple File Sharing (Recommended), and then click the Apply button and finally the OK button. The next illustration shows the Folder Options screen.

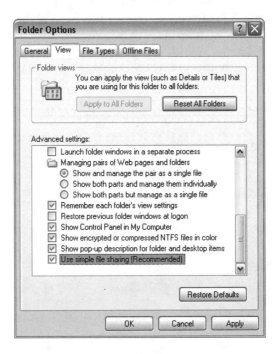

NOTE If you should join your Windows XP Professional computer to a Windows domain, the simplified sharing setting will be disabled.

Now that simplified sharing has been turned off, we will walk through the process of creating a new file share on your Windows XP Professional computer. The steps below will carry you through the process.

1. Click the Start button and click My Computer.

2. Select a disk (C:\ for example) and a folder to share.

3. Right-click the folder and select Sharing and Security from the context menu that appears.

4. In the Properties window that appears, click the bullet next to Share this Folder.

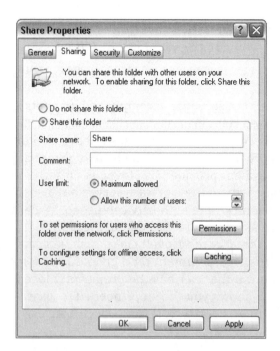

TECH TALK

Sharing Services with HTTP

Another useful method of providing users access to shared resources is via the Hypertext Transfer Protocol and File Transfer Protocol. HTTP and FTP are used to provide widespread file access in many internal networks in the form of intranet web servers. If you are using any of the Windows server products since NT, you will have Internet Information Server (or a derivative) and you will be able to enable and configure FTP and HTTP services with little effort.

One of the nice things about providing access to files in this manner is that any client using a compatible web browser or FTP client will be able to gain access to the files. This allows an administrator to add any kind of client to the network and provide access almost instantaneously—and without the use of specialized services to translate file formats from one system (server) to another (client). Another benefit of sharing information in this manner is the easy integration with other web server-based services.

The 6.x and 5.x releases of Novell NetWare also come with an HTTP server, a third-party product called Apache. Apache has a greater feature set and is far more widely used than IIS, but the configuration of Apache can be intimidating for a novice user.

5. From here, you can alter the share- and file-level security in the same manner as you would in the Windows 2000 process described earlier.

NETWARE 5.X

File sharing on a NetWare server is accomplished in a notably different manner than its Windows-based counterparts. Each Windows-based client computer that will connect to the NetWare file server needs to have a client piece of software installed. Microsoft provides a client in the form of Client Services for NetWare, but in most cases the client provided by Novell is preferred because they allow not only basic connectivity to the NetWare server, but also management tools that a user with the appropriate authority can use to create new folders and modify their "trustee assignments" (access privileges).

Any Windows PC that has the Novell client installed can use the following steps to check the trustee assignment for a given file or folder, and change the trustee assignment if the user has the proper privileges (administrative rights). The following shows you the steps needed to access and, if needed, alter the user rights of a file on a NetWare server from a Windows 2000-based client:

1. Double-click Network Neighborhood.
2. Double-click the Entire Network icon.
3. Locate the file you want to access and right-click, selecting NetWare Rights from the menu that appears.
4. Click the user account within the Trustees box.
5. In the right-hand portion of the window, the user's rights to the file or folder will be displayed.

In order to make changes to the access rights on the NetWare server, you will need to be using an account that has administrative rights to the NetWare server. NetWare file sharing and access control is explored in more detail in Chapter 11.

TROUBLESHOOTING

Top Three Reasons Users Cannot Access Shared Resources

Sooner or later you will have user(s) that cannot access one of the shared resources that you have created. You'll find it's useful to keep in mind these common sources of file access problems:

- **Access list inconsistencies**   Make sure that the user has the appropriate access on the Access Control List of the resource. Especially look for groups that may have been implicitly denied access to the resource. On a Windows-based server, the Deny attribute will take precedence over all other rights.

- **Network connectivity**   Next to access-right-related issues, network communications errors are probably the most common culprits in inaccessible network shares. Congested network segments, failing network adapters, and electromagnetic (EM) interference can all result in disrupted communication that may be crippling or intermittent.

- **Share permissions**   Make sure users have needed share-level permissions. For the most part, you should leave share permissions at the default setting that allows full control to all users. Should you need to modify share-level permissions beyond this, you will need to be careful to ensure the resulting combination of ACL and share-level rights do not conflict with each other.

RESOLVING USER RIGHTS ISSUES

Over time, it is possible that users may end up with contradictory access to some of the network resources—for example, where a user expects to be able to edit a file, they can only read or delete it, or something similar. These kinds of issues tend to arise on networks that have added and removed users somewhat frequently and have perhaps rearranged the user groups a time or two. Solving these kinds of issues is not very difficult if they are approached methodically.

PERMISSIONS CONFLICTS

Most permission conflicts take one of two forms. The first form occurs when the file access permissions (Windows ACL) specify one level of access and the share-level permissions provide a more restrictive level of access. The net result is that a user can log on to a server locally and accomplish what they need to do, yet over the network the user finds that they do not have the ability to perform whatever task is needed. The simplest solution to this kind of issue is to reset the share-level permissions back to the default setting, allowing full control to everyone and testing to see if the user has regained functionality. It is almost always better to allow wide share-level permissions and then restrict the user access at the file level. This will restrict both the network-based rights and, should the user log on to the server locally, the local rights.

The second form of permission conflict arises when a user is a member of more than one user group and the groups have conflicting access rights. For example, a user could be a member of a group that has full control over a folder and also a member of a group that has been implicitly denied access to the resource all together. The net result is that the user will have no access. This may be intentional or accidental. The solution to this conundrum is to place the user in what would be a single group with the correct access rights to the resource. You could then also add the user back to previous groups until the issue again manifests and then decide if the group needs access level changed, if the user needs to be removed from the problematic group, or if another solution must be sought. Because of the potential for conflicting permissions, it is generally not a good idea to implicitly deny a user access to a resource.

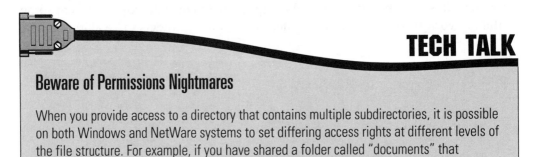

TECH TALK

Beware of Permissions Nightmares

When you provide access to a directory that contains multiple subdirectories, it is possible on both Windows and NetWare systems to set differing access rights at different levels of the file structure. For example, if you have shared a folder called "documents" that contains the subfolders "text," "spreadsheet," "images," and "web," it is possible to

Beware of Permissions Nightmares (continued)

assign a user access to the "web" folder, but not the root of "documents" or any of the other subfolders. Sometimes this kind of arrangement is used to allow a group of users—say, the marketing department of a company—to have space for users to store data that only they have access to. The problem with this arrangement is that it is difficult to centrally track who has access to which resource. If permissions issues arise, you may need to reset permissions on all of the files and folders by changing the permissions at the root of the shared directory and then propagating changes down to all subfolders and files. One potential hang-up to this solution on NetWare 5.x (and later) systems is this: filters can be defined at a subfolder that will prevent propagated permissions from taking effect. Use groups to assign access wherever possible, and make your configurations as simple as possible, and life (with regards to this topic) will be more enjoyable.

On a Windows 2000/XP Pro or .NET system, you can make use of a fairly handy command-line-based tool to change the NTFS ACL, known as CACLS.exe. While this tool is text-based and perhaps a bit less user friendly than using the graphical interface to modify file and folder permissions, it can be used to automate the management of ACL settings. A good example is the following Tech Talk element. While there are a few common command switch options for the CACLS command, the list that follows itemizes and explains all of them just in case. The syntax of the CACLS command is cacls *filename/foldername/options*:

- **/E**   Edits the existing ACL rather than replacing it. Unless you specify the edit options, the existing ACL will be removed and your new options applied when you use the CACLS command.

- **/T**   Changes the ACL for the specified target and all of the files and subfolders within the target, if the target is a folder.

- **/G *username:permission***   Used to specify a user (*username*) who will receive the specified user right (*permission*). Possible permissions options include R for read access, W for write access, C for change, or F for full control. For example, cacls C:\MyFolder /G ddalan:F would give the user ddalan full control of the folder C:\MyFolder.

- **/R *username***   Revokes the specified user's rights to the folder or file specified by the cacls command. This option is only valid in conjunction with the /E option. If it worked without the /E option, you would remove the access rights of all users since (without/E specified) the existing ACL is deleted.

- **/D** *username*   Used to implicitly deny a user access to the specified resource.

- **/P** *username:permission*   Used to replace the user's existing ACL settings with the permissions specified. The same options are available with this switch as with the /G option.

- **/C**   This allows CACLS to continue processing files in the event that it encounters an error while working with multiple files and folders.

The CACLS command makes use of wildcards, if you like. For example, you could change the access rights to all of the files within a directory without changing the directory or contained subdirectories' access rights. You can specify multiple users in a single instance of the command as well. If you combine these features and the available command options, you could implement complex and far-reaching access list changes with a single command.

In addition to creating file shares, you may need to share printers from your Windows 2000 system. Any printer that is configured and installed on the server can be shared out as a network resource. To share a printer on Windows 2000, complete these steps:

1. Log on as a user with the ability to create file shares, such as a member of the administrators group.

TECH TALK

Automatically Changing Rights

Sometimes you might find it useful to make ACL changes to a large number of computers using scripts and/or batch files rather than making manual changes. Fortunately, the CACLS command can be used in this capacity to automate the changing of an access list for a file or directory. For example, if you opened a command prompt and entered the command cacls *filename* /E /G administrator: F, you would be granted the full control right to the administrator account to the file *filename*. To see all of the syntax options for CACLS, open a command prompt and type **cacls /?** and press ENTER.

2. Double-click My Computer and then double-click Control Panel.

3. From within the Control Panel, double-click the Printers icon.

4. Pick any installed printer and right-click it, selecting Sharing from the context menu that appears.

5. The Printer Sharing window will allow you to name the printer, designate the printer as shared, and modify which users have rights to print to and manage the printer (under the Security tab). If you decide to take advantage of the option to list the printer in the directory (creating an Active Directory object), users can search the AD database and locate your printer based on the information such as printer type and location.

PAINFUL LESSONS I'VE LEARNED

Little Mistakes Making Big Problems

Problems that occur as the result of improperly configured permissions can be subtle at times. In one instance, I was responsible for supporting and installing a complex application that was really a large number of individual applications merged into a single "mega-app." This software was used as a supplemental education tool for elementary schools, including curriculum and testing components. Much of the program's operation depended on users having full control of most of the program files and directories. A few selected directories had to be restricted to read only for all users to prevent data corruption. As you may have guessed by now, permissions problems were somewhat common since the requirements were very particular. In one instance, I thought that I completed an installation and due to an emergency at another site, left it to the local technology staff (at the site where the software was installed) to complete the permissions configuration. Unfortunately, the technology staff failed to follow the somewhat complex and time-consuming instructions, and they accidentally set one of the data directories to read only. The net result? The program worked flawlessly, except for one minor detail. The testing components of the software never recorded the results of any of the software users. So after a year of use, the users had nothing to show for all of the work the students had done. We solved the problem going forward, but fixing the relationship with the customer took considerable time.

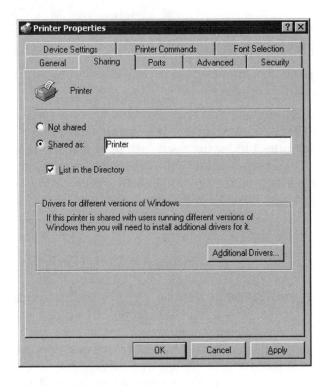

In order for your network clients to make use of the printers shared from your Windows NT/2000 server, you need to make sure that the appropriate drivers are installed on the server. In order to make sure your server has drivers for all of the clients on your network, you will need to obtain the appropriate driver files and then install them for the shared printer. Once you have the driver files handy, you need to open the Control Panel and then the printer applet. Right-click the printer you need to install additional drivers to and select properties from the context menu that appears. Under the Sharing tab, click the Additional Drivers button. A window will open that allows you to select which drivers you want to add. Check the appropriate boxes and then provide the driver files when prompted.

AUDITING USER ACCESS

Having the right information at your disposal can be very useful when trying to resolve access problems, such as permissions conflicts. One way to ensure that you can find out rapidly what has been occurring in and around a specific shared network resource is to enable auditing of that resource. Windows 2000 provides options for enabling auditing for a particular user or for every user

TECH TALK

Attach to Network Printers the Easy Way

Many Windows users are familiar with the process of using the Add New Printer Wizard to add local and network printers. If you are using Windows 2000 or Windows XP as a client operating system and you need to attach to a network printer, there is an even faster method than using the wizard. You can attach to any shared printer in three simple steps. First, open Windows Explorer and browse to the server that your network printer is shared from—for example, \\printserver. Locate the printer you want to attach to and right-click it. Select the Connect option from the context menu that appears. That's it! The printer will now appear in your Printers folder (in the Control Panel) and it will be selectable when you print from any of your Windows applications.

that gains access—or even attempts to access—to a resource. You can keep track of everything from authentication attempts to attempts to change the ACL for a particular resource, regardless whether or not the attempt was successful.

In order to audit user access, you will need to select a target folder that resides on an NTFS partition. You will also need to enable auditing on either the local computer or for all systems if they are members of a domain. To enable domain-wide auditing, you will need to log on to a domain controller as an administrator. If you are working with a member or stand-alone server, you will also need to log on to that system as an administrator. To enable auditing functionality, follow these steps:

1. Open the Administrative Tools and locate the Local Security Policy or Domain Security Policy object and open it.

2. Click the plus symbol next to the Local Policy entry and then click the Audit Policy entry. These steps are the same for both the domain and local versions of the Security tool.

3. You will see a list of entries in the right-hand portion of the Security Console (see Figure 7-2). The options are somewhat self-explanatory, and to enable any of them you will need to right-click the object, select Security from the menu that appears, and then check the boxes relating to the features you wish to enable.

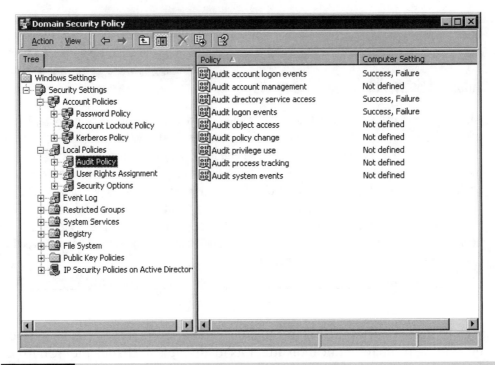

FIGURE 7.2   The Domain Security Console

Now that you have enabled security on your local system or your domain, you can configure auditing on your server. If your server is part of a domain (such as a member server), you will need to reboot the system so that it obtains the new security policy you have defined. The following steps will walk you through the process of enabling auditing on a resource:

1. Log on as a user with administrative privileges.

2. Browse to the folder that you wish to use for the purpose of testing auditing.

3. Right-click the file or folder and select the Properties entry from the context menu that appears.

4. In the window that opens, select the Security tab. Click the Advanced button.

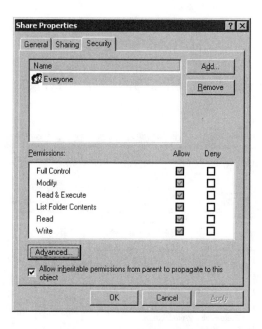

5. In the window that appears next, click the Auditing tab.

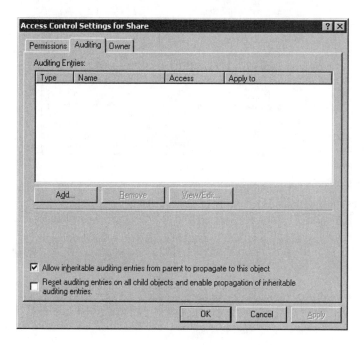

6. From this screen, click the Add button. In the User Selection window that appears, simply select the "everyone" group.

7. Once you have selected a group or a user, the Auditing Options window will appear and you can see that there is a dizzying array of options you can choose to track.

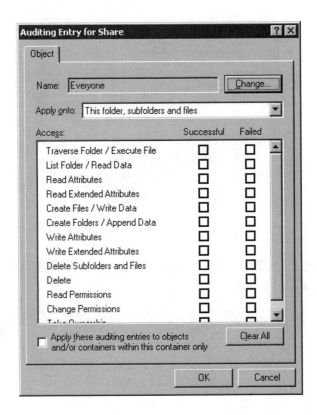

NOTE Auditing does have its dark side. Tracking every little thing that happens on a resource eats processing time and RAM. If you have detailed auditing on a large number of resources or a resource that is frequently accessed, you could seriously degrade the performance of your server. Auditing is best used when you are trying to gather information about a problem with a particular user or resource. Once the information has been collected, the auditing should be stopped.

TROUBLESHOOTING

Quick Fix with the "hosts" File

If you should find yourself in a situation where a host or a server is having trouble resolving the IP address of another host or server and time is tight, there is a quick temporary fix you can implement until you have time to find the source of the problem. By editing the hosts file, located in the C:\WINDOWS\system32\drivers\etc directory (Windows XP) or C:\WINT\ system32\drivers\ect (Windows 2000), you can specify the IP address associated with a particular hostname. By opening the hosts file in a text editor such as Notepad, you can make the needed mapping. Examples of the appropriate syntax are present in the file, and once you have made your changes and saved the file, you should restart the computer in question— and your resolution problem is "duct taped" until you have the time or the resources for a more thorough solution.

DISK QUOTAS

The process of enabling hard drive storage quotas is particularly useful if your users are prone to storing transitory data. Transitory data is not needed in the long term and can (and should) be deleted as soon as it is safe to do so. Quotas can help your users manage their disk usage, since they will not have the illusion of infinite server disk space capacity. On a Windows 2000 Server, disk quotas are an option only available for the whole disk, and the quota menu will not appear if the following outlined steps are attempted on individual files or folders. As with most management functions, you will need to have the appropriate user rights in order to establish or manage disk quotas. To keep things simple, you should make use of an administrative user account (can be a local administrator) when working with disk quotas.

In addition to enabling disk quotas for the drive in question, you will need to then create individual entries for particular users to actually establish quotas. Like the enabling of disk quotas, the setting of user limits must be done from the root disk and will apply to the user's usage of the entire disk. These steps will walk you through the process of enabling quotas on the C:\ drive of a Windows 2000 Server.

1. Log on as an administrative user.
2. Open My Computer and right-click the C:\ drive.
3. Select Properties in the menu that appears.
4. Select the Quotas tab.
5. Check the box next to Enable Quota Management.
6. Click Apply and then click the OK button.

Now that disk quotas can be used on the C:\ drive, we will walk through the steps for creating a quota entry for a particular user:

1. Right-click the C:\ drive, or any other drive where disk quotas have been enabled.
2. Select Properties in the menu that appears.
3. Select the Quotas tab.
4. Click the Quotas Entries tab.
5. In the window that appears, open the Quota menu (upper-left corner) and select New Quota Entry.
6. Select the user from the Accounts Manager, such as Guest, and click the OK button.
7. In the next window, select the bullet that allows you to set a quota and set both a quota and a warning limit for the user, as needed. Since the default quota limit is not appropriate for all (in our case, 1KB), you will need to make certain you configure the limits appropriately.

PHYSICAL SERVER MANAGEMENT

There are two very important ideas that relate to the physical location of the servers that you will use to share files, run your applications, or provide printing services. One of the topics is how you locate your servers to ensure the most efficient operation for your users. The other topic of concern is deciding what precautions need to be taken to protect your servers from physical harm, theft, or up close and personal intrusion attempts.

LOCATING SERVERS ON THE NETWORK EFFICIENTLY

When you have dozens or hundreds of users accessing the resources of a single server, where that server is located on the network relative to the users is very important. For example, if your heavily used file server has two routers between it and the network segment where your users are primarily located, you will be missing out on the potential performance that would result in relocating the server closer to the end users.

In many cases the issue is not one of the server being a great distance from all of the end users, but more likely that some users will be closer to the server than others. Ideally, you want shared resources as close as possible to the users and (though sometimes difficult) the same distance from any and all of the users. By distance, it is meant that each user would have to traverse the same number of network devices or interfaces (generically called "hops"). This ensures that the level of service is consistent across all of the server's users. For example, assume that you have a multiport Ethernet switch (48 10/100 Ethernet ports) in the main distribution frame (MDF), where your core network devices are stored, and several 16-port switches at various locations throughout your facility that all connect to your MDF switch. You would want to connect your file server to the high-density switch in the MDF, primarily because most of the users would presumably be connected to the distributed 16-port switches. The net result would be balanced access to the server housed in the MDF.

TROUBLESHOOTING

Improving Performance of Shared Resources

If your users report sluggish access to shared files, there are a couple of things you can change and/or investigate to improve performance. First, you can disable compression if it is in use. Delivering compressed files to network users requires significantly more resources than serving uncompressed files and thus degrades overall performance. If you have the

---

Improving Performance of Shared Resources (continued)

option for a major server overhaul, you can add faster hard drives or construct a Redundant Array of Inexpensive Disks (RAID) configuration to improve the speed at which the hard disk can deliver requested files. In most cases, the hard drive is second only to the network adapter as the slowest component when it comes to serving files to network users. This brings us to the last general suggestion, increasing the bandwidth to the server. Gigabit Ethernet is widely available and many vendors produce network hardware, such as switches and Gigabit-capable network adapters.

PHYSICALLY SECURING SERVERS

When one thinks of physical server security, most often images of ill-intending hackers breaking into server rooms come to mind. But the "cat hacker" is not nearly as relevant a threat as the electrical failure, fire, flooding, employee theft, and accidental damage from vendors and employees. To address these threats, you will need to accomplish several tasks. First off, servers should be (if at all possible) secured in a room where no one but the network maintenance personnel have ready access to them. Commonly, phone systems, electrical systems, and network systems share the same facility. This can be a reasonable arrangement if all of the previously listed systems are protected against accidental or intentional damage or theft resulting from human actions or errors. This addresses the human element for the most part, but to ensure that fire, water, and electricity do not become the destroyers of your servers, you will need to accomplish a few more things.

Fire extinguishing systems (that is, sprinklers) should not use water if they are located in the network operations systems. Several kinds of systems now exist that use either a solid or gaseous fire retardant, and one of them should be used. A small fire somewhere other than the server room could end up triggering your sprinkler systems. If they are water-spraying sprinklers, your entire network infrastructure could be instantaneously destroyed. (Funny thing about network hardware and computers—they are not fond of being submerged while powered on!)

Keeping reliable and regulated power available for your networking infrastructure is also important. Not only will you need high-quality uninterruptible power supplies (UPS) and surge protectors, but you may need line conditioners that will help clean up "dirty power" that may periodically behave in a manner outside of the specifications of your networking and server equipment. Many devices have been destroyed by poorly performing power sources that run out of phase or vary amplitude or voltage. Invest in the hardware before you find yourself without a critical resource due to electrical disruption.

Since some disasters simply cannot be planned for, perhaps the most important thing you could do to prepare is have (1) regular backups and (2) copies of the most recent backups in an off-site location. If your facility is destroyed in an earthquake or burned down, it would do little good to have recent backups in the building that just burned down or was otherwise destroyed. Banks or other facilities with hardened vaults are great places to store critical backups that could make the difference between an irritating disaster and the end of the company that you work for.

SHARING FROM WORKSTATIONS

Sharing printers and files from an individual user's computer tends to be a double-edged sword. In smaller networks (where dedicated IT staff may be few and far between), this behavior can give end users greater flexibility for getting their jobs done. However, as networks grow in size, any attempt to manage a veritable soup of shared resources is bound to lead to headaches in all but the most iron-willed people.

WORKGROUP (SMALL) NETWORKS

If a network is a small collection of computers attached via basic networking equipment but lacking in central management and file storage resources, providing shared resources from the workstation may be the only option. Sometimes in small businesses there is no funding for dedicated servers, extensive networking hardware, or anything similar. As long as the users can keep straight which files are where and a process is put into place for ensuring that computers housing shared resources remain accessible (that is, turned on), this solution can work very well for sharing files and printers.

The potential downside is that hardware failure could cause the loss of a portion of the shared data. It would be difficult to maintain the regular backup of various workstation-class computers. This is especially true if the backups depend on the users for intervention. End users are often more concerned with getting their jobs done (since that is what they are paid to do) than they are in playing the role of technician. Because cost is often a factor in this kind of scenario, expensive automated backup devices and software are probably no more an option that a centralized file server would be.

There are some options that could alleviate the potential downside of distributed sharing. Devices such as the Quantum SNAP server and other inexpensive network storage devices make the possibility of centralized file storage more realistic where financing is a concern. Considering 30GB units can be obtained for less than $400 (ready to connect to the network and use out of the box), this option should definitely be considered in this kind of situation. Single-purpose print servers—barely more than a parallel interface and a network adapter in a little box—offer the same kind of solution for network printing.

MEDIUM TO LARGE NETWORKS

This section will be brief, because large networks simply are not well suited to distributed file and printer sharing. It is difficult to plan for network changes or manage existing bandwidth when the impacts of file transfers and printing are widely distributed. At a minimum, this situation calls for a fixed storage device such as the SNAP server, dedicated file servers, and networked print servers. Ideally in a large network, high-speed network backbones would connect powerful servers to the network to ensure smooth and responsive performance from your networked resources.

TECH TALK

Saving Space

If adding additional hardware is not an option at a time you find you are running out of disk space, your Windows-based server can make use of file compression. In the past, file compression was generally a very poor idea because the compression was imperfect and sometimes data corruption could occur. You still should not compress a drive that houses the operating system files, as that will degrade the performance of the whole server. File compression can be used to gain some additional storage capacity, but it should be used as a short-term solution. If you need additional space in the long term, you have two choices: either delete extraneous files or additional storage space should be added.

WRAPPING UP...

In our exploration of creating and managing network shares, we looked at many different pieces of the shared resources puzzle. First off, we walked through the process for creating file and printer shares on some of the more common scenarios that exist in networking today. We also walked through the process for enabling and defining disk quotas on a Windows 2000 Server to prevent users from consuming disk space needlessly. We looked at ways to alter user rights, how to troubleshoot shared resources that do not appear to provide the access intended to a given user, and ways to eliminate (or at least reduce) the potential for user rights–related problems.

We then looked at some less direct methods of supporting file services and monitoring them for troubleshooting and even security purposes. We walked through enabling auditing for a resource on Windows 2000 Server, and we examined the impact of the physical placement of server resources on the accessibility and performance of the server. We then looked at reasons for carefully selecting the configuration of the facility used to house the server and associated networking equipment. Finally, we closed this chapter with an exploration of the benefits and problems of sharing resources from end-user workstations in various networking environments.

WORKING WITH WINDOWS 2000 NETWORKS

8

Windows 2000 was a revolution for Windows networking. Network management, scalability, and overall usage was much more limited and even more complicated in the days of Windows NT, but Windows 2000 brought many changes to Windows networking. Obviously, Windows 2000 is not perfect, and future releases of Windows 2000 Server will no doubt make additional changes to the Windows networking design. If you are working in a larger network, the odds are quite good that you are working in a Windows 2000 network, a NetWare network, or a UNIX-based environment. Windows 2000 networks have gained a lot of ground during the past few years, and in this chapter we'll take a look at the fundamental design and functions that make Windows 2000 networks tick. If you are working in a Windows 2000 network, your understanding of the concepts and features presented in this chapter will make your work easier. In this chapter, we'll…

- Explore sites, domains, and organizational units
- Examine Windows 2000 domain controllers
- Configure Windows 2000 group policy

WINDOWS 2000 DOMAINS, SITES, AND ORGANIZATIONAL UNITS

Windows 2000 networks are made up of domains, sites, and organizational units. This structure gives Windows 2000 the flexibility and scalability necessary in today's networking environments. Indeed, you can use Windows 2000 to implement a network of only a few hundred computers or a network containing thousands upon thousands of computers. In order to understand this network structure, you must have an understanding of Windows 2000 domains, sites, and organizational units, and in the following sections we'll take a look at these features.

UNDERSTANDING WINDOWS 2000 DOMAINS

A domain is a logical grouping of users, computers, and resources that makes up a security and administrative boundary. As you are working in Windows 2000 networks, you'll hear the term "domain" thrown around a lot, and rightly so—the domain is one of the core components of Windows 2000 networking. The domain is not a physical entity—it doesn't identify the actual network topology or physical locations of the network, but it defines a boundary. A domain can be a grouping of users, computers, and resources in one office building containing a few hundred users, or it can be a grouping of users, computers, and resources spread over several offices around the globe and containing thousands of objects. In the same manner, the domain serves as a security boundary. Security policies are applied to the domain and desired security standards can be used across the entire domain. So, the domain is used to define both a security and an administrative boundary.

In the days of Windows NT, domains were limited to the number of objects they could physically hold. This resulted in Windows NT networks having multiple, and often confusing, domain structures. In Windows 2000 networks, domains are essentially unlimited in terms of scalability (they can hold millions of objects), so the structure of Windows 2000 domains is much simpler than it was in Windows NT. In a Windows 2000 network, all domain (as well as site and organizational unit) information is held in the central repository—the Active Directory. Network data and configuration information, along with user, group, and resource data, are all found in the Active Directory and replicated to domain controllers throughout the domain.

THE WINDOWS 2000 NAMESPACE

In order to understand Windows 2000 domains, we must also understand the Windows 2000 namespace. As you are probably aware, Windows 2000 networks are built on the Domain Name System (DNS). In the past, Windows networks used NetBIOS as the naming scheme, but DNS is the most scalable naming system in existence (it holds the entire Internet), and Windows 2000 is completely integrated with DNS. You must install and use DNS in order to install and configure the Active Directory—the two cannot be separated. Because of this, the Windows namespace (or the naming area that can be resolved) is entirely built on DNS. Therefore, Windows 2000 domain names are DNS names. For example, xprod.com could be the name of an Internet web site, but it is also a domain in a Windows 2000 network. Juser@xprod.com is an Internet e-mail address, but it is also a username in a Windows 2000 network. As you can see, the Windows 2000 namespace is seamless with Internet names, simply because they are all built on the same naming system—DNS.

Because the Windows 2000 network is built on the DNS namespace, all domains in a Windows 2000 network follow the DNS naming structure. As I mentioned, a company called Xprod could implement the Active Directory using their company name for the namespace. As such, the first domain that is created, called the forest root domain, could be named xprod.com. From this root domain name, all other network names are then built. However, let's say that Xprod later purchases two other companies, one named ZSoft and one named Meridian. The network engineers need to keep the two new companies separate, using different administrators and different security standards, but also include them in the original company's network. The answer in this scenario is to create child domains. The child domains, once installed, can then be named zsoft.xprod.com and meridian.xprod.com. This structure forms a contiguous namespace. As you can see in Figure 8-1, the child domains get their DNS name from the root domain.

PAINFUL LESSONS

I'VE LEARNED

DNS and the Active Directory

Because DNS is tied to the Active Directory, an Active Directory implementation is only as strong as DNS. Case in point—Active Directory can work with other versions of DNS rather than Microsoft DNS (such as BIND); however, the DNS implementation used must be able to support Service Locator Resource Records (SRV) and should support Dynamic Update Protocol. Environments that attempt to use versions of DNS other than Microsoft DNS with the Active Directory often run into a number of configuration problems and issues, so it is important that environments implementing Windows 2000 pay close attention to the DNS structure.

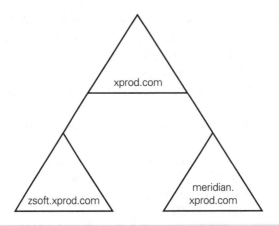

FIGURE 8.1 Child domains derive their name from the root domain.

NOTE Additional child domains can be added anytime as needed, and you can even have multiple levels of child domains, such as production.meridian.xprod.com. Of course, network planners should take care when designing a domain structure. Domains are expensive both in terms of hardware and management, so the fewer domains, the better.

TECH TALK

Root Domain Issues

Windows 2000 networks are designed by network engineers and administrators. You may, however, find yourself involved in a new Active Directory implementation, beginning with the root domain. The process of physically installing the root domain is actually quite simple—on the first Windows 2000 Server that you want to be a domain controller for the domain, you run the dcpromo.exe wizard and answer the questions that appear. However, before installing the forest root domain, careful planning should occur. Keep in mind that the root domain should encompass the entire business, so even the name can be complicated. Also, at present, you cannot change the root domain name without reinstalling the Active Directory, so choose the root domain name with care. Later versions of the Active Directory will provide the ability to change domain names without reinstalling, but at the time of this writing you are simply stuck if you want to change the name later. So, the root domain name should be carefully considered and discussed before moving forward with the Active Directory implementation.

UNDERSTANDING FORESTS AND TREES

As I mentioned, the Active Directory namespace is made up of a root domain and any child domains that may be necessary. Along with the domain concepts, there are two additional concepts you should know. First, an Active Directory implementation is called a "forest." The forest holds "trees," which is simply the root domain and additional child domains. The importance of the forest and tree concepts is simply this: each Active Directory forest contains one configuration, one schema (which defines what objects can be held in the Active Directory), and one global catalog that lists all of the objects. However, you can have more than one tree in the forest. For example, let's say that a company, xprod.com, acquires another company, Anderson Toys. Anderson Toys has its own network, but the network engineers want both networks in the same Active Directory forest. In this case, the new company can become andersontoys.com. This new tree does not have a contiguous namespace with xprod.com, but they can exist in the same forest and share information between them. Obviously, this design is not commonly used, but is provided in the case where two companies merge but need to keep separate identities.

TRUSTS BETWEEN WINDOWS DOMAINS

In order for users in one domain to access resources in another domain, the two domains have to trust each other. In Windows NT networks, trust relationships between domains could be a real headache. One domain could be the trusting domain while another domain could trust that domain, but some domains were only trusted while some are trusting—and the whole network could become one confusing access problem if you were not careful. Trust relationships in Windows 2000 networks have been greatly simplified. In fact, trust relationships between domains within the same tree are automatically configured as two-way transitive trust relationships. This means that DomainA and DomainB both trust each other, and should there be a DomainC that DomainB trusts, then DomainA automatically trusts that domain as well. This design removes the trust relationship problems between domains in the same tree.

UNDERSTANDING WINDOWS 2000 SITES

As I mentioned in the previous section, a domain is a logical grouping of computers, users, and resources for administrative and security purposes. A site, on the other hand, is a physical grouping of computers, users, and resources. A site is not a part of the Active Directory namespace, and as an administrator, you typically do not work directly with sites. Sites are used by domains to manage traffic. For example, say a domain is based at your company headquarters in Dallas. All users, computers, and resources are physically located in that single location. To the Active Directory, the offices make up one site because they are all contained on well-connected subnets. In other words, there are no WAN links. The site, then, defines the geographical locations of the domain. In many cases, there may simply be one site. However, what if your domain spans three different cities in different states, or even several different countries, as shown in Figure 8-2.

The Active Directory then uses a site for each physical location and the information you provide it to determine the speed, reliability, and availability of the WAN links that connect these sites. To administrators and domain users, it appears as though everyone is located in one place, but in reality the users, computers, and resources are spread out over several different geographical locations.

Why not make multiple domains, then? The answer comes back to administration and security. Keep in mind that multiple domains cost more because more domain administrators are required, and more domain controllers— not to mention the implementation of security and potential for more problems with access to resources. A single domain environment is always preferred, and because of this design, the Active Directory uses sites to manage the physical locations that may be contained in a single domain.

SECRET
Domains are a part of the Active Directory namespace and are used to build an Active Directory infrastructure—sites are not. Think of sites as the physical underworkings of a domain.

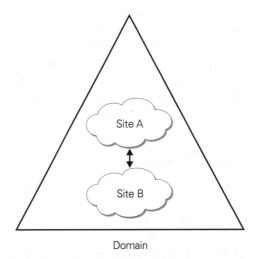

So, how does the Active Directory determine these sites? Site information is gathered through information that administrators provide. The key point to keep in mind is that the Active Directory considers a "site" to be a collection of "well-connected" subnets. More simply put, the Active Directory considers a site a location that has fast and readily available bandwidth, such as a typical LAN. In order for the Active Directory to manage traffic over WAN links, the Active Directory must know what sites exist and have information about the speed and availability of the WAN links between them. Let's consider an example. Let's say that your network has a LAN in Dallas and a LAN in New York. There is a T1 link connecting the two sites as well as a 256-Kbps link that is used for backup purposes. Administrators use the Active Directory to basically "instruct" the Active Directory about the existence of the two sites and the two links that connect them. Using the Active Directory, administrators can assign a cost to each link so that the faster T1 link is always favored over the 256-Kbps link. This way, the Active Directory knows to use the 256-Kbps link for backup purposes. Why does the Active Directory need to know about the two sites if there is only one domain anyway? The answer is all about traffic.

Network traffic between clients and domain controllers occurs frequently. After all, clients must be authenticated and they must access network resources. On the other hand, domain controllers frequently communicate with each other, replicating changes that have occurred in the Active Directory so that each domain controller has an accurate copy of the database. The problem with WAN links, however, is that bandwidth is often not freely available. Because of this, the Active Directory must understand how sites are configured and how much available bandwidth exists between sites. This way, the Active Directory can control traffic over site links, and even control when replication occurs. With sites configured, the Active Directory can prevent a user from being authenticated by a domain controller in New York when the user actually resides in Dallas. The Active Directory can use the site and site link data to keep traffic localized on the LAN as much as possible, thus reducing traffic over costly and often slow WAN links.

NOTE   In order to manage sites and site links, the Active Directory provides a tool called Active Directory Sites and Services, which exists on all domain controllers. Administrators can manage sites and site links from any domain controller using this tool. The good news is that if only one site exists, the Active Directory automatically configures itself—there is nothing administrators have to configure.

As I mentioned, sites are connected by site links (as they are called in the Active Directory), although you may refer to them as WAN links. These links can be high-bandwidth expensive links, such as T1 or T3, or in the case of satellite offices, the link could be a simple 256-Kbps connection or even a 56-Kbps modem connection—this all depends on the site design of your network and how much money your company has spent on network infrastructure. Regardless, the Active Directory needs to know what links are available and some information about those links in order to be able to use them appropriately. For this reason, administrators can configure a couple of different options to help the Active Directory understand the link and how to best use it:

- **Cost** In order for the Active Directory to know how to use site links, you must assign a cost to the link. For example (as mentioned previously), let's say you use a T1 link between two sites, but there is also a backup link of only 256 Kbps. You want the Active Directory to always use the T1 link if at all possible. In order for the Active Directory to know to use the T1 link, you must assign a lower cost to it. So, cost is simply a value that you assign to a link. The Active Directory favors lower-cost links over higher-cost links, so your T1 link might have a cost of 10 while the 245-Kbps link might have a cost of 50. Using the cost, the Active Directory will always prefer to use the T1 link over the 256-Kbps link because the T1 link has a lower cost. Aside from bandwidth, though, keep in mind that cost can be used even when the two links have the same bandwidth. For example, let's say that you have two 256-Kbps links between two sites, but one link tends to be less reliable. To make sure the Active Directory favors the more reliable link, simply assign a lower-cost value to the more reliable link. As you are thinking about cost per link, keep in mind that "cost" in and of itself is an arbitrary value that you assign. There is no right or wrong numerical value, but the Active Directory simply sees lower number values as "less expensive," so it always tries to use the lower-cost link. The cost is assigned using the Active Directory Sites and Services tool, as shown in the following illustration.

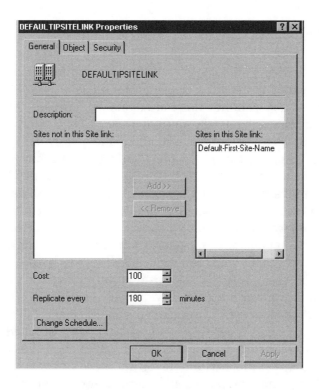

- **Usage**   When a site link is created in the Active Directory, administrators can control the usage of the site link or the frequency of its use. The concept applies to replication. On a LAN, replication occurs frequently between domain controllers. However, over site links, you may want to control the time that replication can occur. Using the Active Directory Sites and Services, you can have replication occur every 15 minutes, every hour, or even every three hours, depending on your needs. As a practice, you want replication to occur as frequently as possible, but site link availability is always a tradeoff between frequent replication and link usage/availability. See the "Understanding Active Directory Replication" section next to learn more about replication.

- **Schedule**   Replication within a site occurs without a schedule and it occurs frequently. However, over site links, you may want replication to occur at certain periods of the day when site link traffic is at its lowest. Using the Active Directory Sites and Services tool, you can create a replication schedule so that replication occurs over the site link only when you want it to.

UNDERSTANDING ACTIVE DIRECTORY REPLICATION

In our discussion of sites, I have mentioned replication several times. Replication is the process of updating domain controller database information. In an Active Directory environment, there isn't a single master domain controller that holds the Active Directory database; rather, there are domain controllers that function in a peer-to-peer fashion—each domain controller holds a copy of the Active Directory database and updates to the database can be made on any domain controller. Because changes or updates can be made on any domain controller, the domain controllers must replicate with each other; otherwise, the Active Directory would become inconsistent and eventually become a big collection of useless data. So, replication occurs to keep each domain controller consistent. For example, let's say that you create a new user account on a certain domain controller. Once the account is created, that domain controller begins a replication process with other domain controller partners, who then replicate with their partners, and so forth. The replication process copies the new user account attribute to each domain controller. When the new user logs on, any domain controller can authenticate the user because each domain controller maintains an exact copy of the database. This kind of replication, where a peer-to-peer approach is used, is called "multimaster" replication because there is no single master domain controller.

Replication occurs at the attribute level, and here's what I mean by that statement. Let's say that you have a shared printer configured in the Active Directory. The printer is considered a database *object*, while the qualities about the printer (such as make, model, printing speed, color, and so forth) are all called *attributes*. Attributes basically define the object. When a change is made in the Active Directory, replication occurs at the attribute level. For example, let's say you change a user's password. When replication occurs, only the password attribute must be replicated—not the entire user account. Because attribute replication occurs, replication traffic is kept much smaller than it would be if the entire object was replicated each time a change was made. Of course, if a new object is created, it must be replicated, but after that, only attribute changes to the object are replicated.

Now, in a multimaster replication system, there is always the possibility of duplicate or conflicting replication. Because this problem can occur, update sequence numbers (USNs) are used to identify the current attribute change. USNs are 64-bit numbers, and when an object or attribute is changed, the USN is updated to reflect that change. Because the USN is updated, all other domain controllers now have an outdated USN number. When replication occurs, domain controllers learn that the old USN is outdated and the object needs to be updated through replication. Each domain controller maintains a USN table listing the current USNs, and the table is checked for outdated USNs during replication.

If you access the Object tab of an object's properties dialog box, you can see its original USN number and the current USN number, which will be different if the object has changed, as shown in the next illustration.

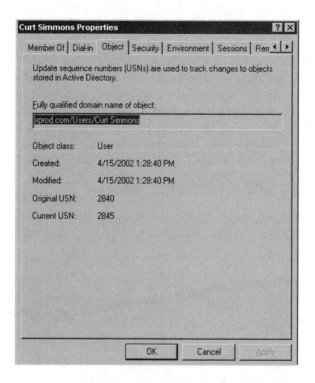

Because USNs are used, timestamps are generally not needed, although they are maintained for tiebreaking purposes. However, timestamps, which are used in some replication models, present their own problems because each domain controller's clock must be synchronized with the others. With USNs, the number value determines the current object rather than a timestamp.

It is important to understand that replication between domain controllers occurs in a partner fashion, which is also called "store and forward." When a change to the Active Directory is made on one domain controller, that domain controller then notifies its replication partners of the change. The partners can then request the replication data. Those domain controllers then replicate the changes to their replication partners, and so forth, until all domain controllers have the replicated data. The Active Directory creates partnerships between domain controllers automatically and without any configuration from administrators through the knowledge consistency checker (KCC), which is a built-in process running in the Active Directory. Within a site, the Active Directory uses the KCC to create partnership connections between domain controllers. Should one domain controller become unavailable or be removed from service, the KCC can automatically detect this change and make adjustments in the replication topology. The same is true if a new domain controller is added to the domain. The KCC is also used between sites, but the process uses the data you provide about sites and site links to generate the replication topology. The good news is that all of this is performed in the background, although administrators can use the Active Directory Sites and Services tool to manually make adjustments in replication between sites. As a general rule, though, the Active Directory takes care of its own replication topology, which is certainly helpful to busy administrators.

UNDERSTANDING ORGANIZATIONAL UNITS

So far, you have learned that domains are a logical grouping of computers, users, and resources. Sites are used by domains to determine the physical location

TECH TALK

Understanding Replication Protocols

Like all network traffic, replication occurs through the use of protocols. There are two protocols that can be used to move replication traffic from one domain controller to the next. The first and primary protocol is Remote Procedure Calls (RPC) over Internet Protocol (IP). RPC/IP is a synchronous process where domain controllers poll replication partners for database changes. The remote procedure call requests updates to the database, then RPC is used over the IP network. This feature allows for fast replication to occur within a site or between sites. Intrasite (within a site) replication always uses uncompressed RPC/IP.

Intersite (between sites) replication, however, can use compressed RPC/IP, or it can use Simple Mail Transfer Protocol (SMTP) when communication occurs between different domains. SMTP is considered asynchronous transfer. Replication traffic is sent over a WAN link when it is possible to send the data, rather than waiting on a remote procedure call. SMTP is slower and causes more database latency, but it is useful when unreliable WAN links are in use. As a general rule, though, RPC/IP should be used when at all possible. Like all things concerning sites and replication, the use of SMTP or RPC/IP in intersite replication can be configured using the Active Directory Sites and Services tool.

of those computers, users, and resources, and to manage traffic. Under the Windows 2000 design, a domain is essentially unlimited in size. For example, the domain could contain a few thousand objects or, potentially, hundreds of thousands of objects. In larger domains, the problem then becomes management. In other words, in a large domain with hundreds of thousands of objects, how do you organize the domain so that different administrators manage different portions of the Active Directory, or even different groups of users, computers, and resources? The answer is the organizational unit, also referred to as an OU.

The organizational unit is simply a container, much like a folder, within the Active Directory where different objects can be stored. Certain administrators can be delegated control over the different OUs as needed. This design gives

TROUBLESHOOTING

How the Active Directory Solves Replication Problems

Although the replication *process* in the Active Directory is rock solid, there is still the possibility that replication *problems* can occur. The first potential problem is replication conflicts. Let's say that an administrator makes a password change to a user account on one domain controller. At the same time, an administrator makes the same change on a different domain controller. When the replication process occurs, there will be a conflict because the same attribute is being replicated. The Active Directory recognizes the conflict as a collision, and takes the appropriate steps to solve the collision. First of all, the Active Directory will view the timestamp of each change to try and determine which change occurred last. If the timestamp can be used, the latest change is the one that will be replicated.

Another potential replication problem is repeat replication. Since replication occurs at a partner level, it is possible that the same data could be replicated twice. To avoid this problem, a process called "propagation dampening" is used. Propagation dampening uses two vectors to track a replication change. When the replication data reaches the last domain controller, propagation dampening ensures that the replication cycle is essentially stopped so that the last domain controller does not "loop" back to another replication partner. As you can see, these built-in processes ensure that replication problems are managed internally by Windows 2000.

networks a lot of flexibility without the expense and difficulty of configuring and managing multiple domains. For example,

- A network could organize all users into one OU that is managed by certain administrators, or all printers into one OU that is administered by certain administrators.

- A network could organize its domain by its company needs. For example, there could be a marketing OU and a sales OU. Different administrators could manage the OUs, including all of the users and resources for those company divisions.

- A network could be organized by location. There could be a Paris OU or a Dallas OU, where administrators in those locations manage the users and resources while still belonging to a single domain.

As you can see, there are a number of different options that can be configured, and they all are based on the organizational needs of a particular network. However, aside from basic organization, there are some additional things you can do with OUs. First of all, OUs serve as an organizational boundary, but they also serve as a security and management boundary. Within an OU, an administrator can place different restrictions on resources and users, and you can even use a group policy at the OU level (which we'll explore in more detail later in this chapter). With delegation of control, one administrator can manage a particular OU but have no administrative power over another one. As you can see, OUs are a way to subdivide a domain into more manageable pieces.

However, there are two important points to keep in mind about the OU. First, OUs are invisible in terms of DNS. Let's say you have resources in an OU called "resources," located in the xprod.com domain. The resources are still found in the xprod.com domain—not resources.xprod.com. Secondly, OUs are specific to the domain and can only contain objects held within that domain. An OU cannot contain any resources that reside in another domain.

As network administrators and planners determine the need and use of organizational units, it is important to keep in mind that you can have as many OUs as you need and OUs can be "nested," which means they can reside within other OUs. For example, consider the graphic shown in Figure 8-3. As you can see, the first-level OU resides at the domain level. From that point, you can also create additional OUs within the OUs to the second and third levels. OUs that exist after the third level are referred to as "deeply nested OUs."

As you can see, there is no real limit to the number of OUs and sub-OUs that can be created, but administrators should carefully plan and implement an OU structure so that it does not get out of control. Like most things in life, simplicity is usually best, and excessive numbers of OUs tend to be more confusing than

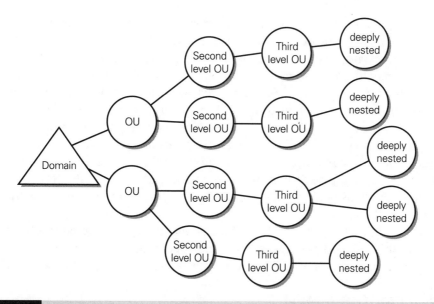

| FIGURE 8.3 | OU hierarchy |

helpful. Also, deeply nested OUs can affect group policy. Group policy is implemented at the site, domain, and OU levels, but you may see group policy performance problems at the deeply nested OU level, and you may also see slower user logons. Also, OUs function on an inheritance system, which means they inherit the properties of parent OUs. In deeply nested OU's, inheritance problems can cause administrative difficulties as well as performance problems. The point is to use OUs as needed—but do not use more than necessary.

UNDERSTANDING WINDOWS 2000 DOMAIN CONTROLLERS

In our previous discussion of domains, sites, and OUs, I mentioned several times that Windows 2000 domain controllers hold and maintain the Active Directory database. The Active Directory database contains all of the objects and information about those objects and attributes within a network. Domain controllers, then, are simply Windows 2000 servers that are configured to function as domain controllers for a particular domain. Windows 2000 Server can function as a stand-alone server, a member server of a domain, or a domain controller. Member servers are used for Web, print, DNS, DHCP, and file services primarily, while domain controllers are used to manage and provide the Active Directory, as well as user authentication.

In the olden days of Windows NT 4.0, there was a primary domain controller that held the only writable database, and backup domain controllers, which received a nonwritable copy of the database. Because of this design, the size of the domain was limited and caused Windows NT networks to grow in terms of domain numbers. In Windows 2000 networks, because multiple domain controllers are used, all of which have writable copies of the Active Directory database, domain size is virtually unlimited. Each domain controller holds a writable copy of the Active Directory database, and administration to the Active Directory can be made on any domain controller. Changes to the database are then replicated, as we discussed, and this design provides much greater flexibility than was seen in Windows NT. This design, called multimaster domain management, is the basis for Windows 2000 functionality.

However, networking in Windows 2000 is also not quite that simple, and in addition to this peer design, there are some specialized roles that must be held by domain controllers as well. The following sections examine these.

GLOBAL CATALOG SERVER

Global catalog servers contain object data about what is located in the domain and what is located in other domains (if they exist). More specifically, the global catalog server contains a full replica of all Active Directory objects within its own domain and a partial replica of all objects found in other domains in the forest. A partial replica means that the Active Directory is aware of the objects found in other domains and contains the most common attributes for those objects. The goal is that a user can search the Active Directory, and the global catalog server can locate objects in the residing domain as well as other domains within the forest. For example, let's say that a user searches for a shared folder. The global catalog server contains a full replica of all shared folders in the residing network and a partial replica of all shared folders in other domains. The partial replica contains enough information that the user can locate the shared folders in the remote domains and connect to them, assuming the user has the necessary permissions to use the resource.

Aside from providing a full or partial replica for all objects, global catalog servers are also required for user logons. Global catalog servers provide information about universal groups that may exist in the forest, because universal groups can span more than one domain.

SECRET

Global catalog servers are necessary for user logons only if the domain is running in native mode. Windows 2000 provides a mixed mode feature so that older Windows NT BDCs can be used during the migration process to Windows 2000. Universal groups are not supported in mixed mode, so there is no need for a global catalog server unless the network is running in native mode.

By default, the first domain controller installed when you are creating a new domain is the global catalog server. However, if you want to switch the global catalog server role to another domain controller at a later time, you can do so using the Active Directory.

SINGLE MASTER ROLES

Aside from the global catalog server, there are also some additional roles that must be played. Although a multimaster network resolves many problems, there are simply some roles that do not function well in a multimaster network. In order to accommodate these issues, the Active Directory provides flexible single-master operations (FSMO) roles. FSMO roles primarily have to do with replication, which we discussed earlier in this chapter. Although multimaster replication functions very well in Windows 2000, the FSMO roles are needed to provide certain services that do not function well in a multimaster state. There are five different FSMO roles, each individually providing some unique network service that is necessary in the domain. The five FSMO roles are

- **Schema master**   The schema is the schematic or blueprint of the Active Directory—it defines what objects and attributes can be held in the database. There is only one schema master in the entire Active Directory forest, and is held by default on the first domain controller in the first domain of the forest. Modifications to the schema can only be made on this particular domain controller, and only by members of the Schema Admins group.

- **Domain naming master**   The domain naming master manages the names of domains within the forest. Each time a domain is added or removed from the forest, the domain naming master keeps track of the data in order to make certain there are no duplicate names. There is only one domain naming master in the entire forest.

- **PDC emulator**   The PDC emulator role is just as it sounds—the role allows a Windows 2000 domain controller to act like a primary domain controller to Windows NT 4.0 backup domain controllers as well as down-level clients, such as Windows 9x and Windows NT 4.0 workstations. Because Windows NT networks expect to find a PDC, the PDC emulator "acts like" a Windows NT PDC to the BDCs and down-level clients. Aside from these tasks, the PDC emulator also assists in some replication processes. Each domain has one PDC emulator.

- **Relative ID (RID) master**   When a new user or computer (or group) is added to a domain, it is assigned a security ID (SID) that includes a relative ID (RID). The RID master holds all of the possible RIDS that can be assigned in the domain. This domain controller ensures that RID numbers assigned do not overlap with RID numbers in another domain. There is one RID master in each domain in the forest.

■ **Infrastructure master** The infrastructure master manages group memberships within multiple domains. In other words, the infrastructure master is responsible for updating the cross-domain group-to-use reference. Let's say you add some new members to a group and they reside in different domains. The infrastructure master records the change to make sure that all group memberships are kept accurate. There is one infrastructure master in each domain in the forest.

THE BRIDGEHEAD SERVER

When a new site is created, the Active Directory automatically assigns the role of "bridgehead server" to one domain controller in the domain (through the KCC). The bridgehead server sends and receives replication data for that particular site. You can think of the bridgehead server as a gateway between remote sites. Rather than different domain controllers in one site replicating with domain controllers in another site, all replication traffic has to flow through the bridgehead server. When the bridgehead server receives data from a remote site, it is then replicated to the bridgehead server's replication partners within the domain, and so forth, as shown in Figure 8-4.

As I mentioned, one domain controller is automatically configured in each site as a bridgehead server, but you can select a different bridgehead server and you can configure additional bridgehead servers. Although only one bridgehead server can function at any given time, the additional bridgehead server(s) can be used in the event that the primary bridgehead server should be offline.

EXPLORING GROUP POLICY

Group policy is a powerful feature, first introduced in Windows 2000, that provides a highly effective method of managing computers, users, and even software on the network. Using group policy, administrators can place restrictions on users and computers, implement security standards, customize the Windows 2000 desktop, and even install and remove software without any intervention from the user. All of this can be done through group policy, administered by the Active Directory. As an A+ technician in a Windows 2000 network, group policy may very well be an area that you help implement and manage, and if you are new to Windows 2000 networking, you should certainly get your feet on solid ground with group policies. In this section of the chapter, we'll take a look at the structure of group policies and how you can put them to work on your network.

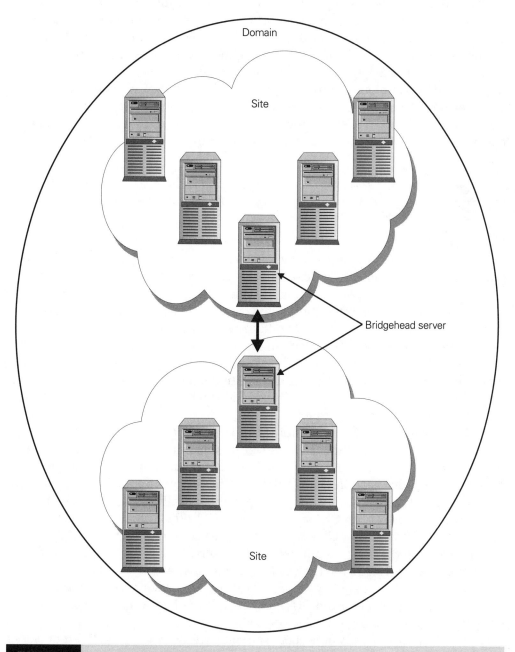

| FIGURE 8.4 | The Bridgehead server |

UNDERSTANDING GROUP POLICY

In essence, a group policy is simply a collection of settings that are applied to a computer when it boots, or to a user when the user logs on. These settings impact the look, use, and functionality of Windows 2000 Professional and Windows XP Professional computers in a Windows network. Group policies can be implemented at the site, domain, or OU level, or at the local computer level. Because you can implement group policies at various network levels, the concept of "inheritance" is in effect. Inheritance simply means that settings are inherited from a parent OU. So, in this case, the structure is inherited from the local computer policy to the site policy, site to the domain, then the domain to the OU.

 Don't let the term "group policy" be a source of confusion. You cannot apply policies to actual groups or users, but only to sites, domains, or OUs, where they affect users and computers residing in the sites, domains, or OUs.

Let's consider an example. Let's say that you want to implement a network-wide group policy that applies to all users. In this case, you can configure a site policy. The site policy is inherited to all domains, then to all OUs. If certain computers have a local group policy configured, it is overridden by any site, domain, or OU policies that exist. Or, let's say that your network has two domains. You want to use different policies in each domain. In this case, you would create a group policy for the one domain and implement it at the domain level, then create another group policy for the second domain and implement it in that domain at the domain level. Any computer or user within the domains will receive the domain policy within the domain they belong to.

However, what if you have multiple group policies at different levels? Let's say there is a site policy that affects several domains, but one domain has its own group policy. In this case, an "override" feature is automatically in effect. First, the site policy is applied, then the domain policy is applied. Any policies in the domain that conflict with the site policy automatically override the site policy. Or, what if there is also an OU policy in the mix? In this case, the site policy is applied, then the domain policy, which overrides conflicting settings of the site policy. Then, the OU policy is applied, which overrides conflicting policies from the domain policy. Here's the trick to keeping it all straight: by default, the policy closest to the user is the policy he or she receives. If a user account resides in a certain OU, the settings for the OU policy will be applied, along with any site or domain policies that do not conflict.

Let's look at a specific example. Let's say you have a simple site policy that blocks the use of the Run command. There is also a domain policy that implements several other settings, including customized Internet Explorer settings. Finally, there is an OU policy that has more specific Internet Explorer settings. For a user residing in the OU, what settings does the account receive? The user receives all of the settings, but the settings closest to the user override any conflicting settings from above. So, the user is prevented from using the Run command and receives the Internet Explorer settings specific to the OU because those settings override the domain Internet Explorer settings.

Now, let's muddy the waters even a bit more. Let's say you have a site and domain policy in effect. However, there is a particular OU that has specialized needs. You want to implement a group policy at this OU, but you do not want the site and domain policies applied at the OU. What can you do? For situations such as this, group policy has a "block inheritance" feature so that you can block inherit from higher policies. In this case, you would choose the block inheritance option at the OU level so that the site and domain policies are not applied. Simple enough, but there is one other issue to consider. Because site or domain administrators may have more control than an OU administrator, higher policies such as site and domain policies have the option to configure "no override." This means that the policy will be applied all the way down to the lowest level and cannot be overridden by another policy. For example, let's say you configure a site policy that removes the run line from all computers. However, a domain administrator configures a domain policy that allows the run line. What happens? By default, the domain policy overrides the site policy, so the run line would be allowed. However, if the site administrator has configured no override, then the domain policy would not

"Don't Override Me!"

PAINFUL LESSONS

I'VE LEARNED

Block inheritance and no override are both important features that give you some flexibility in the group policy inheritance structure. You can think of these settings as exceptions—in some cases, they are needed for specific purposes. As a general rule, though, these settings should be used when absolutely necessary and carefully considered. In your environment, if the block inheritance and no override features are used regularly, this is typically a sign that the group policy structure needs some work. No override and block inheritance can cause a number of group policy problems, so it is important that you realize the full impact of these settings before they are used. Otherwise, you can end up with a difficult group policy structure that is complicated to troubleshoot. Like many options in Windows 2000 networking, you should always start with a pencil and paper and map out your network goals before implementing group policy settings. This can save you a lot of time and problems down the road.

override the setting and the run line would not be available. A bit confusing, but keep in mind that the settings are all about an inheritance order—and control on the part of senior administrators.

CREATING A GROUP POLICY

Because group policy is configured at the site, domain, or OU level, you (once again) return to your Active Directory tools to configure it. For site policies, you can open the Active Directory Sites and Services tool. Right-click the desired site in the console and click Properties. On the Group Policy tab, shown in Figure 8-5, you can click New to create a new group policy. If you want to create a group policy at the domain or OU level, open Active Directory Users and Computers and right-click the desired domain or OU and click Properties. Then access the Group Policy tab, which will look the same as the tab you see in Figure 8-5. Notice the "block inheritance policy" check box in Figure 8-5. Notice that the option is grayed out in this figure. This is because you are looking at the site policy dialog box, and because there is no higher policy in the inheritance order, there is nothing to block at the site level. This dialog box appears enabled when you access it from the domain or OU level.

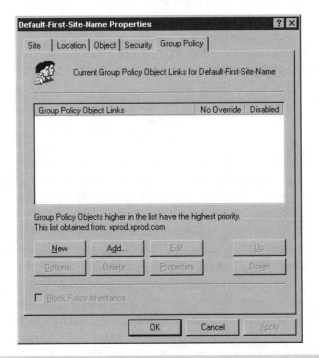

FIGURE 8.5   Group policy

To create a new group policy, click the New button. The policy appears in the window. Notice that you can now click the Options button. This provides the Object Options dialog box, shown in the following illustration. You can choose to disable the group policy at any time, or use the no override feature as we discussed. Remember that when you use the no override feature, lower-level group policies will not be able to override any of the settings found in this group policy—they can add to those settings with additional settings, but they cannot override the policy in any way.

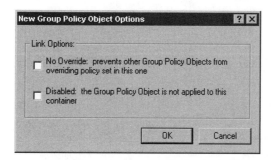

EDITING A GROUP POLICY

Once you have created the group policy, you are ready to edit it. When you create the group policy, all policy settings are set to their default level. Now, you must click the Edit button in order to actually invoke policy settings. When you click the Edit button on the Group Policy tab, the Group Policy console, shown in Figure 8-6, appears.

I should also mention here that you do not have to use the Active Directory tools to open the Group Policy console—you can do so manually by opening the Group Policy snap-in, which you may find easier, depending on your needs.

You can quickly open the local Group Policy console by typing **gpedit.msc** at the run line. This opens the local console where you can configure a group policy for the local computer. If you need to configure a site, domain, or OU policy, follow the provided steps.

To Start the Group Policy Console Manually, follow these steps:

1. Click Start | Run, type **MMC**, then click OK.

2. Click Console | Add/Remove snap-in.

3. On the Add/Remove snap-in window, click the Add button.

4. From the snap-in list that appears, select Group Policy and click OK.

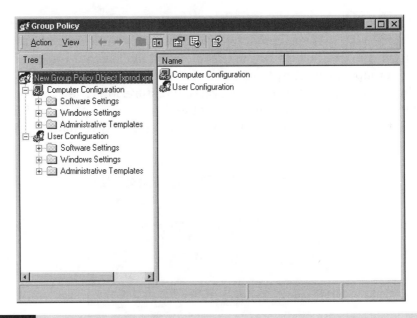

FIGURE 8.6   The Group Policy console

5. The Select Group Policy Object window appears. The default selection is the local computer, but since you want to edit a site, domain, or OU policy, click the Browse button.

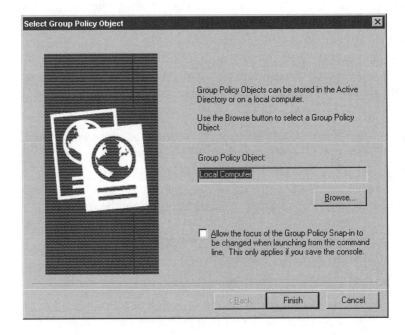

6. The Browse for a Group Policy object window opens. You see tabs for Domain/OUs, Sites, Computers, or All. You can browse the tabs and open the desired policy, then click OK.

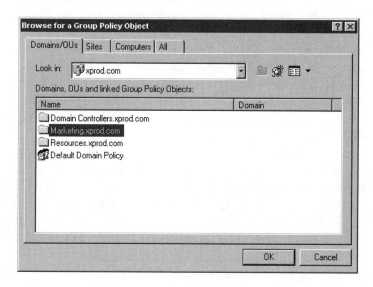

7. Click the Finish button, then click Close on the Add Standalone snap-in window, then click OK to open the snap-in.

NOTE To create a group policy, you must be a member of the Administrators group or the Group Policy Creator Owners group.

Either way, once you open the Group Policy console, you can then configure the group policy object. You can configure either the user object or computer object (or both) by clicking the icon in the left pane to expand them. You'll see that the categories are the same for the user and computer, and you'll even find that many of the policies overlap. Keep in mind that computer configurations apply to computers and are employed when the computers boot. User policies apply to users and are configured when the user logs on.

CONFIGURING THE COMPUTER CONFIGURATION

The computer configuration in the Group Policy console has three containers: Software Settings, Windows Settings, and Administrative Templates. Each container holds policies you can configure that are applied to the computer. The following sections consider what is available in each of these.

SOFTWARE SETTINGS

The Software Settings container contains a software installation icon. If you select the icon, you can see any configured software packages displayed in the right pane. You can also create a new software package by selecting Software Installation in the left pane and clicking Action | New | Package. The software installation option only works with Windows Installer Packages (.msi) files that you must create prior to using the software installation feature. Of course, most Microsoft software ships prepackaged as .msi files, but keep in mind that only .msi software packages can be used. Any installer packages you add to the console will then become a part of the group policy and installed on client computers to which the policy applies.

There are two concepts concerning software installation that you must remember. You can either publish or assign software. Published software applies to users. When the user logs on, the available software that can be installed is listed in "Add New Programs" in Add/Remove Programs in the Control Panel, and the user can choose to install that software if he or she wants to. If you assign software, it is installed on the computer automatically without the user's choice or intervention. You can either publish or assign software to users, but you can only assign software to computers.

If you select Software Installation in the left console pane then click Action | Properties, you see the property dialog box appear. On the General tab, you have a few basic options that you can configure for software deployment. You can choose to display a deployment software dialog box and you can choose to display either a basic or maximum user interface while installation is occurring. You also see an option to publish. This means that you want the new package to be published with the standard package options. As you can see in the following illustration, the published option is grayed out. This is because you can only publish to users, not computers. You can also choose to uninstall any applications when they fall out of the scope of management. For example, if software is installed under an OU policy and the computer is moved to a different OU, the software would be automatically uninstalled.

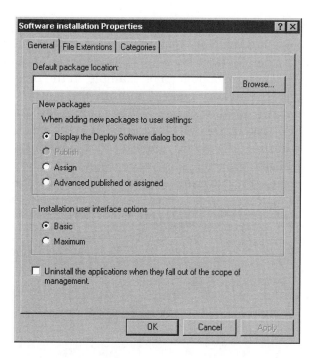

The File Extensions tab enables you to associate all extensions with particular applications. This option is useful for custom applications so that correct files can be associated with them. The Categories tab enables you to add custom categories to Add/Remove Programs on the user's computer. These custom categories can store corporate software applications.

WINDOWS SETTINGS

If you expand Windows Settings, you see two categories: Scripts and Security Settings. Select Scripts in the left pane, and you see startup and shutdown options appear in the right pane. If you select one of the options and then click Action | Properties, you can choose to use a desired script or you can add one as needed. When you add scripts, or remove them for that matter, the scripts become part of the group policy and will be run when the user boots the computer or shuts down.

If you expand the Security Settings container, you see a number of subcontainers that house different kinds of security policies. For example, if you select Account Policies in the left pane, the Password Policy and Account Lockout Policy containers appear in the right pane. If you double-click one of the policy containers, you see a list of actual policies. For example, under Password Policy, you see such policies as enforce password history, maximum password age, minimum password length, and so forth. If you double-click one of the policies, a simple dialog box appears where you can define a policy. For example, in the next illustration you see the enforce password history policy. To define the policy, simply click the check box and enter the number of passwords a computer should remember, then click OK. Notice that, by default, most policies are not defined. You only need to access and define the policies you want to implement. In other words, you do not have to disable policies that you do not want to use because they are not enforced by default. You have to configure them for use in the policy.

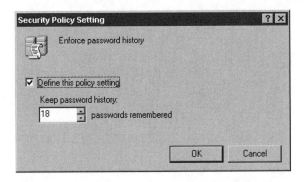

As you can see, there are a number of different policies that you implement concerning security, so you'll have to look around a bit to find the policies that you want. Fortunately, the policies are organized by container under the security object, so you can browse them rather quickly and easily. Here are the categories you find:

■ **Account Policies** Contains subcontainers for password policy and account lockout policy.

■ **Local Policies** Contains subcontainers for audit policy, user rights assignment, and security options.

■ **Event Log** Contains policy settings for the event log.

■ **Restricted Groups** Contains security access policies for restricted group access.

■ **System Services** Contains security policies for system services on the computer, such as DHCP Client, FRS, and so forth. This feature enables you to set security on various system services to prevent user tampering.

■ **Registry** Contains security policies for registry access and editing.

- **File System**   Contains security policies for file system configuration.

- **Public Key Policies**   Contains subcontainers for encrypted data recovery agents, automatic certificate request settings, trusted root certification authorities, and enterprise trusts.

- **IP Security Policies**   When IP Security (IPSec) is in effect, these policies define security settings for client and server IP traffic.

ADMINISTRATIVE TEMPLATES

The Administrative Templates container contains a number of templates and different categories that you can use to configure various system components. You can also import other templates as desired. Fortunately, policy templates all look basically the same. When you double-click the template, you have a Policy and Explain tab. On the Policy tab, you can choose Enabled, Disabled, or keep the policy Not Configured. It is important, however, to note that Not Configured does not write any changes to the registry. Both the Enabled and Disabled options write registry changes, so when you do not want to implement a policy, simply leave the setting as Not Configured.

As you can see, you have a number of different administrative templates that you can use to enable or disable policies as needed. Again, you'll need to browse the categories and templates to find what you need, but use the following bullet list for a quick reference:

- Under Windows Components, you can configure policies for NetMeeting, Internet Explorer, Task Scheduler and Windows Installer.

- Under System, you can configure Logon, Disk Quotas, DNS Client, Group Policy, Windows File Protection.

- Under Network, you can configure Offline Files and Network and Dial-up Connections.

- Under Printers, you have a number of templates that determine what users can do with a local printer when logged onto the computer.

USER CONFIGURATION

The group policy user configuration places management restrictions or permissions on items directly associated with the user account. You have the same Software Settings, Windows Settings, and Administrative Templates containers as you saw in the previous sections, so I'm only going to point out information that is different in the user configuration.

First, under Windows Settings, you have a few additional categories, which are

- **Internet Explorer Maintenance**   This category of policies enables you to configure a number of custom Internet Explorer options, such as a custom title bar. You can also use animated bitmaps, custom logos, preconfigured connection settings, preconfigured URLs, security settings, and program settings.

- **Remote Installation Services**   This category gives you a Choice Options icon that presents you with a simple window so you can define the level of user interaction during a remote installation, such as using custom setup and so forth.

- **Folder Redirection**   Folder redirection enables a user to log on to any workstation and receive his or her files and folders. You can choose the target location on the user's computer to redirect the folders.

Under Administrative Templates, you also have categories for:

- **Start Menu & Task Bar**   Enables you to configure Start Menu and taskbar items.

- **Desktop**   Enables you to control desktop settings including the Active Desktop as well as Active Directory searches.

- **Control Panel**   Enables you to manage and control Control Panel items.

PAINFUL LESSONS I'VE LEARNED

Too Many, Too Late

Group policy is a powerful feature, but a little goes a long way. Keep in mind that the purpose of group policy is to enforce settings that are necessary for your organization—it is not designed as a method for playing "Big Brother." I've worked in environments where group policies were ridiculously complex, and the result is a lot of administrator time, a lot of user complaints, and generally a lot of problems. The key point here is to implement the policies that you need, but don't implement anything that is not absolutely necessary. Keep your group policy configuration neat, lean, and clean and you'll have a much more effective policy and a more effective network.

WRAPPING UP...

Windows 2000 provides highly effective networking tools and designs for today's large and complicated networks. Using the Active Directory, large LAN and WAN environments can build an effective Active Directory structure using sites, domains, and OUs. In Windows 2000 networks, domain controllers function in a multimaster design, giving you more networking and management flexibility. Group policy is an effective network tool for managing network clients and adding and removing software. With these designs, Windows networks have become very popular and continue to grow.

MANAGING WINDOWS 2000 SERVER

9

As an A+ technician working in a Windows network you are likely to get your hands dirty with Windows 2000 Server, depending on your job description and your assigned tasks. Even if you came aboard as a hardware technician, you may find yourself working with Windows 2000 Server and managing network services. The good news is Windows 2000 is a robust operating system—the bad news is there can be a rather lengthy learning curve if you are new to Windows networking. If so, see Chapter 7 for a Windows networking primer, then turn your attention to this chapter to dig into Windows 2000 Server. I should note here that there are obviously entire books just on managing Windows 2000 Server (some in excess of 1,500 pages), so it is not possible for me to cover everything in this chapter. However, I have focused this chapter on the issues and tasks that you are likely to face as an A+ technician. In this chapter, we'll be…

- Working with the Active Directory
- Working with DHCP
- Managing DNS
- Working with Terminal Services

WORKING WITH ACTIVE DIRECTORY

The Active Directory is Microsoft's flagship directory service, which pervades most areas of network management when working with Windows 2000. Using the Active Directory, you configure user and group accounts, managing shared folders and printers, shared applications, and just about anything else you might want to make available on the network. The Active Directory runs on Windows 2000 domain controllers, and as a part of your job as an A+ technician, you may have delegated permission to manage certain portions of the Active Directory. Like Windows 2000 Server, there are entire books just on the Active Directory, and the configuration of it can be rather complex. However, the day-to-day management of the Active Directory most likely befalls junior administrators or A+ technicians like yourself, and the following sections show you how to manage resources within the Active Directory using a Windows 2000 domain controller.

ADDING USERS AND GROUPS

In a Windows 2000 domain, user and group accounts are managed in the Active Directory. When you add a user or group account, the data is recorded in the Active Directory and replicated to other domain controllers. This ensures that each domain controller has an exact copy of the Active Directory, including changes and additions as they are made. Replication is performed automatically in the background, so all you have to work with is the Active Directory interface on a Windows 2000 domain controller.

User accounts can be from one to twenty characters in length and must be unique to all other names on the network. You can use any combination of letters, numbers, and symbols, except "/\{};:| =,+*?<>." As you are creating the account, you can assign a default password and have the users change it. You can also require certain passwords, if needed, and specify certain password lengths or complexity rules. Windows 2000 networks use a group policy to require certain password lengths or complexity rules.

Creating a user account is easy using the Active Directory Users and Computers, and the following steps show you how.

1. On a Windows 2000 domain controller, click Start | Programs | Administrative Tools | Active Directory Users and Computers.

2. Select the desired organizational unit or container and click Action | New | User.

3. In the New Object – User dialog box, enter the desired information for the user account and click Next.

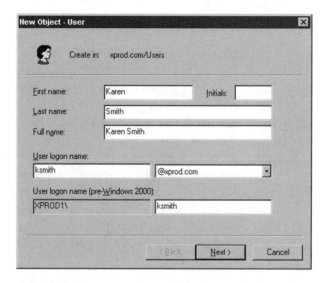

4. In the next dialog box, enter a desired password and confirm it. Use the provided check boxes to have the user change the password at the next logon, prevent the user from changing the password, choose the Never Expire option, or even disable the user's account. Click Next.

5. Click Finish. The new account now appears in the Active Directory Users and Computers and will be replicated to other domain controllers.

NOTE Once the account is created, you can right-click the Account icon found in the OU or container where it was stored and click Properties. You can then configure additional account information, such as addresses, phone numbers, locations, and so forth.

Aside from creating user accounts, you can also configure group accounts in the same manner. Select the location (OU or container) where you want to store the group account and click Action | New | Group. Enter a group name and choose the group scope (domain local, global, universal) and group type (security or distribution).

CONFIGURING ORGANIZATIONAL UNITS (OUS)

An organizational unit (OU) is a management tool that allows you to group certain items together in much the same way you use folders. Within each OU, you can place any Active Directory resource, such as user accounts, shared folders, printers, and even other OUs. Like a file folder, an OU does not have any functionality on its own, but it is designed to hold other resources.

OUs are used in the Active Directory as an administrative and organizational boundary, as well as a group policy boundary. They can effectively take the place of Windows NT resource domains, and in fact, many NT networks with several domains can effectively upgrade to the Active Directory model and become one domain with several OUs. As you might imagine, the use of OUs requires some planning and careful consideration. If you are new to Windows 2000 networking, you would benefit from reading a book about Windows 2000 network architecture. The actual process of creating a new OU is rather easy, but you should be aware of the planning issues to do before actually creating and using new OUs.

As with user, group, and computer objects, OUs are created and configured using the Active Directory Users and Computers tool. Simply open the Active Directory Users and Computers console, then click Action | New | Organizational Unit. Enter the name for the new OU and click OK. Once you have created the OU, you can see it in the Users and Computers console. At this point, you can be moving resources into the OU as necessary.

Like user and group accounts, you can also access the OU Properties dialog box by right-clicking the OU and clicking Properties. You'll see standard General, Managed By, Object, Security, and Group Policy tabs (and possibly a Permissions tab) that you can manage as needed.

PUBLISHING CONTACTS

A contact is much like a business card—it contains information about a person or even a company that can be stored in the Active Directory. This person or company is not a network user that has an account, but one whose information may be accessed by network users. When a user searches for the person or company, the Active Directory can recall the person's or company's contact information. However, the line between a contact and a user can get fuzzy because contacts can also have a user account, and they can be members of groups within your organization. The point is simply that the contact object provides you a way to include people and businesses in your Active Directory even though those people or businesses are not directly a part of your network.

You can create contacts in any OU or container using the Active Directory Users and Computers console. To create a new contact, click Action | New | Contact. Enter the contact's name and click OK. The properties sheets for the contact object contain several different tabs that enable you to configure the contact as desired. The tabs you'll find, such as General, Address, Telephones, and so forth simply give you a way to enter more information about the contact that can be accessed by Active Directory users.

NOTE   It is important to keep in mind that the contact feature is designed for companies and even users that are not a part of your network. In other words, the contact feature is a way to provide contact information for Active Directory users. Not every vendor with whom your company does business needs contact data, so use this feature on an "as needed" basis.

PUBLISHING PRINTERS

Network printer information can be stored in the Active Directory so that users can find the printer that they need to use and automatically connect to it. The network user does not have to know which server the printer is connected to and they do not need to know anything about the network topology in order to use the printer.

You can publish printer objects in the Active Directory connected to either Windows 2000 computers or down-level computers, such as NT and 9x. However, the publication method for Windows 2000 and down-level computers is different. Windows 2000 computers can automatically publish shared printers in the Active Directory without configuration from the Active Directory administrator. In Windows 2000 computers (either Server or Professional) and Windows XP, you have the option to automatically list the printer in the Active Directory when you share the printer (it's found on the Sharing tab). Click the check box to list the printer in the directory. Once you click OK, the printer information is sent to a domain controller for publication in the Active Directory.

Down-level computers, such as Windows NT or 9x, can also publish shared printers in the Active Directory so that other users can locate and access them; however, down-level computers cannot automatically publish the printer. For down-level shared printers, an administrator must manually add the printer object in the Active Directory. To add a printer, open Active Directory Users and Computers, then select the OU or container where you want to store the printer object. Then, click Action | New | Printer. In the New Object-Printer window, enter the UNC path to the shared printer, such as \\server_name\share_name, and click the OK button. Once you click OK, the Active Directory checks for the network share and adds the printer object to the directory if it is available. If the printer is not available or is not shared, you receive an error message telling you the printer does not exist.

TECH TALK

Printer Management and the Active Directory

The Active Directory only stores information about the printer, such as the network location and some additional property information you can enter. The Active Directory does not manage the printer. The Active Directory acts as a pointer to the printer object. When a user searches for a printer, discovers a desired printer, and then connects to the printer, the Active Directory simply redirects the request to the computer that holds the share. This process is invisible to the end user, who is not aware of the server or computer that actually manages the printer. This feature enables users to access network resources without having to know which server or computer holds which shared printer. Think of the Active Directory as a phone book—the directory's job is to list a resource so that users can find it, but the directory does not actually manage that resource.

PUBLISHING SHARED FOLDERS

The Active Directory does not physically contain shared folders, but simply the pointers to those shared folders and resources. Users can search for shared folders using keywords and locate the folders they need, which contain the actual resources they need to use. Shared folders function in the Active Directory the same way as printers in terms of Active Directory objects. When you publish a shared folder, you are simply publishing pointer information that redirects a user to the computer that holds the shared folder. Just as a printer share redirects the user to the server or computer where the shared printer is attached, shared folders redirect the user to the computer that actually houses the shared folder.

Shared folders are not published automatically, but must be manually published by an administrator. With this thought in mind, your network may need to create guidelines to determine the requirements for sharing a folder in the directory (or the number of shared folders can get out of hand). Also note that all configuration and security for a shared folder is performed on the computer that physically holds the share. The Active Directory does not provide any security for any shared folder, but simply redirects user requests for access to the computer that holds the share.

To publish a shared folder, open Active Directory Users and Computers, select the OU or container where you want to place the shared folder object, then click Action | New | Shared Folder. In the New Object–Shared Folder window, enter a name for the shared folder and the UNC path to the shared folder, such as \\computer_name\share_name.

As with printer objects, you can enter share information on the General tab, which you can access by right-clicking the object and clicking Properties. The information you enter on the General tab enables you to define the shared folder object in more detail and enables users to more accurately locate the shared folder they want to use. You can enter a description of the shared folder. If you click the Keyword button, a dialog box appears where you can enter a list of keywords. Use the Add button to enter the keywords and create the list, and use the Edit and Remove buttons to make changes to the list.

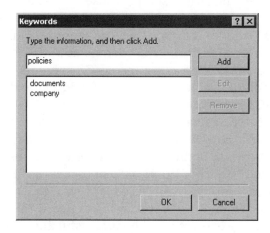

WORKING WITH DHCP

Dynamic Host Configuration Protocol (DHCP) is a server service that dynamically leases IP addresses and related IP information to network clients. At first glance, this may not seem like an important task, but you have to remember that on a TCP/IP network, each network client must have a unique IP address and an appropriate subnet mask. Without these, the client cannot communicate on the network. Also, two clients cannot have the same IP address. If two clients have the same IP address, neither will be able to communicate on the network. Since each client must have unique addressing information, static management of IP addresses is not practical.

NOTE   Keep in mind that although APIPA can be used to automatically assign IP addresses to workgroup clients, this Windows feature is designed for workgroups only—not large domain environments.

DHCP works by leasing IP addresses and IP information to network clients for a period of time. For the lease to happen, a "negotiation" process occurs. During the boot process, a client computer that is configured as a DHCP client sends out a broadcast packet called DHCPDISCOVER. The Discover packet contains the client's MAC address so the DHCP Servers can respond to it. DHCP servers on the network respond to the broadcast with a DHCPOFFER, which contains the IP address to be leased, the subnet mask, and the default gateway. If several DHCP servers respond to the request, the client accepts the first offer it receives. The client responds via a broadcast message called a DHCPREQUEST. If other DHCP servers made offers, they also see their lease offers were not accepted by the broadcast message. The DHCP server whose offer was accepted responds with a DHCPACK message, which acknowledges the lease acceptance and contains the client's IP address lease as well as other IP addressing information you configure the server to provide. The client is now a TCP/IP client and can participate on the network. If, however, the DHCP server is not available, then the client computer autoassigns itself an APIPA address and continues to try and contact the DHCP server.

Keep in mind that a lease is for a period of time. Typically, a client can keep its IP address for several days, depending on how you configure the DHCP server to lease addresses. Once half of the lease time expires, the client attempts to gain a second lease for the IP address. When a client obtains an IP address, it attempts to keep the lease by requesting a new lease for the same IP address. If the DHCP server is not available when the client is trying to renew the address, the client continues trying until the lease is up. If unsuccessful, the client simply has to get a new IP address lease.

In order to have a Windows 2000 Server function as a DHCP server, you must install the DHCP server service. You install DHCP in the same manner you install other networking components in Windows 2000 Server—through either Add/ Remove Programs in the Control Panel or through the Configure Your Server tool. Once installed, you can open and begin configuring DHCP by clicking Start | Program | Administrative Tools | DHCP. DHCP does not begin leasing IP addresses and it is not functional until it is first configured by an administrator and authorized in the Active Directory by an enterprise administrator. You can learn how to configure DHCP for operation in the following sections.

CREATING DHCP SCOPES

A scope is the full range of IP addresses that can be leased from a particular DHCP server. Each DHCP server has its own scope of IP addresses that are appropriate for the subnet on which the DHCP server leases addresses. DHCP servers do not share scopes and their scopes must not overlap with each other.

This action would result in the same IP addresses being leased to different network clients, which would cause the clients to lose network communication ability. There are three different types of scopes that you can configure: standard scope, superscope, and multicast scope.

CREATING A STANDARD SCOPE

A standard scope is simply a grouping of IP addresses that can be leased to network clients in a particular domain. Most of the time, you will configure standard scopes on DHCP servers. As you might imagine, scope configuration takes some planning on the part of network administrators to ensure that the correct range of IP addresses is made available to network clients. The following steps show you how to create a standard scope.

1. Click Start | Programs | Administrative Tools | DHCP.

2. Select the server in the console tree, click the Action menu, then click New Scope. The New Scope Wizard begins.

3. Click Next on the Welcome screen.

4. In the Scope Name dialog box, enter a name for the scope and a description, if desired. Click Next.

5. In the IP Address Range window, enter the starting and ending IP addresses of the full scope for this server, then enter the subnet mask for the IP subnet in the Subnet Mast dialog box. Click Next.

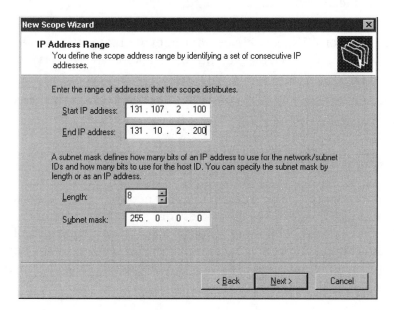

6. In the Add Exclusions window, enter any exclusion ranges desired by entering the starting and ending IP addresses of the range(s). Click the Add button to add it to the list, and repeat the process to define more exclusion ranges, then click Next.

7. In the Lease Duration window, enter the desired lease duration in the provided boxes. The default lease time is eight days. If you have primarily mobile computers, you may wish to reduce the lease times to free up more IP addresses when those computers are not connected. For stable desktop networks, longer leases are fine. In most cases, the default setting is best. Make your selection, then click Next.

8. The Configure DHCP Options window appears. DHCP options allow you to specify additional IP addressing information that is returned to clients with an IP lease, such as the address of the default gateway, WINS, and DNS servers. Click the Yes button, then click Next.

9. In the Router (Default Gateway) window, enter the IP address(es) of the routers for your subnet. The default gateway allows IP traffic to flow between different subnets. Make your entries if desired, then click Next.

10. In the Domain Name and DNS Servers window, enter the name of the parent domain and DNS server(s) name and IP addresses, as desired. The parent domain provides the name of the domain that clients use for DNS resolution, and the server names and IP addresses point the clients to appropriate servers. Use the Add button to enter the addresses you provide, then click Next.

11. The WINS Servers window appears. Enter the server name(s) and IP address(es) of WINS servers on your network that you want sent to your client computers. Click the Add button to add the WINS servers to the list, then click Next when you are done.

12. The Activate Scope window appears. Click the Yes button, then click Next.

13. Click Finish to complete the wizard.

CONFIGURING A SUPERSCOPE

A superscope contains several individual scopes, grouped for management purposes as one scope. In some cases, you may need to extend the scope to provide additional IP addresses due to network growth. Instead of creating additional subnets with additional scopes, you can use a concept called multinets. A multinet allows you to combine several scopes so they appear as one scope on an IP subnet. This scope combination is called a superscope.

The multinet allows you to create logical IP subnets where only one physical subnet exists. This is an administrative solution to extend the IP address range of a subnet without creating a new subnet. You can easily configure a superscope in DHCP manager, but as with all aspects of networking, careful planning must take place first to ensure that your multinet will meet your administrative needs and ensure client connectivity. To create a superscope, follow these steps.

1. In the DHCP Manager, select the server in the console for which you want to create a superscope, click the Action menu, then click New Superscope. The New Superscope Wizard begins.

2. Click Next on the Welcome screen.

3. In the Superscope Name window, enter the name of the superscope and click Next.

4. In the Select Scopes window, the available scopes appear. Select one or more scopes to add to the superscope and click Next.

5. Click Finish to complete the wizard.

CONFIGURING A MULTICAST SCOPE

Multicasting is the process of sending the same message to a group of network clients. In much the same way you can send an e-mail message to a group of people, multicasting allows a group of clients to appear as one client. Multicasting is used for a variety of purposes. For example, a multicast group can be configured so that a videoconference is sent over the network to all members of the group. By using the multicast features in DHCP, the multicast IP address can be automatically assigned. Multicasting is accomplished using a class D IP address range that is reserved for multicasting purposes. The address range is 224.0.0.0 to 239.255.255.255. The class D address allows you to use multicasting on your network without interfering with typical IP communication. In other words, multicast clients have a typical IP address appropriate for their subnet and they also have a multicast IP address. To create a multicast scope:

1. In the DHCP Manager, select the desired server where you want to create a multicast scope, click the Action menu, then click New Multicast scope. The New Multicast Scope Wizard appears.

2. Click Next on the Welcome screen.

3. Enter a name for the multicast scope and a description, if desired, then click Next.

4. Enter a valid IP address range for the multicast, which must fall in the 224.0.0.0 to 239.255.255.255 range. You can also enter a time to live (TTL), which is the number of routers that multicast traffic passes through on your network. The default is 32. Make your selections, then click Next.

5. In the Add Exclusion window, enter an exclusion range, if desired, by entering the start and ending IP addresses of the exclusion range. Click the Add button to add the exclusion range to the list and click Next.

6. In the Lease Duration window, enter the desired multicast lease duration. The default is 30 days. Configure the lease duration depending on your multicast needs, based on the amount of time a multicast group may need to exist. Click Next.

7. In the Activate Multicast Scope window, click Yes to activate the multicast scope and click Next.

8. Click Finish to complete the wizard.

AUTHORIZING THE DHCP SERVER

Once you have configured the desired scopes for your subnet, your next step is to authorize the DHCP server in the Active Directory. DHCP Servers cannot lease IP addresses in Windows 2000 networks without being authorized. In most cases, domain controllers that function as DHCP servers will be automatically authorized by the Active Directory, but member servers must be authorized manually. Authorization is a security precaution that ensures only authorized DHCP servers operate on the network. This prevents unauthorized, or "rogue," DHCP servers from coming online and issuing IP addresses. This security feature prevents DHCP servers from "accidentally" coming online and leasing incorrect or inappropriate IP addresses to network clients. When a DHCP server is authorized by the Active Directory, its IP address is added to a list of authorized servers.

To authorize a DHCP server, select the DHCP server you want to authorize in the DHCP Manager console, click the Action menu, then click Authorize. The authorization process may take a few moments. Click the Action menu, then click Refresh (or simply click F5) to refresh your server to see if authorization has taken place. If it has, the server object in the console appears with a green icon. The server can now lease IP addresses to clients.

MANAGING SCOPES

Each scope that you configure has a property dialog box so that you can make changes to the scope without having to re-create it. Select the scope in the console, click the Action menu, then click Properties. The General tab contains the scope name, starting and ending IP address, and the lease time. All of this information was configured when you created the scope, but you can easily change it as needed on the General tab. The DNS tab allows automatic updating of DNS with DHCP client information. The default options here are typically all you need. The Advanced tab contains three radio buttons. You can choose to assign IP addresses to DHCP clients only, BOOTP clients only, or do both. If you choose to lease IP addresses to BOOTP clients, you can set the lease duration for them on this tab as well. You can also use the Action menu to delete or deactivate a scope. If you deactivate a scope, you can use the Action menu to reactivate it, but the scope will not be able to lease IP addresses to clients as long as it is deactivated.

If you expand the scope in the console tree, you see several subcontainers appear. The following bullet list tells you what you can do with each:

- **Address Pool**   If you click Address Pool, your current address pool is displayed in the details pane. If you click the Action menu, you can add a new exclusion range if desired.

- **Address Leases**   If you click Address Leases, a list of leased IP addresses and the clients who hold the leases appear in the details pane as well as the lease expiration dates.

- **Reservations**   If you click Reservations, a list of your current reservations appears in the details pane. You can add a new reservation by clicking the Action menu and selecting New Reservation.

- **Scope Options**   If you click Scope options, you can configure additional IP options for the scope. The options for 003, 006, 044, and 046 are the ones most commonly used.

MANAGING THE DHCP SERVER

You can manage the DHCP server by selecting it in the console and using the Action menu. You have two major options. First, you can click Display Server Statistics. Server statistics give you statistical information about the server and provide such information as leases, releases, the percentage of the scope that is in use, and so forth. The Server Statistics option is a good way to gain quick information about the server's DHCP functions.

You can also manage the server by accessing the server's properties, found on the Action menu. The server properties sheet has three tabs: General, DNS, and Advanced.

On the General tab, you have three check boxes you can select or deselect. The first is to automatically update statistics. The default is every 10 minutes. Next, you can enable DHCP logging. This option is selected by default, and this feature writes a daily file that you can use to troubleshoot and monitor the DHCP service. Finally, you can show the BOOTP table folder. Use this option so you can see the BOOTP table folder if your network uses BOOTP clients. BOOTP clients are diskless workstations that obtain their IP addresses and boot program from the server. BOOTP is an older technology solution that is supported in Windows 2000 for backward compatibility.

On the DNS tab, you can make some selections about how the DHCP server interoperates with DNS. DNS and DHCP are integrated in Windows 2000, and due to the dynamic nature of Dynamic DNS, DHCP can automatically update DNS when a client's IP address changes.

On the Advanced tab, you have a few configuration options. First, you can set conflict detection, if desired. Conflict detection allows the DHCP server to attempt to detect IP lease conflicts before leasing an IP address to a network client. Under normal circumstances, this option is not needed, and if you choose to use conflict detection, the leasing negotiation between the server and client will operate more slowly.

You can also use the Advanced tab to change the audit log file and database paths if desired. The default is C:\WINNT\System32\dhcp. In addition, you can click the Bindings button to change the server network connection that communicates with network clients. This feature is useful for servers that have multiple network interface cards (NICs), and is there so you can select which network adapter card the DHCP server can assign IP addresses.

MANAGING DNS

Domain Name System (DNS) is an industry standard for resolving hostnames to IP addresses. DNS is integrated with Windows 2000, providing the namespace for the organization. Why, you might ask? The answer is simple. DNS is highly extensible and scalable. Millions of computers can fit within the namespace (it makes up the entire Internet), so there are virtually no limits to the naming convention used in your organization—unlike the olden days of NetBIOS. Windows 2000 networking with the Active Directory is based on DNS and all

Active Directory names are DNS names. This approach provides a global naming system so that the local network naming structure is the same as the Internet. So, in short, you can't separate Windows 2000 and DNS.

TECH TALK

Understanding DNS

In order to understand DNS, you have to understand the DNS namespace. A namespace is an area that can be resolved. A postal address on a letter follows a namespace in that the letter contains a ZIP code, state, city, street address, and name. All letters follow this namespace so that out of the millions of possible addressees, your mail reaches only you (we hope, at least!). The namespace can be resolved by first examining the ZIP code, then the state, then the city. This narrows the resolution to one geographical area. Next, the address is resolved by narrowing it to one street and one street number, and the final portion of the resolution process is your name. This system works because all mail follows this namespace. If letter writers put whatever information they wanted on the envelope, your mail would probably never reach you. A namespace, then, is an area that can be resolved.

DNS functions in the same manner. By following a namespace, hostnames can be resolved to IP addresses. www.microsoft.com is a hostname that represents an IP address. Since computers must have this IP address to communicate, the host must be resolved to an IP address. This is accomplished by first considering the root domain, which is represented by a period ("."). Next, the address is read beginning with the top-level domain, such as com, edu, mil, gov, org, net, and so forth. For example, microsoft.com is a part of the "com" first-level domain, so at this point in the resolution process, all other first-level domains are excluded. Next, the second-level domain is usually a "friendly" name of a company, organization, or even person. Microsoft is an original, unique, friendly name, so it is resolved next. At this point, a particular server or group of servers, called third-level domains, can be resolved. For example, sales.microsoft.com, may point to a particular server. Using this method, any DNS name can be resolved to the host computer so its IP address can be retrieved. The name resolution process on the Internet usually requires a number of different domain servers. For example, "com" servers would be used to resolve Microsoft, and so forth.

WORKING WITH DNS ZONES

To subdivide DNS duties and administrative control, DNS zones are often used in DNS networks. DNS name resolution occurs through the use of DNS database files. Different servers in a network hold portions of the DNS database file so that name resolution can occur. In small networks, a DNS server may even hold the entire name- to-IP-address database file. When a DNS server is queried for name resolution, it checks its database file to determine if there is an entry for the query. If not, it can forward the request on to another DNS zone. For example, prod.xprod.com and mkt.xprod.com could be DNS zones. Servers in the production zone hold all DNS records for the zone, while DNS servers in the marketing zone hold all records for the mkt zone. This feature allows different administrators to manage DNS servers in different portions of the namespace. The zone is a way to partition the DNS namespace so it is more manageable.

There are two kinds of DNS database files within a zone: a primary database file and a secondary database file. One server in the zone contains the *primary zone database file*, and all other DNS servers in the zone contain copies of that primary database file, called *secondary zone database files*. Only the primary zone database file can have updates or changes made to it. Any changes made to the primary zone database file are replicated to the secondary zone database files through a process called *zone transfer*. The server that holds the primary zone database file is called an *authoritative server* because it has "authority" over the DNS servers in the zone. Secondary database file servers in the zone are used to reduce the traffic and query load on the primary zone database server.

SETTING UP DNS

You install DNS just as you would any other Windows 2000 server service. You can use either the Configure Your Server tool in Administrative Tools to install it, or you can use Add/Remove Programs in the Control Panel. Then Select Add/ Remove Windows Components.

SECRET DNS is automatically installed on domain controllers if no DNS implementation is currently in place because DNS must be present for the Active Directory. It is not automatically installed on member servers, however.

Once DNS is installed, it is not operational until you set up the service. A wizard is provided to help you configure your DNS server for the role you want it to play in your DNS network. To set up DNS:

1. Click Start | Programs | Administrative Tools | DNS.

2. In the tree pane, select your DNS server, click the Action menu, then click Configure the Server. The Configure DNS Server Wizard appears.

3. Click Next on the Welcome screen. The system collects setup information.

4. The Root Server window appears. In a DNS network, there must be a root server. If this is the first DNS server on your network, select the appropriate radio button, and if other DNS servers are already running, select the appropriate radio button and enter an IP address.

5. If you chose to create a root server, you are prompted for a decision concerning a forward lookup zone. A forward lookup zone is a name-to-IP-address database that helps computers resolve names to IP addresses and contains information about network services. You are encouraged to create the forward lookup zone now. Click either Yes to create it or No.

6. In the Zone Type window, you can choose to either create an Active Directory integrated zone (if the Active Directory is installed on the network), a standard primary zone, or a standard secondary. In pure Active Directory environments, this option should be selected so that all zone and database data is stored in the Active Directory. Selecting the standard primary creates a new zone where the database is stored locally, and selecting standard secondary allows your server to become a secondary server in an existing zone. Make your selection and click Next.

7. In the Zone Name window, enter the name of the zone and click Next.

8. In the Zone File window, you can choose to either create a new zone database file or use one you have copied from another computer. Make your selection by clicking the appropriate radio button, then click Next.

9. You are next prompted to create a reverse lookup zone. A reverse lookup zone allows a computer to resolve IP addresses to DNS names. Under normal circumstances, DNS names are resolved to IP addresses instead of the reverse manner. You can choose to provide this, however, or you can always create a reverse lookup zone later. Make your selection and click Next.

10. If you chose to create a reverse lookup zone, the Zone Type window appears. If not, a Summary window appears. Review your selections and click Finish.

CONFIGURING SERVER PROPERTIES

If you select your DNS server in the tree pane, click the Action menu, and then click Properties, you are presented with seven tabs. You have a number of configuration options in the properties sheets.

On the Interfaces tab, you can determine which IP addresses your DNS server listens to for DNS queries. The default is for your server to listen to all IP addresses, but you can select the Only the Following IP Addresses radio button and enter the desired IP addresses. This feature is useful if you want your DNS server to only service a select group of computers.

On the Forwarders tab, you can click the check box to enable "forwarders." Forwarders allow your DNS server to forward unresolved queries to other DNS servers you specify on this tab. If your server is the root server, the option will not be available since your server is already at the top of the hierarchy.

The Advanced tab, as seen in the following illustration, presents you with several server options you can select by clicking the appropriate check box. By default, BIND secondaries, enable round robin, and enable netmask ordering are selected. You can also disable recursion, which prevents a DNS server from carrying the full responsibility for name-to-IP-address resolution (allows forwarding). Besides this option, you can choose to fail when the DNS server starts if bad zone data is detected, and you can use a cache method that prevents pollution from occurring.

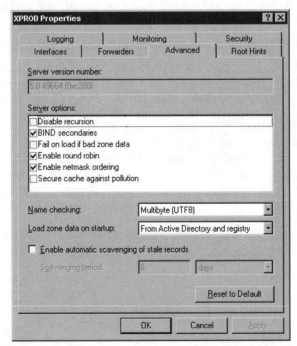

Under Name Checking, you can use the following methods:

- **Strict RFC**   Strictly enforces the use of RFC-compliant rules for all DNS names. Non-RFC names are treated as errors.

- **Non RFC**   Any names that are not RFC-compliant can be used.

- **Multibyte**   Uses the Unicode 8-bit translation encoding scheme.

- **All Names**   Allows all names to be used with the DNS server.

You also choose how you want zone data to be loaded at startup. You have the option of using the Active Directory and registry, registry, or from a file (Boot.dns in %SystemRoot%\System32\DNS). Depending on your network configuration, you can make the appropriate selection.

Finally, you can also use this tab to enable automatic scavenging of stale records. This feature allows the server to automatically clean old records out of the database at an interval you select on the tab. The default automatic scavenge interval is every seven days.

The Root Hints tab contains DNS servers and IP addresses that can be used for query resolution. The Root Hints tab allows you to enter the names and IP addresses of other DNS servers that your server can contact for name resolution, or edit and remove them as necessary. By default, Root Hints contains 13 root DNS servers that are used to resolve names outside of the authoritative DNS zone. This feature helps an authoritative zone server to find servers above it in the hierarchy.

The Logging tab gives you the option to log a number of events, such as query, notify, update, and so forth, as shown in the following illustration. The logging feature allows you to specify the kind of DNS activity you would like written to dns.log in %SystemRoot%\system32\dns. This feature is useful for troubleshooting purposes. However, logging should only be enabled for monitoring particular problems or events. This feature consumes a lot of disk space and you may see performance problems on the server, so keep in mind that logging of DNS events is for troubleshooting only.

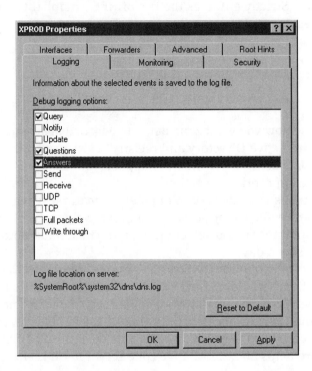

Finally, you have both Monitoring and Security tabs. The Monitoring tab allows you to perform simple DNS tests against your server so you can verify its configuration. The Security tab is like all others in Windows 2000 Server where you can configure who can access and configure the DNS service on this server.

DATABASE MANAGEMENT

There are a few database management options you should be familiar with, all available from the Action menu in the DNS console when you select your DNS server. These actions essentially keep the database clean and working properly.

- **New Zone**   This action launches the New Zone Wizard, which you saw during the initial server configuration. You can use this feature to configure new zones as needed.

- **Set Aging/Scavenging for All Zones**   This feature gives you a properties sheet, shown in the next illustration, where you can scavenge stale resource records. Scavenging is a server task that cleans old records out of the DNS database. You can configure the no-refresh and refresh intervals (both of which are seven days, by default). The no-refresh interval is the time between the most recent refresh of a record timestamp and the moment when the timestamp may be refreshed again, while the fresh interval is the time between the earliest moment when a record timestamp can be refreshed and when it can be scavenged.

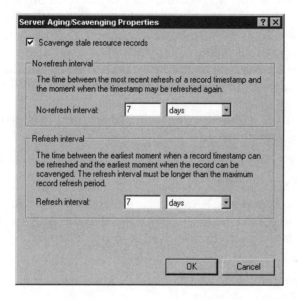

NOTE   As a general rule, the seven-day default is the best setting. If you use a setting that is too low, you cause undue work on the server and on replication between DNS servers. If the setting is high, you may have records that are too old and cause network problems. So, think twice before changing this setting.

- **Scavenge Stale Resource Records**   This action allows you to manually scavenge the database. You do not need to perform this action since the database scavenges itself every seven days by default, but you can use it if you believe the database has old records that need to be cleaned.

- **Update Server Data Files**   Data files are normally updated at predefined intervals and when the server is shut down. You can manually force the action by using the Action menu, which causes the DNS service to write all changes to the zone data files immediately.

MANAGING ZONE RESOURCE RECORDS AND ZONE PROPERTIES

Resource records are commonly used by DNS servers as a way to help the server resolve DNS queries. When a new zone is created, there are two default resource records that are automatically created. The first is the Start of Authority (SOA), which defines the authoritative server for the zone. The second is the Name Server (NS) record, which lists all DNS servers operating in the zone.

Aside from the SOA and NS records, there are several other records you can create. You can easily create these records by expanding the DNS server in the tree pane and selecting the appropriate zone, then clicking the Action menu. There are a lot of possible records that you can create, but I've included the most commonly used ones in the following bullet list. Again, the resource records are used to point to specific servers that host certain services.

- **Host (A)**   An A record provides a host-to-IP-address mapping for a forward lookup zone.

- **Pointer (PTR)**   A PTR record is an IP-address-to-name record.

- **Alias (CNAME)**   A CNAME (canonical name) record allows a host to have a different name. CNAME records are often used for load-balancing purposes and contain a host's alias as well as the fully qualified domain name. CNAME records can be used to group DNS servers so they appear as one server.

- **Mail Exchanger (MX)**   An MX record identifies a mail server with a particular host or domain.

Concerning zone properties, you can access the properties sheets for each zone by expanding the zone in the tree pane, selecting the desired zone, clicking the Action menu, and then clicking Properties. There are a few different options you should keep in mind, which I've summarized in the following bullet list:

- The General tab lists the status of the zone (such as running or paused) and the type of zone (primary, secondary, and so forth). If you click the Change button, you are presented with the Zone Type window that you originally saw in the Create New Zone Wizard. You can change zone type to either Active Directory integrated, primary, or secondary, as necessary.

- The Allow Dynamic Updates drop-down menu allows you to select Yes or No. This feature should be enabled so dynamic updates can occur.

- The Start of Authority (SOA) and Name Servers tabs provide the resource records for the start of authority and name server records. These are configured automatically when you create a new zone, but you can make changes as needed using these two tabs.

- The WINS tab allows you to use WINS to resolve name-to-IP-address mappings that DNS cannot resolve. This is a useful feature in networks that contain down-level clients and servers (such as NT, 9x, and so forth). Typically, you do not need this feature if your network is a pure Windows 2000 network.

- The Zone Transfers tab allows you to enable zone transfer to occur (which is enabled by default). You can specify that zone transfers be sent to any server in the zone or only to servers you specify.

WORKING WITH TERMINAL SERVICES

Terminal Services, which has been around practically forever in the computing world, continues to be an important server service offered in Windows 2000 Server. Terminal Services provides remote access to a server desktop through software that serves as a terminal emulator. This feature transmits the user interface to the client. The client then manages the interface through keyboard and mouse clicks that are returned to the server for processing. A terminal server can host many sessions at one time, and each session user sees only his or her manipulation of the interface. The good news about Terminal Services is that Windows 2000 can host terminal services from Windows clients as well as Macintosh and UNIX with additional third-party software. This feature gives networks more flexibility when working with applications that simply need to run on the terminal server instead of the client desktop.

Windows 2000 Server supports two different terminal server modes. You can deploy terminal services in remote administration mode or application server mode, but not both at the same time. In remote administration mode, you can access your server from any terminal on your network and administer it remotely. In application services mode, terminals that might not be able to run Windows can connect to the terminal server and run applications as needed.

INSTALLING TERMINAL SERVICES

You install Terminal Services just as you do any other Windows 2000 component, through either Add/Remove programs in the Control Panel or through the

Configure Your Server tool. When you choose install Terminal Services, a window appears asking you to select one of two modes, either remote administration mode or application server mode. Once you install Terminal Services, you will need to reboot your computer. You read about using both modes in the next several sections.

REMOTE ADMINISTRATION MODE

Remote administration mode is used to remotely manage your Windows 2000 Server from virtually any computer on your network. When you install in this mode, the terminal service runs on the server and you can connect to the server from a client computer and then manage the server remotely. In this mode, you do not need to enable Terminal Services licensing. Once you install Terminal Services in remote administration mode, you can install Terminal Services on the desired client computer so that you can remotely administer your server. In remote administration mode, only two members of the administrators group can access the terminal server at a time.

To install Terminal Services on the client, you need to make the installation disks by clicking Start | Programs | Administrative Tools | Terminal Services Client Creator. Follow the instructions that appear, and you will need two floppy disks. You can also install the tools by simply sharing the folder.

Use the two floppy disks to install the client Terminal Services on the desired client computers. Once the installation is complete, launch the Terminal Services Client application from the Programs menu, then enter an administrator username and password. The terminal appears on the remote computer where you can administer the terminal server.

APPLICATION SERVER MODE

Application server mode allows users to connect to your terminal server and run applications. Keep in mind that all of the processing is performed on the server's end and users are simply provided a graphical interface. When you choose to install Terminal Services in application server mode, a window appears where you can select permissions compatible with Windows 2000 users or permissions compatible with Terminal Servers 4.0 users. The Windows 2000 option provides the most secure environment. By default, users have the same permissions as members of the Users group, which may prevent them from running some legacy applications. If you are using legacy applications, you can choose to use permissions compatible with Terminal Services 4.0 users. When you select this option, users have full access to critical registry and file system locations, which is required by many legacy applications. However, this can be a dangerous scenario as you can see.

You should consider the impact on system resources that several sessions can create. The server's processor and system RAM must be able to handle running multiple applications and processes when clients connect to the terminal server. In short, use the application server mode on a server that has high system resources and is not responsible for a multitude of other network tasks.

Terminal server licensing for the application server mode can apply to either an enterprise or domain, depending on which option you selected during setup. Also, terminal servers can only access domain license servers if they are in the same domain as the license server. Terminal Services has its own method for licensing clients that log onto the terminal server. Clients must receive a valid license before they are allowed to log on in application server mode. The license must be activated by Microsoft, which uses Microsoft Clearinghouse, a database to maintain and activate licenses. However, Terminal Server allows unlicensed clients to connect for 90 days. After that time, Terminal Services will not allow clients to connect without appropriate licenses. You can use the Terminal Server Licensing tool available in Administrative Tools to activate the license with the Microsoft database.

NOTE You can use the Terminal Services Manager to manage user sessions, such as disconnect users, send a message, reset the connection, and examine status. You can access the Terminal Services Manager from Administrative Tools.

TROUBLESHOOTING

Application Sharing Issues

Once you have installed Terminal Services in application server mode, you can set up applications for use with Terminal Services. There are a couple of important tips to keep in mind as you work:

- You can use Add/Remove programs in the Control Panel to install the desired applications. You can also use the change user command at the command prompt before and after installing the program. The change user command ensures that program files are

Application Sharing Issues (continued)

installed in the systemroot rather than in the windows subdirectory of the user's home directory. The change user / install command places the system in install mode and turns off the .ini file mapping. After the program is installed, the change user / execute command returns the system to execute mode, restores the .ini file mapping, and redirects user-specific data to the user's home directory. Add/Remove Programs automatically runs the change user command in the background, so it is the preferred method for installing applications on a terminal server for multisession use.

■ Applications that were installed before you installed Terminal Services application server mode will need to be reinstalled so they will be available to users in multisession mode.

■ It is important to test your application installations. Some 16-bit programs may have problems working with Terminal Services, so you should test all installations before deployment.

You may find the terminal server command line commands listed in Table 9-1 useful as you work with and manage terminal server.

change logon	Temporarily disable logons to the terminal server.
change port	Changes COM port mappings for MS-DOS program compatibility.
change user	Changes the .ini file mapping for the current user.
cprofile	Removes user-specific file associations from a user's profile.
dbgtrace	Enables and disables debug tracing.
flattemp	Enables or disables flat temporary directories.
logoff	Ends a client's session.
msg	Sends a message to one or more clients.
query process	Displays information about processes.
query session	Displays information about Terminal Services sessions.

TABLE 9.1   Working with Terminal Server Commands

query termserver	Lists terminal servers on the network.
query user	Displays information about users logged on to the system.
register	Registers a program so that it has special execution characteristics.
reset session	Allows you to reset a session from the terminal server.
shadow	Allows you to monitor or remotely control an active session of another user.
tscon	Connects a client from a Terminal Services session.
tsdiscon	Disconnects a client from a Terminal Services session.
tskill	Terminates a process.
tsprof	Copies user information and changes profile path.
tsshutdn	Shuts down a Terminal Services server.

TABLE 9.1   Working with Terminal Server Commands *(continued)*

WORKING WITH REMOTE ACCESS

Remote Access Service allows remote network clients to establish a dial-up connection to a remote access server. Once authenticated, clients can then begin using network resources just as though they are locally connected. Due to the portable nature of many environments, RAS continues to be an important service provided by Windows 2000 Server.

As you might imagine, RAS management can be a complicated issue—there are entire books on the subject. In this section, I want to provide an overview of Windows 2000 RAS and look at a few of the configuration issues you are likely to run across.

RAS is installed by default on Windows 2000 servers when you perform an initial installation. However, it is not enabled. In order to set up and implement RAS, you have to enable it, and this can be accomplished through the Routing and Remote Access Server Setup Wizard. The following steps show you how to enable RAS.

1. Click Start | Programs | Administrative Tools | Routing and Remote Access.

2. In the console, select your server, click the Action menu, and then click Configure and Enable Routing and Remote Access.

3. Click Next on the wizard's Welcome screen.

4. On the Common Configurations window, you can choose Remote Access Server, VPN, Router, and Internet connection server. For this lab, select Remote Access Server and click Next.

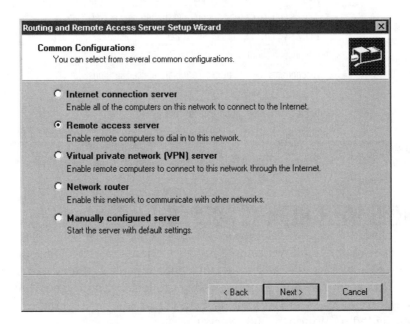

5. Verify the required protocols in the list provided. Typically, you need TCP/IP, but you may need others depending on your network clients. Click Next.

6. In the IP Address Assignment window, select how you want remote clients to be assigned an IP address. Click either the Automatically radio button or the Specified Range radio button, then click Next. If you choose automatic, remote clients are provided an IP address through DHCP. If you click the specified option, you enter an IP address range to assign to remote clients.

7. Next, you can choose to enable RADIUS or not. Click either No or Yes, then click Next. Remote Authentication Dial-In User Service (RADIUS) provides a central authentication database for multiple remote access servers and collects accounting information about remote connections. This window allows you to set up this remote access server to use an existing RADIUS server if you so choose.

8. Click the Finish button. Windows 2000 starts the Routing and Remote Access Service.

Once RAS is enabled, you can further configure the server by accessing the server's properties sheets. In the Routing and Remote Access console, select your server, click the Action menu, and then click Properties. The following sections point out the configuration options available to you.

CONFIGURING THE GENERAL TAB

The General tab, shown in the next illustration, gives you two options. First, you can choose to enable your server as a router. If you select this option, you can choose to allow only local LAN routing or you can choose to allow LAN and demand dial routing. Next, you can choose to enable your server as a remote access server. This option simply allows you to use your server as both a routing and a remote access server, or either one, as desired.

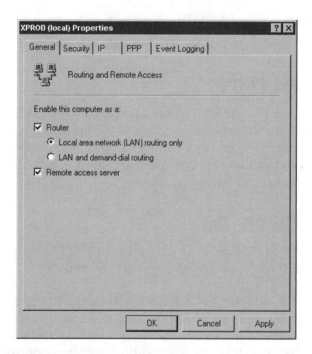

CONFIGURING THE SECURITY TAB

The Security tab allows you to choose the authentication and accounting provider. You can select either Windows authentication and accounting or RADIUS authentication and accounting. If you choose to implement RADIUS, use the Configure button to connect to a RADIUS server.

For Windows authentication, you can click the Authentication Methods button and select the type of Windows authentication you want to use for remote access. The following list tells you what options you have:

- **Extensible authentication protocol (EAP)** Allows the use of third-party authentication software and is also used for Smart Card logon.

- **MS-CHAP V2** Generates encryption keys during RAS authentication negotiation.

- **MS-CHAP** An earlier version of CHAP that provides secure logon.

- **Shiva Password Authentication Protocol (SPAP)** Used by Shiva clients connecting to a Windows 2000 RAS Server. SPAP is more secure than cleartext, but less secure than CHAP.

- **Unencrypted password (PAP)** No encryption required.

- **Unauthenticated access** No authentication is required.

CONFIGURING THE IP TAB

The IP tab allows you to enable IP routing and allow IP-based remote access and demand dial-connections. You can choose to implement either DHCP IP leases for remote clients or you can enter a static IP address pool. These are the same options you configured with the RAS Setup Wizard, but you can use this tab to make changes as necessary.

CONFIGURING THE PPP TAB

The PPP tab, shown in the following illustration, gives you three main check boxes for Point-to-Point Protocol features that you can enable:

- **Multilink Connections** This feature allows you to use multilink, which connects several modems or adapters together to increase bandwidth. You can also choose to use dynamic bandwidth control with Bandwidth Allocation Protocol (BAP) or Bandwidth Allocation Control Protocol (BACP). These protocols allow the multilink connection to dynamically add or drop PPP links as necessary for the traffic flow.

- **Link Control Protocol (LCP) extensions** Used to manage LCP and PPP connections.

- **Software Compression**   Uses the Microsoft Point-to-Point Compression Protocol (MPPC) to compress data sent on the remote access or demand-dial connection.

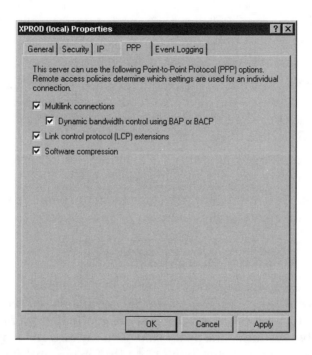

CONFIGURING THE EVENT LOGGING TAB

The Event Logging tab provides you an effective way to monitor your remote access server through the use of log files. The Event Logging tab offers several radio buttons so you can choose to log the kind of information desired, such as errors, warnings, PPP logging, and so forth. If you are experiencing problems with your remote access server, these different logging options can help you pinpoint the problem.

CREATING A REMOTE ACCESS POLICY

Remote access policies define how remote access can be used by remote clients. The policies create "rules" that must be followed for different remote access rights and permissions. For example, you specify certain dial-in numbers, dial-in hours, and even numbers a user must dial-in from. You can create remote access policies by selecting Remote Access Policy in the Routing and

Remote Access console, clicking the Action menu, and then clicking New Remote Access Policy. This action leads you through several steps in order to create the new remote access policy.

1. Select Remote Access Policy in the console tree, then click Action | New Remote Access Policy.

2. Enter a friendly name for the policy, then click Next.

3. In the Conditions window, click the Add button to see a list of conditions you can use to create the policy. Select the desired condition(s), then click Add. You may be asked to enter additional information, depending on the option you selected. Click Next.

4. On the Permissions window, choose to either grant or deny remote access permission, based on your attribute selection. Click Next.

5. Click Finish. The new policy now appears in the details pane of the Routing and Remote Access console.

CONFIGURING A REMOTE ACCESS PROFILE

For each remote access policy, you can configure the remote access profile. The profile defines settings for users who match the conditions you specify in the policy. You can create/edit a profile when you first create the first profile by clicking the Edit Profile button during the policy steps. You can also edit it by accessing the Properties of the policy and clicking the Edit Profile button. This action opens the Profile window that contains six tabs. The following sections give you a brief overview of the options you have.

CONFIGURING THE DIAL-IN CONSTRAINTS TAB

The Dial-in Constraints tab allows you to set restrictions for the dial-in policy. You can choose to disconnect the connection if it is idle for a certain period of time, restrict the maximum session time, or restrict access to certain days and times. You can also choose to restrict the kind of dial-in media used by the client.

CONFIGURING THE IP TAB

The IP tab allows you to set a specific profile for the policy, such as a server-assigned or client-requested IP address. By default, the Server Settings Define Policy radio button is selected.

CONFIGURING THE MULTILINK TAB

You can also define multilink settings for this particular profile. By default, the profile uses the server settings, but you have the option to define multilink settings for this profile. You can choose to either allow or disable multilink and use BAP, if desired. If you choose to use BAP, you specify when a link is dropped by the percentage of bandwidth usage and period of time. Additionally, you can require BAP for dynamic multilink requests.

CONFIGURING THE AUTHENTICATION AND ENCRYPTION SETTINGS

You configure authentication and encryption settings for the RAS server by accessing the RAS server's properties. You can also configure authentication and encryption settings for a policy's profile. This feature allows you to implement different encryption and authentication settings for each profile, if desired. The Authentication and Encryption tabs both provide you with a list of check boxes where you can select the desired authentication and encryption settings.

CONFIGURING THE ADVANCED TAB

The Advanced Profile tab allows you to specify additional attributes to be returned to the Remote Access Server. If you click the Add button, you can see a lengthy list of attributes you can select. The Add Attributes option allows you to specify additional information for certain network client configurations.

WRAPPING UP...

The configuration and management of Windows 2000 Server is a complicated topic, depending on the portion of Windows 2000 you are assigned to configure. Keep in mind that as an A+ technician, you are most likely to be assigned the management task of some server service within Windows 2000. Of course, there is no substitute for hands-on practice, and as you work, keep in mind that there are many additional books and online documentation options available to help you with Windows 2000.

NETWORKING WITH WINDOWS XP

10

Windows XP, which has been rather popular in both professional networking environments and home/small office networks, provides a number of networking features that are important in large and small networks. In fact, if you are working in a network that uses Windows XP, you have likely faced the task of working with these features. The good news is Windows XP is perhaps the easiest Microsoft operating system to manage and configure, which is good news for A+ technicians. In this chapter, we'll take a look at the major networking features of Windows XP. We'll especially focus on newer technologies and configurations that you are most likely to need. If you want to learn more about Windows XP in general, be sure to check out the *A+ Technician's On-the-Job Guide to Windows® XP*. In this chapter, we'll…

- Explore Windows XP's networking features
- Set up a home or small office network
- Use ICS and ICF
- Connect to a Windows domain
- Use Remote Desktop
- Configure wireless networking

EXPLORING WINDOWS XP'S NETWORKING FEATURES

Windows XP gives you more graphical interfaces than any previous version of Windows, and the same is true with networking components. You can gain more information and do more through the graphical Windows XP environment. In terms of networking, most of your work is confined to the Network Connections folder, found in Control Panel, and in many cases directly from the Start menu. When you open Network Connections, you'll see an icon list of any connections that are currently configured, such as a network connection, a dial-up connection, a VPN connection, and so forth. The good news is Network Connections gives you more information about the status of connections than ever before. In order to get information about the local area connection, or any of the connections for that matter, simply double-click the connection icon. A status dialog box, which is shown in the following illustration, opens where you can view the connection status, the current speed, and the current network access. You can even access the Properties dialog box or disable the connection should the need ever arise.

In the past, if you wanted to find out more detailed information about a connection, you had to dig around a little in the interface or use a command line utility. Windows XP provides this information directly to you on the Support tab, shown in the next illustration. If you click the Support tab, you can take a look at the IP address, the subnet mask, and the current default gateway. Windows XP also contains a new "repair" feature, also available from the Support tab. If the connection is not working, you can click the Repair button and Windows XP will attempt to contact the DHCP server for a new IP address. In addition, the repair option also flushes the Address Resolution Protocol (ARP) cache, the NetBIOS cache, and the Domain Name System (DNS) cache. During the repair process, the computer also reregisters with the WINS and DNS servers on the network.

If you click the Details button, you'll also see the Media Access Control (MAC), or physical address of the NIC.

NOTE You can easily manage the local area connection also by right-clicking the icon and accessing such options as disable, status, repair, and bridge connections.

MANAGING TCP/IP

Transmission Control Protocol/Internet Protocol (TCP/IP) is the networking standard used in modern networks today. As you learned in Chapter 1, TCP/IP is made up of standard components, such as an IP address, a subnet mask, and a default gateway. These IP standards and your basic work with TCP/IP are no different using Windows XP than any other version of Windows or even other operating systems. In other words, the same old TCP/IP rules apply.

Like Windows 2000, Windows XP can automatically configure TCP/IP when used in a home network or even small office network that does not employ a DHCP server. This automatic addressing, called automatic private IP addressing (APIPA), is designed to provide TCP/IP networking without the hassles and headaches of configuring IP. When APIPA is used, Windows XP first looks for a DHCP server in order to obtain an IP lease. On a home network or small office network where no DHCP server is used, the server obviously does not answer the computer. When no DHCP server responds, Windows XP uses APIPA to autoassign itself an IP address in the private IP address range of 169.254.0.1 to 169.254.0.254. Before assigning itself an IP address, a broadcast message is sent over the network to see if another APIPA client is using the desired IP address. If another client is using the IP address, the client tries another one. The client computer will try to locate an available address up to ten times. When a unique address is found, the client assigns itself the address and it can begin communicating with other APIPA clients. When self-assigning an address, the

---

PAINFUL LESSONS

I'VE LEARNED

DHCP and Windows XP

In a DHCP environment, or an environment that uses routers, you might not want APIPA to be used at all. In fact, APIPA really doesn't help clients connect in a DHCP environment because the IP address assigned by APIPA will most likely not be the correct IP address range or subnet mask assigned by the DHCP server. In this case, you can disable APIPA by editing the registry. Navigate to HKEY_LOCAL_MACHINE\System\CurrentControlSet\Services\Tcpip\Parameters\Interfaces\<adapter card? and add the regkey IPAutoconfigurationEnabled.

TROUBLESHOOTING

APIPA in a DHCP Network

APIPA is designed for use in a home network or small office network where no DHCP server is employed. So, what happens when APIPA is used in a larger network—by accident? For example, let's say that Windows XP is used in a Windows domain where a DHCP server is used to lease IP addresses. The DHCP server is taken offline for repairs. During that time, a few Windows XP clients need to renew their IP address leases, or some new computers are configured. What will happen? Because the DHCP server is not available, the clients will autoconfigure an IP address using APIPA. However, the IP address range used by APIPA is not likely to be the same as the IP address range used on the network. The result is that the clients will be orphaned from the rest of the network because the IP address range and subnet mask provided by APIPA do not match up to the rest of the network. So, as you are using Windows XP, keep in mind that APIPA is designed for small networks with no DHCP server—it is not a replacement for the DHCP server in a Windows domain.

computer assigns an IP address and an appropriate subnet mask. Because APIPA assumes that the computer is on a local subnet only, no default gateway is configured. After an APIPA address is configured, the computer still sends a Discover message every five minutes looking for a DHCP server.

To use APIPA or DHCP:

1. Click Start | Control Panel | Network Connections.
2. Right-click the Local Area Connection and click Properties.
3. On the General Properties tab, select Internet Protocol (TCP/IP) in the list and click the Properties button.
4. On the Internet Protocol (TCP/IP) Properties General tab, ensure that the Obtain an IP Address Automatically and the Obtain DNS Server Address Automatically radio buttons are selected. Once these are selected,

Windows XP Professional looks for a DHCP server. If no DHCP server is found, an APIPA address is configured.

Because manual configuration of an IP address and subnet mask is not practical in large networks, DHCP was developed to provide IP addresses to network clients and make certain that all clients have unique IP addresses. In the same manner, APIPA is used to ensure that clients on small networks can use TCP/IP without having to be reconfigured (since most end users are not even aware of TCP/IP). However, there may be cases where you want to configure a manual, or static, IP address for a certain computer. For example, let's say that you are using a Windows XP Professional computer as an intranet web server. You want the computer to always have a certain IP address. Since DHCP and APIPA use dynamic IP addresses that can change, you can simply configure a manual address for the computer. Under most circumstances, you will not configure static IP addresses, but when a static IP address is needed, Windows XP gives you the same TCP/IP configuration Properties dialog box you have likely seen in other versions of Windows. The following steps show you how to manually configure TCP/IP properties.

1. Click Start | Control Panel | Network Connections.

2. Right-click the Local Area Connection and click Properties.

3. In the Local Area Connection Properties window, select Internet Protocol (TCP/IP) in the list and click Properties.

4. On the Internet Protocol (TCP/IP) Properties window, click the Use the Following IP Address radio button and manually enter the desired values for the IP address, subnet mask, and default gateway. If desired, you can also enter a preferred and alternate DNS server IP address in the provided boxes.

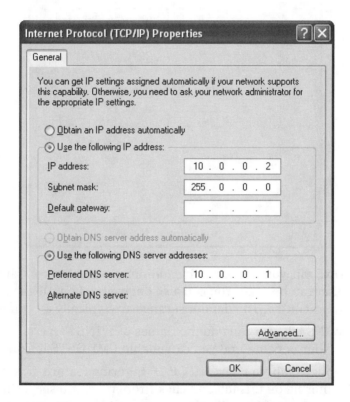

5. If you click the Advanced button, you can configure some additional TCP/IP settings. On the IP Settings tab, you can add, edit, and remove IP addresses and default gateways for the computer, in the case where multiple configurations are needed. This feature may be especially

helpful in the case of a laptop computer that you move from one network to the next.

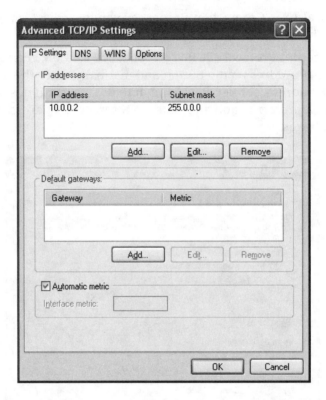

6. On the DNS tab, you can enter the additional addresses of other DNS servers that can be used. You can also determine how DNS handles names that are unqualified. The default settings are typically all you need here.

7. On the WINS tab, you can add the names of WINS servers, if they are still in use on your network and you can enable LMHOSTS lookups.

8. On the Options tab, you have a TCP/IP Filtering feature. If you select TCP/IP Filtering on this tab and click Properties, you see a simple TCP/IP Filtering window. TCP/IP filtering functions like a miniature firewall where you can allow or deny traffic on desired TCP and UDP ports, or on a protocol basis. Click OK and OK again once you have configured these options.

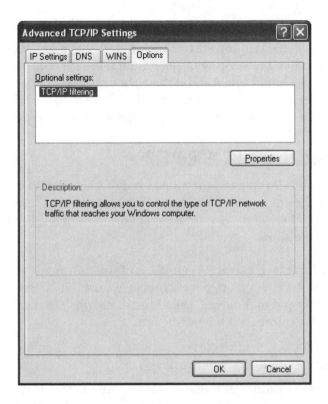

NOTE There are several command line troubleshooting tools that you can use with Windows XP. See Chapter 13 to learn more.

SETTING UP A HOME OR OFFICE NETWORK

As an A+ technician, your first thought might be that home and small office networking is beneath your skills. However, don't assume things are that simple. How about a small office network with 50 Windows XP clients, a single Internet connection, and a network that spans several rooms? How about adding laptop computers to that mix that need to travel from room to room? Or, what about a home network of five computers, each one running different versions of Windows and even using different types of networking components?

Small office and home networking has become very important during the past several years as even the smallest of offices have joined the networking revolution. While Windows domains provide much more functionality than a small office network, the cost of implementing a domain is often too great for smaller organizations, even those who need a network of 50 or more computers. In those environments, Windows XP is the operating system of choice because home and small office networking is easier and more flexible than ever before. As an A+ tech, you should understand the options and process of configuring a home or small office network (which can certainly lead to additional jobs for you). The next few sections explore the options Windows XP provides.

HOME AND SMALL OFFICE HARDWARE

At its most basic level, you need the same kind of hardware to configure a home or small office network that you need when using Windows XP in domain networks. The topology and the hardware needs are much less complex, but the basic needs are the same:

- **Network interface cards**   Regardless of the network, each computer must be outfitted with a network interface card (NIC). Before purchasing NICs, you'll need to determine the kind of network that will be used, which we'll explore in the next section.

- **Cabling**   You'll need the correct cabling in order to connect computers on a home or small office network.

- **Hub or access point**   A hub is a central connection device in which all computers connect in a home or small office network. The hub manages traffic between the computers, and some hubs even provide DSL/cable connections and firewall functionality.

- **Routers and residential gateways**   A router or residential gateway manages traffic coming onto the network from the Internet as well as traffic flowing from the network to the Internet. You can think of a router or a residential gateway as a gatekeeper between the workgroup and the Internet. Routers and residential gateways often provide firewall services and even Network Address Translation (NAT) functions. Using Windows XP, you can bypass the need for a router or residential gateway by using Internet Connection Sharing, (see "Using Internet Connection Sharing" later in this chapter).

CHOOSING A TYPE OF NETWORK

Before purchasing the equipment to create a home or small office network, you'll first need to determine the kind of network that you want to create. Using Windows XP, there are three standard types of networks that you might consider using, and the following sections review these options. You can also learn more about these in Chapter 2.

ETHERNET

Ethernet is a networking standard, and the most popular kind of network in use today. When I say "standard," this means that Ethernet networks conform to certain networking characteristics, which are adhered to by each manufacturer of networking equipment. Ethernet NICs connect to RJ-45 cables, and you'll need an Ethernet hub, router, or residential gateway, depending on your needs. Ethernet can provide three different speeds—10 Mbps, 100 Mbps, and Gigabit Ethernet—depending on the networking hardware that you purchase. Ethernet is the most common standard, and you'll find all kinds (and prices) of Ethernet NICs and hubs at any computer store.

HOMEPNA

When home networking first became popular, hardware manufacturers wanted a way to make home networking easy in any home without a bunch of cables or expensive home remodeling. The answer? Use the home's existing phone lines. HomePNA networks use PCI or USB NICs, but each NIC connects to a standard phone jack in the home or small office using standard RJ-11 phone cable. Rather than using a hub and having wiring running everywhere, you simply use the existing phone lines in the home as the network. Even though the computers are connected to the phone lines, you can still have voice conversations at the same time the network is functioning. This design allows you to have computers in any room of the house, as long as a phone jack is available. Without a hub or cabling, the home network is simple, neat, and very easy to set up. However, HomePNA are limited to 10-Mbps transfer. This speed is fine if you are only sharing files and printers, and accessing the Internet, but if you need to run large multimedia files over the network or play network games, the speed is a little slow. HomePNA, however, is very flexible and you can even combine an Ethernet or wireless network with a HomePNA network using Windows XP's new network bridge feature. See the "Using Network Bridges" section later in this chapter for details.

WIRELESS NETWORKS

Windows XP brings a lot of wireless networking capabilities to the table, making it easier for you to configure and use wireless networks than ever before. Since this is a newer kind of network and one that requires a little more thought, I've devoted an entire section to wireless networking later in this chapter (see "Wireless Networking").

SETTING UP A HOME OR SMALL OFFICE NETWORK

As you are preparing to create a home or small office network, you'll need to gather the hardware that you'll need and determine the kind of network that you want, such as Ethernet, HomePNA, or wireless. If you have an existing network and you want to create a different network using a different network type, such as Ethernet and HomePNA, you can use a Windows XP Professional computer as a network bridge, which is explored in the next section. Before you get started configuring Windows XP for networking, install any necessary NICs and gather cables (if needed). Then, arrange the physical topology of the computers and connect the network cabling (if needed) to the hub, router, or residential gateway. You should review any documentation and instructions that accompanied the hardware. Once the computers are all wired and connected, you are ready to configure Windows XP for home or small office networking. Windows XP makes this easier with the Network Setup Wizard.

To configure the first Windows XP computer on the home or small office network:

1. Click Start | Control Panel | Network Connections. In the Network Tasks pane of the Network Connections window, click the Set Up a Home or Small Office Network link.

2. The Network Setup Wizard appears. Click Next on the Welcome screen.

3. On the Before You Continue page, read the instructions and make sure that all network components are connected and working. If you want to set up the ICS host at this time, connect to the Internet.

4. In the Select a Connection Method window, select the first button option if the computer will function as the ICS host. If not, choose the second button option if there currently exists another ICS host. If neither of these options applies to you, click Other. Make a selection and click Next.

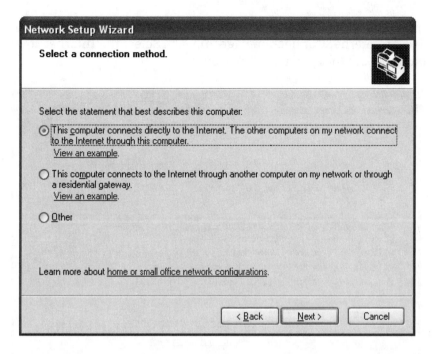

5. If you chose the Other option, the next window allows you to select

   ■ This computer connects to the Internet directly or though a network hub. Other computers on my network also connect to the Internet directly or through a hub.

   ■ This computer connects directly to the Internet. I do not have a network yet.

   ■ This computer belongs to a network that does not have an Internet connection.

6. In step 4, if you determined that the computer should function as the ICS host, an Internet Connection page appears. Select the Internet connection that you want to share and click Next.

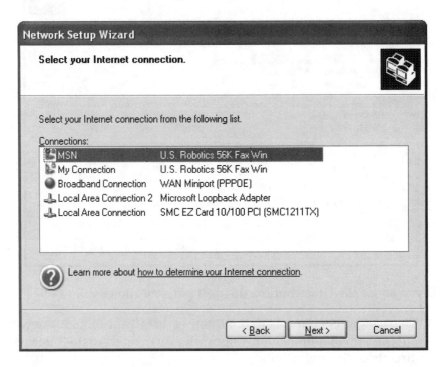

7. If you have multiple LAN connections installed on your computer, a page appears asking if you want to bridge those connections. You can choose to allow Windows XP to automatically bridge the connections by selecting the provided button option, or you can choose the button option so that you can choose your own bridge connections. Make a selection and click Next.

8. If you chose to select your own bridge connections, a page appears so that you can select the connections to bridge. Do not choose any Internet connections—you cannot bridge a LAN connection with an Internet connection, and doing so presents a serious security breach on your network! Make your selections and click Next.

9. On the next page, give the computer a name and a description. The name you assign the computer should be a friendly name that is easily recognizable on your network. However, if you are using a broadband connection, your computer may have a required name (often true of cable modems). In that case, do not change the name. See your ISP documentation for additional details. Click Next.

10. In the next page, assign a name for your network by typing it in the provided dialog box. By default, your workgroup is named MSHOME. However, you can change it to anything you like. The name should be friendly, and all computers on your network must use the same workgroup name. Click Next.

11. Review the settings you are about to apply on the next page. When you are sure they are correct, click Next. Use the Back button to make any necessary changes.

12. Windows XP configures the computer for networking, and you see a "waiting" page while the computer is configured.

13. When prompted, you can choose to create a network setup disk to use any down-level clients. Make a selection, if necessary, and click Next.

14. Follow any additional instructions to create the network setup disk and click Finish. If all of the clients on your network are Windows XP clients, you will not need a network setup disk.

Now that the first computer is installed, you are ready to begin installing the other Windows XP computers. Simply follow these same steps to install the networking software on the additional client computers. If you are using ICS, keep in mind that the Network Setup Wizard will ask you to choose how the computer connects to the Internet. Select the option to connect through another computer, and the Network Setup Wizard will locate the ICS host and proceed with setup from there. See the next section to learn more about ICS.

Windows 98, Windows Me, Windows NT 4.0, and Windows 2000 clients can also natively function in your workgroup with your existing Windows XP clients. Windows 95, Windows 3.x, and earlier versions of Windows NT are not supported. These clients, collectively called down-level clients, can be configured manually for networking, or you can run the Network Setup Wizard on these clients as well. To use the Network Setup Wizard, you can either use the floppy disk that you created when you configured the Windows XP clients, or you can use the Windows XP installation CD-ROM to run the Network Setup Wizard.

To install down-level clients:

1. Insert the Windows XP CD-ROM into the down-level client's CD-ROM drive.

2. On the Welcome screen that appears, click the Perform Additional Tasks option.

3. In the next window, click the Set Up a Home or Small Office Network option.

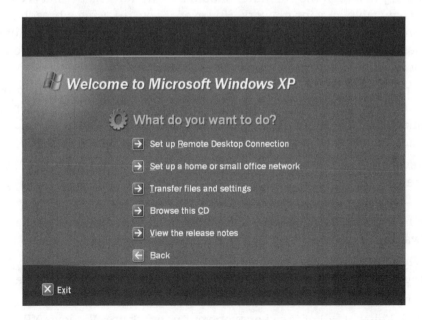

4. Depending on the operating system version you are using, the Network Setup Wizard may need to copy some additional files to your computer and restart it. Click Yes to continue.

5. At this point, the Network Setup Wizard Welcome page appears. Click Next to continue. The remaining steps are the same. See the steps earlier in this section for instructions.

USING INTERNET CONNECTION SHARING

Let's say you are configuring an office network consisting of ten computers and one DSL connection. Your client does not want to pay for Internet connections for each computer, but would like for all the computers to have Internet access. Rather than purchasing a residential gateway or even some kind of proxy server, you can use Windows XP's Internet Connection Sharing, or ICS. ICS enables you to have one computer connected to the Internet and all other computers on the network share the Internet connection. With this design, only one connection to the Internet is needed, you don't have the expense and aggravation of additional hardware, and all clients can use the Internet seamlessly—just as if they were directly connected.

ICS will work with any kind of networking hardware, such as Ethernet, HomePNA, or even wireless networks. You can set up ICS with the Network Setup Wizard when you first configure networking, or you can configure it at a later time by rerunning the Network Setup Wizard. When you use ICS, one computer acts as the ICS host, which is simply the computer that holds the Internet connection, and all other network computers are considered ICS clients. ICS is supported on Windows 98, Windows Me, Windows NT 4.0, Windows 2000, and Windows XP computers. You cannot use Windows 95 or earlier versions or other operating systems, such as Macintosh.

NOTE   You don't have to use the Windows XP computer as the host—you can use a different computer, such as Windows Me, but you will have fewer operational problems if the XP computer is the ICS host. Also, note that ICS does not work with some versions of AOL. Check with AOL to see if your version is supported.

When you set up the ICS host, the local area connection for your internal NIC is configured as 192.168.0.1 with a subnet mask of 255.255.255.0. If the ICS host has more than one NIC for your workgroup, such as in the case of a multisegment network, you need to bridge those connections so that both network segments can use ICS.

When ICS is configured, the ICS host configures and begins using a few services that provide clients access to the host, and basically allow the ICS host to function as a DHCP server of sorts. The first service is the DHCP Allocator service. When additional network clients are added to the network, the DHCP Allocator assigns those clients IP addresses, ranging from 192.168.0.2 through 192.168.0.254 with a subnet mask of 255.255.255.0. A DNS proxy is also used so that no additional DNS servers are required on your network. These services run automatically and in the background, and require no additional configuration from you. If a modem connection is used on the ICS host, autodial is turned on by default so that the connection is automatically dialed when an ICS client makes a request to the Internet. Also, Internet Connection Firewall (ICF) is automatically used on the shared connection, which you can learn more about later in this chapter (see the "Using Internet Connection Firewall" section).

SETTING UP ICS

You can easily configure ICS when you first create the network using the Network Setup Wizard. Or, if you decide to use ICS on an existing network, simply run the Network Setup Wizard again on the computer that will function as the ICS host. See the previous steps to run the Network Setup Wizard.

Once you have run the Home Networking Wizard on the XP computer, you need to run the wizard on each computer that you want to include in the home network. If you need to configure down-level clients, such as Windows 2000, Me, and 98, use the Windows XP installation CD-ROM. You'll find the Network Setup Wizard appears in the Other Tasks category. Or, you can choose to create the network setup disks option that appears at the end of the Network Setup Wizard. You can then run the wizard on your client computers. When you run the wizard on the client computers, choose the option to connect to another computer or a residential gateway. The wizard will then locate the ICS host and configure the client computer to access the Internet through the ICS host.

NOTE ICS only works with Internet Explorer 5.0 or later. Users in your network may try to use Netscape or Opera, but these browsers will not work with ICS.

MANAGING ICS

Once ICS is configured, the service is designed to take care of itself without intervention from you. There are only a few settings for ICS that you may need to change, and these are found on the shared Internet connection by opening Network Connections. Right-click the shared Internet connection (appears with a hand under it), and click Properties. On the Properties dialog box, click the Advanced tab.

On the Advanced Settings window, shown in the following illustration, you have three check box options concerning ICS:

- **Allow other network computers to connect through this computer's Internet connection**   This option essentially turns ICS on or off. If you want to stop sharing the connection at some point in the future, clear the check box.

- **Establish a dial-up connection whenever another computer on my network attempts to access the Internet**   If the shared connection is a dial-up connection, this option allows Windows XP to automatically dial the connection when another client attempts to use the Internet. If this selection is cleared, ICS clients will only be able to use the Internet if you manually generate a dial-up connection on the ICS host, which basically defeats the automated nature of ICS.

- **Allow other network users to control or disable the shared Internet connection**   This feature, which is new in Windows XP, allows the ICS clients to essentially control the connection. In a small home or office network, this setting may work well. With this option enabled, client users can disconnect a dial-up session and access statistics about that session.

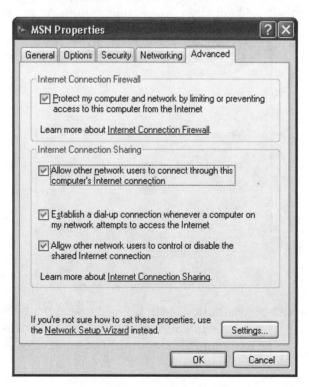

As I mentioned in the previous section, a new feature in Windows XP's ICS is client management. By default, clients on an ICS network can manage the Internet connection. This includes connecting to and disconnecting from the ISP as well as accessing connection statistics. In a small office environment, this feature may be helpful, because users can generate a connection through the ICS host—but also disconnect that session when they are done so as not to tie up phone lines. However, you can stop clients from controlling the Internet connection and accessing information by simply clearing the Allow Other Network Users to Control or Disable the Shared Internet Connection check box found on the Advanced tab. If you want to allow clients to manage the connection, clients will see an Internet Gateway icon in the Network Connections folder, representing the ICS host, as shown in Figure 10-1.

NOTE Keep in mind that the purpose of ICS is to share a single connection. However, this configuration does not stop other network computers from having their own dial-up connections or even broadband connections. For example, you may have a shared DSL connection, but clients can also have a dial-up connection that can be used should the shared connection be unavailable. This option makes certain that the client has some kind of Internet access available at all times.

If you double-click the icon, you see a Status dialog box. You can view the status, duration speed, and activity of the connection using the dialog box.

If you click the Properties button, a simple window appears telling you what connection you are using. Click the Settings button. The Services dialog box appears, as you can see in the next illustration. These services work with ICF to

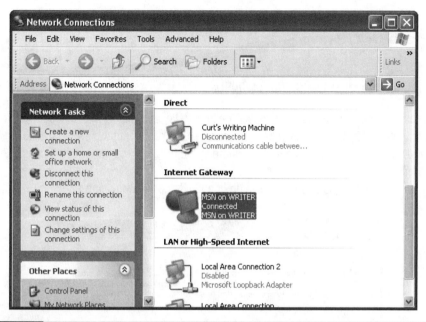

FIGURE 10.1   Internet Gateway

allow certain kinds of Internet traffic that would otherwise not be allowed. See
the next section to learn more about ICF.

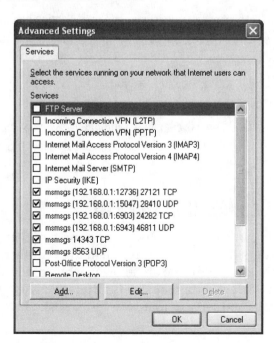

TECH TALK

Moving the ICS Host to Another Computer

Let's say that your current ICS host has a really bad day and the hard drive crashes. While the computer is being repaired, you want to use a different computer as the ICS host. What can you do? Windows XP will not allow another computer on the network to become the ICS host until you remove ICS sharing on the original host. If you try to enable another computer as the ICS host, you'll receive an IP address conflict error message.

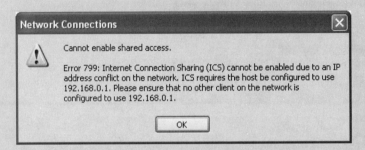

So, to change the ICS host to another computer, you need to do the following:

1. First, disable the ICS host computer by clearing the ICS option on the Advanced tab of the Internet connection's properties sheets. This will clear the former ICS host's IP address. If the former ICS host is down or turned off, you don't have to worry about this step.

2. On the new ICS host computer, run the Network Setup Wizard again and choose the option to share the Internet connection.

3. Once the setup of the ICS host is complete, rerun the Network Setup Wizard on the client computers so that they will be configured to use the new ICS host.

USING INTERNET CONNECTION FIREWALL

A firewall is any piece of computer software or hardware that protects a network from intruders. The firewall is designed to basically filter TCP/IP traffic so that certain kinds of traffic are allowed while other kinds of traffic are not. The firewall can detect certain kinds of intruder activity and completely block TCP/IP protocols and services that pose certain risks. In today's environment

Firewall Protection

Don't underestimate the importance of firewall protection in the home or small office network. With the explosive growth of broadband connections (DSL, cable, satellite), the need for a firewall becomes very important because these computers are always connected to the Internet, and therefore always exposed to danger. In a network situation where ICS is used, the entire network is open to attacks from the Internet since all computers connect to the Internet through the ICS host. Without firewall protection, your entire network is exposed.

of heavy Internet usage and network hacking, firewalls are commonly used and very important for all kinds of networking environments, including home and small office networks. Windows XP also includes its own firewall to help protect local computers from malicious people when you're on the Internet. You can think of the firewall found in Windows XP as a "personal firewall," and indeed other companies even produce firewalls for the typical home or small office user (such as Norton Internet Security). Although the Windows XP firewall provides basic firewall protection, it does not have the flexibility and caching services provided by other third-party firewall products. If you want more firewall flexibility and control, you might consider using a third-party product. Of course, ICF is already built into Windows XP, so it is certainly more convenient to use.

UNDERSTANDING HOW ICF WORKS

ICF is a software solution built into Windows XP. ICF examines traffic that flows out of your computer and traffic that flows into your computer from the Internet. Because ICF inspects traffic as it occurs, it is considered a "stateful" firewall. When you make a request to the Internet, ICF logs this request. When traffic arrives from the Internet to your computer, ICF checks its log to determine if the information was requested. If it was, the traffic is allowed to pass. If the traffic was not requested, it is dropped at the firewall and does not enter the computer. The result is data from the Internet that you request, such as web pages, are allowed to enter your computer, and anything that should arrive at the firewall (such as a hacker attack) that was not explicitly requested is not allowed to enter the firewall. ICF does not specifically block certain protocols or activity—it simply blocks any traffic that was not explicitly requested. The end result is nothing enters the computer that you didn't ask for. Blocked traffic is simply dropped, and this is done automatically without any intervention from you. In fact, ICF doesn't even tell you when communication from the Internet has been dropped.

An important point to remember concerning ICF is that ICF blocks nonrequested traffic—it is not a protective measure against viruses or Trojan horses. Windows XP does not provide any software to protect against these very real and common threats, so it is imperative that you install antivirus software on all computers on your network and keep that software up-to-date at all times.

ISSUES WITH ICF

ICF is designed to meet certain needs and provide a certain service; therefore, it is important that you keep a few issues in mind as you are working with it. First of all, ICF should be enabled on any shared Internet connection in your home or small office network. You do not have to use a home or small office network to use ICF—if you only have one computer and you want the additional protection, ICF works great on one computer too. ICF is not designed for use on a Windows domain where Windows 2000 Servers, DHCP servers, or DNS servers are in use—it is a home or small office networking solution only.

ICF works on a per-connection basis. For example, let's say your computer has a DSL connection and a modem connection. You use the modem connection in the event that the DSL connection goes down. You need to enable ICF on both the DSL and modem connections to have full protection. ICF is per connection—not per computer. In a small network setting using Internet Connection Sharing (ICS), you should certainly enable ICF on the ICS connection. However, if other computers on the network have other ways to connect to the Internet (such as through modems), you need to enable ICF on each of those connections as well.

In the same manner, each ICF connection stands alone. Any configuration changes you make to ICF are only for that particular connection. For example, if you have two connections and ICF is enabled on each of them, you must individually configure each connection as needed.

ICF should not be enabled on any computer's network adapter card that is used to connect to local computers. Doing so will prevent connectivity. ICF should only be used for connections to the Internet—not connections between computers on your private network. Also, ICF interferes with file sharing and other networking services, so you typically should enable ICF on VPN connections.

Outlook Express will work with ICF and will continue to automatically check for and download mail. Microsoft Office applications such as Outlook 2000 will not be able to check mail automatically because remote procedure calls (RPCs) are used with the mail server. The mail server must be able to contact the Outlook client, but in the case of ICF, direct communication like this will be blocked.

TURNING ON ICF

You can enable ICF through the Internet connection's Properties dialog box, or when you run the Network Setup Wizard. If you have configured ICS, then you were prompted to enable ICF as well. If you right-click any Internet connection found in the Network Connections folder and click Properties, you will see the Properties dialog box for that connection. Click the Advanced tab and you see the ICF check box. To turn on ICF, just enable the check box and click OK.

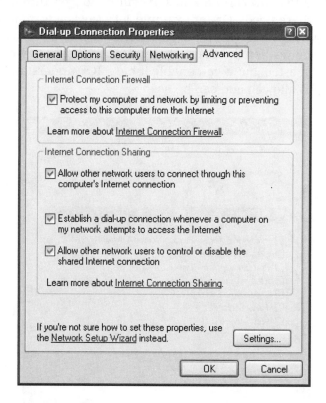

CONFIGURING ICF SETTINGS

For basic ICF use, you don't need to do anything except turn ICF on. However, there are some additional configuration options you may need. If you click the Settings button on the Advanced tab, you see advanced settings that govern how ICF works and what kinds of applications and services it allows. Again, you typically do not need to configure anything here if you are simply using the

Internet and accessing Internet mail. However, if you are using certain applications or you are providing certain types of content to the Internet, you may need to configure some of these settings.

The first tab is the Services tab, shown in the following illustration. ICF blocks all of the services you see listed here by default, because these services send information to your computer without being requested. For example, let's say that you are running a web server on your Windows XP Professional computer. If ICF is in use, you need to check the web server (HTTP) and possibly the secure web server (HTTPS) check boxes so that Internet users can access content on your web server. When you click these check boxes and click OK, ICF basically reconfigures itself to allow certain kinds of content to pass through the firewall in order to meet these needs. Or, for example, let's say you want to use Remote Desktop sharing with someone on the Internet. By default, ICF will not allow this kind of communication because communication is sent to your computer without being requested, but if you enable it here, ICF understands that Remote Desktop sharing is allowed and can be used.

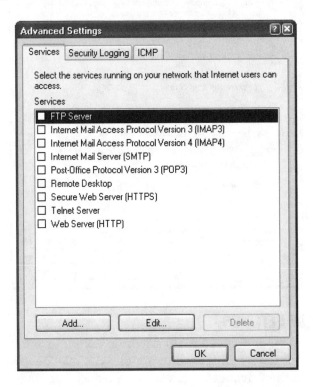

If you want to enable one of the services listed on the Services tab, just click the desired check box. An additional window appears where you must enter the name or IP address of the computer on your network that runs the service. Under most circumstances, you do not need to change any of the port information because Windows XP configures this information on its own. The computer name or IP address tells Windows XP which computer runs the service so that only that computer receives the service traffic—not other computers on your network. As you can see, this is an additional security feature that keeps service traffic from entering computers that do not offer the service.

If the service that you need to allow is not listed on the Services tab, you can click the Add button and enter the service name and TCP/IP port numbers on which the service communicates. Obviously, this is an advanced configuration, but the option is provided for networks that use custom applications or those who want to provide custom services to Internet users.

NOTE   The service options that you see here allow you to provide additional functionality. Basically, these services weaken the firewall by allowing certain kinds of traffic that are not initially allowed. While using these services is fine, do not enable anything that you are not directly using, because the use of services always increases the chances of a firewall breach.

The next tab is Security Logging. The security log is a simple text file where you can log successful connections, unsuccessful connections, or even both. Because ICF does not alert you when traffic is blocked from the firewall, you can use the security log to keep track of blocked traffic. This feature is a great way to see what the firewall is doing, and provides you a place to check for possible hacker attacks against your computer. By default, the security log is stored in C:\Windows\pfirewall.log, but you can click the Browse button on the Security Logging tab, shown in the next illustration, to change the location. Also notice that the log file has a maximum size of 4096KB by default (4MB). You can increase or decrease this space if you like. To enable logging for unsuccessful inbound or outbound connections, just click the desired check boxes.

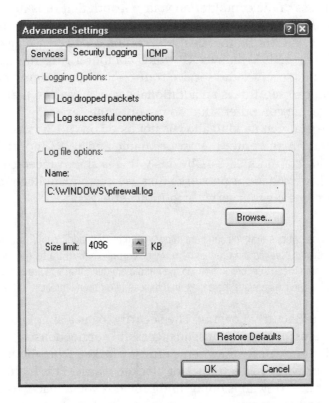

If you want to check out the log file, just browse the location of the file and open it (it will open with Notepad or any other text editor). As you can see in Figure 10-2, the log file contains TCP addressing and port information, and is not exactly easy to read. However, you can see how many firewall drops occurred over a period of time.

NOTE If you are the naturally curious type, you can copy and paste any destination IP address into a web browser and see the site that was accessed. Though not designed for this purpose, you can log all successful connections and see what sites a user has been accessing. Of course, a savvy user can edit this file and delete those sites as well.

The final tab is the ICMP tab. ICMP (Internet Control Message Protocol) is a protocol used on the Internet so that computers can send information to and from each other about network problems or transmissions problems. Ping is an

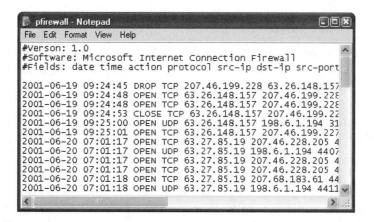

FIGURE 10.2   Firewall log

example of an ICMP tool. However, some attacks from the Internet act like ICMP messages, so by default, no ICMP messages are allowed on your network. Depending on your needs, however, you may want to enable some of these ICMP message types (or all of them). Just click the check boxes on the ICMP tab, shown in the following illustration, and you can select a message type and read more about it in the Description portion of the window.

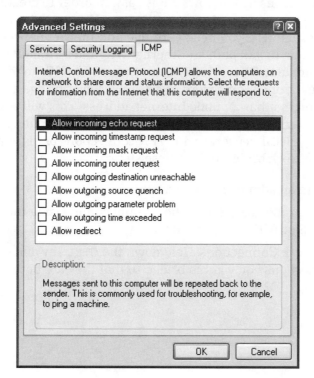

USING NETWORK BRIDGES

One issue that has always been a problem with networks is interoperability. For example, let's say you have two existing networks that use two different topologies. How can you connect the two networks together? This problem, in enterprise environments, can be very difficult and very costly.

However, the same problem can also occur in a home or small office network. For example, what if you have an Ethernet network in an office, but you want to use HomePNA for the rest of the house or add additional networked rooms to the existing network? In the past, you had to choose one topology or the other, but with Windows XP you can keep the existing Ethernet network and add the HomePNA network through a network bridge. A network bridge is a piece of software or hardware that can connect two dissimilar networks or network segments, and Windows XP provides a software bridge that allows a Windows XP computer to connect to dissimilar networks. In our example, the Ethernet and HomePNA networks will not readily communicate with each other, but you can use a Windows XP computer to act as the bridge between the two networks. The bridge basically acts as a translator between the two networks. To the users on the network, the bridge is invisible. Network users simply access network resources across the bridge without having to be aware of any topology issues.

Bridging connections in Windows XP is easy. In order to create the bridge, install a NIC from each network on the Windows XP computer that will act as the bridge. For example, if you need to bridge an Ethernet network and a HomePNA network, install both an Ethernet NIC and a HomePNA NIC on the Windows XP computer. Then, simply connect the two NICs to their respective networks. However, one strong word of warning: Never bridge a private network with a connection that has a public Internet address. This will open your private network to the Internet. Rather, use ICS to connect the computers to the Internet. Also, do not bridge local networks with VPN connections or dial-up connections.

To create a network bridge, follow these steps:

1. Log on with an administrative account.

2. Access the properties pages of both connections. Using the Advanced tab, turn off ICS or ICF if they are in use.

3. Open Network Connections. Hold down the CTRL key and click each of the LAN connections you want to bridge so that they are both selected.

4. Release the CTRL key. Then, right-click the selected adapters and click Bridge Connections.

5. Windows XP creates the network bridge. When the process is complete, the bridge appears in the Network Connections folder, along with the LAN connections that appear under the Bridge category, shown in Figure 10-3.

NOTE   The computer that contains the bridge must be turned on at all times for the two network segments to be bridged. If the bridge is offline, the segments will not be connected.

You can add or remove connections to the bridge at any time by right-clicking the Bridge icon and clicking Properties. You can only have one bridge on a Windows XP computer, but the bridge can support multiple connections (up to 64). For example, you could bridge two HomePNA network and two Ethernet networks all on the same bridge. You can easily add or remove connections from a bridge by right-clicking the bridge and clicking the connection and clicking Remove from Bridge or Add to Bridge, as needed.

FIGURE 10.3   The Network Bridge screen

CONNECTING TO A WINDOWS DOMAIN

Windows XP Professional is designed to function in a Windows domain and take advantage of all that domains have to offer. Although Windows XP Professional is an excellent choice for a home or small office network, it also contains the features necessary in a Windows domain. In a domain environment, the domain controllers hold the local security database and network administrators manage user and computer accounts through the Active Directory from a Windows 2000 or Windows .NET server.

User and computer accounts are configured in the Active Directory by a domain administrator. Rather than logging on using a local account, the Windows dialog box appears and users enter a domain username and password. A Windows domain controller then authenticates the user by checking the username and password with the Active Directory.

Windows XP Professional can be a domain member, but of course Windows XP cannot function as a domain controller. Before joining a Windows XP Professional computer to a domain, you'll need a few things set up and ready:

1. You must be using Windows XP Professional. Windows XP Home edition cannot join a Windows domain.

2. A network administrator must create a computer account for the computer in the Active Directory.

3. A network administrator must create a username and password for the user. You'll need this information, along with the name of the domain, when you configure your computer to join a domain.

4. The computer's TCP/IP settings should be set to Obtain an IP Address Automatically so that a DHCP server can provide a valid IP address for your computer.

5. Your computer must be configured with a NIC and physically connected to the network.

6. You can join a domain with wizard help, or you can do so manually. If you do not have a lot of experience using the manual approach, use the wizard to get you started.

The following steps show you how to join a domain using the Network Identification Wizard. Log on with a local administrator account, then follow these steps.

1. Click Start | Control Panel | System.

2. In the System Properties dialog box, click the Computer Name tab. As you can see, the Computer Name tab gives you a computer description and Network ID and Change buttons.

3. Click the Network ID button. This opens the Network Identification Wizard, which guides you through the rest of the process. Click Next on the Welcome page that appears.

4. The next window asks you if the computer will be a part of a business network (domain) or a home/small office computer (workgroup). Select the business network option and click Next.

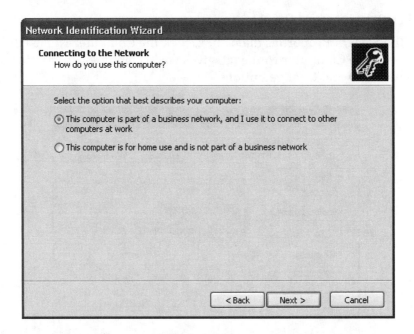

5. In the Connecting a Network page, select the My Company Uses a Network with a Domain option and click Next.

6. The next page tells you about the username, password, domain name, and possibly the computer name information that you will need. Click Next once you have read the page.

7. On the User Account and Domain Information page, enter your username, password, and domain name. Keep in mind that the password is case sensitive. Click Next.

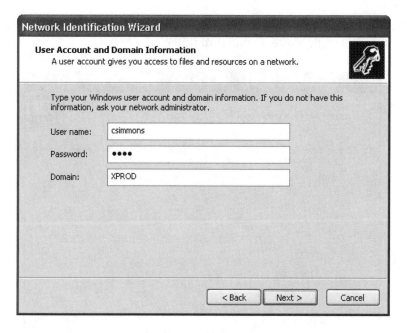

8. You may also be asked to verify the computer and the domain. If so, enter the information in the provided page and click Next.

9. In the User Account window, you can choose to add the domain user account to the local user accounts so that the user can gain access to local system resources. This feature enables you to limit what the user can do on the local machine or even make the user account a local administrator account. For example, I am logging on to a domain using my username, csimmons. However, I also want administrative control over my local computer. So, I simply agree to add the new user account to the local computer. I can then log on locally with my administrative account and make this domain account a local administrator account. Now, I have one

login for the domain that allows me to completely manage my local computer as well. Make a selection and click Next.

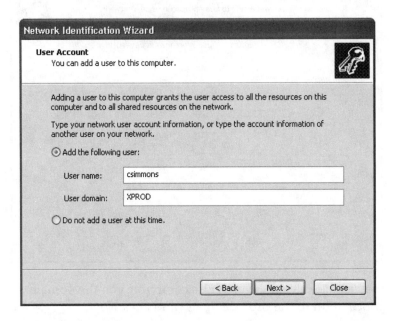

10. If you chose to add the user, choose the level of permission that you want to assign, and click Next.

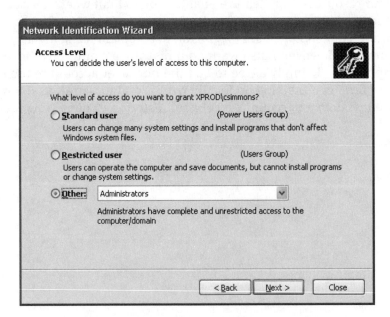

11. Click Finish. A prompt appears for you to restart your computer.

If you want to avoid the wizard approach to joining a domain, you can more quickly do so by using the Change button option on the Computer Name tab of System Properties. This option basically distills the wizard pages to a single dialog box, where you enter the computer name and (if necessary) click the option to log on to a Windows domain, and enter the domain name. Simply click OK to join the domain and enter the username and password for your domain account when prompted. You'll need to restart your computer once you complete the joining process.

USING REMOTE DESKTOP

Remote Desktop is a new Windows XP feature that makes use of terminal services from Windows 2000. Using Remote Desktop, you can connect to a remote Windows XP Professional computer from another client. For example, you could connect to an office computer from a remote office over the local area network or even the wide area network. Or, you can connect to an office computer over the Internet. Remote Desktop gives you more flexibility and allows you to access resources residing on a Windows XP computer from a remote location. When you access the computer remotely, a terminal window appears where you can open files, launch programs, configure system changes, browse folders—basically anything you might do if you were sitting at the computer locally.

Remote Desktop is generally easy to use and set up, but depending on the needed configuration, you might have a few networking snags to work through. Keep in mind the following important points and restrictions concerning Remote Desktop:

■ Windows XP Professional can function as a Remote Desktop host in that other computers can connect to it. You can connect to a Windows XP Professional computer and manage it remotely using Windows XP Professional or Windows XP Home Edition, or by installing the Remote Desktop Connection software on Windows 2000, Windows NT 4, Windows Me, Windows 98, or Windows 95. We'll explore the setup and configuration of the Remote Desktop Connection software (see "Using Remote Desktop" later in this chapter).

■ Remote Desktop allows multiple users to connect to the same computer so that different users can access different resources and run different applications as needed. When a remote user connects to the Remote Desktop host, the local desktop is locked. This prevents anyone from using the computer while you are logged on remotely.

■ Each client accessing the Remote Desktop host must have a direct connection to the host. This can be accomplished using a LAN/WAN connection, a dial-up connection, or a VPN connection, or it can be done over the Internet if the Remote Desktop host has a public IP address. We'll explore these options in the next few sections.

TURNING ON REMOTE DESKTOP

The Remote Desktop software runs on Windows XP Professional, so in order to use Remote Desktop, you must first turn on the service on the Windows XP Professional computer that will act as the Remote Desktop host. Other computers can then access the host remotely. To turn on Remote Desktop on a Windows XP Professional computer, follow these steps:

1. Log on to the Windows XP Professional computer as a member of the Administrators group. You cannot enable Remote Desktop without an administrator account.

2. Click Start | Control Panel | System. In the System Properties dialog box, click the Remote tab.

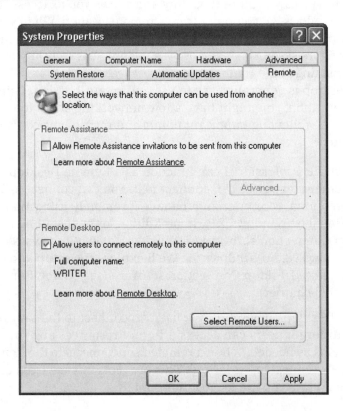

3. Select the Allow Users to Connect Remotely to This Computer check box in order to enable Remote Desktop. Once the setting is enabled, the current user and any member of the Administrators or Remote Desktop groups can access the computer using Remote Desktop. However, you might want to change the default settings to allow/prevent users from accessing Remote Desktop. One important note to remember is that any user who attempts to use Remote Desktop must have a password. Remote Desktop connections do not allow blank passwords. To manage the users that can access the Remote Desktop, click the Select Remote Users button.

4. In the Remote Desktop Users dialog box, you can click the Add button to add users to the Remote Desktop group, or use the Remove button to remove users from that group. Keep in mind that local administrators automatically have access. When you are done, click OK.

Once the Remote Desktop host is configured, you can then connect to the Remote Desktop and start a terminal session. However, before doing so, you'll need to determine how you will connect and work with any networking issues concerning the connection method that you need. The following sections explore your options.

CONNECTING OVER A LAN/WAN   Connecting to a Remote Desktop host over a LAN or WAN is the easiest way to connect. The client computer uses the host computer's IP address to make a direct connection. There is no additional configuration you have to work with.

CONNECTING USING A DIAL-UP CONNECTION   You can connect to a Remote Desktop host through a dial-up connection to that host. For example, let's say your work computer resides in a small office. The computer has a modem and is connected to the phone line. In order to access your work computer from a home computer, you first use the Create a New Connection Wizard on your work computer to configure the computer to accept incoming calls. Then, from your home computer, configure a dial-up connection to dial the work computer's number. You can then dial the work computer directly and create a remote desktop session.

CONNECTING USING THE INTERNET   You can connect to a Remote Desktop host over the Internet, but the process can be complicated. When a computer is connected to the Internet, it is assigned an IP address by the ISP. This public IP address must be used in order to make the remote desktop connection. The problem, however, is that public IP addresses change frequently. For example, if you are using a modem to connect to the Internet, each time you connect you are generally given a new dynamic IP address. Even with broadband connections, such as cable and DSL, the IP addresses may frequently change. There is no direct workaround for this issue; the simple fact is that you must know the IP address of the computer in order to connect to it. To find the public IP address, connect to the Internet, then double-click the connection in Network Connections. Click the Details tab and you'll see the current public IP address. You can then use this IP address to connect to the host from the client computer. If you are using a dial-up connection, you must leave the host computer connected to the Internet in order to make the Remote Desktop connection.

CONNECTING THROUGH A REMOTE ACCESS SERVER   If you need to connect to a Remote Desktop host over the Internet and through a remote access server, you should use a virtual private network (VPN) connection. This will give you the most security when using the Remote Desktop host over the Internet. The RAS must be configured by an administrator to allow VPN traffic. Once you connect to the network, you can start the Remote Desktop session with the host by simply connecting to it using the host's IP address.

TROUBLESHOOTING

Trouble with Firewalls

As you can imagine, firewalls are typically not very friendly to Remote Desktop connections by default. Most firewalls will not, by default, allow Remote Desktop traffic. If you need to connect to a Remote Desktop host that resides behind a firewall, keep these points in mind to solve the firewall issue:

- If you are using Internet Connection Firewall on the host computer, you need to access the Advanced Settings dialog box and enable Remote Desktop traffic. This will allow Remote Desktop traffic to pass through the firewall once the service is enabled.

- If the host computer resides on a LAN that is protected by a firewall, or if another individual firewall product is used, you'll need to ask an administrator to configure the firewall to allow incoming access on TCP port 3389. Remote Desktop uses TCP port 3389, and the connection will fail if the firewall is not configured to allow incoming access on this port. The connecting user has to allow outgoing traffic on TCP port 3389 as well.

CONFIGURING THE REMOTE DESKTOP CLIENT

Once the Remote Desktop host is set up and you have determined how you will connect to it, you can then configure the Remote Desktop client.

In Windows XP, the client software is known as Remote Desktop Connection, which was called Terminal Services Client in previous versions of Windows. The Remote Desktop Connection software enables a client to generate a terminal services connection with the host. If you are using Windows XP Professional or Windows XP Home Edition, there is nothing you need to configure. The Remote Desktop Connection software is already installed and configured on the system. Simply click Start | All Programs | Accessories | Communications | Remote Desktop Connection.

If you are using Windows 2000, Windows NT 4.0, Windows Me, Windows 98, or Windows 95, you must install the Remote Desktop Connection software on those computers. The Remote Desktop Connection software is found on the Windows XP CD-ROM. Insert the CD-ROM in the desired client and choose Perform Additional Tasks, then choose the Set Up/Remove Remote Desktop Connection option. This will install the software. If you do not have a Windows XP CD-ROM available, you can also download the software from Microsoft's web site at http://www.microsoft.com/windowsxp/pro/downloads/rdclientdl.asp. Follow the simple setup instructions that appear.

ESTABLISHING A REMOTE DESKTOP CONNECTION

To start the Remote Desktop connection from a Windows XP client, click Start | All Programs | Accessories | Communications | Remote Desktop Connection. If you are connecting from a down-level client, click Start | Programs | Accessories | Communications | Remote Desktop Connection. The Remote Desktop Connection dialog box appears.

If you are connecting a host that resides on your LAN or WAN, simply enter the computer's name or IP address. If you are connecting through a VPN connection or over the Internet, use the IP address of the remote host. After you have entered the name or IP address, just click Connect. Once the connection is made, the screen turns black and then you see a login dialog box.

Enter a username and password that is a member of the Remote Desktop group or one that has administrative privileges and click OK. Remember that blank passwords cannot be used. You must use an account that has a password. Once the username and password have been accepted, the terminal window provides your remote desktop, as shown in Figure 10-4.

FIGURE 10.4 Remote Desktop session

Remote vs. Local Computer

Keep in mind as you are working with the remote desktop that you can open applications and create and save files. However, the files you create, edit, and save are saved on the remote computer—you are simply seeing a terminal of what is happening on the remote computer. For this reason, you cannot save files to your local client desktop and you cannot drag and drop items from the terminal window (host computer) to your local computer (client computer).

TROUBLESHOOTING

Multiple Users

Windows XP's Remote Desktop allows multiple users, but there are a couple of rules that are followed. For example, let's say that you have a Remote Desktop account to access a computer from your home office. However, sometimes other administrators use the Windows XP Professional computer at the office when you are not there. In this case, one of two things can happen:

- First, if Fast User Switching is enabled on the remote computer, the remote user sees a message stating that the remote user wishes to log on. The user sitting at the computer locally has the ability to reject your message and keep you from logging on by clicking the No button. If no one is actually sitting at the computer (but it is logged on), the local user is logged off because there is no response. However, the local user's session remains logged on because Fast User Switching is enabled, so all applications and all open files remain that way. However the local user will not be able to use the computer until you log off.

- If Fast User Switching is not enabled on the remote computer, you have the option to forcefully log the local user off the computer. However, the local user will not have the

Multiple Users (continued)

option to save any open files. Because of the potential for lost data, it is best to use Fast User Switching with Remote Desktop so that any local users accessing the computer will not lose data. On the other hand, in this same scenario, a local administrator can forcefully log on, disconnecting the remote user. Or, if the same account is used by more than one person, the local user can always disconnect the remote user. The exception, though, is that a nonadministrator cannot forcefully disconnect an administrator who is logged on.

MANAGING REMOTE DESKTOP PERFORMANCE

Because Remote Desktop creates a terminal window of the activity found at the remote computer, performance can be a problem over slow network links. For example, let's say you are using a dial-up connection to connect to a remote desktop. Because of the graphical nature of Windows XP, the Remote Desktop connection may perform slowly. As with most networking performance issues, it all comes down to bandwidth. If you are connecting to a remote desktop over a LAN or WAN, you will likely have plenty of available bandwidth for the connection. Dial-up connections, though, are often slow.

In order to manage the performance of Remote Desktop, Windows XP gives you some configuration options that can help speed up Remote Desktop service, giving you better performance by removing some graphical elements.

To configure the performance options, open the Remote Desktop connection, and in the Remote Desktop Connection dialog box, click the Options button. You see several available tabs. Click the Experience tab, shown in Figure 10-5.

Use the drop-down menu to select your connection speed, then use the check boxes to specify further connection options. By reducing the usage of items, such as Display Background, the amount of bandwidth required to transmit the images to your remote computer is reduced. You can adjust these settings as needed until you find the performance level that meets your needs.

You can also click the Display tab, which will modify how Windows handles the remote session in the terminal window. You can lower the resolution and the colors used in the terminal window in order to lower bandwidth usage.

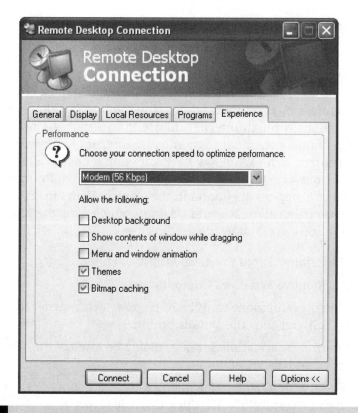

FIGURE 10.5   The Experience tab

The Local Resources tab gives you some configuration options that can also help performance. There are three categories found on this tab for Sound, Keyboard, and Local Resources. You can choose to have sounds downloaded and played locally, such as in the case of Windows events, but this option does consume more bandwidth. The Keyboard option allows you to use special key combinations that will operate when the remote session is open. The options you'll find here are self-explanatory. Finally, Local Resources enables the mapping of client disk drives, printers, and serial port to the remote host. This option allows you to map drives from the remote host to your local computer. For example, let's say you are working on the remote computer but you want to print the document on your home computer (remote client). This feature allows you to do that, or even access information on your local drives from within the terminal window.

USING REMOTE DESKTOP WITH INTERNET EXPLORER

You may find it easier to open a Remote Desktop session using Internet Explorer rather than the Remote Desktop Connection software. In order to use Internet Explorer to open a remote terminal window, you must configure the Windows XP Professional computer that is the Remote Desktop host for web services. This is done through Internet Information Services. Once configured, you can then generate a terminal session using Internet Explorer 4.0 or later.

In order to configure the Windows XP Professional host to allow web connections, you must first install IIS. Use the Add/Remove Programs/Add/ Remove Windows Components option in the Control Panel to install IIS. Then, you can configure IIS to allow Remote Desktop, which runs the Remote Desktop Web Connection software. Follow these steps:

1. Click Add/Remove Programs in the Control Panel.

2. Click Add/Remove Windows Components.

3. In the Windows Components Wizard page, select Internet Information Services (IIS) and click the Details button.

4. In the Internet Information Services dialog box, select the World Wide Web Service and click Details.

5. In the World Wide Web Service dialog box, select Remote Desktop Web Connection and click OK. Click OK twice more and complete the wizard.

Once the Remote Desktop Web Connection component is installed, you now need to set the permissions. Follow these steps:

1. Click Start | Control Panel | Administrative Tools | Internet Information Services.

2. Expand the computer name, then navigate to Web Sites/Default Web Site/tsweb.

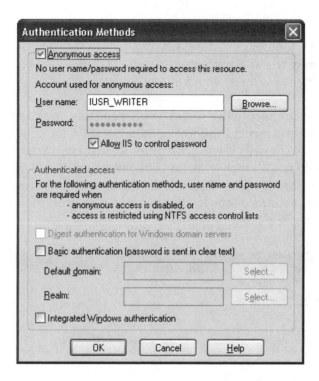

3. Right-click the tsweb container and click Properties.

4. Click the Directory Security tab and click Edit under Anonymous Access and Authentication Control.

5. In the Authentication Methods dialog box, ensure that anonymous access is allowed and click OK. Anonymous access only gives a remote user access to the IIS directory. Once connected, Remote Desktop will still require a username and password.

Once the remote computer is configured to allow web access to Remote Desktop, you can use your client computer to connect. Make sure you are using Internet Explorer 4 or later to make the connection. If you are connecting over the Internet to the remote computer, use the computer's public IP address to connect. Finally, if you are connecting through a RAS, make the connection and use the name or IP address of the remote desktop to generate the connection.

To connect to the remote desktop using Internet Explorer, open Internet Explorer and type the default address, which is http://*server*/tsweb. Again, if you are connecting over the Internet, use the public IP address to connect, as in http://*ipaddress*/tsweb. You'll see a Remote Desktop Web Connection screen, shown in Figure 10-6.

When you first connect to the server, you'll probably see a security warning (depending on your Internet Explorer configuration). The Remote Desktop installs an ActiveX control on your computer, so just click Yes to the security warning (if you do not, Remote Desktop will not work). You'll see the same Logon dialog box. Enter your username and password and click OK. The Remote Desktop sessions opens in Internet Explorer or in full screen mode, depending on your selection.

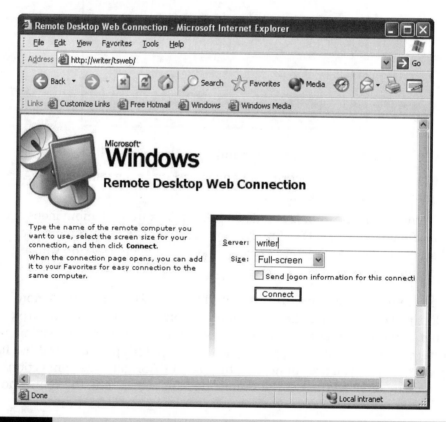

FIGURE 10.6 The Remote Desktop Web Connection screen

WIRELESS NETWORKING

Wireless networking has offered a lot of promise over the past few years, and rightly so—after all, who doesn't want an office without wires and the flexibility to easily move around. However, wireless networking has faced a lot of challenges and has not been widely adopted. However, with recent standards and recent security features, wireless networks are becoming more popular, both in larger networks and even home and small office networks. Windows XP Professional contains all of the wireless networking software you need, and it fully supports the major wireless networking standards available today.

Both Windows XP Professional and Windows XP Home editions support infrared and 802.11b wireless networking. Infrared networking uses an infrared beam of light to transfer information from one computer to another, or from a device to a computer, such as a digital camera to a computer. The infrared transfer works a lot like a direct cable connection—the process is a one-way transfer, and for this reason, infrared is a great way to move data wirelessly, but it is not a true networking solution.

The 802.11b standard, which is also called Wi-Fi, is the most popular wireless networking standard in use today, providing transfer rates of around 11 Mbps. In a Wi-Fi network, you have a range of up to 300 meters, and it provides the best wireless security that is currently available. Because Wi-Fi is the most popular, you'll find plenty of wireless network devices at any computer store that are compatible with Windows XP. If you are shopping for wireless devices, look for compatibility information right on the box. Also, you should see an "802.11b standard" or "Wi-Fi standard" note on the box as well.

UNDERSTANDING INFRARED

Infrared networking is a line-of-sight technology that transfers data over an infrared beam of light, just like a grocery store scanner. Since the technology is a line-of-sight technology, the two infrared devices must be in range and aligned, or pointing to each other. The single infrared beam then transfers the data. Since you have to line up the two infrared ports on the two computers or the device (such as a PDA) and the computer, infrared networking is not as practical as Wi-Fi.

UNDERSTANDING WI-FI

Wi-Fi networks provide two different topologies, or modes, both of which are supported by Windows XP. The two modes, which are called infrastructure mode and ad hoc mode, meet different networking needs. In infrastructure mode, an existing wired LAN, such as Ethernet, extends to include wireless devices. The wireless devices use a hub, called an access point, that connects to the wired LAN's hub. The access point manages all of the traffic between the wired network and the wireless devices, just as a typical hub might do.

The second kind of mode is ad hoc mode. Ad hoc mode allows one wireless computer to connect to another without the use of an access point in a direct connection method. When an access point is not used or is not available, the wireless computers can automatically shift into ad hoc mode so that they can communicate with each other without an access point. Of course, without an access point, the computers cannot access an existing wired Ethernet network. You can also use infrastructure mode and ad hoc mode at the same time, through a process called zero configuration. When in infrastructure mode, all wireless NICs look for an access point. If one is not found, the NICs switch to ad hoc mode so that communication with other computers within range can occur. Windows XP can automatically configure wireless NICs from infrastructure mode to ad hoc mode, and vice versa, without any manual configuration from you.

In order to create a wireless network, you'll need wireless NICs that are compatible with Windows XP, and you'll need an access point if you intend to use infrastructure mode. Of course, no cabling is necessary, with the exception of an RJ-45 cable, to connect the access point to an Ethernet hub. You'll find a variety of wireless devices by different manufacturers at your local computer store or from online stores.

SETTING UP AN INFRARED NETWORK

Infrared technology is a great (and easy) way to transfer data between two computers, or a device and a computer, such as a digital camera or even PDA. This kind of data transfer frees you from wires, but does require a line-of-sight connection. In order for Windows XP to communicate over infrared, the computer must be outfitted with an infrared port. Most laptop computers ship with an infrared port, and if you need one on a PC, you can purchase an infrared port device that connects to the computer via USB. As always, check the Microsoft HCL before purchasing an infrared device. Once you install an infrared device,

TECH TALK

Wireless Security

Security has been a prohibitive issue concerning wireless networking in the past. After all, you can't have a secure network if the data transmitted in the air is not secure. The 802.11b standard contains some basic security features for access points, called the service set identifier (SSID). An SSID is a known security identifier and it is taken from the NIC on each computer. The access point is aware of the SSID, and once it is taken from the NIC, an association with the NIC and the SSID is made on the access point. However, the SSID is not encrypted, which makes it available for theft during transit. As you can see, the 802.11b security standard really isn't that secure.

The standard that is most commonly used today and supported by Windows XP is called the Wired Equivalent Privacy (WEP). This security standard gives you an encryption scheme that provides a 40-bit encryption scheme or 104-bit encryption scheme. The encryption scheme prevents theft of data that is airborne, and this built-in standard provides a great measure of security, especially for home and small office wireless networks. Along with WEP, many wireless NICs also support a standard called 802.1x. The 802.1x standard provides authentication for access to Ethernet networks over a wireless access point. Using 802.1x, the access point authenticates users in conjunction with server software on the Windows network. Most major brands of wireless NICs support both the WEP and 802.1x standards.

you'll see a Wireless Link icon in the Control Panel. If you double-click the Wireless Link icon, you'll, see a few configuration tabs.

On the Infrared tab, you have a few basic options. You can display an icon on the taskbar indicating infrared activity. This option will allow you to see when you are connected to an infrared link and when another computer or device is within your infrared range. You can also choose to play sound when an infrared device is nearby. Using the options you see here, you can allow others to send files to your computer using the infrared beam, and you can be notified when the computer is receiving files. Finally, you can choose a default location in which to store files.

On the Image Transfer tab, you can choose to use the wireless link to transfer images from a digital camera to your computer. Enable the option and choose a default storage location for the picture files as they arrive.

The Hardware tab simply lists the infrared device that is installed. You can see basic information about the device, such as the manufacturer, the COM port location, and the current device status. If you select the device in the window and click the Properties button, the Device Manager properties dialog box opens. You'll see the standard General and Driver tabs, but there is also an IrDA Settings tab that may come in handy. This tab allows you to set the maximum connection rate as well as the COM port. If you are having problems with communications with a certain device, try lowering this value.

Once the infrared connection is configured, you can establish two kinds of infrared connections. The first is an infrared link, which allows the computer to communicate with another computer or device over an infrared link. You can connect with another Windows XP computer, a Windows 2000 computer, a Windows 98 computer, or other devices such as PDAs and digital cameras. This kind of link connection allows you to transfer files from one computer/device to the other computer/device.

To create an infrared link:

1. Move the infrared computers or devices so that the infrared receivers are facing each other and are less than one meter apart.

2. When the infrared device is detected, an icon appears in your Notification Area and the Wireless Link icon appears on the desktop.

3. Right-click the Wireless link icon and click Connect. The connection is made and data can now be transferred.

The second kind of connection is an infrared network connection. The infrared network connection is like the link connection, but it is used between two computers to create a direct connection. This kind of connection works like a direct cable connection—one computer acts as the host and one computer acts as the guest. The guest computer provides a username and password, and then can access shared information on the host computer. The guest computer can even map to shared drives and folders. To set up an infrared network connection between two computers, follow these steps:

1. On the host computer, create a user account for the guest computer if necessary.

2. Align the two computers so that the infrared transceivers are less than one meter apart and are pointing at each other.

3. The Infrared icon appears in the Notification Area and the Wireless Link icon appears on the desktop.

4. To establish the network connection, open Network Connections and click Create a New Connection.

5. Click Next on the Welcome screen.

6. In the Network Connection Type window, choose Set Up an Advanced Connection. Click Next.

7. On the Advanced Connection Options page, choose Connect Directly to Another Computer and click Next.

8. Choose the role of the computer, which is the Host computer in this example. Click Next.

9. On the Connection Device page, choose the infrared port as the connection device. Click Next.

10. In the User Permissions window, choose the accounts that can connect over the infrared port. Click Add if you need to add additional accounts. Click Next.

11. Click Finish. The connection now appears in Network Connections as Incoming Connection.

12. On the guest computer, repeat this same process, but choose the Guest option. When the wizard is complete, both computers can open the connection in the Network Connections folder and click File | Connect to start the infrared network session.

SETTING UP AN 802.11B NETWORK

In order to set up an 802.11b, you'll first need to decide if you want to use infrastructure mode or ad hoc. If you want to use infrastructure mode, you'll need to purchase a wireless access point. If you only want to use ad hoc mode, only the wireless NICs are needed. Keep in mind that if you purchase a wireless access point, you can still use ad hoc mode if needed. As you are shopping for hardware, also keep in mind that some access points can also act as routers or residential gateways for Internet access. Once you install 802.11b NICs, Windows XP configures the NICs automatically to look for an access point. If no access point is found, Windows XP reconfigures the NICs to use ad hoc mode. When the connection to the wireless network is attempted after the NIC is installed, a Connect to Wireless Network dialog box appears, where you can choose the wireless network you want to connect to and provide the WEP key, if required by the network.

In most cases, Windows XP does a good job of automatically managing the wireless network connections and configuration. However, you can also access the NIC's properties pages and manually configure some settings if necessary. The following steps show the options.

1. Open Network Connections and right-click the wireless connection. Click Properties.

2. On the Wireless Networks tab, notice that by default, Windows configures the wireless network settings for you. You see the available networks and the preferred networks. If you need to configure an available network that you want to connect to, select the option in the Available Networks list and click Configure.

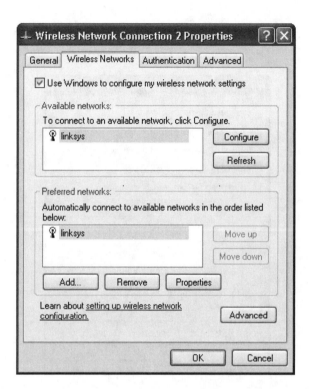

3. The Wireless Network Properties dialog box appears. By default, the wireless data encryption and network authentication is enabled. If you need to enter the network key manually, do so in this dialog box and configure any necessary options. Check the NIC's documentation for details. Under most circumstances, the key is provided automatically and the options here are grayed out. Notice also that if you are using ad hoc mode, you can disable the settings on this tab by choosing the This Is a

Computer-to-Computer (Ad Hoc) Network; Wireless Access Points Are Not Used.

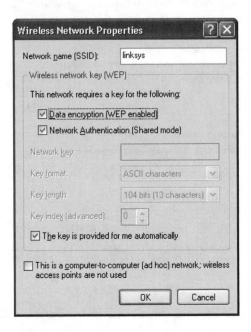

4. In the Preferred Networks list, you can reorganize the list if you have more than one network by using the Move Up or Move Down buttons. Place the network that you use most often at the top of the list in order to speed up your initial access to that network.

5. If you only want to connect to access point networks or you only want to connect to ad hoc networks, click the Advanced button at the bottom of the Wireless Networks tab. You see an Advanced dialog box. By default, any available network (access point preferred) is selected. If you want to restrict the connection to only access points or ad hoc networks, choose the desired option.

WRAPPING UP...

Windows XP Professional provides a number of networking features that bring flexibility to the networking table. Windows XP Professional provides all of the software necessary to create effective home and small office networks, connections to Windows domains, remote networking, and even wireless networking. Now that you have taken a look at networking with Windows XP, in the next chapter we'll focus our attention on networking with NetWare.

NETWORKING WITH NETWARE 5

11

Novell NetWare is a prominent network operating system designed to provide a wide range of networking services. While it has become subordinate in distribution to other NOS options, there are many situations where NetWare is still in wide use. In particular, large businesses, government agencies, and some educational institutions are highly dependent on the NetWare operating environment. Because this NOS is important, we will look a variety of concepts and procedures that will be useful if you are involved in deploying and supporting NetWare 5 in the role of network server. In this chapter, we'll…

■ Install NetWare 5 on a supported server platform

■ Configure NetWare to provide file and printer services to network users

■ Configure NetWare networking services

■ Install the NetWare client on Windows 2000

■ Explore Novell Directory Services and common tools for managing NDS use

OVERVIEW OF NETWARE

NetWare is the flagship network operating system product produced by Novell. NetWare has been developed to play a large number of network server roles, from print and file server to application and web server. By most standards, NetWare has set the trend in NOS capabilities with products such as the Novell Directory Service (NDS)—which has inspired other networking services such as Microsoft's Active Directory. While not as widely popular as it once was, NetWare remains a capable and popular server operating platform.

INSTALLING NETWARE 5

NetWare installation can be an imposing task, especially if you are used to other systems such as Linux or Windows server products. If you keep a couple of basic ideas in mind while considering the installation process, you will end up saving yourself considerable headaches. In this section, we will look at installations as a two-part process. First, you need to plan—deciding how the server will be used, selecting hardware, and making some nontrivial decisions about how users will access the NetWare server from the network. Planning may be a bigger issue if you have a complex existing networking infrastructure, but even if this is the first server on a new network, planning is still important.

One specific example is deciding on what networking protocols you will enable your server to use: the Internet Protocol (IP), Internetwork Packet Exchange (IPX), or both. This particular topic will be specifically addressed later in this chapter since the nature of your networking protocols can have a dramatic effect on network performance, the kinds of networking hardware you can use, and how easy it will be to attach network clients to your LAN or WAN. The second stage is the actual installation. For this part, we will walk through processes for both new server installations and the upgrade of existing NetWare 4.11 servers.

PREPARING FOR INSTALLATION

The first step in your preparation for installation will be the selection of the hardware that will be used to house your server installation. The minimum system requirements for NetWare 5 are outlined here:

- **Processor** Pentium 133 MHz or faster.

- **CD-ROM** Capable of ISO 9660 disks and compatible with the El Torito standard that allows booting from the CD-ROM drive.

- **System RAM**   The system will need 64MB of RAM.

- **Hard disk**   A hard disk with a minimum of a 50GB DOS partition, or 1MB of disk space for every 1MB of RAM installed, as long as it's more than 50MB. Additional 550MB (minimum) available for the NetWare partition.

- **Network adapters**   Ethernet or token ring network adapter.

While these minimum settings will get you up and running, you won't be able to do much with your server. Most modern servers support far more robust systems components. It is highly recommended that you take advantage of this fact when building your server. A recommended configuration for a server that will support 50–100 network users, and that will be used to run server-side applications as well as store user files, should meet the following recommended specifications. Only the items that have different recommendations are included—other unlisted components mentioned in the minimum system requirements are still essential.

- **Processor**   Pentium 4 1.4 GHz or faster. NetWare supports multiprocessing as well, so feel free to make use of multiprocessor-capable systems.

- **System RAM**   You should install at least 512MB of RAM rated at least for 133-MHz operation (PC133). Memory throughput can be a significant limiter in overall systems performance, so you would be wise to use faster RAM technology (DDRAM or RDRAM) if your system has support for such technologies.

- **Hard disk**   A hard disk with a minimum of a 500GB DOS partition and an additional 30–100GB for applications and user data. A good rule of thumb is to allot 100MB of disk space per user for data files alone. If your users work with large data files (CAD or large graphics file), you should allot 1–5GB for each such user.

- **Network adapters**   Fast Ethernet, Gigabit Ethernet, or High Speed Token Ring (HSTR). If users are frequently accessing files on the server or they need to perform large file transfers (multigigabyte), you will be better served by HSTR or Gigabit Ethernet.

After you have obtained the hardware for your server, you will need to collect the information about your existing network, or the planned network. This information will ensure that you are able to interconnect your new or upgraded server with the users it will serve. You will need to collect (and have ready when you perform the installation) a couple of bits of information. If you are monitoring the state of the network with an SNMP monitor, you should have the community name available. You should also have the IP or IPX address of the monitoring station where SNMP events should be sent. If you will make use of the IPX protocol—either alone or in conjunction with IP—you will need to know the network number of your server. This network number and the MAC address of its network card will make up the IPX address of the server. If you will be using IP exclusively or in conjunction with IPX, you will need a bit more configuration information. You will need the IP address of the server, subnet mask, the default gateway, and the DNS name in use on the network (if indeed DNS is in use). Because the choice of networking protocols is an important issue, we will look at the options you have available in the next section.

CHOOSING A NETWORK PROTOCOL

The protocols used on your network will have a huge impact on the scalability—the ability to grow—of your network. Because the protocols used by your servers will for the most part determine the kinds of protocols used on your network, we'll spend some time comparing the supported protocols, IP and IPX.

INTERNETWORK PACKET EXCHANGE (IPX)

The IPX protocol was made popular almost entirely as the result of the NetWare operating system. IPX is a part of a protocol suite, IPX/SPX. Like TCP/IP, the IPX/SPX suite contains protocols designed to handle various parts of the network communications process. IPX is the portion of the suite responsible for addressing the hosts on the network. Like most other networking protocols, IPX requires that all hosts have unique addresses. The IPX address is an 80-bit address that is made up of a network and node (that is, host) portion. The user-specified network number and the Media Access Control (MAC) or physical address are combined to form the network address of the host. Because each network adapter made has a unique MAC address, the resulting combination ensures that all hosts on a particular network can be uniquely identified. The IPX network address is stored as a hexadecimal value, and is far less user friendly than the comparable IP addresses. Though this is the case, it is actually easier to configure an IPX address since the network number is represented as a nice and tidy number such as 0001.

In addition to the network and node address, there is a component known as a socket number. This value directly correlates to the IP port number, and it is used to sort network traffic based on the application using the network.

IPX makes use of a variety of encapsulation types. Encapsulation is basically the method used to wrap data from other processes so that it may be transported across a network reliably. When configuring IPX network adapters, this information is very important since adapters using one encapsulation type cannot communicate with adapters that are not using the same encapsulation type. There are four encapsulation types used by IPX. Those encapsulation types are

- **Ethernet II**   This is essentially the same as the ubiquitous Ethernet specification. The only difference is a gory technical detail—the source and destination address fields are followed by an EtherType field that is used to identify the kind of information that follows the encapsulation header. Essentially, it is employed to recognize the kind of network protocol in use, such as IP, IPX, or ARP.

- **Novell 802.2**   This is the IPX implementation of the Ethernet standard, which basically rearranges the order of the encapsulation fields of the standard Ethernet (or Ethernet II) specification.

- **Novell Ethernet 802.3**   Uses a proprietary IPX header integrated within the standard Ethernet fields to support proprietary methods of communication.

- **Ethernet SNAP**   SNAP specifies a standard method of encapsulating IP communications in a manner necessary to performing three functions: reliable data transfer, connection management (establishing and breaking connections), and maintenance of quality of service (QoS) standards.

There is one other component of the IPX/SPX protocol stack you need to be aware of: the Service Advertising Protocol (SAP). SAP is used by NetWare servers to advertise the resources they have available for client use. For example, SAP is used by NetWare servers to advertise file and printer shares. SAP is also used to identify the IPX address of NetWare servers. SAP uses network broadcasts to distribute information among the network hosts. The information sent out in the SAP transmission includes descriptive information about the services offered by the advertising server in the form of a SAP table. If the server has a large number of shares and other services, the SAP table can become quite large. This behavior is probably the biggest shortcoming of the IPX/SPX protocol suite. Because SAP uses regular broadcasts to pass service-related information between all of the servers on the same network, there is a limit to the scalability of purely IPX networks.

PAINFUL
LESSONS

I'VE LEARNED

Choke the LAN with IPX

When working at a customer site in an effort to troubleshoot problems with a huge software package, I learned the hard way about the negative effect of broadcast-based behavior IPX. The LAN I was working on had ten NetWare servers and 500+ users. Periodically, 50–100 of the users would be running a complex (if poorly built) software package that made large file transfers between the client and the server. Problem was that when more than 50 or 60 users were logged on, the network would slow to a crawl. As it turns out, the SAP traffic from the NetWare servers was slowing network communications just enough to cause some components of the software package in use to time out. The resolution involved many network changes, since converting to a completely IP network was not possible. Comparable network configurations working in an IP-only environment did not experience the same issues. The lesson learned was that we needed to adjust the recommended network settings for IPX-enabled networks to make sure that the product would operate as expected, while recommending IP as the preferred solution.

Without careful planning, a routed IPX network can become overwhelmed by broadcast traffic. One advantage of this behavior is that every client on the network has a list of all available network services at all times, and this speeds the accessing of networked resources compared to comparable IP networks. The performance of IPX is further enhanced by the fact that IPX communications have less overhead than other network protocols and thus move data faster across the network than other contemporary protocols, such as IP.

You're probably going to be better off using IPX over IP if you have a smaller network, where the ease of use is more important than the scalability of IP. Because a small network with few servers will not generate very large volumes of network traffic, the solution could be ideal. If you need IP as well—for Internet access, for example—you can install the Migration Agent on the server so that it can translate between IPX and IP networks.

TROUBLESHOOTING

Troubleshooting IPX

Though IPX is fairly simple to configure, there are occasions where newly configured clients fail to connect to the network. In such cases, you will need to check a couple of critical areas and verify that the settings on the host in question are correct. The first thing to check is the frame type. Typically, there is an option within the IPX settings that allows you to select a frame type of "auto." If this does not work, check the adapter settings on a working network host and implicitly set the failed system to match. Another item you need to check is the network number of the failing host. If the number does not match that of the other workstations, it will continue to fail in connection attempts.

INTERNET PROTOCOL (IP)

Since the topic is covered elsewhere in detail (see Appendix A), we will not spend much time here discussing the details of IP addressing. Instead, we will focus on the strengths, weaknesses, and general role that IP plays as the primary or complementary protocol on your NetWare server. IP is very scalable as a network protocol, and you will easily be able to support networks that range from a few users to hundreds of connected hosts at a time. In addition to the scalability of IP, there are several other key benefits:

- IP is the standard for all Internet-connected computer systems. If computers on your network will access the Internet, they will need to use IP, or a designated IPX-enabled server will need to use IP and migration services.

- IP is supported by every major operating system implementation and operating environment, from the earliest networked operating systems, such as DOS, to the latest operating systems from IBM, Microsoft, and Novell.

If you are upgrading from NetWare 4.11, it is very likely that you have some host that depends on IPX for connectivity. If this is the case, you may be better off with both IP and IPX. One downside to this configuration (IP and IPX) is that you take the performance hit of IPX and still have to deal with the sometimes complex configuration of IP addresses and the associated IP services.

If you are still in need of guidance about which protocol to use, look at it like this: If you have an existing IPX implementation or a very small network, IPX may be a practical solution. However, since there is a limited quantity of IPX-capable routing products, there are serious limitations on IPX scalability, and given the prevalence of IP-dependent software and hardware, you are probably best off selecting IP only or IP and IPX if you are unsure.

NOTE You should not attempt the following procedure on a working system if you will need that system for work-related tasks. This process will wipe clean the hard drive of the system and build a clean installation of NetWare.

PERFORMING A NEW INSTALLATION

Once you have all of the information you need in hand and you have made a decision about how you want the networking components to operate, you are ready to begin your clean installation. The installation process occurs in two phases. The first involves creating a DOS partition that you can use to begin the installation. The second phase is the graphical NetWare installation that uses your newly built DOS partition to get NetWare up and running.

TECH TALK

Creating a DOS Boot Disk

If you find that you need to build a bootable DOS disk, you can use any available DOS system (but not Window 95/98) in order to create a usable disk. In order to accomplish this, you need to insert a blank floppy into your DOS system and from the command prompt run the command sys A:. This command will copy the operating system files to the floppy. After this copy completes, search the computer for the files format.com and fdisk.com. Copy each of these files to the newly created boot floppy and you will be ready to go.

To complete the initial setup of the hard drives in anticipation of installing NetWare, follow the steps outlined here. You will need to use the DOS FORMAT and FDISK commands. If you do not have DOS installed, you can use another operating system to create boot disks as described earlier, or you can use the license floppy that came in your NetWare media package. To prepare the disk, follow these steps:

1. Run the FDISK command and select option 3 to remove the existing partitions.

2. Once the partitions have been removed, exit back to the main FDISK menu and select option 1 to create a DOS partition.

3. Follow the prompt to create a primary partition that is at least 50MB in size, or in line with the recommendations earlier in this chapter. After completing this step, exit FDISK and reboot your PC.

4. Once the partition is created, use the FORMAT /S command to format the new partition as bootable.

This completes the first phase of the installation process. If your system supports booting from the CD-ROM, you can simply insert the NetWare CD and reboot the computer. If the system will not boot from a CD-ROM, you will need to install DOS and the DOS driver for your CD-ROM before you can continue. The following steps will walk you through the graphical portion of the NetWare installation process:

1. If you booted from the CD-ROM, skip to step 2. Otherwise, insert the NetWare installation CD, change to the CD-ROM drive (often D:\), type **INSTALL** and press the ENTER key. In either method, choose the installation language if prompted.

2. Read the licensing agreement and then accept the agreement.

3. On the next screen, select the New Server installation type. Press the F2 key to specify advanced installation settings.

4. When presented with the option, choose to use the CD-ROM via a NetWare driver. If this option is not available, select the option to use the DOS driver. The NetWare driver can often prove to be slightly more reliable, but in most cases you should not encounter problems regardless of the option you select.

5. Specify a server ID for your server. If you have no established requirement or established naming convention for a server ID, you can leave the

default ID in place. Press F10 to accept the configuration changes you made and select Continue.

6. When you have completed the advanced configuration, use the Modify option to change the country, keyboard mappings, and code page settings to the proper settings for your location and hardware.

7. Select the mouse and video type that matches your server's hardware and continue.

8. After copying some drivers, you will be able to specify the system drivers that match your server's hardware. If the detected options correctly match your hardware, you can choose Continue and move to the next step. If some of the hardware has been incorrectly identified, use the Modify option to specify the correct drivers. Once the correct hardware is specified, select Continue.

9. Now you will need to select your network adapters (network boards) and hard disks (storage devices). Again, if the devices have been correctly detected, you need not do anything else. If the driver selected is incorrect, or there is no device shown at all, use the Modify option and specify the correct driver. Within this screen you can specify NetWare Loadable Modules (NLM) that you wish to use during the installation. Unless you have a specific need for an NLM, you can ignore this functionality. When everything is configured as required, select Continue.

NOTE If you will be using a token ring network adapter, you will need to specify the ROUTE.NLM module in step #9.

10. The next screen will prompt you to specify the size of the NetWare volume that will house the SYS volume and the bulk of the NetWare operation files. You should choose a size of at least 1,000MB if there is sufficient disk space to do so. Leftover space can be used to create additional volumes at a later time. Press the F10 key to save the information you set for the SYS volume. Click Continue to commence the rest of the installation process.

After the completion of step 10, the NetWare operating system files will be copied to the newly created SYS volume. After the file transfer has completed, you will see the Installation Wizard. This wizard will take you through the remaining configuration process of your newly created server. The following steps outline those involved in completing the Installation Wizard:

1. Enter the name you will use for this server and click the Next button.

2. If you wish to configure new volumes, you may do so now. You should create at least one additional volume to accommodate user files. To create a new volume, click Free Space in the list of volumes, then click Create.

3. Enter a name for the volume—for example, **User**.

4. Next, choose NSS as the volume type.

5. Enter the size of the volume you wish to create in the Space to Use field and click Apply to Volume.

6. Click OK to return to the volume list, followed by Next.

7. Indicate if you would like the volumes mounted now or after installation. You can specify the location to install some of the add-on products and you will need to mount the volume you created if you wish to use a volume other than SYS.

8. In the Protocol screen that appears, select your network adapter and then select the protocols that you want to use with it: IP, IPX, or both. By selecting IP only, the system will install IPX compatibility mode to ensure interoperability with existing IPX hosts. Click the Next option to continue.

9. Select the time zone settings and daylight saving settings, if needed, and click Next.

10. Next, specify the NDS tree to join or create a new NDS tree and then click Next. If you are building an NDS tree from scratch, you can use any name for the tree and context that conforms to your network's naming conventions.

11. If you have an existing organizational unit to join the server to, use the Browse button to locate it. If not, you can specify a new OU for the server to join.

12. Enter the username, context, and password for the Admin user. If joining an existing NDS tree, use the proper Admin account. If not, you may specify any name, password, and context you desire. Once the Summary screen appears, review the information and click Next.

13. You will be prompted to enter the License diskette—place it in the floppy drive when prompted and click Next.

14. During the final file copy, allow all of the default services to install (you'll see an Option screen) and add Novell Distributed Print Services (NDPS). Click Next when finished. Walk through any additional service-related prompts as needed.

15. From the Summary screen that appears, click Finish. You will be prompted to reboot the server, and you should select the option to do so. Be sure to remove the installation CD and any floppy disks before rebooting. By default, when the server reloads, NetWare will load automatically.

Once the server has been rebooted, and NetWare has loaded, you can verify the availability of network services by installing the NetWare client on one of the network hosts and attempting to connect to the tree and context you specified during installations.

UPGRADING AN EXISTING INSTALLATION

So what do you do if you have an existing NetWare installation that you'd like to upgrade? If you follow the process outlined next, you can move from previous versions such as NetWare 4.11. Keep in mind that the server hosting the older installation will need to meet the minimum system specifications outlined earlier in this chapter. To upgrade an existing NetWare server, follow the steps here:

1. Make a backup of the existing files, such as user files and application data, that are stored on the server. This backup process should also include the copying of AUTOEXEC.NCF and the LAN drivers from the SYS volume so you will have them if you need them later.

2. Bring the existing server offline using the DOWN command.

3. Insert the NetWare 5 installation CD and run the INSTALL program. You can also insert the installation CD and reboot the server, or boot from the CD if your system's BIOS is configured to do so.

NOTE From this point forward the process is essentially the same as when performing a new installation. The steps are included here to identify the steps that differ should you find yourself upgrading a NetWare server.

4. In either method, choose the installation language if prompted.

5. Read the licensing agreement and select Accept Agreement.

6. On the next screen, select the Upgrade from 3.1x or 4.1x option for your installation type. Press the F2 key to specify advanced installation settings.

7. Select the mouse and video type that matches your server's hardware and continue.

8. After copying some drivers, you will be able to specify the system drivers that match your server's hardware. If the detected options correctly match

your hardware, you can choose Continue and move to the next step. If some of the hardware has been incorrectly identified, use the Modify option to specify the correct drivers. Once the correct hardware is specified, select Continue.

9. Now you will need to select your network adapters (network boards) and hard disks (storage devices). Again, if the devices have been correctly detected, you need not do anything else. If the drivers selected are incorrect, or there is no device shown at all, use the Modify option and specify the correct driver. Within this screen you can specify NetWare Loadable Modules (NLM) that you wish to use during the installation. Unless you have a specific need for an NLM, you can ignore this functionality. When everything is configured as required, select Continue.

After the completion of step 9, files will copy and the Install Wizard will launch. The following steps outline completing the Installation Wizard:

1. Indicate that you would like the volumes mounted now. You can specify the location to install some of the add-on products, and you will need to mount the volume you created if you wish to use a volume other than SYS.

2. In the Protocol screen that appears, select your network adapter and then select the protocols that you want to use with it: IP, IPX, or both. By selecting IP only, the system will install IPX compatibility mode to ensure interoperability with existing IPX hosts.

3. Next, specify the NDS tree to join and click Next.

4. If you have an existing organizational unit to join the server to, use the Browse button to locate it. If not, you can specify a new OU for the server to join.

5. Enter the username, context, and password for the Admin user. If joining an existing NDS tree, use the proper Admin account. If not, you may specify any name, password, and context you desire. Once the Summary screen appears, review the information and click Next.

6. You will be prompted to enter the License diskette—place it in the floppy drive when prompted and click Next.

7. During the final file copy, allow all of the default services to install (you'll see an Option screen) and add Novell Distributed Print Services (NDPS). Click Next when finished. Walk through any additional service-related prompts as needed.

8. Click the Finish button from within the Summary screen. Reboot when prompted, making sure to remove the installation CD and any floppy disk before rebooting. NetWare should load automatically.

SECRET

If you have upgraded from NetWare 3.x, you should probably check to make sure that the integrity of the new NDS information is intact. From the graphical interface of the server, press ALT+ESC and reopen the console view (command line). Run the command DSREPAIR. When you are prompted, select the Unattended Full Repair option. This process will ensure that the Novell Directory Service configuration is in proper order.

NOVELL CLIENT

By far the most common method of connecting Windows-based clients to the NetWare network is through the use of the Novell Client. The client comes with the NetWare installation package, but it is also updated on a semiregular basis, so for the most part you would be better off downloading the newest client from Novell's web site. You can get the client at http://download.novell.com/filedist/ PublicSearch. To obtain the Novell Client, open the preceding link. When the web page loads, select the product (Novell Client), select the OS (Windows 2000), and then click Search. On the page that appears next, click the "download link" and follow the instructions for obtaining the self-extracting archive.

INSTALLING THE NOVELL CLIENT

Once you have the self-extracting archive, double-click it to execute the file. The extractor will prompt you for a location to use for extracting the files. Enter in the path **C:\NWC**. And let the extraction begin! Once the extraction is complete, browse to the C:\NWC folder and locate the setup file, named setupnw.exe. Execute the installer and you should see the Novell client installer begin. Select the typical install option, as shown in the following illustration, and click Next. The system will reboot, and upon restart you will be prompted to enter needed configuration information.

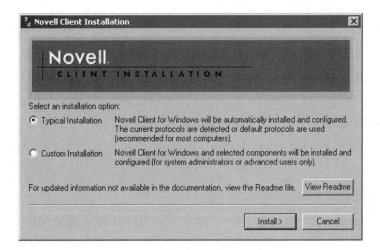

You will be asked to provide the username and password for the server you want to connect to during the installation. Enter your server information and the Admin account information. When the installation completes, allow the system to reboot.

CONFIGURING NETWARE FILE AND PRINT SERVICES

Once your NetWare server is up and running, you will need to go about the task of getting your user access to the server. This is particularly true if you need to provide space for user files on the server. In this section, we will walk through the process of modifying access to NetWare volumes. We will also examine the process for creating a new user account, creating a user group, and assigning a user to said user group. But file sharing is not the only basic service you will want to configure. Network printing is an important role for many network servers. In this section, we will also examine the process for installing and enabling printer services.

ACCESSING FILES ON NETWARE SERVERS

The first step to providing user access to the file structure of the NetWare server is to create an account usable for logging on to the server. If your server is the first one on the network, you may need to create many users. If, however, you have joined an existing network or upgraded an existing server, you will probably have many user accounts at your disposal. Regardless of the scenario, you will probably need to create a user account at some point. The steps that follow outline the process for creating a new user account:

1. If you did not create the User volume during the installation or the upgrade, do so now.

2. Open the NetWare administrator utility by right-clicking the red N in your toolbar and selecting NetWare Utilities (Windows 95/98/2000). Then select the Object Properties entry. In the screen that appears, select the object that will house the new user account.

3. From the Object menu, choose Create. In the New Object window that appears, select the option for User and then click the OK button.

4. Enter the user logon name and last name when prompted.

5. Create a home directory for this user by checking the box next to Create Home Directory, click the Browse button, and then open the container where the user directory will be located.

6. Choose the Create option and click the OK button that appears in the new window.

Now that you have a user, you could assign them as a trustee to an existing directory. What if you have large numbers of users? Managing the trustee rights on a per-user basis could become time-consuming and the source of significant frustration. A better method for dealing with large numbers of users is through group membership. If you create a group and then add the users to that group, you can manage all of the included users' access to any resource by simply modifying the access rights of the group as a whole. The following steps outline the process for creating a new group and assigning users to that group:

1. Open the NetWare Administrator and select the object that will hold the new group.

2. Choose Create from the Object menu.

3. This time, select the Group entry from the New Object window that appears, and enter a name for the new group.

4. Fill the check box that is labeled Define Additional Properties, and choose the Create option.

5. Now open the group's Members page and click the Add button. On the right-hand portion of the current window, select the container with the user you want to add. Once you do this, the user will appear in the left-hand portion. Click the user and then OK.

Now that we have a user and a group, we will examine the process for altering their access rights to a directory on the NetWare server. The first thing you need to do is open the NetWare utility by right-clicking the red N in your toolbar and selecting NetWare Utilities. Then select the Trustee Rights entry. A window will open, as shown here.

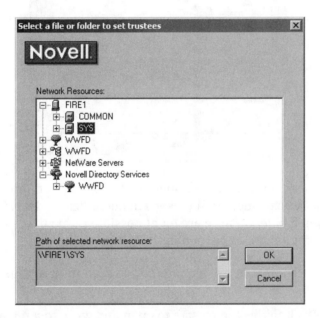

Select the object for which you wish to modify the user access rights. Once you have selected an object, click the OK button. The next window that appears is the NetWare rights window, as shown in the next illustration. The bottom portion of this window contains the objects holding users that you can establish as trustees for a particular resource. Once you have found the user you wish to add, click that username and then click the Add button.

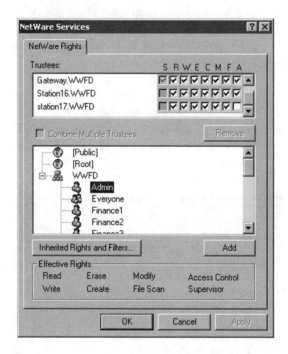

The user will now appear in the upper portion of the NetWare Rights window. The various check boxes next to the user's name indicate which rights the user has to the assigned object. There are eight possible rights that a user can be assigned. These rights are explained in the following list:

- **Read (R)**   Grants the trustee the right to read the contents of a directory or file.

- **Write (W)**   Enables the trustee to open and write to a file or a directory.

- **Create (C)**   Allows a trustee to create subdirectories and salvage deleted files.

- **Erase (E)**   Allows a trustee to delete directories and files.

- **Modify (M)**   Allows the trustee to alter file and directory names and attributes.

- **File Scan (F)**   Allows the trustee to view the names of files and directories.

- **Access Control (A)** Allows the trustee to modify the access rights to the object in question.

- **Supervisor (S)** Grants the trustee complete control over the file or directory.

Once you have added or modified the trustee rights to a resource, you might want to check the inherited rights filters for the object you are working on. If there are inherited rights that conflict with those you have just assigned, problems such as inaccessible resources might arise. Click the Inherited Rights and Filters button and a window similar to the following illustration will appear.

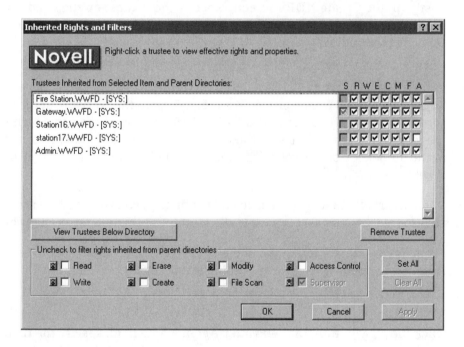

SHARING PRINTERS

Using network printing is a critical requirement for most network users. Because this need is nearly ubiquitous, we will walk through the process of creating a public access printer that network users can use to print documents. The following steps will walk you through the process of creating a network accessible printer. There are two general phases: installing the NDPS (Novell Distributed Print Services) and creating a printer for public access.

1. From any workstation that has the NetWare client installed, log on as Admin and open the NetWare Administrators utility.

2. Open the NetWare browsers screen and locate the NDS object that will contain the NDPS Manager. When selected, use the Object menu and choose the Create option.

3. From the list of class objects that appear, select the NDPS Manager entry.

4. A new screen will appear—the Create NDPS screen. Enter the name you wish to use for this object, then specify the server (Resident Server field) that will house the NDPS information.

5. Lastly (in the Create NDPS screen), specify the volume on the resident server that will house the NDPS database. This information goes in the Database Volume field.

6. Click the Create button. Once you reopen the object's browser, your NDPS Manager object will appear.

7. To load the NDPS Manager you just created, go to the NetWare server console and run the command LOAD NDPSM *name*, where *name* is the name of the Manager you specified in step 4. By including this command in the autoexec.ncf file, your Print Manager will start with the server if it is rebooted.

Now that the NDPS Manager is active and configured, you will need to create a printing resource that users can attach to. To accomplish this, follow the steps here:

1. From any workstation that has the NetWare client installed, log on as Admin and open the NetWare Administrators utility.

2. Double-click the NDPS Manager object and open the Printer Agent List page.

3. Click the New button. In the Printer Agent Name field, specify the name for the printer you are creating.

4. You now need to choose the gateway type for the printer. There are gateways for Xerox and HP printers, as well as a NetWare gateway for other makes of printers. Choose your gateway and click OK.

5. Choose the printer type, printer port, and any other information you need to specify (varies by gateway), and be sure to select the connection type for the printer you are attaching.

6. Make sure that you have selected the printer drivers for all of the operating systems in use on your network, or at least those that will be using the printer. When you are done configuring the drivers, click Continue.

NOVELL DIRECTORY SERVICES (NDS)

NDS is, simply put, a distributed database used to track information about the network. Hosts, printers, servers, users, and groups are all stored in the NDS database as objects. One of the advancements of NDS over the previous method NetWare used to catalog information (called *bindery*) is the ability to organize information based on object properties. The ability to group items makes locating a particular resource far more efficient than the older methodology. The NDS database is maintained by all of the servers on the network. This is a benefit and a detriment at the same time. While the NDS database is very resilient because there is not a single point of failure, there can be a large volume of network traffic associated with NDS replication processes.

NDS TOOLS

There are a variety of tools that come with NetWare, designed to allow detailed management of the NDS infrastructure. The most obvious example is the NetWare Administrator's utility. This utility will allow you to create new NDS objects (as in users and groups), delete objects, search for objects, move objects, change object properties, and rename the object altogether.

If you are maintaining an NDS configuration that must traverse slow WAN links, the replication traffic could easily overwhelm your WAN capacity or at least have a serious negative impact, depending, of course, on the volume of traffic. NetWare has a product designed to manage NDS replication traffic over a WAN. To use this product, you will need to install it first on each server that will communicate across one of the WAN links. Insert the NetWare installation CD and run the NWCONFIG command. Once the Configuration window opens, choose Product Options and then Install Other Novell Products. Once the product is installed, you will be able to implement WAN traffic policies that can restrict replication to off hours or restrict the allowed protocols, among other criteria.

USING CLIENT SERVICES FOR NETWARE

Earlier in this chapter, we discussed the installation of the NetWare Client in order to connect your Windows-based PC to your NetWare server. If you do not want to use the NetWare Client, or if your intention is to migrate from NetWare towards a Windows 2000 Server–based network, there is another client option. Microsoft provides Client Services for NetWare (CSNW) to connect your Windows 2000 Professional systems to NetWare networks. By installing Client Services for NetWare, your client computer will be able to connect to file and printing services provided by the NetWare 5 servers that reside on the same network as the Windows 2000 client.

To make use of CSNW, log on to the Windows 2000 Professional workstation as a user with Administrative rights and complete the steps here:

1. Double-click My Computer and open the Control Panel.

2. From within the Control Panel, double-click the Network and Dial-Up Connections applet.

3. Right-click the connection that you wish to install CSNW on and select Properties from the list that appears.

TECH TALK

Trading Clients to Troubleshoot

Because there are some differences between how the NetWare client and Microsoft's Client Services for NetWare operate, you may find switching from one to the other a useful troubleshooting option. These differences are subtle for the most part and only manifest themselves when customized applications handle the client to server requests in a somewhat nonstandard manner. This being said, either client will connect your Windows 2000, or XP, client system to NetWare resources even though some applications operate more effectively with one client or the other. If you find that a new server-based application will not operate as expected and you have exhausted conventional troubleshooting steps, try switching your client software as a final step and you may on occasion be pleasantly surprised by the result.

4. In the window that appears, make sure that the General tab is selected and click the Install button.

5. In the window displayed next, select the Client entry and click the Add button.

6. Within the next dialog box, select Client Services for NetWare and click the OK button. Files will then be installed and you will be able to enter the NetWare network information that matches your network settings.

When you are configuring the network settings for your client, you will need to know the preferred server or default tree and context. If your network is using NetWare 5, as is assumed here, you will select a default tree and context. The default tree is used when you are connecting to server(s) that are configured to participate in a Novell Directory Services implementation. Every user in an NDS network has an object associated with them that provides a single logon to the NDS tree. The context identifies the location of the user's object that is the container that holds the object the user wants to use to authenticate to the NDS tree.

NOTE   Client Services for NetWare only makes use of the IPX/SPX protocol, and not IP. CSNW does not support the use of NetWare management utilities such as Nwadmin, either. If your NetWare network will be using IP only, or if the client must support all of the NetWare administration tools, you will need to use the NetWare Client.

INSTALLING GATEWAY SERVICES FOR NETWARE

Microsoft's tool collection for integrating Windows 2000 systems with NetWare servers does not stop at client-side software. Windows 2000 Servers can be configured to provide what is called Gateway Services for NetWare. Basically this service allows you to configure a Windows 2000 server to act as an intermediary between your Windows clients and NetWare servers. When these services are active, Windows clients connecting to the GWSN server will be essentially unaware of the existence of the NetWare network. This ability can be particularly useful if you are planning to migrate your current application or file server from NetWare 5 to Windows 2000 Server. To install GSNW, follow these steps. You will need to log on to the server using an account with Administrative privileges.

1. Get into the Control Panel, through My Computer, and double-click the Network and Dial-Up Connections icon.

2. Right-click the LAN connection that will be configured to use GSNW and select Properties from the menu that appears.

3. In the next window, click the Install button.

4. Select the Client entry and click the Add button. In the next window, select the Gateway Services for NetWare. Click the OK button.

Once the installation completes, the server will need to reboot. Upon startup, you can log on and configure the various elements of GSNW. To do this, log on as an administrator, open the Control Panel and then the GSNW applet. At the main screen, shown in the next illustration, you can configure the default tree and context used to connect to the NetWare network.

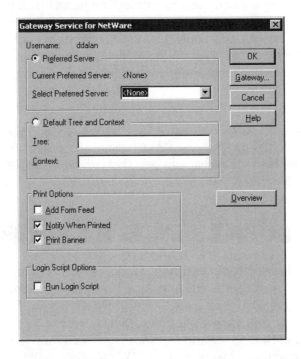

At the bottom of this window is a check box that will allow you to enable your Windows clients to use any available NetWare logon scripts. If you have existing NetWare scripts, you will want to enable this option. There are some other options in this screen, but the most important are the items revealed by clicking the Gateway button. Clicking the Gateway button will reveal the screen shown next.

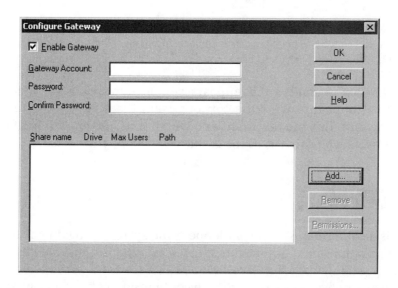

Within the Configure Gateway window open, you can fill in the check box next to the Enable Gateway label. By checking this box, you will be able to specify the user account to be used as a gateway for your Windows clients. This gateway account is used to connect to all of the NetWare servers and their shared resources, such as files and printers. Rather than having each Windows workstation use a NetWare account of its own, this common account will be used. Once a user account has been specified, you can then click the Add button to configure a resource for Windows client access. By adding a resource from a NetWare server, the object will be mounted in a manner on the server that allows the Windows client computers to connect to the object as if it was simply a shared resource housed on the Windows 2000 Server. When you click the Add button, the window shown in the following illustration will appear.

NOTE   The account used for the GSNW service should not be a user with administrative privileges on the NDS network. Permissions can be set to restrict or expand the privileges of the gateway account as needed without providing undue access to the NetWare network in general.

In the New Share window that appears, you need to specify the name of the share as it will appear to Windows network users, the network path to the resource, the local drive letter to use, and whether or not you will limit the number of users who can access the resource.

WRAPPING UP...

NetWare is a comprehensive network operating system, providing flexible file, printer, application, and authentication services. Whether installed as a new server or upgrading from NetWare 4.x/3.x, NetWare 5 will prove to be a useful addition to any network. NetWare can be configured to utilize a large range of hardware options in a relatively painless installation and configuration procedure. While NetWare 5 makes use of IPX for many tasks, there is robust support for the Internet Protocol and it allows the administrator a lot of leeway when choosing how to use one, the other, or both of these networking protocols. Once the NetWare client is installed, performing daily management tasks is a snap. From creating users and groups to modifying trustee rights and sharing printers, this compact tool accomplishes a lot from any workstation where it's installed.

WORKING WITH INTERNET INFORMATION SERVICES

12

If you are working with any of the currently available Microsoft operating systems, or you plan to, you have at your fingertips a powerful, integrated web service platform. This platform is called Internet Information Services (IIS). While the feature set available varies depending on the particular operating system you are using, IIS normally provides at least HTTP (web) and File Transfer Protocol (FTP) services. In addition to these "core services," IIS can be used to provide Simple Mail Transfer Protocol (SMTP) and Network News Transfer Protocol (NNTP). While some controversy exists about the fitness of IIS for providing commercial-grade web services, most of that concern has centered on security and is an issue that is easily overcome with regular maintenance and careful planning. If you are using IIS to provide web services, you need to make sure that you keep your server current with the latest service packs and patches. Once any concerns have been addressed, IIS can be used to provide a flexible suite of web services. In this chapter, we'll…

- Install the IIS service for Windows 2000 (IIS 5.0) and XP (IIS 5.1)

- Examine changes present in the .NET implementation of IIS (IIS 6.0)

- Create and test a basic web site configuration using the HTTP server

- Create and test a basic FTP site using the FTP server
- Troubleshoot common connectivity and authentication problems
- Configure IIS for secure operation

INTERNET INFORMATION SERVICES

For some time now, Internet Information Services has been the flagship web services platform for the Windows NT family of operating systems. Windows NT 4.0 (called Internet Information Services), Windows 2000, Windows XP Professional, and .NET Server 2003 all support one of several versions of IIS. In this chapter, we will examine IIS 5.0 on Windows 2000 Server and IIS 5.1 on Windows XP, and we'll take a brief look at the new features of IIS 6.0 on Windows .NET Server. Within each version we will explore the use of the "subservices" available, including HTTP, FTP, SMTP, and NNTP server services.

In order to access the master configuration settings for any particular service (under Windows XP/.NET), right-click the service (only works for Web and FTP) and select Properties from the context menu that appears. The configuration options that are displayed, known as master properties, will affect all of the elements of that particular service. For example, if you are using Windows 2000 Server and you make a global change to your web service, then all of the individual sites within the web server will take on the new configuration element that has just been set globally.

If you are working with IIS 5.0 on Windows 2000 Server, you will need to go about changing global settings in a different manner. From within the IIS service in the MMC, right-click the Internet Information Services entry, not one of the individual services, and select Properties from the context menu that appears. The window next displayed will be the Internet Information Services Properties window, as shown in Figure 12-1.

In this window, you can select either the Web Server service (HTTP server) or the FTP server by clicking the drop-down (highlighted in Figure 12-1), and then manage the global settings by clicking the Edit button. Another very handy feature, if you decide you need it, is the bandwidth throttling option. By filling the associated check box (shown in Figure 12-1), you place a cap on how much of the network bandwidth the web services on the configured server will be allowed to consume. Keep in mind that you will probably use this feature to minimize the use of your Internet connection, which typically will have a capacity of 128 Kbps to 45,000 Kbps (45 Mbps). Also keep in mind that this setting affects all web, FTP, NNTP, and SMTP sites on the server you are configuring. If you

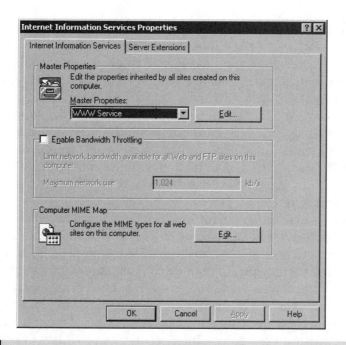

FIGURE 12.1   The IIS 5.0 Properties window

restrict this setting globally, be sure you leave enough room for all of the sites you have hosted.

The HyperText Transfer Protocol (HTTP) server is used to provide web page hosting support. It is HTTP that specifies how to handle the documents that your web browser downloads, interprets, and then displays as web pages. HTTP is most commonly used as the protocol that lets you experience web sites such as www.yahoo.com and others as something other than plaintext. HTTP has a range of other uses as well. For example, companies use HTTP to build intranets—private mini-Internets that help workers and managers access information easily and even allows them to collaborate online on projects. Needless to say, HTTP is fairly important in the day-to-day lives of many computer users. This service is available in all IIS implementations. Server operating systems such as Windows 2000 Server and .NET Server will support the hosting of multiple web sites on a single server, while other operating systems (Windows XP Professional, for example) will support a single site and a limited number of simultaneous connections.

File Transfer Protocol (FTP) is used to perform basic file management tasks with as little network overhead as possible. FTP can be used to create and remove directories and files. As the name suggests, FTP can also be used to transfer files. Because there is not a great deal of overhead with the protocol, files can generally be moved slightly faster with FTP than with other protocols. Not only does the remote client download/upload files more efficiently, but the server providing access does not have to work as hard as it would if there were a more complex protocol in use. Simply put, FTP is very efficient at performing file transfers. Like HTTP, FTP is supported in all implementations of IIS. Also, FTP only has multisite capabilities when a Server version (2000 and .NET) of the Windows operating system is in use.

The Network News Transfer Protocol (NNTP) is used to allow remote users to post messages to a kind of electronic news group. Basically, a user connects to a news server and then selects from the available groups, each relating to a specific topic, and then begins to read existing messages, post replies, and create new postings on the relevant topic. For example, a music enthusiast might connect to a news server and locate alt.music.guitar, and then browse the messages for information about their favorite guitar player or about playing the instrument. Most news servers are provided by Internet service providers or colleges, but they certainly can be used to provide support for discussion groups in all kinds of settings—from corporations to community service groups. Access to these services may be public or private, like most other IIS services. NNTP is only available in the IIS versions that accompany a Windows Server family operating system, which also includes the .NET Server family.

The last of the "core" IIS services is the Simple Mail Transport Protocol (SMTP). These services provide electronic mail relay services. The purpose of the SMTP virtual server is to provide basic mail relay and delivery. Microsoft has another, more feature rich, e-mail/productivity package called Exchange. The IIS SMTP server will not provide the advanced user management possible with Exchange and other e-mail applications. If you just need a place for others to send mail and a means of forwarding your outgoing e-mail, though, the IIS SMTP service should work just fine. This tidy e-mail enabler is present in both the Windows 2000 Server implementation and the package distributed with Windows XP Professional and .NET Server.

TECH TALK

Windows 2000 Server vs. Windows XP Professional: Making a Choice

So you need to implement an IIS server, but which version of IIS do you need? Which operating system should you use? It all depends on how many users will access your web site and if you will need multiple sites of one kind or another. Windows 2000 Server will provide you with the ability to support thousands of user connections and more web and FTP sites than most people could ever want. Windows XP Professional will be useful if you need to provide web services for a small workgroup of users. Windows 2000 and XP Professional have limited feature sets. For example, they will support a single FTP and/or web site, and the licensing agreement restricts the number of inbound connections to ten simultaneous users, where the Windows 2000 Server version can support multiple instances of HTTP and FTP servers and virtually unlimited inbound connections.

INSTALLING IIS ON WINDOWS 2000 SERVER

Now we will take a tour through the process of installing IIS when you are using Windows 2000 Server. In the following list, all of the steps you will need to complete are outlined. Keep in mind that IIS is installed by default. If the user did not opt to skip IIS installation when the server software was installed, then IIS will already be installed. You can still perform these procedures, but you will not actually install or remove IIS if it is already present.

1. Double-click the My Computer icon on the desktop.
2. Double-click the Control Panel entry.
3. Double-click the Add/Remove Programs icon.
4. Click the Add/Remove Windows Components button.

5. Within the window that appears next, select the Internet Information Services package by checking the box if it is unchecked. If the box is already checked, clearing it will eventually result in the removal of IIS.

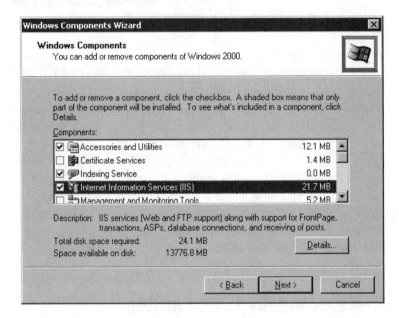

6. While the IIS entry is selected, click the Details button. Make sure that all of the available options (check all boxes) are selected, as they are in the following illustration.

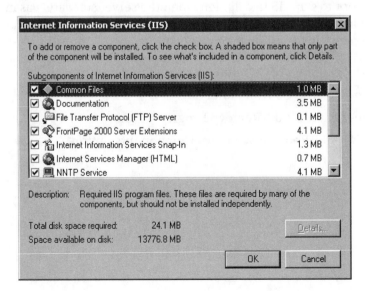

7. Click OK when all of the items in the Details window are selected.

8. Press the Next button.

9. The IIS components will install.

INSTALLING IIS ON WINDOWS XP PROFESSIONAL

While the version of IIS available with Windows XP Professional is less feature-rich than the version that accompanies Windows 2000 Server, it can still be very useful for a number of things. Of course, if you will be making use of IIS with your Windows XP Professional system, you will need to install IIS first. The following steps outline the process for installing IIS. In this case, we will summarize the steps. Though the screens will look slightly different, these steps are virtually the same as those for the Windows 2000 system.

1. Open the Add/Remove programs tool in the Control Panel. Click the button to add a new Windows component.

2. Select the option to add the Internet Information Services package by filling in the check box.

3. While the IIS entry is selected, click the Details button. Check all of the boxes to ensure that all components are installed.

4. Click OK and Next until the installation has completed.

Once you have completed the installation steps for the platform of your choice, it will be time to configure your server to provide only the services you will use. In the following section, we will examine the procedure for starting and stopping IIS services, and the basic configuration of the four common IIS services: HTTP, FTP, SMTP, and NNTP.

STARTING, STOPPING, AND CONFIGURING IIS SERVICES

With IIS and the web service installed, you should be able to point any web browser to the NetBIOS name, IP address, or the loopback (127.0.01) IP address of your IIS system and see an "Under Construction" page. If you use a browser on the IIS system itself, you will see the IIS administration page as well as the help file. All of the other IIS services will behave in a similar manner, revealing only the most basic default access. For example, the FTP server will allow anonymous access, but there won't be any content to access. In order to make the web sites do something, or have your SMTP and FTP servers authenticate users, you will need to make a few initial changes.

TECH TALK

IIS Installation Extras

There are several default changes that you should be aware of since they will be in existence after you complete the IIS installation. First off, there are two user accounts that are created: IUSER<computername> and IWAM<computername>, where <computername> is the name of the system using IIS. For example, a server named websrv would get two accounts, IUSER_WEBSRV and IWAM_ WEBSRV. The IUSER account is used to control access by anonymous users to your IIS server for all of the services. The IWAM account is used by the IIS server to execute scripting such as Common Gateway Interface (CGI) and Active Server Pages (ASP). The other thing you need to be aware of is the kinds of services that are running, whether you're ready or not. By default, the Web server, FTP, IIS Administration, and SMTP (if available) will be running.

HTTP (WEB) SERVER

When using IIS in conjunction with Windows 2000, IIS version 5.0, you will have several options for configuring your web server. The following steps will get you from your desktop to the configuration interface for the HTTP server:

1. Right-click the My Computer icon.

2. Select Manage from the context menu that appears.

3. The Microsoft Management Console (MMC) will open. Locate the Services and Applications entry and click the plus (+) symbol next to it to expand the item.

4. In the newly expanded list, find the Internet Information Services entry and click the plus (+) symbol next to it to open it. You should see something similar to that shown in Figure 12-2.

5. Locate the Default Web Site entry and right-click it, selecting Properties from the context menu that appears.

6. The Default Web Site Properties window will now be visible.

Within the Default Web Site Properties, there are ten categories where configuration changes can be made. These categories are

- Web Site
- Operators
- Performance
- ISAPI Filters
- Home Directory
- Documents
- Directory Security
- HTTP Headers
- Custom Errors
- Server Extensions

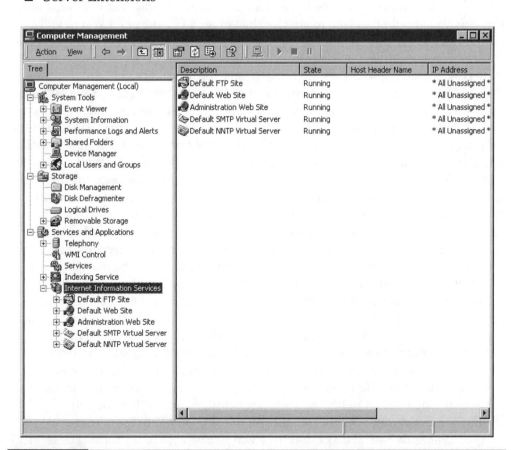

FIGURE 12.2   Individual IIS services

NOTE Not all of these fields or their suboptions are available in the IIS distribution that accompanies Windows 2000 Professional or Windows XP Professional. The configuration information that follows will accurately address those elements shared by IIS 5.0 (2000) and IIS 5.1 (XP). The configuration options available with IIS 5.1 are almost a perfect subset of the configuration options available with IIS 5.0. If FrontPage server extensions are installed, you will see an associated Configuration tab.

Under the Web Site tab there are three options that are fairly critical. The first important element is the Web Site Identification. This identifies the web site using a name that you specify. For example, if you had a web site www.superfoo.com, you might change the description to read "SuperFoo." When you find that you have large numbers of sites hosted on your server, clear, concise, and meaningful descriptions can save lots of time when trying to manage configurations and troubleshoot problems.

The next important element is the IP Address configuration option. For the default site, this value should be left as (All Unassigned); however, if it is the only web site, you should feel free to specify the server's IP address if you need to. The (All Unassigned) option will ensure that any web request sent to the server's IP that is not targeting a hosted site will be delivered to the default web site of the server. If multiple web sites are being hosted, host headers are used in addition to IP addresses. This set of capabilities can prove to be very useful. Say you have a single IP address on your web server and three web sites: foo.com, superfoo.com, and realultimatesuperfoo.com. Since all of the hostnames would have DNS records pointing to your server's single IP address, IIS would use host header information to determine which content to serve. To configure the host header information for a site, click the Advanced button next to the IP Address field. By selecting an entry in the upper portion of the Advanced Multiple Website Configuration window that appears, you can use the Edit button to enter a host header and change port numbers and IP settings for your site. Information you place into the host header field will be the web site's URL—for example, www .foo.com or mycoolsite.foo.com. If the header field does not match the URL requested by a user searching for your web site, IIS will not be able to provide the needed content.

The next two options on the Default Web Site Properties window are the Operators and Performance tabs. The Operators tab allows you to specify which user accounts on your Windows 2000 domain will have the ability to manage the web site for which this option is configured. For the default site, the default settings are best left alone if you will be hosting multiple web sites. Web site operators will be able to change site access permissions, enable logging, change the default document, modify the footer, set content expiration, and enable/disable content rating options. In addition to these specific rights, there are some occasionally useful tasks that they will not be able to perform. These restricted actions include configuring the anonymous user account, creating or managing virtual directories, throttling bandwidth, changing the identification of the web site they have access to, or changing the application isolation settings.

The Performance tab allows you to manage how the IIS should respond to heavy usage loads. You can control how network bandwidth is used by limiting the amount of bandwidth available for any single web site (throttling) and placing limits on how much of the available CPU capacity can be consumed by the web site in question. You can also prepare IIS by estimating the number of hits, or web page requests, you think the site will encounter. Unless you are sure your site will be receiving a large volume of visitors or you pay for Internet access based on usage, the performance options can be left at their default settings.

The next three tabs of the Default Web Site Properties window are ISAPI Filters, Home Directory, and Documents. ISAPI (Internet Server Application Programming Interface) Filters are Microsoft's answer to server-side scripting such as CGI and Perl. Support for a variety of scripting engines can be added into IIS operation by adding and configuring them within the ISAPI tab.

Home Directory is exactly what you might think it is: a tool for specifying the home directory of the web site. This directory will be the location that the web page designers will need to place files in if they want users to have access to them through a browser. These directories are defined on a per-site basis, so there is no option for configuring a global default directory location. There are three different options. You can locate the directory on the local computer or connect it to a share on a different computer. The last option is to redirect to a different URL. When you are connecting to a share on another computer, you will need to enter the security credentials that will be used to access the share. In addition to the location for the web site source files, options within this tab will allow you to control the kinds of customized applications and scripting, and to a degree the kinds of user access allowed. This directory and all files and subdirectories will be "exposed to the Internet," so choose carefully. Generally speaking, the folder selected should not have any subfolders that are not intended to be a part of the web site.

The Documents tab contains two configurable subitems. The first item allows the configuration of the default documents and the second is the Enable Document Footer option. A default document will be provided by default when a web browser does not specify a specific document. Clients requesting a default document will be served the file that matches one of the types (index.htm, default.asp) listed in the Default Documents window. The items in this list are processed in order from top to bottom. By checking or clearing the Document Footer option on the default documents sheet written in HTML, you can designate the location of a file that will be appended to the end of all of the documents served.

Our next stop in the default configuration page is the Directory Security tab. Within this tab there are a series of fairly intuitive controls for managing user access from within the IIS service. These controls will work in addition to any NTFS file-level permissions you have already configured, which can result in some confusion. If you have a folder configured to allow only administrator accounts and for some reason then make it a web page home directory, and you then enable anonymous access, anyone will be able to (via the Web) access the directory you created. If anonymous access is not allowed—though it will be for the vast majority of publicly accessible web servers—you can specify what kind of authenticated access to use.

Under the HTTP Headers tab, you can configure when HTTP header content expires, whether or not to use custom headers, and if you wish to support content ratings and MIME types. These options come together to ensure that time-sensitive information remains up-to-date (if you set the older content to expire), and other content-related features are available should you need them. For example, if content expiration is enabled, end-user browsers will be instructed to drop previously cached information after a specified period of time.

The last two tabs in the web site properties are Custom Errors and Server Extensions. The Custom Errors tab allows you to configure customized error messages. That sounds pretty simple, and it is. Messages such as the common "Error 404: Page not Found" and others are installed and available by default. You could even add your own custom error messages if you so desire. The Server Extensions tab allows you to decide if there will be general support for dynamic content and identify which programming language will be supported. Because other helper applications can be installed and configured, this tab provides only the most basic functionality.

FTP SERVER

Just like the HTTP server, IIS has several configurable options that can be used with the FTP server. To access the FTP site configuration controls, use the following steps. These are essentially the same steps used for accessing the HTTP configuration interface.

1. Right-click the My Computer icon.

2. Select Manage from the context menu that appears.

3. The Microsoft Management Console (MMC) will open. Locate the Services and Applications entry and click the plus (+) symbol next to it to expose the subitems.

4. Locate the Internet Information Services entry and click the plus (+) symbol next to it to expand the listing.

5. Locate the Default FTP Site entry and right-click it, selecting Properties from the context.

6. The five-tabbed Default FTP Site Properties window appears.

Within the Default Web Site Properties, there are five configuration categories where changes can be made. These categories are

- FTP Site
- Security Accounts
- Messages
- Home Directory
- Directory Security

The first tab on the site properties sheet will allow you to specify the name of the site, the IP address, the TCP port number to use, and restrictions on the maximum number of connected users, if needed. Logging options can also be accessed through this interface. You can simply enable logging or you can use the Properties button to access extended options to choose which items to log and how often to generate a new log file, among other things.

The Security Accounts tab enables you to alter the basic authentication types allowed on the FTP site in question. For example, you can allow anonymous access, force all users to connect anonymously, or require users to authenticate to the server using their Windows domain account usernames and passwords. This is generally unwise, especially if the web site is accessed beyond a private LAN, since the usernames and passwords delivered in this manner will be sent without the benefit of any kind of encryption. The information will be sent across the network in a clear text format. You can also designate a site operator in this sheet. The Messages tab allows you to create custom welcome, exit, and "server full" messages that will be shown to users connecting to your FTP server.

The Home Directory and Directory Security tabs will allow you to specify the location of the directory that is to be used with the FTP site. This can be a directory located on this computer or a share located on another computer. The Directory Security option will allow you to establish filters that can block or grant access based on the IP address of the computer attempting to connect to your server.

SMTP SERVER

An SMTP server is used to facilitate the orderly delivery of e-mail. The SMTP server will take the message sent by a client and deliver that e-mail to the proper receiving host—another e-mail server. The receiving server typically uses either POP or IMAP services to receive and store e-mail for client delivery. Once the SMTP server is enabled, you will be able to use your IIS server to deliver e-mail from your e-mail application. To access the configuration console for the IIS SMTP server, and begin the process of using the SMTP server, follow these steps:

1. Right-click the My Computer icon.

2. Select Manage from the context menu that appears.

3. The Microsoft Management Console (MMC) will open. Click the plus (+) symbol next to the Services and Applications entry.

4. In the expanded list, click the plus (+) symbol next to the Internet Information Services entry.

5. Locate and right-click the Default SMTP Virtual Server entry and select Properties from the menu that appears.

6. The Default SMTP Virtual Server window will now be visible.

Within the Default SMTP Virtual Server Properties window, there are six tabs that will allow you to alter the various parameters of the SMTP server. The tabs available are listed here:

- General
- Access
- Messages
- Delivery
- LDAP Routing
- Security

On the General settings tab, you can configure basic settings such as the logical name for your virtual server and the IP address that the SMTP server should listen to for incoming SMTP (e-mail) connections. In addition to the general information, you can also specify the number of incoming and outgoing connections that the SMTP server will allow at one time, and you can specify the location and level of detail used when logging access to the SMTP server.

In the Access tab that is next, you can specify the connection and authentication rules used when hosts connect to the server. For example, you can require encryption, configure certificate services (which support secure connectivity), or filter access to the server based on the IP address of the client attempting to connect. Lastly, you can enable or disable e-mail relay. If you don't know of a reason why you want to allow other hosts to relay mail through your server, it's best to make sure that this feature is not available. One unfortunately common use of e-mail relay is masking the source of e-mail spam.

The next tab is labeled Messages and contains configuration options that will allow you to limit the size of messages sent through your SMTP server as well as the number of users that may be addressed by a single message. If you limit the number of addresses that a message can be targeted to, you can help reduce the impact of mass mailing viruses and worms as well as prevent superfluous forwarding by your users, because there will be a cap on how many users any single e-mail can reach.

The last three tabs—Delivery, LDAP Routing, and Security—are useful for nonstandard configurations and troubleshooting. Should you need to alter the delivery behavior of the server, such as how long the server will attempt to deliver a message that is not reaching the intended host before giving up, the Delivery tab includes the needed options. LDAP (Lightweight Directory Access Protocol) is used to integrate server information with a range of database services such as Microsoft's Active Directory service. In the LDAP Routing tab, you will be able to specify the LDAP type, server name and IP, and authentication information, if appropriate. Like the Security tab in other IIS services, the SMTP Security tab allows you to also designate user accounts on your server or the Windows domain that will be allowed to alter the operating behavior of your SMTP server.

NNTP SERVER (2000 SERVER ONLY)

The NNTP server present with Windows 2000 Server has a fairly compact set of configuration options. This is due in large part to the fact that NNTP is a fairly task-specific service and extensive configuration options would be of little use. To access the NNTP configuration interface, follow the steps outlined here:

1. Right-click My Computer.

2. Select Manage from the menu that appears.

3. Locate the Services and Applications in the MMC window and click the plus (+) symbol to view the subitems.

4. From within the Internet Information Services entry, click the plus (+) symbol and right-click NNTP Virtual Server Properties, and then select Properties from the menu that appears.

5. The NNTP Virtual Server Properties configuration panel should now be visible.

There are four general configuration groups within the NNTP server service that you can tinker with. The groups are listed here:

- General
- Access
- Settings
- Security

The General tab provides the same configuration options as the SMTP configuration interface. You can assign a logical name to the NNTP instance, specify an IP address for the NNTP server to listen to for incoming connections, and configure connection rules. The Access, Message, and Security tabs all perform the same functions in the NNTP service that the corresponding tabs in the SMTP service do. Features within these tabs give you control over what kind of connections will be allowed and how large messages posted can be, in addition to other features.

SECURITY AND IIS

IIS comes with a number of built-in security features. Some of the key features are common to both IIS 5.0 and 5.1. These features include various data encryption and access filtering techniques. In addition to these shared security features, the 5.1 implementation of IIS has some new security enhancements. In this section, we will examine the general security features of the IIS.

NOTE   IIS services that are unused should be disabled. All of the IIS services are designed to allow remote users access to your server. If you are not going to actively manage and configure any of the default IIS services, you can improve system security by simply shutting them off.

IIS makes use of the Secure Socket Layer (SSL) standard to enable private, secure communications. One particular use of this technology is in e-commerce. SSL creates an encrypted session between the web server and the client. IIS comes with an extension of the SSL package known as Server-Gated Cryptography (SGC). SGC uses specialized certificates to enable 128-bit encrypted communications with export versions of IIS. To actually make use of SGC, however, an SGC security certificate must be obtained from a certificate authority. The use of SSL and encryption certificates in general is enabled within the individual web site configuration settings.

As mentioned in previous configuration sections, IIS can implicitly grant or deny access from Internet-based IP addresses or domains, thereby restricting which domain names and/or IP subnets are allowed to access the IIS server. These features operate in addition to any available local security settings such as local file permissions. These new restrictions will allow you to restrict access to your IIS server based on the client's fully qualified domain name (host.domain.com) or IP address.

SECURITY FEATURES NEW IN IIS 5.1

One of the most obvious changes present in IIS 5.1 is a distinct increase in the number of easy-to-follow security wizards that now exist for many security features. One example is the Permissions Wizard, which is designed to make

TECH TALK

Monitoring Usage with Log Files

Each of the supported IIS services (HTTP, FTP, NNTP, and SMTP) has a logging option that can be used to collect a great deal of information. You can collect information about which users have connected, when, and which services they used. This information can be used to identify potential security issues. Log files are also particularly useful in the quest to solve some common access and performance problems. The only restriction on logging is disk space. If you have the room, you would be wise to enable very detailed logging for all of the services you provide, long enough to collect a baseline for normal performance once the server goes live. If an issue occurs, you can then collect new data and compare it to the old as a part of the troubleshooting process.

the assignment of user access rights on virtual FTP and HTTP directories and files as painless as possible. One of the most powerful benefits of the new security wizards is the integration of IIS security and NTFS file permissions. This integration ensures that there are not two separate (and possibly conflicting) sets of access permissions for the content associated with the web or FTP site. In fact, most of the security configuration options present in IIS 5.1 will be configured via a wizard interface.

IIS version 5.1 makes full use of the Secure Socket Layer (SSL) version 3.0 standard and a feature known as transport layer security (TLS). Each of these features individually allows the secure transfer of information between web servers and their hosts. The product of these technologies is the ability for the IIS web server to identify the user prior to the user providing a username and password. When the user initiates a connection to the web server, security certificates are examined by the server to identify the client uniquely. IIS has the ability to map the user certificate to a Windows domain user account. This allows the control of access privileges by certificate rather than by username and logon information.

Perhaps the most advanced new security feature present with IIS 5.1 is Advanced Digest Authentication. Advanced Digest Authentication is used to enable a wide range of secure communications. Advanced Digest Authentication allows users connecting from the Internet or other networks to authenticate across network devices such as firewalls without requiring client-side software or the transmission of user credentials in a cleartext format over public networks. Keep in mind that in order to make use of Advanced Digest Authentication, both the IIS server and Windows domain controller must be using either Windows .NET (domain controller or IIS system) or Windows XP (IIS system).

TECH TALK

IIS Lockdown and Cumulative IIS Patch

There are two especially critical options provided by Microsoft that will help you secure your web server. The first is a tool, the IIS Lockdown tool, which can be found via Microsoft's download page at http://www.microsoft.com/download. When this tool is run, many of the weak default settings that exist for the default installation of IIS are remedied. The tool uses templates for a particular IIS server role, such as a public web server, and disables features not required in the fulfillment of that role. There is a wealth of options

---

IIS Lockdown and Cumulative IIS Patch (continued)

with this frequently updated tool. For detailed and current information, check out the security tools site at http://microsoft.com/technet/security/tools/tools.asp.

One of the most prevalent complaints voiced by IT folks in charge of IIS systems is the difficulty in keeping up with the regular product updates. A simple solution was made to help users play catch-up. This solution, our second option, is the IIS cumulative patch. By downloading and installing the patch, your IIS system will receive all of the service releases for IIS that existed as of October 30, 2002. To locate this patch, visit http.microsoft.com/downloads and search for "IIS cumulative patch." Once the patch is installed, your system will be a veritable fortress. Additional updates can be obtained for your server by visiting http:// www.microsoft .com/ technet/security/current.asp and searching for the hot fixes for IIS (4.0, 5.0, 5.1, and eventually 6.0) and applying them to your server.

PREVIEW OF INTERNET INFORMATION SERVER 6.0

Windows .NET Server brings with it a new iteration of Internet Information Services, version 6.0. This latest release features a series of improvements to the existing IIS products, version 5.x. The most noteworthy improvement relates to process isolation. This isolation reduces the impact of one IIS-related process on other IIS-related processes and the server system as a whole. This isn't just the web and FTP service we are talking about, but the individual processes spawned by these processes as well. For example, something like a newly developed web application that unexpectedly fails (taking the web server service and maybe the server with it) is far less likely to disrupt operations when it fails. Specifically, this isolation protects the core IIS processes from being negatively affected by other user-initiated and nonessential processes. The Web Administration Service (WAS) is the tool used to police traffic between user processes pertaining to configuration and management tasks and the core processes of the IIS server. The duty of WAS is simply to make sure that client processes (such as a script of some kind) are started, monitored, recycled (terminated), or restarted.

Next is the "worker isolation mode." This mode ensures that all of the individual pieces of application code are run in isolated memory spaces. A big improvement over previous IIS implementations is that the performance impact of isolating services is greatly minimized. This feature compliments WAS in that it further reduces the possibilities that a failed subprocess will cause other components to fail. In addition to protecting the IIS core processes, any group of subprocesses that has one of the members fail will most likely be able to restart that process without disrupting other processes—and therefore users of the web server. Another advantage of the isolated operation is that each process can be given its own operating priority, and operating system–level features such as CPU throttling can be managed on a per-application basis.

The previous items are far from the only improvements in IIS from 5.1 to 6.0. The following list is a brief description of some of the other key process improvements present in the latest implementation of IIS 6.0:

- WAS "process health monitoring" that keeps tabs on the status of all client-initiated processes. This constant communication between WAS and the client processes ensures that WAS is instantly aware if any of the client services should stop responding. If a client process does fail, WAS will then generate a duplicate process and then restart the failing service. The net result is that, hypothetically, the client will not notice any loss of service whatsoever while WAS is working behind the scenes.

- Improved handling of idle client processes via the idle timeout process. If a client process stays idle for a period of time longer than the administratively configured value, a request is sent to end the process. This design element has been added to ensure that system resources are not unnecessarily used by processes that are consuming resources but not actually doing anything.

- In the event that a client process fails, it will subsequently end communication with the "process police" (a.k.a. the WAS process). In previous IIS implementations, the IIS server processes would log the error and then attempt to restart the process. Sometimes a client service will simply fail again once it is restarted, especially if the conditions causing it to fail are still present when the process restarts. The net result is a cyclical failure that can have a dramatic impact (for the worse) on system resources. IS 6.0 resolves this issue by using the WAS process. WAS is used to automatically disable client processes that repeatedly fail. This process is known as "rapid-fail protection."

- If the WAS service is unable to restart a failed client process, it can initiate what is known as the "orphaning worker processes." In this scenario, a client process that has failed to respond to inquiries by the WAS service for a predetermined period of time, and has not been successfully ended/restarted by WAS, will be abandoned. A new replacement service will be started. The old "orphaned" process is left alone and the new process takes over the handling of the client requests.

- The IIS 6.0 process isolation mode can be configured to restart client processes in order to manage faulty applications in what is called the "recycling worker process." If a process fails, no portion of the IIS server needs to be restarted—the individual defective process is "recycled" instead. This recycling involves shutting down and restarting the involved process (such as the HTTP server for a particular site). There are many criteria used to determine when a process is recycled, including, but not limited to, daily schedules (same time each day) and elapsed time since last recycle.

SECURITY IMPROVEMENTS

Security components of IIS 6.0 are focused on locking out the commonly exploitable components while minimizing the impacts of any new attacks by adopting an adaptive approach to security. One component of this new security approach is the development of the IIS Lockdown Wizard. This tool, providing the same service as the IIS Lockdown tool now available as a download for previous IIS versions, is designed to provide an easy-to-use interface for making appropriate IIS security configurations. Unlike previous versions of IIS, now only the ability to provide static content will be enabled by default. No scripts or dynamic content will operate without intentional administrative intervention and configuration.

The account used to provide IIS 6.0 with its access to system resources is now severely limited in the scope of its privileges. In the past, this access account had administrative-level access. Most of these privileges have been removed in the IIS 6.0 implementation. This change will likely prevent a catastrophe should the IIS service become compromised by malicious users using new attack strategies.

WORKING WITH DIRECTORIES AND CONTENT

If you need to use IIS to support multiple web or FTP sites, you need to take into careful consideration the arrangement of the directories used to store content for those sites. You'll also need to be very familiar with the process for creating new web sites and virtual hosts, and the process for delegating access to those various features. If you have multiple web sites, you may or may not be responsible for actually creating and uploading the content for the various sites. Either way, you will need to be familiar with the processes involved. Most of the concepts explored in this section, especially site creation and testing, will apply equally to single-site and multisite server scenarios.

PLANNING FOR MULTIPLE WEB SITES

One of the most important tasks that will need to be completed on a multiple web site server is the creation of directories to house content. IIS can be configured to use any local directory as the document folder for a configured web or FTP site. Each web and FTP site can be configured to use a unique directory for its content. This ability allows you to configure access rights differently on each folder and organize content in such a way that it is easy to find the content directory for a particular web site. Since we know that we will need a number of folders, let's review the process for creating a new directory. In addition to the Windows Server implementations of IIS, this process will work on both Windows 2000 Professional and Windows XP, with operating system–specific differences noted:

1. On Windows 2000, double-click the My Computer icon on the desktop. If you are using Windows XP Professional, click the Start button and then My Computer.

2. Find the hard drive where you want to create the new directory.

3. Double-click the Hard Drive icon to open.

4. Click the File menu and select New | Folder.

5. Enter a name for the new folder and press the ENTER key.

Now that you have created the needed directory for the multisite configuration, let's explore the steps needed to configure IIS to make use of the new directory. The following steps assume that the site will be accessible by anonymous users, that the content will be stored in the "C:\sample" directory, that the site name is www.2foo4u.com and www.2foo4u.net, and that you are working with Windows 2000 Server:

1. Open Computer Management and locate the IIS service. Click the IIS entry to highlight it.

2. Click the Action menu (upper-left corner of the MMC), select New | Web Site from the menu that appears.

3. The Web Site Creation Wizard will appear. Click Next.

4. In the description box, type **sample1** and click Next.

5. Leave the IP and port settings at their default values and enter the host header **www.2foo4u.com**. Click the Next button.

6. In the next window, enter the path to the source C:\sample. Make sure that the check box indicating you wish to allow anonymous access is filled and click the Next button.

TECH TALK

Giving Developers the Power

If a web page designer that is using your server needs to develop additional web sites, you can accommodate the need in a relatively painless manner. First, you need to make sure that the web page designer has permission to write to the directory where they will store the web site content. No web site information should be stored in this folder. Instead, create a subdirectory for each individual site that the designer will be working with. Configure each new web site on IIS (for this designer) to point to the appropriate subdirectory in the folder you created. If at a later time your designer needs space for additional sites, you can simply create a new folder alongside the other directories. The new folders will inherit the NTFS permissions of the parent folder by default. Because the permissions work for the other sites (and they will if the designer can edit the sites and users can access them), you should be ready to go once IIS has been configured to use the new directory for the new site. In addition to removing the need to set user rights each time, you will have a well-organized structure. Each developer's content will be located under that developer's folder, making it easy to copy, back up, or otherwise manage the content.

7. In the Web Site Access Permissions window that appears next, allow only Read and Run Scripts, which are the default settings. Click the Next button.

8. Click the Finish button to exit the wizard.

PAINFUL
LESSONS

I'VE LEARNED

Moving from Testing to Production

It was a common practice of mine to configure web servers to use nonstandard ports on unused IP addresses when a web site configuration was being tested prior to "going live." On one occasion, a long time ago, I had a working web site for the company intranet and when I tried to go live, my users could not gain access. I thought I had a permissions issue, but in fact I failed to complete a simple dummy check. The server was configured to listen on port 8080, and unless a user could somehow magically divine this, they had no hope of accessing the site. Once I changed back to port 80, presto! Everything began to work normally.

TROUBLESHOOTING

Addressing Overutilization

If your server is heavily utilized and users complain of slow response time, there are three critical areas you should check out to begin correcting the problem. The first one is bandwidth, then available memory, and, finally, CPU utilization. Using Windows Performance Monitor will allow you to see the level of utilization for CPU and memory. If either one is the problem, you can take one of two approaches: increase the performance (faster CPU, more memory) or remove some of the web site services (such as scripting support) if practical to do so. If bandwidth is the issue, you can purchase more bandwidth, restrict the number of simultaneous connections, or place bandwidth caps on each of the supported web sites. This will result in an even distribution of bandwidth among the hosted sites and should improve bandwidth utilization issues.

Another method for housing content is through the use of virtual roots. Virtual roots are commonly used with FTP implementations. Basically, an existing network share is used rather than a new or existing local directory. If your web server is used to provide telecommuters access to local network resources, this can be very handy indeed. For example, if an outside sales representative needs to have the ability to upload and download files from a sales (or any other) share on the network, that share can be designated as the *virtual* root of an FTP site on your web server. By using the network resource as the root of an FTP site, authorized users can get the needed access from virtually anywhere.

NOTE If your web server is used to provide public services, you are strongly encouraged to avoid using virtual roots. In order to use a virtual root, your web server will need to have some kind of access to the network where the virtual root resides. If this is your private network, then virtual roots introduce a serious potential risk. Should a malicious user gain control of your web server, they will most likely have some kind of access to the network housing the virtual root as well. If you need to use virtual roots on a remotely accessible server, you should require encrypted connections to the network the server is on, such as virtual private networking (VPN), and restrict general public access.

IMPLEMENTING AND TESTING SITES

So, now you have been exposed to an overview of IIS as well as the process for accessing and tweaking the configuration options for the various services. In this section, we will walk through the process of building and testing a basic web and FTP site. Since Windows XP Professional supports only a single FTP and web site (the default ones that exist when IIS is installed), the following steps will be performed—assuming Windows 2000 Server is in use.

BUILDING A NEW WEB SITE

Follow these steps to create a new web site on your Windows 2000 Server. We will use the default documents in this case, so a successful site implementation will only provide the "Under Construction" error message to users attempting to connect to the site. Prior to executing these steps, create a folder on the root of any attached hard drive—called "sample," such as C:\sample. Ensure that the Everyone group has at least read access to this folder.

1. Right-click My Computer.
2. Select Manage from the menu that appears.
3. Locate the Services and Applications entry in the MMC window and click the plus (+) symbol to view the subitems.
4. Right-click the Internet Information Services entry and select New | Website from the menu that appears.
5. The New Web Site Wizard will appear—click Next to continue.
6. Enter a web site description (foo.com in this case) and then click Next.
7. In the next window, specify your server's IP address, port 80, and a host header value of www.foo.com. Click the Next button.
8. Specify the home directory as C:\sample. Click the Next button.
9. Leave the default access permissions in place and click the Next button. Click Finish to exit the wizard.

To test this configuration, you will need to have a DNS record created that will point requests to www.foo.com to the IP address of the newly configured server. Once that is done, any computer using the DNS server that has the appropriate record in place should now be able to access your site by entering www.foo.com into a web browser.

PAINFUL
LESSONS

I'VE LEARNED

Dueling Web Sites

My first introduction to the usefulness of HTTP host headers came in the typical manner—painfully. I had created a number of web sites on a Windows 2000 server with three IP addresses. When I was done, many of the sites would not respond to requests. I had configured the corresponding DNS records to direct the appropriate URL to the configured server IP address. But with multiple sites configured on a single IP and no host headers attached, IIS had no idea where to direct incoming requests. A little bit of research and some header additions solved the problem just in time.

Once you have completed the following steps, you will have a new FTP site that allows anonymous users to access the content with read-only permission. This configuration will be designed to provide connectivity based on the IP address of the server and not the logical hostname. In order to ensure that hosts can use the configured hostname, you need to make sure that the DNS services used by the clients have the proper information to resolve the desired hostname to the actual IP address used by the server.

1. Right-click My Computer.

2. Select Manage from the menu that appears.

3. Locate the Services and Applications entry in the MMC window and click the plus (+) symbol to view the subitems.

4. Right-click the Internet Information Services entry and select New | FTP Site from the menu that appears.

5. The FTP Site Creation Wizard will appear—click Next to continue.

6. Enter a description for the FTP site. In this case, we'll use **ftp.foo.com**. Click the Next button to continue.

7. In the next window, specify the IP address of the server and leave the default port at the value of 21. Click the Next button to continue.

8. Specify the C:\sample directory (or other directory of your choosing) as the home directory for the web site. Click the Next button to continue.

9. Leave the site access permissions at the default values and click the Next button to continue. Click Finish to exit the wizard.

TESTING YOUR SITES

In order to make sure that your FTP and HTTP server configurations are working as expected, you can perform a couple of simple tests to make sure that the server is reacting to incoming requests appropriately. To test your new web site configuration, perform these steps:

1. Open the WINT\system32\drivers\etc folder and open the hosts file with Notepad. Within the hosts file, create an entry for your server IP address and then the hostname www.foo.com. There is a sample entry in the file using the 127.0.0.1 IP that you can use as a formatting example. Save and close the file.

2. Open a web browser on the system with the customized hosts file and enter the web site address **www.foo.com**.

3. You should see either a page not found message or the default document, if any is present.

If you are prompted for a logon name and password, your file and/or directory security settings are possibly too restrictive. Guidance for correcting this kind of issue is provided in the "Solving User Access Problems" section later in this chapter.

Now that you have tested your web site configuration, we will check out the FTP site for proper operation. Once the following steps have been completed, you will know for certain if your FTP site is working as expected:

1. While logged onto your server, click the Start button, then select the Run command. In the window that appears, type **cmd** and press the ENTER key.

PAINFUL
LESSONS

I'VE LEARNED

Changing Two Things at Once

One of the more common mistakes I am prone to make when working with IIS and FTP sites is messing with the NTFS permissions as well as the IIS security settings, and completely fouling the operation of the site. If users will need more than read-only access, it is necessary to configure the specific FTP directory to allow read and write access via the NTFS permissions and use the IIS security settings to restrict access, if needed. This way, one of two components is eliminated.

2. At the command prompt, type **ftp** and then press the ENTER key.

3. Next type **open *ipaddress*** where *ipaddress* is the IP address you specified for the new site you created.

4. When prompted, provide the logon name of anonymous and a password of me@mail.com. You should now have access to the FTP server as an anonymous read-only user.

Once these steps have been completed, you should be connected to the FTP site. If the site in general is not accessible, you will receive an error message that says the connection attempt failed after you try step #2. If you receive an error message after providing a username and password, you will need to double-check your FTP site security settings and the NTFS file permissions on the FTP home directory.

SOLVING USER ACCESS PROBLEMS

One of the common issues that occur when you have a newly created site (FTP or web) is some kind of user access problem. Either the user cannot log on or they cannot gain access to the content desired once they are logged on. There are two ways to address this issue. First, you can run the Permissions Wizard on the site in question. To do this, open the MMC and right-click the web or FTP site that is experiencing problems. Select All Tasks and then Permissions Wizard. Follow the prompts of the wizard, select the kinds of access you desire, and have the wizard replace all of the existing security permissions. If using the Permissions Wizard does not correct the access issue, check the NTFS file-level permissions for any setting that might restrict access. If the user can read files but not write, you will need to check both IIS and NTFS security settings because either one can restrict users to read-only access.

WRAPPING UP...

Internet Information Services is available with most of the current Microsoft operating systems and can provide a range of services, including web serving, FTP, news, and e-mail. While IIS exists in many of Microsoft's operating systems, only the Server version of Windows supports multiple instances of web and FTP sites. Server versions of IIS also allow virtually unlimited numbers of users to connect to the services offered. Nonserver versions such as Windows XP

Professional can accommodate a single instance of any of the available services, and are restricted to ten simultaneous connections at a time.

Much of this chapter was dedicated to installation configuration of the various IIS services. Each service has a wealth of security, usage, and policy-related options you can configure on a per-site basis. Many of these services are enabled by default once IIS is installed, and any of them that you do not plan to actively use should be disabled.

TOOLS AND TROUBLESHOOTING TACTICS

13

No IT worker is complete without a solid repertoire of systems software and network tools. There are all kinds of tools available—from external hardware units to freeware applications. Having a variety of them at your disposal can be invaluable when you are in the middle of a bad situation. Our focus here will be on working with software tools that are readily available with your operating system or are easily obtained. In this chapter, we'll…

- Explore the usage of Windows 2000 command line utilities
- Configure Windows 2000 Server to provide a variety of remote access services
- Use the NetWare 5 disk management tools to create and mount server volumes
- Examine common networking issue types
- Create and Manage NetWare user accounts

WINDOWS 2000 SERVER TOOLS

There are a large number of tools available at your disposal with Windows 2000 Server, from disk and user management to enabling and controlling enhanced services such as web and remote access services. In this chapter, we will focus on the tools that will be useful in troubleshooting network and server-related issues.

COMMAND LINE TOOLS

Windows 2000 Server has thankfully kept, and even expanded upon, the command line functionality of other operating systems. A host of tools exist that, used from the command line, can identify the status of connections between host's the utilization of a particular network segment, or view a host's routing table just to name a few. In this section, we will explore some of the more useful tools and their usage options. In order to use these tools, click the Start button and select the Run icon. In the Run dialog box that appears, type **cmd** and press ENTER. If the host running the command is configured to use DNS services, either the DNS hostname (www.foo.com) or the IP address (127.0.0.1) can be used. Each of the tools outlined next has the capability to make use of a variety of parameters, or switches, which will modify the behavior of the command in question. The switches that are the most useful are explained following the command itself. To view the full complement of all available switches, you can use the switch "/?", which will display the command syntax and the purpose of the available switches.

TRACERT

The tracert command is used to determine the routers, or hops, that exist between the host where the command is run and the target specified during the execution of the command. In addition to the hops between the hosts, tracert calculates the time it takes for data to reach each hop and then return to the host. This is done three times to ensure that an accurate sample is obtained. See Figure 13-1 to view the output of the tracert command. Large (over 200 ms) round-trip times can indicate a point of network congestion. The list that follows contains the common switches that can be used with the tracert command, what those switches will accomplish, and an example of their use:

- **-d**   Keeps tracert from resolving IP addresses into hostnames. Example: tracert –d www.foo.com or tracert –d 206.16.6.52

- **-h**   Allows you to specify the number of hops to examine. For example, tracert –h 4 www.foo.com will only examine the first four routers between the host running the command and the remote target.

```
C:\WINNT\System32\cmd.exe                                    _ □ ×

C:\>tracert www.stonecreeknetworks.com

Tracing route to www.stonecreeknetworks.com [64.85.73.31]
over a maximum of 30 hops:

   1    <10 ms    <10 ms    <10 ms   cigate.ci.walla-walla.wa.us [209.74.210.1]
   2    <10 ms     50 ms     30 ms   198.239.158.249
   3     60 ms      *         30 ms   198.239.158.74
   4     40 ms     71 ms     80 ms   198.187.0.66
   5     50 ms     40 ms     40 ms   198.187.0.178
   6     40 ms     50 ms     40 ms   198.187.0.162
   7     40 ms     40 ms     80 ms   198.187.0.218
   8     40 ms     50 ms     50 ms   ccar2-wes-FE1-2-1-0.pnw-gigapop.net [198.107.144
.9]
   9     70 ms     90 ms     60 ms   cnsp2-wes-GE0-1-0-0.pnw-gigapop.net [198.107.151
.7]
  10     60 ms     61 ms     50 ms   bpr1-ge-5-3-0.SeattleSwitchDesign.cw.net [208.17
3.49.33]
  11     30 ms     40 ms     60 ms   acr1-aso-0.Seattle.cw.net [208.172.83.186]
  12     30 ms     50 ms     60 ms   bhr1-pos-0-0.Tukwilase2.cw.net [208.172.83.130]

  13     50 ms     40 ms     70 ms   csr11-ve240.Tukwilase2.cw.net [216.34.64.34]
  14     40 ms     91 ms     60 ms   m1.dnsix.com [64.85.73.31]

Trace complete.

C:\>_
```

FIGURE 13.1   Tracert output

The tracert command is useful when you are trying to target the source of a network communications problem. If, for example, you are managing a routed network such as a large LAN or WAN, you might run into a situation where tracert would be useful. If users are having trouble accessing a resource such as a printer or file server, tracert can be used to determine if there is a communications bottleneck on the network. By running a trace from the affected client computer to the resource in question (or the other way around), you will see the response time and routing path between the two endpoints. You may discover that the client is using an incorrect gateway or that one of the routers is directing traffic inefficiently. This is especially common after significant router changes have been made, or if new routers have been recently added. It is also possible that you may see excessive round-trip times. Times consistently greater than 20 ms on a LAN or 200 ms on a WAN indicate there is a problem in the capability of the router (or the resource itself) to respond to client requests.

PING

The ping command is probably familiar to you if you have done any kind of work that involves connecting host PCs to the network. The ping command will allow you to determine if a remote host is accessible by sending an ICMP echo reply request. If the host is available and has not had its capability to respond disabled, a response will be sent. The results of this command include an output labeled "time". This number indicates the amount of time it takes for the packet to reach the remote host and then return to the host where the command was executed. High values, over 200 ms, indicate network congestion is occurring. There are several optional switches that can be used with the ping command, and the most useful of them are outlined here:

- **-t** Configures the ping command to continuously send requests to the target host until you use the CTRL-C escape sequence. For example, ping –t 192.168.1.34 will continually send ICMP requests to the host 192.168.1.34 until you use the escape sequence.

- **-n** Allows you to specify the number of echo requests to send to the target host. For example, ping –n 2 192.168.1.34 will send only two requests to the intended host, 192.168.1.34.

PATHPING

The pathping command is basically the ping and tracert command combined and enhanced. While it will provide greater information, it can take a little more time to complete, so it may not be appropriate for all situations. That being said, pathping is very useful when assessing the state of communications between the host where the command is run and the specified target host.

In its most basic form, the command will determine the routers between the sending host and the target (a la tracert) and then ping each step in the process to determine the rate at which packets are dropped by any of the identified routers (ping). The result is a list of the routers involved and the percentage of packets sent to each router that was dropped. Some routers are configured to refuse any ICMP echo reply requests, and they will reflect this with 100-percent packet loss. There are a large number of switches available with this command, many of which are common to ping and tracert commands. To access the full list of options, run the pathping command with no target host specified. To test pathping on a host, use the form "pathping *hostname/IP*" where *hostname/IP* is the name or IP address of the intended target.

TELNET

The telnet command will allow you to connect to a telnet server. Telnet servers are common managed network devices such as routers, switches, and some specialized network storage appliances. The telnet command can be used to connect to either the standard telnet port on a host (TCP port 23) or any other port available by making use of the port command option. For example, you could connect to the standard telnet port on a host at 200.34.56.78 by issuing the command "telnet 200.34.56.78". If the telnet server is running on a different port, such as 3546 (which is a good idea if the server is publicly accessible), then use the command "telnet 200.34.56.78 port 3546."

There are two scenarios where this tool is particularly useful. The most obvious use involves connecting a telnet server, and the secondary use involves testing the functionality of various network services. In their most common manifestation, telnet servers will allow a remote administrator to make changes to the server's operating environment. Typically, the user cannot transfer files, but they can usually edit configuration settings or start and stop system services, among other things. Many network devices, including many popular models of routers and switches, can be configured to provide telnet server services so that network managers can monitor and manage these devices remotely.

The telnet command can be used to perform basic testing of network services. For example, the default TCP port for the HTTP service (web server) is port 80. If you are having a connectivity problem and you are unsure if hosts can connect to the HTTP port of a server, you can add the port number as a switch to the telnet command. For example "telnet *IPAddress* 80" would make a connection to port 80 on the host using the IP address specified if the HTTP service is running on the target. This "trick" works for other common services such as SMTP (e-mail, port 25) and FTP (port 21).

FTP

FTP is really very similar to the telnet command except that, of course, it allows you to make a command line connection to an FTP server. Rather than explain all of the options, the following steps will walk you through the process of connecting to a fictional computer 192.168.234.77 using some of the common options available. This list of steps assumes that the FTP server is using the standard TCP port (20 and 21) and allows anonymous access. Feel free to replace the fictional server with the IP (or hostname) of a real server that allows anonymous access.

1. Open a command prompt and run the command "ftp 192.168.234.77".

2. When prompted, enter the username **anonymous**.

3. Most systems will then prompt you to use your e-mail for a password, and you will need to supply one to log on.

NOTE   This FTP logon process is not a secure one, as the username and password are passed between the client and server as cleartext. If someone happens to be sniffing network traffic when the logon occurs, the username and password could easily be stolen.

4. Once the logon has completed, type **bin** and press the ENTER key. This will configure the session to allow binary file transactions.

5. To download a file, use the get command and then specify the name of the file. For example, "get filename.zip."

You can use the dir command to view directory contents and cd to change directories.

NETSTAT

The netstat command will display connection information, including connected hosts and the ports that the server is listening to for incoming connections. For example, the netstat –a command will show all of the ports of the servers services (http=80, ftp=21 and so forth) as well as any connected users. This command is particularly useful if you want quick and concise information about the services running on the server and the users that are in the process of using those services.

GRAPHICAL TOOLS

In addition to the command line tools that accompany Windows 2000 Server, there are several graphical tools that you will find useful when configuring and troubleshooting network services. Since your Windows 2000 Server has the capacity to provide a number of network services, we will focus on tools that will give you configuration and operational information about some of the more powerful networking features.

ROUTING AND REMOTE ACCESS (RRAS)

Windows 2000 Server comes with a powerful routing, dial-up access, and VPN access solution called Routing and Remote Access (RRAS). RRAS is a Windows 2000 service that can be used to configure a wide range of services. First off though, you will need to configure and activate the RRAS service. In the steps that follows, you will enable the RRAS service and configure your server to act as a router on your LAN:

1. Click the Start | Programs | Administrative Tools. Locate the Routing and Remote Access (RRAS) icon and click it to open the RRAS console.

2. Once you have the RRAS console open, you should see your server in the list. After clicking the server you will see a small red symbol next to it indicating the RRAS service is not active. See Figure 13-2.

3. Right-click the server and choose Configure and Enable Routing and Remote Access from the context menu that appears.

4. The next window displayed is the RRAS Wizard. Click the Next button to continue.

5. By default, the radio button next to the Network Router entry will be selected. Leave the default setting as is and click the Next button again. Select TCP/IP as the supported protocol and click the Next button.

6. Select No when prompted to use demand dial services, then click the Next button again.

7. After clicking the Finish button, the RRAS service will start and you will see, as in Figure 13-3, that your server now has a small green icon next to it in the RRAS window and various services are visible in relation to the server.

Once you have RRAS enabled and your Windows 2000 Server is acting as a router or as an Internet gateway, there are two critical network management elements you can implement: static routing and IP filtering. Both of these features

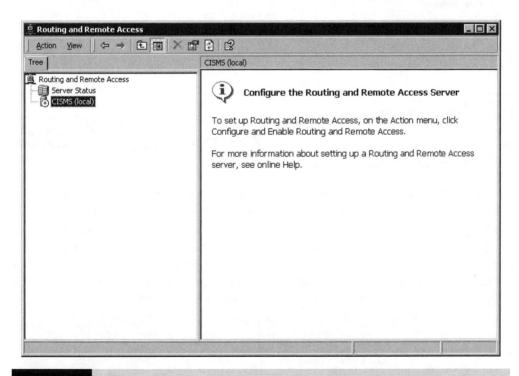

FIGURE 13.2   RRAS console

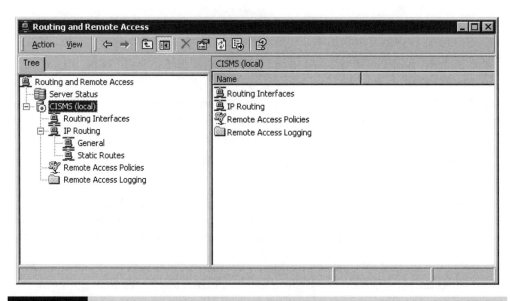

FIGURE 13.3 RRAS enabled

are accessed from within the RRAS console. A static route forces the router to push network traffic destined for a given network or host in a predetermined location. Take, for example, a Windows 2000 Server that has two network

TECH TALK

Cutting Network Abuse

Many large-scale networks, from office buildings to educational institutions, have users that inappropriately use network resources for less than productive purposes. Two of the biggest culprits are streaming media and online games. Depending on the number of users, a large quantity of the available WAN (Internet) capacity may be consumed. One simple solution is to block TCP/IP ports used by the services that, as long as they are not "work related," are consuming the most bandwidth. For example the Real Audio player uses port 7070, and the popular online game called Half-Life uses ports 2710 and 2715. If other services are in use, you can usually enable logging at the WAN router to capture the kinds of ports being used by network clients. By sorting through this list, you can identify ports that are used by forbidden services.

adapters—one is connected to the private network (network A) and the other is connected to the Internet. If another router on the network connects to yet another network (network B) your Windows 2000 Server can be configured with a static route that will forward all requests it receives for network B to the appropriate router. To add a static route to your RRAS server, follow these steps:

1. Open the RRAS console and expand the IP Routing container.

2. Right-click the Static Routes object and select New Static Route from the menu that appears, and the static routes interface will appear.

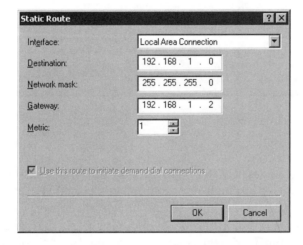

3. Select the interface that this route should apply to. You may either select a particular interface by selecting one of the Local Area Connections, or all interfaces by selecting Internal.

4. Next enter the network ID or specific host that you are providing access to, its network mask, and the IP address of the gateway that will provide a route to the network in question.

5. Lastly, you will need to enter the gateway address used to reach the IP you have specified. The gateway address must reside on one of the networks that your router (Windows 2000 Server) is connected to; otherwise, your router will have no means of delivering traffic to the gateway.

6. Once all of the information has been entered, click the OK button and your route will appear in the right-hand portion of the RRAS console, as shown in Figure 13-4.

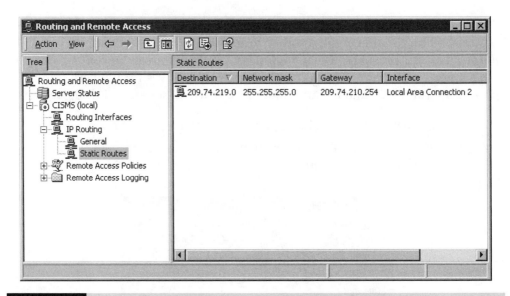

FIGURE 13.4   Static route information

The RRAS service provides the capability to filter inbound (coming into the router) and outbound (from the router to other networks) IP traffic. This filtering will allow you to enact granular control over how traffic moves about your network, as well as prevent some security risks by blocking ports that you may not want authorized or unauthorized users using/accessing. In addition to implementing some control over how network traffic is secured, blocking certain ports such as those used by streaming web-based radio can help you reduce the utilization of your often costly links to the Internet. The following steps will allow you to create a basic IP filter that allows incoming traffic on TCP port 80 only:

1. Open the RRAS console, then click the plus symbol (+) next to IP Routing.

2. Click the General entry. In the right-hand portion of the console, all of the available routing interfaces will appear.

3. Right-click one of the interfaces and select Properties from the context menu that appears. The IP Interface window is displayed.

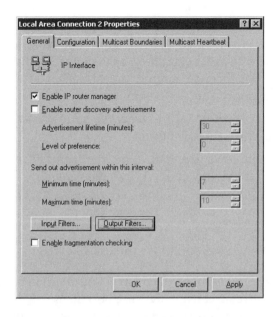

4. From within the IP Interface window, you can click the Input Filters or Output Filters buttons. Both of these tools will allow you to do the same thing—configure filter rules—except that one binds to inbound connections and one to outbound connections.

5. Click the Inbound Filters button. The Filter window will appear.

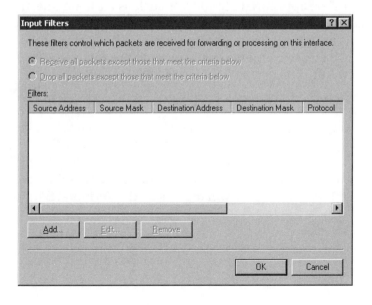

6. Click the Add button. In the Add IP Filter dialog box that appears, you can decide to filter IP traffic based on the source network address, destination address, both source and destination as well as specific TCP and UDP ports. If you do not specify a source or destination address, the rule will be applied to all source and/or destination addresses.

7. In the Protocol box, select TCP and set the source and destination ports to a value of 80. Click the OK button.

8. The Add Filter windows will vanish and the Input Filters window will now show the rule that you have added. To make sure that your configuration allows only port 80 traffic (and does not block all port 80 traffic), make sure the bullet next to Drop All Packets Except Those That Meet the Criteria Below is selected.

9. Click OK and then OK again. Close the RRAS console.

The same process could be used to construct outbound filters for your router. You could, for instance, restrict users to using port 80 only. This would effectively allow them to connect to web servers, but not other resources. This might be appropriate if the next hop beyond the filtered interface was the router connecting the LAN to the internet, but for intra-LAN connectivity this is probably a poor idea since most of the LAN traffic is not going to be targeting port 80.

Because another of the features of RRAS is the capability to support dial-in connections over a modem, we'll briefly explore this feature. Installing dial-up support requires the appropriate hardware, such as a phone line and installed modem. You will also need to select the appropriate option during RRAS configuration (select the Remote Access Server option). This service behaves much like VPN, because they essentially provide the same service. Dial-in connections typically are easy to implement because there has been extensive standardization of modem protocols. Dial-up connections to the LAN are useful in two regards: users that have to travel frequently can use the service to access local network resources, and it offers one of the most secure options for remote network management. When you dial in to the server, you will not be sharing a public network segment. If you use encrypted services (VPN) in addition to dial-up, then you have a mobile and secure remote access solution. This can be combined with the service we will discuss next—Terminal Services.

TECH TALK

Making a VPN Server with Windows 2000 Server

To enable virtual private network (VPN) services on your Windows 2000 Server, follow the process outlined next. You will need to be logged on to your Windows 2000 Server as a user with administrative privileges in order to complete these steps.

1. Click Start | Programs | Administrative Tools.

2. Locate the Routing and Remote Access application and open it.

3. Click the Action menu and select Disable Routing and Remote Access. This will erase your current RRAS configuration.

4. Click the Action menu and select Configure and Enable.

5. When the RRAS Wizard opens, click the Next button to continue.

6. Click the bullet next to the Virtual Private Network Server entry.

7. Select the supported protocols (TCP/IP) and click Next.

8. Specify the connection to use for incoming VPN connections, then click Next.

9. Select a static pool to assign addresses.

10. Specify the IP address pool to use and click the Next button.

11. Unless you know you need RADIUS support, click Next.

12. Click the Finish button and the RRAS service will start.

TERMINAL SERVICES

Windows 2000 Terminal Services allows a user to connect to a Windows 2000 Server in a manner that simulates direct access. For example, if a remote user connects to a Widows 2000 Server that has Terminal Services installed, that

TROUBLESHOOTING

Solving Dial-Up Access Problems

If you or your users are having trouble using your Windows 2000 Routing and Remote Access Server for dial-up services, there are a couple of simple checks that will either resolve the issue or at least help you identify the source. The first step is to check and see if the available dial-in connections are in use. Log on to the RRAS server and open the RRAS applet. You will be able to immediately see if there are any users connected. If there are connections available, and fewer users are connected than there are modems available, you will need to dig a little deeper. If the user is dialing in from a hotel or similar setting, they may need to dial 9 to get an outside line, or there may be too much line noise to make a connection. If the computer in question has not connected previously, then double-check both the dial-in client's configuration (phone #, protocols, and so forth) as well as the user account being used. Make sure that the user has been granted permissions to dial in and that they are not in conflict with any time-based dial-in restrictions. Logging is probably your best hope for resolving truly confounding connectivity problems. If you configure RRAS to log the connection attempts (can work for VPN or dial-up), you will be able to see if the user is actually able to establish a communications session. If they can get a session connected, you should be able to identify where the (probably authentication related) issues are occurring. If the issue is not configuration based, you can restart the RRAS server, reset the modems if they are external, and reboot the remote client.

user can connect to the server and create a virtual session. When the session is active, the user will see the desktop of the server and then can interact with it just like they were physically sitting in front of the server. The advantages of this capability are numerous. For example, an administrator in charge of maintaining multiple Windows 2000 Servers can take advantage of Terminal Services to keep tabs on all the various servers from a single location. This reduces the time needed to enact repairs or to collect information about potential server failures.

There are two modes that can be used with Terminal Services: application server mode and remote administration mode. The application server mode will allow you to connect large numbers of users to the terminal server for the purpose of sharing applications and so forth. This option requires that you have a terminal server licensing server to manage user connections, but for our purposes the remote administration mode is more practical. With the remote administration mode in use, only users who are members of the local or domain administrators groups will be able to access the server and launch a terminal services session, and only two users at a time will be able to make use of the service.

In order to make use of Terminal Services, you will, of course, need to install the feature first. The steps outlined next will install Terminal Services in administrative mode on your Windows 2000 Server:

1. Open the Windows Control Panel and launch Add/Remove Programs.

2. In the window that appears, click Add/Remove Windows Components.

3. Locate the Terminal Services entry and fill in the associated check box. Do not fill in the check box next to the Terminal Services Licensing entry as it is used only for the application server mode. Click the Next button.

4. In the Terminal Services Setup window that appears, select the remote administration option and click the Next button. The installation will proceed and Terminal Services will start.

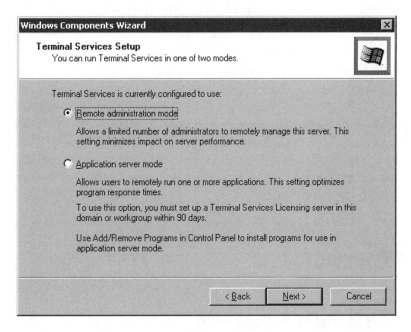

Once you have Terminal Services installed, you will need to perform a simple client-side configuration to make the connection. While your Windows 2000 Server can be used to create Terminal Services client installation disks, there is a much easier method for getting the client files installed. By visiting the Microsoft

Windows XP download site at http://www.microsoft.com/windowsxp/pro/downloads/, you can obtain a new version of the client software, now called the Remote Desktop Protocol (RDP) client. RDP client tools work with both Terminal Services and the new RDP service provided with Windows XP and .NET server. This compatibility makes the RDP client the client of choice. To obtain and install the RDP client, follow these steps:

1. Open a web browser and enter the URL, **http://www.microsoft.com/windowsxp/pro/downloads/**.

2. Scroll down to the Handy Tools heading and click the link titled Remote Desktop Connection Software.

3. On the page that appears next, there is a link to the file msrdpcli.exe. Click the link and select the Save option when prompted. Select a location and download the file.

4. When the download completes, locate and run the msrdpcli.exe executable.

5. Step through the Installation Wizard using the default settings.

6. Once the installation is completed, click the Start button, go to Programs, then Accessories. Find the Communications folder and launch the Remote Desktop Connection application.

7. With the RDP application, pictured in Figure 13-5, you can enter all of the information needed to connect to your Terminal Services–enabled server. If you do not see the same options as shown in Figure 13-5, click the Options button to expand your choices. Only the configuration information under the General tab is critical. The other tabs contain visualization and other such information that does not have to be changed from the default settings to allow connectivity.

TROUBLESHOOTING

Using Terminal Services to Work from Home

Here is the scenario: You're the network administrator and you have at least one Windows 2000 Server with Terminal Services installed. Since you are occasionally on call at all hours of the night, or sometimes at home sick, you would like to use the Remote Desktop client to

Using Terminal Services to Work from Home (continued)

connect to the server and manage your network. When tested on the network, you find that the client connects fine, but from home you get an error message indicating the Terminal Services host is inaccessible.

To get your remote access up and working, you will need to configure an inbound port on your Internet firewall to direct Terminal Services traffic on TCP port 3389 to the server that has Terminal Services running. Because there is a significant risk from exposing your server to the Internet, you should use VPN to make an initial encrypted connection to the LAN, and then make the RDP connection over that VPN link. If the link between your home PC and the server is not encrypted, it will be possible for a determined hacker to sniff packets sent between your computer and the server and possibly obtain information such as your logon and password. An even more effective configuration is to use RDP over a dedicated dial-up connection to the server providing the Terminal Services functionality. Since you would have a direct connection to the terminal server, there is less risk to network security.

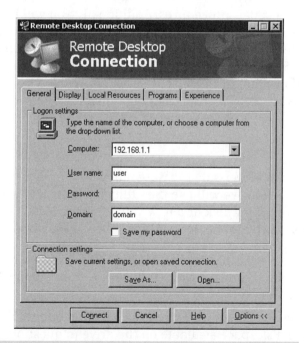

FIGURE 13.5   Remote Desktop connection

NETWARE TOOLS

Just like Windows 2000 Server, Novell NetWare 5 has a wealth of server and network tools. In Chapter 11, we took a long look at the networking and implementation processes associated with NetWare 5. The tools in this section focus more on the daily operation of the NetWare server and include two general categories: file management and user account administration. Because the vast majority of general network evaluation and monitoring will occur at the client side (at the administrator's workstation), specific network analysis tools will not be examined here. Because each client (such as Windows, UNIX, or Apple workstations) will have its own tools available, it would be prohibitive to attempt to address them all. Of course, Windows analysis tools are covered in some detail in this and other chapters, so for the vast majority of users the relevant topics are present in this text.

FILE MANAGEMENT TOOLS

The tools outlined next will allow you to configure the hard disk on the server and enact basic disk repair procedures. Additionally, you will be able to explore the process for recovering deleted data and permanently removing deleted files. In order to complete the various processes outlined in this section, you will need to have administrative rights to a NetWare server and have the NetWare Administrator application installed. The services provided by Windows Client Services for NetWare (CSNW from Chapter 11) will not provide the needed functionality.

NWCONFIG.NLM

NWCONFIG.NLM is a server-side NetWare utility used for many disk management purposes. In this section, we will use the utility to create a new volume. This can be a new volume on a new disk or a new volume using existing disk space on an installed hard disk. To build the new volume, follow these steps:

1. Log on to the NetWare server and load NWCONFIG.NLM. When prompted, select Standard Disk Options and then Modify Disk Partitions and Hot Fix.

2. Next, choose the Create NetWare Disk Partition option. You will see the current free disk space available on the drive in question.

3. Enter the size of the new partition and leave the rest of the settings at their default values for the Hot Fix and Redirection Area settings.

4. To commit the changes you have made, press the F10 key on your keyboard and then choose Yes when prompted.

5. Go back to the Hot Fix screen and choose the NetWare Volume Options setting.

6. Press the INSERT key to see a list of the configured volumes and free disk space. In this view, you should be able to see the partition that was just created. Select the newly created partition and press the ENTER key.

7. When prompted, select the option titled Make this Segment a New Volume and then enter a name for the new volume.

8. Press F10 to save the current configuration.

MOUNT UTILITY

In order to use new volumes, or work on existing volumes, you will need to make use of the MOUNT and DISMOUNT utilities. To mount a volume newvol, execute the following command from the prompt at the NetWare server: mount newvol. The dismount command uses the same syntax and, of course, accomplishes the exact opposite of the mount command.

VREPAIR.NLM

If hardware issues arise with one of the server hard disks, it is possible that critical volume information will become corrupted. The result might be inaccessible (unmountable) volumes—disk read errors or bad hard disk blocks that result in inaccessible data. Because the data on server disks tends to be important, NetWare comes with a tool for attempting repairs of afflicted volumes. VREPAIR.NLM is normally invoked automatically when the server encounters disk errors. If for some reason the NLM is not invoked automatically, the steps outline how to run the utility manually.

This is not a procedure that should be performed (for practice anyway) on a system that is currently in production use. If you would like to practice the procedure outlined next, it is highly recommended that you either make sure you have a working backup in the event that there is a problem or, better yet, practice on a nonessential server that, if it becomes inoperable, nobody will care if you inadvertently render the system inaccessible.

1. Before going forward, dismount the volume you will be working with.

2. From the console of the server, load VREPAIR.NLM.

3. Choose the volume you want to repair by selecting Option 1 and specifying the target drive.

4. Press the ENTER key and then select Option 2 to have VREPAIR log any errors it finds to a log file for later examination. Enter a name for the log file and press the ENTER key.

5. Select Option 4 to proceed with the repair and press the ENTER key.

6. Once the VREPAIR process has completed, you will be asked to write any repairs to the disk. Select Yes to implement any needed repairs.

7. If there were errors detected, you will need to run VREPAIR again to ensure that all of the defects were detected and corrected. Continue running VREPAIR until errors are no longer detected.

If issues with the volume persist, you may need to delete the volume and re-create it. Any data stored on that volume will be lost and must be restored from any backups that are available.

TECH TALK

Purge and Salvage NetWare Files

As you may or may not know, a network client will not be able to permanently delete files that are stored on a NetWare server unless they have administrative privileges. This is a fail-safe of sorts, but can present some perplexing problems since these files occupy space and thus an administrator needs to play a role in removing older files to free additional disk space. The flip side is that if a user accidentally deletes a needed file, you will be able to help them recover the information in a relatively painless manner. Follow these steps to purge or restore a deleted file from your NetWare server:

1. Open the NetWare Administrator on your client system.

2. Locate the directory containing the files that need to be purged or restored.

3. Click the Tools menu, then select the Salvage option.

4. In the Include field of the window that appears, specify the files to act on.

5. Using the Source drop-down menu, choose where to place restored files.

6. Click the List button to display the files you have chosen to work with.

7. Select the files (click them) and then click the Purge button to remove.

8. If you want to restore files, click them and click the Salvage button.

Files restored from a deleted directory will appear in the DELETED.SAV directory in the root of the server.

USER ACCOUNT TOOLS

Creating and managing accounts can be a daily chore for the network administrator. Fortunately, the NetWare Administrator tool simplifies two of the more common activities: creating user accounts and managing user rights.

CREATING A USER ACCOUNT

To create a new user account, you will need to create a home directory for the user in question on your NetWare 5 server and then follow these steps:

1. Launch the NetWare Administrator.
2. Select the container that will be used to house you new user by clicking it.
3. Click the Objects menu and select the Create option.
4. In the New Objects window that appears next, you must select the User option and then click the OK button.
5. The Create User windows will appear. Fill in the Login Name field.
6. Fill in the check box next to Create Home Directory and click the Browse button. Locate a directory where the user's home directory should be located and select the appropriate entry.
7. The window that appears next will allow you to define additional information that will be associated with the user's account. If you are curious, explore these options. When you have made any desired changes, click the OK button.

CHANGING INDIVIDUAL FILE ACCESS RIGHTS

Obviously, you will occasionally need to alter the kinds of rights assigned to a user in relation to the files and folders. If you need to change or add users as trustees (users that have access rights) to a folder or volume on your NetWare server, you can use the NetWare Administrator tool to accomplish this. The steps outlined next will walk you through the process of changing the access rights a user has to a volume or an object:

1. Open the NetWare Administrator.
2. Within the Administrator browser, select one of the objects available.
3. Open the Objects menu and then select the Trustees of This Object option.
4. The Trustee window will appear and the users that have been assigned access rights to the object in question will be displayed in the upper

portion of the window. Click one of the users and the lower portion of this window will populate with the rights assigned to that user.

5. To add or remove a user right, you can fill in (add) or clear (remove) the check box associated with a particular user right, such as browse, create, rename, delete, and so forth.

SOLVING COMMON PROBLEMS

Now that we have examined some of the tools at your disposal, we'll look at some basic techniques that can be used in conjunction with these tools to help you actually solve problems on your network. One of the most valuable techniques for dealing with network issues is using preventative measures. By making use of regular monitoring, baseline creations, and regular data backups, you can seriously reduce the impact of server-based problems. The following list outlines some easy ways to implement preventative measures on your network servers:

- Schedule, maintain, and keep off-site regular backups of user data.

- Create a performance baseline for network hardware and server performance that includes utilization during peak and off-peak times.

- Log server and network hardware utilization on a regular basis. Regularly compare the collected information to existing baselines.

TROUBLESHOOTING

Using Disk Imaging

If a user's workstation fails, you may be able to have them up and running in minutes if you have a usable disk image of the workstation configuration. A disk image is made with a program such as Norton Ghost and is literally a snapshot of all of the data on the hard disk that has to be "imaged." If a virus, hardware failure, or other mishap should corrupt the software on the imaged machine, then the previously created image can be restored to the system and the user can be up and running in no time. In order for this solution to be really useful, the user's data files need to be stored on a network share or on removable media of some kind. Since imaging will eradicate any of the remaining data, it is not advised if the user's documents are stored locally on the workstation experiencing the software failure.

NOTE   Baselines typically include information like CPU utilization, network transmission statistics such as collisions, percent of whole traffic that is broadcast/multicast, and segment utilization rates. This information is used for comparative purposes so that a network manager can identify areas where increased utilization or some kind of software/hardware failure may lead to future problems.

Because even the best preventative measures will not forestall all possible issues, you will of course need to prepare for the worst. Applications that rely on networks and centralized servers can be especially prone to problems if the environment they operate in is not stable, or if the conditions change. Add to that the possibility of server and client operating system upgrades that require the migration of your older applications to new and perhaps untested platforms, and the complexities increase.

When a networked application fails, user data may be lost or corrupted. Corrupted data files can usually be repaired with a recent backup of the data, but if the application continues to fail, the resulting downtime could be costly and will almost certainly be frustrating to the end user. Often, the failure of a network

TECH TALK

Migrating Older Applications

Sometimes custom applications installed on older systems must be migrated when the server housing the application is upgraded. The application files and any data records may need to be preserved. Very old applications, such as early 16-bit DOS applications, may not be guaranteed to work on a replacement platform. In many cases, the vendor can offer a replacement product if the product is still supported and the vendor is still in business. If possible, the data should be exported to a common format such as a comma- or tab-delineated text file. Some applications actually store data in this manner, so importing the data into a SQL-based application, for example, is usually straightforward.

If using common formats is not a viable option, then you will need to migrate the application from one server to another. The easiest method involves trying to reinstall the application on the new server. If the installation completes, you can copy the data from the existing server and attempt to open the data on the new server. Should the installation of the legacy application fail, you can try a wholesale copy of the old application and its data. You should attempt to keep the drive letter the same from old system to new, and maintain the same directory structure exactly. If the product was installed on C:\application\source, you should move it to C:\application\source on the new device. Many old applications make use of hard-coded paths and will infrequently work if the paths have changed during the move.

application is the result of either excessive communications delay in network communications or intermittent link failure. On an Ethernet-based network, excessive delay in network communications is the result of several factors. If LAN segment utilization exceeds 40 percent of available bandwidth or if the percent of broadcast traffic exceeds 20 percent, serious degradation can occur. Finally, because of the way Ethernet operates, data collisions can occur. A collision results in lost data and a host that has its data wiped out must resend the missing information. If the number of collisions grows large, network communications can be slowed to a crawl.

The previous causes are collectively known as media contention issues. The solution to these kinds of problems involves adding or expanding the presence of switching on the network. Switching improves the responsiveness of the

TROUBLESHOOTING

Restoring from a Backup

If a user that has files stored on your Windows 2000 Server inadvertently deletes or corrupts a file, you can make use of an existing backup to restore a previous version of the file. If you have been using the Windows backup utility to perform regular backups, you can restore the missing information by collecting the most recent backup and following the procedure outlined here.

1. Click the Start button, then select Programs | Accessories | System Tools and click the Backup icon.

2. When the backup utility opens, click the Restore tab.

3. Select the media containing the backup in the leftmost portion of the window. Once the media has been accessed, you can browse the media for the file or directory that contains the items you wish to restore.

4. Click the check box next to the item(s) you want to restore.

5. Once the items have been selected, click the Start Restore button.

network by providing a new physical network segment on each port of the switch. Because each port is its own segment, there is no media contention.

Network link failures can also result from a number of issues, but you are most likely to encounter this issue if you are accessing resources across a WAN connection or the host/server has a network adapter that is failing. A failing network card is a relatively simple fix—you replace the ailing hardware. Failing network adapters are also relatively easy to identify since most of the network operations passing through the failing device will periodically (or permanently) fail. Fixing issues with intermittent WAN links can be more difficult and costly. If you have verified that the WAN link is dropping, your first step should be to contact the service provider responsible for your service and have them address the connectivity loss. Sometimes due to remote locations, changing line conditions, or dial-up WAN connections, there is not much a service provider can do. Dial-on demand WAN connections, such as ISDN, may need to be replaced with more reliable data services if there are continued connectivity issues.

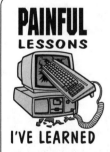

PAINFUL LESSONS I'VE LEARNED

I Swore that the Backup Was Running

One of the shortcomings with Windows backup is that it does not do a real good job of informing you of errors in the backup process. When I first made use of the Windows backup utility I scheduled a weekly normal backup and then daily incremental backups on the same media: a 200GB tape device. Being relatively new at the "backup game," I kind of forgot about the whole process, assuming that all would be well. Several weeks later, I decided to check on the backup since a recent server upgrade had left us with some missing data files. When I checked the tape, it appeared that the last update had occurred over a week prior and the tape was full. When I checked the logs, it turned out there was a pile of messages indicating that backups were failing. Fortunately, the missing data was essentially old and archived anyway, so it was recoverable. To prevent a real disaster, a process was developed where multiple tapes were cycled to ensure that there were several weeks of reliable backups.

TROUBLESHOOTING

Reviving Old Faithful

If you have a file server that is beginning to respond to client requests slower than it used to, there are a couple of simple things you can do to improve the situation. Most server response problems are the result of a performance bottleneck of one kind or another. Typically, the network adapter is the bottleneck for file servers. Where database, web, and application servers tend to consume system resources such as memory and CPU cycles, file servers are far more dependent on the capacity of the network adapter to service clients. To improve the performance of the file server, you can upgrade the section of the network hosting the server. If your switching equipment supports it, you can add a Gigabit Ethernet interface to the switch, and then add a complementary interface on the server. If the existing network equipment will not support faster interfaces, you can obtain a new device that will interface the existing network infrastructure with the faster server backbone. For example, a Hewlett Packard 4000 series modular switch with a 1-Gbps module installed will support large numbers of users (or other switches) as well as the high-speed server backbone.

Problems with Generic Memory

If a server is built using generic memory modules that do not make use of high-quality components, a slew of insidious issues can arise. For example, one of the company web servers that I was managing was experiencing some peculiar scripting errors. Some clients, when running database queries, would get either meaningless results or some kind of error message. Other servers accessing the same information did not experience the errors and logging revealed errors occurring during heavy usage periods. Since I did not want to rebuild the server or replace significant hardware components if I did not have to, I began to eliminate potential points of failure. I decided that since the errors were occurring in a kind of pattern (during heavy usage), I could rule out the CPU as a source. Really, that left me with network-bandwidth-, memory-, or hard-disk-related issues. Since other servers were operating normally under similar loads, I did not think the bandwidth was an issue. Replacing the hard disk would be very time-consuming since the server was not making use of RAID, so I decided to replace the memory modules. As it turns out, the memory modules were very low-quality components. When I replaced them with server-quality (high-speed w/ECC) memory modules, the problems disappeared.

General network communication errors may not be the result of hardware or software failure. As mentioned earlier, network utilization can be a serious problem as well. Users do not have to consume all of the available network bandwidth to cause issues. If there are a large number of network connections in use, the responsiveness of the network can be greatly degraded. This can be a particular problem if users are reliant on slow-speed WAN connections. Since this kind of connection can be easily overwhelmed, it is important that you keep tabs on how the network capacity is being used. Tracking how the WAN link, such as a network's connection to the Internet, is being used can be as simple as installing a proxy server or other application on the WAN gateway that will log the destinations of user-generated traffic. By analyzing the results of this logging, you can identify inappropriate network usage and take the steps needed to correct the errant behavior.

PAINFUL LESSONS

I'VE LEARNED

Giving a User an Inch Who Took a Mile

It is very important to be consistent with the management of network policies. Giving users leeway to drift beyond the defined network policies can lead to abuse that could have otherwise been easily prevented. A friend and sometime coworker of mine once managed the LAN for a network consulting firm and allowed a couple of the engineers to use the network to play LAN games. This seemed reasonable since the network had additional capacity, the users were housed in a secluded location from other users, and sometimes the downtime became unbearable. Unknown to my associate, the users had begun to join Internet-based game servers. This was especially unfortunate since the Internet connection used at that site was a metered leased line with a monthly bandwidth cap. Needless to say, the gaming became frequent and the bandwidth cap was exceeded several times. When questions arose about how the cap was being exceeded so regularly when the cap had never been exceeded before, the truth came out. Because my associate had shown complicity in allowing the abuse to begin in the first place, and that abuse had resulted in significant bandwidth usage costs, he greatly compromised his future with the employer and in fact had several of his job duties assigned to other administrators.

WRAPPING UP...

The main focus of this chapter was on tools that accompany Windows 2000 Server and Novell NetWare 5 that will help you manage server and network resources. Many command line utilities are present with Windows 2000 Server. Some of the tools, such as PathPing, can be used to assess the status of the network between the Windows 2000 Server and a remote resource. Other command line tools can be used to connect to FTP and telnet services, which gives the user the ability to interact with many networked devices—including routers, switches, and network storage devices. In addition to the text-driven utilities available with Windows 2000 Server, there are also many graphical utilities available. The Routing and Remote Access service allows your Windows 2000 Server to act as a VPN server, a router, and a remote access device. Additionally, the Windows Terminal Service can be used to permit sophisticated remote management of your Windows 2000 Servers.

NetWare 5 comes with a host of utilities usable for configuring server disks, user accounts, and user access rights to the files stored on the server. Much of the work for configuring NetWare hard disks can be accomplished with the combination of the NWCONFIG.NLM and MOUNT tools. Should hard disk errors arise, the VREPAIR.NLM tool can be used to rebuild critical volume information and hopefully restore access to the affected device. When it comes to managing accounts, the primary tool for configuring user settings is the NetWare Administrator. This utility can be used to both create new users and modify file access rights.

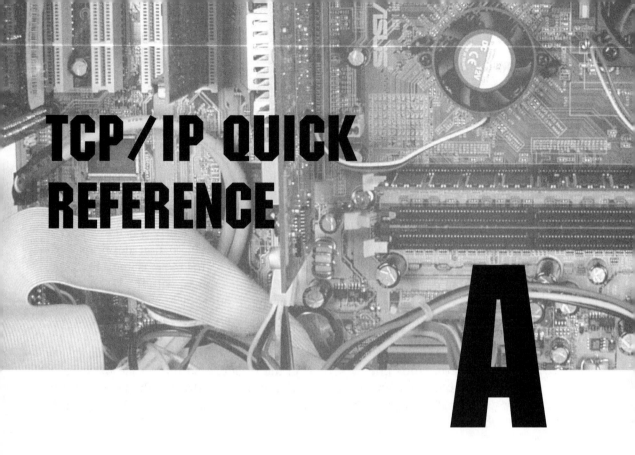

TCP/IP QUICK REFERENCE

A

Internet Protocol (IP) is quite literally the most important protocol in networking today. Support for IP is required for any computer to communicate with other hosts on the Internet and IP has the widest support of any networking protocol. Because it is a virtual guarantee that any network administrator or manager will encounter IP in some form or another, understanding IP addressing is critical. It is also the case that only the smallest of IP networks can be deployed without a decent understanding of IP addressing. In this appendix, we'll take a look at how TCP/IP operates and some ways you can put it to work!

INTERNET PROTOCOL

The Internet Protocol address contains, in its most basic form, information about two network components. The IP address of any given device contains information identifying the network ID where the host/computer resides as well as the host ID of the device itself. IP addresses are 32 bits in length and are stored as binary numbers.

NOTE Binary numbers use a series of 1s and 0s to represent larger and more complex numerical values. These binary numbers make up the native language of the microcomputer.

In an attempt to make IP addresses user friendly, they are most often displayed in "decimal delimited" format. The 32-bit address is segmented into four 8-bit clusters, known as *octets*, in a format that looks like "number.number.number.number." Each of these four octets can contain a whole number value of 0–255. The net result is an address that looks like (using random values) 210.254.23.22.

Earlier, I mentioned that IP addresses identify both the individual network and the ID of the particular node on that network. In order to clearly specify which portion of the IP address identifies the network and which portion identifies the node, a component known as the *subnet mask* is used. This mask is another 32-bit decimal-delimited address that is mathematically combined with the IP address to identify the node and network portions of the IP address. Each IP address is also a member of a class (explained in detail later), and each class has a default subnet mask. For example, the default subnet mask for the IP address 4.215.244.35 would be 255.0.0.0. Simply put, the numeric 255 in the first octet of the subnet mask indicates that the entire first octet of the IP address (in this case, 4) is the network portion of the address. The remainder of the address is the host ID. If the subnet was 255.255.0.0, the network portion of the IP address would be 4.215 and 244.35 would be the host ID.

IP ADDRESS CLASSES

In order to manage the structure of IP addresses and to establish a standard for interpreting them, IP classes were developed. There are five address classes, A–E. The IP address classes A, B, and C are available for anyone to use in networking on a regular basis. Class D addresses are reserved for multicasting and class E addresses are reserved for research purposes. The following table shows the basic features of the three major classes of IP addresses:

Class	Mask Interpretation	Address Range
Class A	Network.Node.Node.Node	1.0.0.0–126.0.0.0
Class B	Network.Network.Node.Node	128.0.0.0–191.255.0.0
Class C	Network.Network.Network.Node	192.0.0.0–223.255.255.255

Using the information in the table, we can now begin to explore the interpretation of subnet masks.

Using the previous IP address example of 4.215.244.35, we can see how the subnet mask works. Using the previous table, notice that any address beginning with 4.x.x.x is a class A address. Also, it is known that the default mask for this address is 255.0.0.0. Right now, it is important to reemphasize that any value present in the subnet mask address indicates that all or part of a corresponding octet in the IP address is referring to the network identifier. A zero in one of the subnet mask address octets indicates that the corresponding octet in the given IP address is available for assignment as part of the host ID.

Here is another example: The IP address 194.215.244.35 has a subnet mask of 255.255.0.0. The first and second octet of the mask is 255. The corresponding octets in the IP address are 194 and 215, respectively. Because the first two octets of the mask are filled (maximum value of 255), the entire first and second octet of the IP address is referring only to the network ID. Our network ID is 194.215. The remaining two octets of the mask are zeros. This means that the node portion of the IP address (our node or host ID) is 244.35. Here are some additional examples to clarify the way masking works to subdivide the IP address for any given host.

IP Address	Subnet Mask	Network ID	Host ID
16.25.47.89	255.0.0.0	16.0.0.0	25.47.89
19.56.254.1	255.0.0.0	19.0.0.0	56.254.1
188.54.25.1	255.255.0.0	188.54.0.0	25.1
216.9.49.57	255.255.255.0	216.9.49.0	.57
194.25.47.89	255.255.0.0	194.25.0.0	47.89

NOTE IP addresses and their subnet masks are most often displayed in the form address/mask, 10.200.33.12/255.0.0.0. A simplified notation method is becoming widely accepted that uses the format address/masked bits, where the previous example would be 10.200.33.12/8. The 8 indicates that the first 8 bits of the subnet mask octet (255 in the previous example) are set to a value of 1. Class A addresses take the form Network.Node.Node.Node/8, class B is Network.Network.Node.Node/16, and class C is Network.Network.Network.Node/24.

Notice that the last address in the preceding list has a different mask and is therefore (even though the address is identical to the first address in the list) a member of a different network. In this difference, is the power of a subnet mask. It is the manipulation of this subnet mask that allows subnetting to take place. Before tackling subnetting, it is important to examine a few special groups of IP addresses known as private addresses.

Not only class D and E addresses are reserved for special uses. Additionally, there are three IP address groupings reserved for use on private networks. The existence of these reservations means any host directly connected to the Internet cannot use one of these special IP addresses as its publicly recognizable address. The addresses are for internal network use only. There is a special reserved IP grouping for each of the standard address classes: A, B, and C. The following list shows the range for each of the private IP groups.

- **Class A**   10.0.0.0–10.255.255.255

- **Class B**   172.16.0.0–172.31.255.255

- **Class C**   192.168.0.0–192.168.255.255

As mentioned earlier, these address groups are designed to be used on private (or internal) networks only. The reservation of these address groups allows many private networks to use the same IP addresses inside their local area or wide area networks (LANs/WANs) and thus avoid the possibility of IP address exhaustion. Because there are a finite number of IP addresses available, and because the use of the Internet has grown rapidly, it is hypothetically possible to exhaust all of the possible IP addresses. Using private IP addresses on internal networks increases the number of IP addresses available for use on the public Internet by allowing redundant address assignment.

One last address has a very special purpose. If you look at Figure A-1, you will notice that none of the address classes include any addresses between 127.0.0.0 and 127.255.255.255. The address 127.0.0.1 is universally known as the "loopback" address, and the majority of TCP/IP implementations recognize any IP address with the first octet of 127 as one of the loopback addresses.

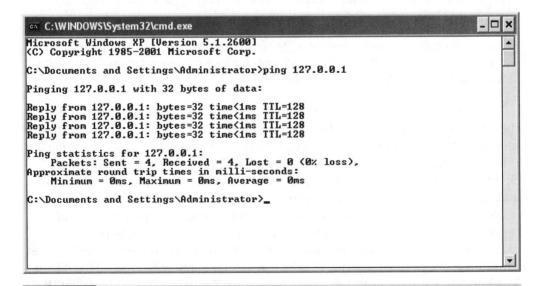

```
C:\WINDOWS\System32\cmd.exe
Microsoft Windows XP [Version 5.1.2600]
(C) Copyright 1985-2001 Microsoft Corp.

C:\Documents and Settings\Administrator>ping 127.0.0.1

Pinging 127.0.0.1 with 32 bytes of data:

Reply from 127.0.0.1: bytes=32 time<1ms TTL=128
Reply from 127.0.0.1: bytes=32 time<1ms TTL=128
Reply from 127.0.0.1: bytes=32 time<1ms TTL=128
Reply from 127.0.0.1: bytes=32 time<1ms TTL=128

Ping statistics for 127.0.0.1:
    Packets: Sent = 4, Received = 4, Lost = 0 (0% loss),
Approximate round trip times in milli-seconds:
    Minimum = 0ms, Maximum = 0ms, Average = 0ms

C:\Documents and Settings\Administrator>_
```

FIGURE A.1   127 address class reservation

As you can see in Figure A-1, executing a ping command on any IP in the 127.0.0.0 group results in a resolution to the loopback address 127.0.0.1. Because this address is used for internal diagnostics and is known by nearly every network device as an internal address only, the whole range 127.0.0.0 is generally ignored to prevent confusion between internal and external functions. The loopback address is most commonly used to determine if the TCP/IP software components of a computer are properly installed and configured.

Each address class (class A, B, or C) of a network can be further subdivided into smaller networks, properly known as *subnetworks* or commonly just *subnets*. One of the essential benefits of subnetting is broadcast control. Routers are devices that connect different networks together, and they do not pass broadcasts (traffic destined for all hosts on a particular network) unless they are specifically configured to do so. If an administrator has a network consisting of a large number of hosts generating network broadcasts, subnetting will allow the administrator to reduce the size of the network segments. This will prevent undue consumption of network capacity from excessive broadcast traffic.

When an existing network is subnetted (16.52.23.45, for example), networks outside of this IP address pool see no outward change. To the rest of the world outside of the subnetted network, the network is a single entity. This allows the reorganization of network IDs as needed, without having to be concerned about the impact on other (external) networks. Any routers involved in communications between networks are aware of the routes needed to forward traffic between subnets. If one of those known networks was locally subnetted, the routing entries would not have to change except in the case of the router interconnecting the new subnets.

USING SUBNETS

How subnetting works requires us to briefly explore binary numbers. Recall that IP addresses and subnet masks are really collections of binary numbers divided into octets. The following example shows you what those octets look like in decimal and binary form:

Decimal Form	Binary Form
16.128.10.10	00010000.10000000.00001010.00001010

Each of the eight bits in the binary form can be a 1 or a 0. Each of those spaces has then a logical numerical value. From left to right, they are 128, 64, 32, 16, 8, 4, 2, and 1.

Here are some numbers and their binary equivalents:

128	10000000
192	11000000
224	11100000
240	11110000
248	11111000
252	11111100
254	11111110

The same system applies for subnet masks as for the IP addresses. Taking this into consideration, subnets are handled in a similar manner:

Class A mask	255.0.0.0 (decimal form)
Equals	11111111.00000000.00000000.00000000 (binary form)

Class B mask	255.255.0.0 (decimal form)
Equals	11111111.11111111.00000000.00000000 (binary form)

Class C mask	255.255.255.0 (decimal form)
Equals	11111111.11111111.11111111.00000000 (binary form)

Again, the subnet mask is used to differentiate between the network and node portions of the IP address. In binary terms, any location in the subnet mask that has the values of 1 signifies that that part of the IP address is reserved for the network portion of the address. As you will see in the examples following, the binary values of the subnet mask must be consecutive 1s from the left to right. This means the lowest value a subnet mask octet can have is 128 since the leftmost portion of any octet is the placeholder correlating to the value of 128. Another way to look at it is this: when viewing a subnet mask in binary form (and reading the numbers from left to right), the first bit equal to 0 is the end of the subnet mask. All bits not used for the network portion of the address may be used for the nodes on that network. The bold 1s in the following example represent bits reserved for the network portion of the IP address. The rule for binary addition is fairly straightforward: 1 + 1 = 1, 1 + 0 = 0, and 0 + 0 = 0.

Class A IP	10.128.10.10 (decimal form)	00001010.10000000.00001010.00001010 (binary form)
Mask	255.0.0.0 (decimal form)	11111111.00000000.00000000.00000000 (binary form)
Combined	10.0.0.0 (decimal form)	00001010.00000000.00000000.00000000 (binary form)

Class B IP	4.32.10.10 (decimal form)	00000100.00100000.00001010.00001010 (binary form)
Mask	255.255.0.0 (decimal form)	11111111.11111111.00000000.00000000 (binary form)
Combined	4.32.0.0 (decimal form)	00000100.00100000.00000000.00000000 (binary form)

Class C IP	221.192.10.16 (decimal form)	11011101.11000000.00001010.00010000 (binary form)
Mask	255.255.255.0 (decimal form)	11111111.11111111.11111111.00000000 (binary form)
Combined	221.192.10.0 (decimal form)	11011101.11000000.00001010.00000000 (binary form)

Now suppose that the network administrator is using the class B network ID 135.44.0.0. There are a large number of nodes and with a default subnet mask of 255.255.0.0, the last two octets are available to use for host ID assignment. On this hypothetical network, it is decided that subnetting is required, and that at least three subnets need to be created. One will be used for general users, another for the company servers, and the last one for remote access clients. One of the benefits sought will be a reduction of the overall effect of broadcast traffic on the network. Also, subnetting will allow tighter security to be implemented on the network by controlling access with special configurations (IP filters and access lists) on the routers that will be needed to interconnect the new subnets.

In order to subnet, the administrator must claim some of the bits currently available for host ID assignment and use them for the network ID instead. In decimal notation form, the default subnet mask for the address previously mentioned is 255.255.0.0., or in binary:

11111111.11111111.**000**00000.00000000

Notice that in bold are the three bit positions that will be removed from the node assignable portion of the mask and given to the network portion of the address. When subnetting begins, the bits are thus transferred:

11111111.11111111.**111**00000.00000000

Looking at the mask in user-friendly decimal form, the subnet mask that was, by default, 255.255.0.0 is now 255.255.224.0. With this reallocation completed, the resulting mask allows for more networks to be created, though each network will have fewer host IDs available than the previous (default) mask allowed. This is the trade-off—network ID space can be gained while total number of available host IDs is lost. Now the need for subnetting is addressed. There are still important matters to resolve. Not every IP address available under the old (nonsubnetted) address scheme is available for use anymore. The trick is calculating the new network ID and available (valid) host IDs.

To perform the needed calculations, it is necessary to convert our addresses from their easy-to-use decimal forms to the sometimes strange-looking binary form. Remember that each bit in each octet identifies the value of a larger number. Keeping this in mind, making the needed conversion is relatively simple. Here is a refresher on how binary numbers operate:

(128) (64) (32) (16) (8) (4) (2) (1)

10100000 = 128 + 32 = 160

11001111 = 128 + 64 + 8 + 4 + 2 + 1 = 207

00000111 = 4 + 2 + 1 = 7

NOTE   Here is something to keep in mind about the type of binary number that IP addresses utilize: they are but one of many mathematically possible forms. IP addresses use a particular type of binary number known as *base 2*. The values of the bit positions are based on the squaring of the value of the number 2: $2^0 = 1$, $2^1 = 2$, $2^2 = 4$, $2^3 = 8$, $2^4 = 16$, $2^5 = 32$, $2^6 = 64$, and, finally, $2^7 = 128$ for an 8-bit octet. What this means is that other values can be used for the base number, though not with IP subnetting—for example, base 3 ($3^0 = 1$, $3^1 = 3$, $3^2 = 9$, $3^3 = 27 \ldots$).

When working with subnetting a network, there are a group of questions that need to be answered concerning the new networks created. What is the broadcast address? What is the subnet number? How many IP addresses can be used for actual hosts/nodes per network? The answers to these questions can be derived from a series of mathematical formulas. Though sometimes confusing at first, once the user becomes familiar with how they work, the equations are usually quite manageable. Be sure to examine each example carefully. The following is a description of key calculations anyone utilizing subnetting will want to know.

Calculating the Number of Subnets Derived from a New Mask:

IP address	177.240.154.5	Class B
Subnet mask	255.255.248.0	Default is 255.255.0.0

Convert subnet mask to binary form: 255.255.248.0 = 11111111.11111111.11111000.00000000
Apply this formula to find out how many networks have been made from the single original network:

$$\text{Subnets} = 2^{(\text{number of additional 1s in subnet address})} - 2 = 2^5 - 2 = 30$$

Calculating the Number of Host IDs Available:

IP address	177.240.154.5	Class B
Subnet mask	255.255.248.0	Default is 255.255.0.0

Convert subnet to binary form: 255.255.248.0 = 11111111.11111111.11111000.00000000
Apply this formula:

$$\text{Nodes (number of assignable IPs)} = 2^{(\text{number of 0s in subnet address})} - 2 = 2^{11} - 2 = 2046$$

Calculating the Subnet Number:

IP address	177.240.154.5	Class B
Subnet mask	255.255.248.0	Default is 255.255.0.0

Subtract the value of the subnetted octet in the subnet mask (248 in this case) from 256:

256 – 248 = 8 = First subnet number.

All subsequent subnet numbers are found by adding the initial subnet number to itself until the nearest value below that of the subnetted octet (248) is reached. This configuration's subnet numbers would be 8, 16, 24, 32, 40, 48, 56, 64, 72, and 80, and so forth up to and including the final subnet of 240.

Each subnet number marks the beginning of a new range of valid IP addresses, so our ranges here would be 8.0–15.255, 16.0–23.255, and 24.0–31.255 all the way up to the last range of 240.0–247.255. The upper value of each range is the broadcast address (15.255, 23.255, 31.255, and 247.255 in this example) and the lowest value is the subnet address or network number (8.0, 16.0, 24.0, and 240.0 in this example). The numbers between the subnet number and the broadcast address are the valid IP addresses available for use with network hosts.

NOTE   Subnet addresses generically identify the network in use. For example, 10.0.0.0 would identify all hosts with IP addresses between 10.0.0.1 and 10.255.255.255. Broadcast addresses are defined as the network ID where all available node bits are set to 1. This is a special address that is used to direct data to all members of a subnetwork rather than a specific host.

Using our previous example, the valid IPs for hosts to use would be: 7.1–15.254, 16.1–23.254, and 24.1–31.254. Notice we could essentially ignore the last octet because it is entirely available for hosts (1–254). The example IP used earlier (177.240.154.5) would reside on the 177.240.152.0 network, with a broadcast address of 177.240.159.255, and it would be accompanied by the usable IP addresses 177.240.152.1–177.240.159.255.

Here is a list of information about the other networks created when the original network (177.240.0.0/16) was subnetted. This list shows the usable IP addresses, subnet address, and broadcast address of each new subnet.

Subnet 177.240.8.0 = 177.240.8.1–177.240.15.254

Subnet address	177.240.8.0
Broadcast address	177.240.15.255

Subnet 177.240.16.0 = 177.240.16.1–177.240.23.254

Subnet address	177.240.16.0
Broadcast address	177.240.23.255

Subnet 177.240.24.0 = 177.240.24.1–177.240.31.254

Subnet address	177.240.24.0
Broadcast address	177.240.31.255

Subnet 177.240.240.0 = 177.240.240.1–177.240.247.254

Subnet address	177.240.240.0
Broadcast address	177.240.247.255

A network administrator should largely be able to subnet without the use of an IP calculator, especially if subnetting or managing subnetted address schemes are required on a regular basis. On the other hand, there are widely available IP calculators that will do most, if not all, of the work of calculating subnet values. The catch is that the person using the calculators needs to know what to input into the calculator and how to understand what comes out. The other catch is that some of the IP calculators do not produce dependable results. Some of the IP calculators available do not work as advertised. Most often, this results in a user being provided invalid subnets in the results. An administrator using such tools should be able to identify mistakes if they occur.

NOTE   Subnetting can be a difficult topic to understand; because of this, it is often useful to look at the topic from as many different approaches as possible. The sites http://support.microsoft.com/default.aspx?scid=kb;EN-US;q164015 and http://www.learntosubnet.com provide written and streaming video explanations on the subject of subnetting.

HELPFUL TOOLS AND DOWNLOADS

B

In this appendix, a wide range of networking tools will be examined. These tools go beyond the built-in components that accompany most operating systems. The purpose of these tools generally includes gathering information about how the network is configured and monitoring your network performance. Because there is no "one size fits all" network tool, we will examine the features of a variety of both hardware and software tools. Some of the software tools are commercial and can be somewhat expensive, while others are shareware/freeware with low or no cost. The goal here is to provide a working cross section of the kinds of third-party networking tools available. From mapping your network to testing network cables, these tools will address most network maintenance and troubleshooting needs.

HARDWARE TOOLS

Hardware tools include devices that range from the most basic telecommunications tools, such as wire computers and strippers, to complex monitoring and analysis devices that are essentially task-specific computers. Because most users are familiar with wire stripper/crimper tools, and because such tools are widely available at most hardware and electronics stores, we will focus more on the multifunction devices. These multifunction devices offer, in most cases, three critical benefits over software-based solutions. These benefits are

- **Operating system independence** Dedicated hardware devices will work in all areas of your network regardless of the type of operating system that the network hosts are using. If the dedicated device can connect to your LAN via a compatible network interface (such as Ethernet), you should be able to test connectivity, identify connected hosts, gather performance statistics, and make use of any other supported features of the device.

- **Extremely high "up time"** Because the devices are task specific, make use of a "no frills" operating system, and depend more on hardware than software to operate, they rarely experience any kind of failure. Where PC-based utilities are dependent on the sometimes fragile operating systems in order to operate, these dedicated devices can run (displaying real-time data) literally for years without interruption if they need to do so.

- **Many forms of these devices are highly portable** Devices such as the Fluke One Touch can be dragged all over the place without much risk of serious damage to the unit, and can be collecting data and identifying problems in minutes. All you need is a network interface and (if you need long-term use) a power supply and you're ready to go. That being said, there are dedicated hardware monitoring devices that are designed to be rack mounted in a server closet. Of course, these units are not very mobile, if at all, but they do share the operating system independence and high uptime of other task-specific network monitors.

Where might these devices come in handy? The mobile units are particularly useful if you will support users in distributed locations. If you have users in remote locations, such as branch offices or specialized facilities, a portable network meter can help you find a solution without having to tote around a fragile laptop with software meters or spend time guessing where the network fault is located. However, users don't have to be many miles apart for network meters to be useful. Any user that is having connectivity issues that seem to result from network performance can be helped with a network monitor. By taking the monitor to the user's computer, you can connect to the network at the user's access point and rapidly determine if the user's connection is working as it should be. Because a problem connecting to a networked resource can have any of a number of causal factors, the ability to quickly identify or eliminate potential problems can really make a difference between a long troubleshooting session and a quick fix.

In addition to the value of these devices as field tools, portable and rack-mount devices can monitor network traffic in real time. If users should complain about the speed connection quality when accessing a certain resource (such as a server), you can use the meter to assess the state of the network as a whole. Most of the meters will allow you to identify the major traffic generators (which client is using the most bandwidth) as well as the number of collisions and how much broadcast traffic is being generated.

NOTE Most hardware-based network monitors are, at least out of the box, designed for use with Ethernet and Fast Ethernet networks. If your network uses token ring as the primary means of connectivity, this is something to keep in mind. While the units can attach at any Ethernet interface available, none of them will be able to directly attach to the token ring interfaces or hardware. You can still monitor network performance, from said Ethernet interfaces, and test cabling if the cables have RJ-45 interfaces and use CAT5 or 6 cabling. If you need diagnostic tools specifically designed for token ring, you should contact the vendor of your token ring equipment for guidance.

FLUKE

Fluke Networks produces a variety of network testing and management products. From portable LAN products to Voice over IP (VoIP) and DSL testers, Fluke makes a tool for virtually every network task.

OPTIVIEW INTEGRATED NETWORK ANALYZER

The Optiview Integrated Network Analyzer is the most feature rich, with three models available, produced by Fluke. The three models are the Standard, the Pro, and the Pro Gigabit. The Standard model comes with many useful features. Along with a robust feature set, this Ethernet-capable unit has a large color screen that displays the collected information on a large and easy-to-read display. The Standard model can attach to an Ethernet/Fast Ethernet network via an RJ-45 interface. The following list outlines some of the key features included in the Standard model:

- Active network discovery that can locate active hosts across a switched network. The functionality includes mapping hostnames to IP address and MAC addresses.

- SNMP device analysis that will discover and collect information about all of the configured SNMP communities on your network. This functionality will catalog and display all of the collected SNMP information held by capable network devices.

- Traffic generation capability that will allow you to simulate a variety of network traffic conditions. This feature allows you to use a variety of options to simulate network utilization levels, packet and frame sizes, and other network conditions. This feature is particularly useful for identifying congestion-related network problems.

- The Optiview also provides a complete cable testing solution. It can identify faults in wiring and incorrectly wired network jacks, and identify the location of wiring problems such as severed lines.

The Pro models add extra functionality, including the ability to directly interface with 100BASE-FX (fiber optic), capture and analyze packet traffic (packet sniffer), and utilize Remote Monitor (RMON) II monitoring to analyze (among other things) the kind of application traffic using the network. The Pro Gigabit model adds the ability to test Gigabit media and signaling on top of all of the Standard and Pro model features.

A couple of optional components are also available, including the WAN Vision Option. This option adds the ability to analyze WAN link utilization and collect information about currently active protocols as well as autodiscovery of most WAN media types. This includes support for ATM, T1, ISDN, and frame relay. The other optional component is the Wireless Network Analyzer. This option includes, among other things, a wireless network adapter and software that allows the Optiview to see wireless LANs (WLAN), attached clients, and various wireless network settings such as the presence of the Wired Equivalent Protocol (WEP) and network signal strength.

ONETOUCH SERIES II

The OneTouch Series II handheld network analyzer is a "little brother" to the more robust Optiview. Where the Optiview has just about every feature you could want for use with your LAN, WAN, or WLAN, the OneTouch Series II possesses a core feature set needed to monitor your LAN. This Ethernet/Fast Ethernet–compatible device makes use of a high-contrast monochrome display and four key abilities to make keeping on top of network operations easy and efficient. The OneTouch Series II can rapidly detect active network interfaces and IP and MAC addresses, as well as SNMP community name and individual link speed. Once this information is collected, alarms are generated for problems such as duplicate IP addresses and physical network transmission problems. While the information obtained by the OneTouch is not as expansive as that collected by the Optiview, it collects and displays several critical forms of information in real time. The information includes segment utilization (percent of total), data collisions, transmission errors, and the percentage of total traffic that is broadcast or multicast in origin. In addition to the logical network information, the OneTouch Series II also provides a complete set of cable-testing features, including the ability to identify opens, cable length, crossed wires, and split pairs. The OneTouch Series II can also be used to generate a tone for cable identification. This feature will allow you to connect the OneTouch to a network cable, initiate the tone generator, and use a specialized receiver to follow the tone along the cable. In this manner, you can accurately identify a single wire based on the strength of the tone.

WAVERUNNER WIRELESS TESTER

The WaveRunner is a limited-scope network analysis device. This modified Compaq iPaq uses a wireless LAN adapter and Linux operating system to run wireless network monitoring software. If you are planning to deploy wireless access points, or you are concerned about the potential for unauthorized wireless access points, this tool could be the solution. In addition to identifying local wireless networks, the WaveRunner has ping, throughput analysis, and specialized web tools that will allow you to see key devices, test connectivity, and determine if Wireless Equivalent Protocol (WEP) is in use.

CRIMPING TOOLS

Though full-featured network analysis devices are invaluable, alone they are not enough to master your network. You will probably need a tool that allows you to work with the physical components of the network such as the network cabling components. For example, if you need to run a network cable to a location where there is no existing wiring, you have two choices: pay someone else to do it or run the wire yourself. If you choose to run the wiring yourself, you will need tools to get the wiring installed and tested. An RJ-45 crimper and wire-stripping tool is used to attach the RJ-45 adapter end onto a compatible, eight-wire network cable such as Category 5 unshielded twisted pair (CAT 5 UTP).

AGILENT FRAMESCOPE 350

The FrameScope 350 is a network meter/tester that has a great deal of configuration options and flexibility. The base unit performs a wide array of logical network tests as well as extensive cable and media testing, though some cable types such as fiber optic cabling will require an additional probe or media adapter in order to connect to them. The key properties of the base unit are outlined here:

- Logical network testing capabilities include an Autotest feature that verifies and rates the performance of SMTP, HTTP, file, DNS/WINS, DHCP, FTP, and print servers. Along with testing these functions, the autotest will evaluate Windows domain controllers and Novell NetWare servers to assess responsiveness and the general ability to service user requests. Of course, the FrameScope can also query SNMP-enabled devices such as routers and switches to obtain configuration and utilization information.

■ The traffic generator allows you to simulate various network activities and utilization levels to determine how your network infrastructure will behave under the tested conditions. For example, you can simulate large numbers of simultaneous user requests to port 80 (HTTP) to see how much your web server can take before beginning to slow down. This is very handy when you are trying to build a baseline for your network.

■ The FrameScope 350 is remote controllable when attached to the network. If left in place as a static monitoring device, you can use any web browser to access the features and information collected by the FS 350. This makes the unit extremely useful since it can be used at a fixed location to collect real-time information. As a semimobile unit, it can access information via the web interface; a fully mobile unit, it can be taken into the field.

■ The FS 3350 has a full-color touch screen that is fairly unique in this smaller class of network analysis device.

As mentioned earlier, there are numerous expansion options with the FrameScope 350. These options include network probes that allow fiber-optic (single-mode and multimode) testing, coaxial cable testing, and full CAT 6 cable certification. These features, combined with the logical network testing and monitoring components, will allow this unit to operate in virtually any network environment.

COMMERCIAL SOFTWARE TOOLS

Sometimes it is more practical to use a PC-based software product to monitor the network. In particular, some manufacturers of networking hardware such as routers and switches make specialized monitoring and management software that offers features unavailable with other monitoring solutions such as remote configuration and custom reporting. Some routers and switches contain proprietary reporting and configuration interfaces that the right software suite can take advantage of to either configure or monitor the router or switch. Another key benefit of many commercial network monitoring software products is that they can use a wide range of technologies for the purpose of delivering administrative alerts. For example, should a critical router or switch fail, the software could be configured to send an SMS message to the network administrator's cell phone to notify the admin of the problem.

BLACK BOX NETWORK SERVICES: LANVUE

The LanVue network security management software, by Black Box network services, is a robustly featured network monitoring package. LanVue will operate on any computer that is capable of running one of the supported operating system platforms, including Windows 95/98/Me and Windows 2000/XP.

The tools available with this package are varied and include the ability to:

- Analyze IP packets in real time
- Identify IP port scanners and identify the source
- Monitor for known network attacks
- Analyze network traffic to identify potentially vulnerable systems
- Identify unauthorized connection requests
- Monitor traffic going to and coming from designated network hosts

While Black Box bills LanVue as a "Security guard that protects your network," LanVue can be used to monitor your network when security is not the primary concern. LanVue can be used to collect network protocol information as well as physical layer information for Ethernet, Fast Ethernet, and token ring. LanVue also contains the utilization analysis that other software and most hardware solutions provide. LanVue can collect information such as network segment utilization, percentage of traffic that is broadcast-based, and the rate at which communications errors are occurring. In order to test network performance, LanVue can also simulate network conditions via a traffic-generating feature.

LanVue can be configured to monitor specific resources and then send alerts in the event that a specified threshold is exceeded. For example, LanVue can be configured to monitor traffic to and from a server and send an alert if a client from an unauthorized network (IP subnet) attempts to access the monitored resource. Another example would be a network segment exceeding a specified utilization level. Once either of the two examples occurs, an alert can be sent to an administrator via SMS, e-mail, or a text-capable pager.

For additional information about LanVue and other Black Box products, you can view the product catalog and browse informational documentation at http://catalog.blackbox.com.

QUEST SOFTWARE: BIG BROTHER

The Big Brother product produced by Quest Software, http://www.quest.com/bigbrother, is a very capable network management product. Big Brother is actually one component of several complementary and interoperable products. The Big Brother component is the multipurpose monitoring package designed to accomplish two tasks. The first task is to monitor the traffic on the network and attached hosts, and the second task is to deliver notification via SMS or text messaging to an administrator when a configured threshold has been exceeded.

NOTE The full name for SMS is Short Message Service. This service is used to deliver brief text messages to cell phones that have the needed capability and services present.

Big Brother is useful for collecting a wide range of networking information and has one real advantage, shared by many of the commercial networking products. Big Brother can be used to set up basic monitoring and maintenance, and if at a later time there is a need to upgrade the capacity of the service, additional software can be installed that will complement Big Brother's services. Because of this, you can start out small with basic monitoring, which provides information with less initial investment, and later expand capacity, if needed. But what abilities are present with Big Brother? The following list outlines the key features:

- Collects and displays information about the process and general machine configuration (operating system, installed software) on monitored systems, which can include routers, switches, and network-attached computers.

- Web-based monitoring interface shows easy-to-read status information about monitored devices. Color-coded entries indicate the status of monitored elements such as FTP, HTTP, and NNTP services (red is a fault, green is normal operation), and the presence of configured alerts.

- Support for custom scripting that allows you to develop your own monitoring processes.

- Maintains a historical record of the last 50 measurement intervals. This will allow you to catch information about a network fault even if you are not actively watching the monitor when the failure occurs.

As mentioned earlier, Big Brother integrates with other Quest Software products to expand the functionality. There are several integration-option products available from Quest, but one of the most noteworthy is the product called Foglight. Foglight offers the ability to add powerful and expansive network monitoring.

FOGLIGHT

Foglight is used to monitor an extensive number of components that affect the performance of applications running on the network. This software package monitors local system performance, individual processes such as database services, and operating system components. The result of this holistic approach is the ability to identify current and potential problems in the process of getting resources from the server to the client. On top of the detailed monitoring and alerting options, Foglight can be used to track historical data. As your network grows and changes, Foglight's ability to use historical data will ensure that the transition from one network configuration to another is smooth.

HEWLETT PACKARD: VANTAGEPOINT FOR WINDOWS

VantagePoint is a member of the expansive remote monitoring and management suite known as OpenView. VantagePoint uses a client/server arrangement on a Windows 2000 or .NET domain to manage the performance of critical systems. Monitoring software is installed on the server and separate management console software is installed at a management station. VantagePoint is used to perform, among other things, the following tasks:

- Monitor configured nodes and generate alerts when a specified event occurs.

- Provide a graphical information display for both viewing the status of monitored hosts and configuring the setting of the monitoring software.

- Generate multilevel physical and logical network maps. These maps can be used to perform impact analysis and assess the potential benefits and problems associated with proposed network service changes.

- Collect real-time network statistics (utilization, broadcast percentage, and so forth) for on-demand network management.

- The management software can be configured to implement certain configuration changes on monitor servers if particular events occur. For example, a server could be configured to redirect network traffic towards a backup network link in the event that a primary network link fails.

One of the problems with VantagePoint when compared to other networking products is the considerable size of the OpenView suite. While you can start with the VantagePoint component and expand functionality at any time as needed with additional components, it can be intimidating at first to identify which additional components are available. This complexity also comes at a fairly steep price, both monetarily and temporally. Not only are the product prices relatively high when compared to other monitoring software packages, but there are often extensive implementation costs because even experienced administrators often need to attend product training or contract the services of OpenView consultants to get the product working at its full potential.

CISCO SYSTEMS: CISCOWORKS FOR WINDOWS 6.1

If your network makes use of Cisco networking products, this tool will be an essential component of your management arsenal. All you need is a Windows NT/2000/XP–based PC and CiscoWorks to get started managing your Cisco equipment dynamically. This version of CiscoWorks is a collection of web-based applications that provides information about the status of the Cisco network hardware, performance statistics, and detailed configuration information. CiscoWorks for Windows will work on the routing, switching, access server, and hub devices produced by Cisco. Within the collection of applications, there are tools for a variety of tasks. The tools in this collection include

- Cisco View version 5.4, which provides a rich graphical display that emulates the front and back of the monitored device. This display reveals status information and allows device configuration (by clicking a port, for example). This tool can monitor and access a single device at a time.

- The network management package WhatsUp Gold 7.0 from Ipswitch software. This tool displays a network topology map of all connected devices, which allows monitoring of all of the applicable devices from a top-down perspective. Included is the ability to discover network devices, generate network maps, and create alarms when network devices experience problems.

Of the many individual functions that these software components provide, there are probably two that are more noteworthy than the others. First is the ability to execute the Cisco IOS show commands without having to recall the sometimes complex syntax of the individual commands. This capability can be used from within either the CiscoWorks desktop application or the WhatsUp application from Ipswitch. The capability is called a Threshold Manager. This tool allows you to easily set the monitoring thresholds on Cisco devices that support the RMON configuration interfaces. Because this capability can be used to automate some of the monitoring of network devices and lets the devices notify the monitoring station when an error occurs, the effectiveness is increased while reducing the load on the network from monitoring overhead.

FINDING USEFUL SHAREWARE AND FREEWARE

Sometimes you need only basic functionality from your network tools, or you are looking for a tool to accomplish a specific task. If this is the case, you just might be able to find a free or nearly free product to fit the bill. Many small publishers, students, and independent researchers produce a variety of network tools. New tools for network management are being developed on a fairly regular basis. On top of that, existing tools often undergo revision and expansion. To locate these tools, there are several good sources, some of which are outlined in the following sections.

DOWNLOAD.COM

Download.com is a clearinghouse of all kinds of downloadable software products. Many software companies will release demo or time-limited versions of their software here in addition to the large volume of freeware and shareware. Software stored here is organized into various categories, and each category is searchable. This makes the content manageable since there are literally thousands of individual programs available. To find a software tool on this archive—for visually tracing a network route, for example—you simply enter the applicable search terms in the search box. One trick to this web site is sorting the results, since initially they appear in a less-than-useful manner. By clicking the Total Downloads link of the results page, you will sort the list with the most popular selection first.

TUCOWS.COM

The Tucows.com web site, http://www.tucows.com, is another clearinghouse for freeware and shareware applications, much like download.com. Like other software distribution sites, you can select the platform for which you need a tool, from Windows to UNIX, and search for the kind of tool you need.

EDUCATIONAL INSTITUTIONS

Many educational institutions have resources for redistributing software of all kinds. In particular, universities with computer science departments can be an excellent source for both information about a particular process, such as collecting network packets, and student- or professor-built tools for performing various tasks. In addition to these extremely customized utilities, many university web sites or FTP servers act as mirrors for other software distribution sites. By searching the university web or FTP site, you can often locate the desired tool.

The combination of information and access to file archives sets this source apart from most others.

NEWS GROUPS AND SUPPORT FORUMS

If you are familiar with network newsgroups, you have another valuable asset for finding information about networking tools. By posting an inquiry to the appropriate news group, you may potentially receive responses from hundreds of experienced professionals.

SELECTED FREEWARE AND SHAREWARE

With so many software products available, it can be difficult to determine which of the products will prove genuinely useful. In this section, we will examine some of the tools that have proven to be useful with some fairly unique applications.

NETPEEKER

NetPeeker is a task-specific tool that reveals the source of network traffic on the system where it is run. When the application loads, it identifies the process using the network connection, shows the amount of bandwidth that is being consumed, and provides the user with the option to terminate the process. If you have workstations that you believe have extraneous processes running that are consuming bandwidth, this tool quickly identifies candidate processes and allows you to end them. Once you have identified the process, you can disable any startup behavior or uninstall the related application to prevent the problem from resurfacing.

RADARPING

RadarPing is designed to monitor the availability of network hosts and generate an alarm should one of the monitored hosts become inactive. If the latter occurs, RadarPing uses SMS or text to speech to notify an administrator. In addition to measuring the responsiveness of network devices, RadarPing generates network maps using vector and other professional- quality graphics components. Since RadarPing constantly checks on the status of networked devices, it can also store the information (round-trip time between hosts, for example) and make use of a statistical analysis component to sort through the collected historical data.

NETWORK PROBE

This tool, produced by Object Planet, is used to display network protocol statistics in real time. Elements such as utilization, collisions, errors, and mappings of which processes are operating on the network are displayed. This tool does not collect information, and thus is really only useful as a complement to other tools, or if you need a cost-effective method for monitoring network traffic in real time.

INDEX

INTERNATIONAL CONTACT INFORMATION

AUSTRALIA
McGraw-Hill Book Company Australia Pty. Ltd.
TEL +61-2-9900-1800
FAX +61-2-9878-8881
http://www.mcgraw-hill.com.au
books-it_sydney@mcgraw-hill.com

CANADA
McGraw-Hill Ryerson Ltd.
TEL +905-430-5000
FAX +905-430-5020
http://www.mcgraw-hill.ca

GREECE, MIDDLE EAST, & AFRICA
(Excluding South Africa)
McGraw-Hill Hellas
TEL +30-210-6560-990
TEL +30-210-6560-993
TEL +30-210-6560-994
FAX +30-210-6545-525

MEXICO (Also serving Latin America)
McGraw-Hill Interamericana Editores S.A. de C.V.
TEL +525-117-1583
FAX +525-117-1589
http://www.mcgraw-hill.com.mx
fernando_castellanos@mcgraw-hill.com

SINGAPORE (Serving Asia)
McGraw-Hill Book Company
TEL +65-863-1580
FAX +65-862-3354
http://www.mcgraw-hill.com.sg
mghasia@mcgraw-hill.com

SOUTH AFRICA
McGraw-Hill South Africa
TEL +27-11-622-7512
FAX +27-11-622-9045
robyn_swanepoel@mcgraw-hill.com

SPAIN
McGraw-Hill/Interamericana de España, S.A.U.
TEL +34-91-180-3000
FAX +34-91-372-8513
http://www.mcgraw-hill.es
professional@mcgraw-hill.es

UNITED KINGDOM, NORTHERN,
EASTERN, & CENTRAL EUROPE
McGraw-Hill Education Europe
TEL +44-1-628-502500
FAX +44-1-628-770224
http://www.mcgraw-hill.co.uk
computing_neurope@mcgraw-hill.com

ALL OTHER INQUIRIES Contact:
Osborne/McGraw-Hill
TEL +1-510-549-6600
FAX +1-510-883-7600
http://www.osborne.com
omg_international@mcgraw-hill.com